THE
SERIOUS
PACIFIC
ANGLER

Advanced Secrets of the Eagle Claw Fishing School

by Ron Kovach

MARKETSCOPE
BOOKS

119 Richard Ct.
Aptos, CA 95003
(408) 688-7535

ISBN 0-934061-21-1

Cover Design: Electric Art Studios
                Mountain View, CA

Illustrations: Meredith A. Kovach

Cover Photo: Rick Wannomac

Acknowledgments

I would especially like to thank the Wright and McGill Company, manufacturers of Eagle Claw Fishing Tackle, for their support of our unique on-the-water seminar program. Thank you, Lee McGill, Don Hoben, and Ron Mount for helping make the Eagle Claw Fishing Schools a reality.

I am also grateful to the following professional anglers and boat captains for assisting me with the *Serious Pacific Angler*:
Captain Buzz Brizendine, Mike Callan, Steve Carson, Captain Nick Cates, Abe Cuanang, Angelo Cuanang, Charlie Davis, Ron De La Mare, Mike Gardner, Captain Steve Giffin, Captain Irv Grisbeck, Leonard Hashimoto, Captain Russ Izor, Captain Bill Lescher, Bill Miyagawa, Captain Tom Schlauch, Captain Billy Stevens, and Bob Suekawa.

Above all, thank you, Linda, my lovely wife, whose vision of establishing an on-the-water saltwater curriculum became the Eagle Claw Fishing Schools in 1989.

About the Author

Ron Kovach is one of the foremost angler-educators in the country. He is the founder and director of the Eagle Claw Fishing Schools and Penn Fishing University. He is also a renown outdoor writer and consultant to the sporting goods industry.

Preface

Fishing the Pacific Coast from Seattle to Cabo San Lucas can be a tough proposition at times. Whether you target salmon or marlin, catching the multitude of diverse Western species requires both skill and expertise. There are days when it is just as hard to get the rockfish to bite in Monterey Bay as it is to catch a limit of barracuda at Catalina Island.

In my writing, lectures, and seminar programs, I stress over and over that 10 percent of the anglers are catching 90 percent of the fish. The explanation is simple: not luck—but education.

I founded the Eagle Claw Fishing schools in 1989 with the idea of creating the most dynamic fishing education program on the West Coast. My dream of providing recreational fishermen with an on-the-water forum has turned into a full-time, year-round saltwater school.

This text is based on the curriculum of the Eagle Claw Schools. These are the actual lessons we have both taught and learned from our on-the-water seminars. Although much of our emphasis is on offshore angling on a charter or party boat, many of these strategies have equal application for small boat owners and coastal fishermen. *The Serious Pacific Angler* is meant to be a "sampler" of sorts of the terrific opportunities that await the adventurous fisherman here on the West Coast!

Contents

Contents (cont.)

West Coast Anglers Go to School

The Problems

The majority of people who fish along the West Coast try their luck in saltwater. In Southern California alone, there are 17 landings from Malibu to San Diego and an armada of sportfishing boats from which to choose. Too often many people find their experience on the water to be a frustrating one, encountering too many fishermen, too little information and, often, less than ideal conditions.

Overcrowding

As metropolitan density increases in the West, and crowded weekends continue to impact freshwater fishing, more and more people are heading to the Pacific to try their luck. Over the years, the focus of my guiding, writing and education programs has shifted from freshwater to saltwater. I wanted to accommodate the interests of the ocean fisherman who has plenty of water nearby, fish within a short drive from home, and wants to learn how to master this fishery.

Many anglers along the Pacific Coast grew up fishing the "party" or "cattle boats" at local landings. These boats are typically 55 to 90 foot vessels and pack in anywhere from 25 to 80 passengers for a half- or full-day trip. In the past, many weekend anglers have complained that it is difficult to become a proficient saltwater fisherman under these less-than-optimal conditions.

Lack of Information

Many novices own limited tackle and have no idea what equipment is best to buy for challenging the variety of marine species. One type of tackle is required for popular pelagic species such as calico bass, bonito, and barracuda. Other equipment is needed for larger gamesters like albacore and yellowtail, and still more for deepwater rockfish. The beginner may not always be able to find a reliable resource for information on which equip-

ment will best serve his own needs, and buying the wrong tackle can be an expensive mistake. On the other hand, rental tackle is available, but may not be in the best condition or may not be suited for the fishing on a given day, since it is often "general purpose."

Even more experienced fishers, I have discovered, may have difficulty in finding the information they need on tackle and techniques. This is true no matter if you are fishing for salmon out of Coos Bay, rockfish at San Francisco's Farallon Islands, or tuna south of San Diego. Most insider information is gathered by word of mouth through friends and fellow fishermen or through trial and error. Much of this information may not be accurate. Many anglers who have been working the "big pond" for years often admit that much of their success or failure is due to luck rather than skill.

The Party Boat Community

Most fishermen are out on the water for a day of serious sportfishing. There can be problems, however, on any party boat with fishermen who are more interested in drinking than fishing. There are others who may take over the prime fishing area on the stern and refuse to move. When a boat is crowded, there may be fishermen who have not been educated in common boat courtesy. They may continually cause crossed lines and tangles, leading to wasted time and money as well as frustration. Other times, "deadheads" may cause considerable problems. These are local fishing pros who are invited to fish for free on some party boats in exchange for upping the fish counts. These reports are published in local newspapers daily and are important in attracting customers to the boats. These fishermen often stake out the best spots on the stern, where the chumming occurs which draws the fish in, and refuse to budge. Beginners may be too intimidated to challenge these "pros." Deadheads may also have an informal agreement with the deckhands who give them the "primo" anchovies for bait while the paying passengers are stuck with the lesser quality "pinheads."

The Idea

Since 1985, I have been conducting seminars and lectures on both fresh and saltwater fishing throughout California. Although I was able to share considerable information with my students on tackle and techniques, I realized that what they needed was a place to try out and practice what they had learned. Since most students did not have access to a private craft, party boats were the most likely option. These vessels too often provide a less-than-ideal situation for the beginner. Students might have to wait several weeks before being able to try out the techniques learned in class, and then they might well encounter the adverse conditions described above. What was needed was a on-the-water school where students could practice their newly learned skills.

To meet this need, I began to conceptualize a plan for providing the typical weekend saltwater angler with an environment that would be educational, as well as generating a friendly, positive atmosphere for the beginner desiring to learn how to fish on the ocean.

Thus, the Eagle Claw Saltwater Fishing Schools were born.

The Boats

Before such an educational program or—"school"—could be implemented, I had to find boats, captains, and crews that would reflect my strong concern for anglers trying to master the sport.

Captain Buzz Brizendine owns and operates the 65 foot Sportfisher, Prowler, out of Fisherman's Landing in San Diego. He is a longtime veteran and authority on the complex fishery that centers on the Los Coronados Islands, located 14 miles south in Mexican waters.

Brizendine is also schooled in marine biology and has studied the movements of pelagic gamefish on the outer banks, sometimes over 100 miles out to sea. These are the so-called "glamour" species, including yellowtail, albacore, dorado, yellow and bluefin tuna.

He is committed to providing the optimal experience for the fisherman on his boat. When I approached him

with the idea for my schools he was immediately interested and we decided to give them a try.

Brizendine and I announced our first on-the-water school in October 1989. This program, like those which followed, was be a limited load, open to only 35 students. We emphasized that there would be no crew fishing permitted. Deckhands would be on board strictly to assist the student-passengers. In addition to the crew, Buzz and myself, we recruited a variety of instructors with skill in both fishing and education to provide small group and one-to-one education for our students. This would be the initial blueprint for the many Eagle Claw Schools that followed at other landings on a variety of other boats.

The Curriculum

I was familiar with other successful freshwater fishing schools conducted by such companies as Orvis. Implementing a curriculum for a saltwater program proved to be somewhat more complex. For one thing, due to the distance the boat must travel to the prime fishing grounds, most schools would consist of overnight trips. Thus, the plan would be to have students board the night before at 9:00 p.m. for check-in and a series of brief mini-seminars on basic angling techniques to prepare them for the next day's fishing. Departure would be at 11:00 p.m.

Once underway, the students receive additional pointers while the boat travels to various fish-holding spots. My team of instructors roam the boat from bow to stern throughout the day to provide one-on-one education for anglers desiring individual instruction.

The novice as well as the more advanced fisherman is thus able to receive instruction based on his individual needs and interests. This could include bait selection, proper casting technique, setting up a trolling outfit, effectively using soft plastic lures, or even how to play a fish down the side of a crowded boat.

The Instructors

Putting together a team of professional anglers to teach weekend fishermen required considerable forethought. I wanted not only individuals who were technically competent, but also "people-oriented" like myself and the various captains of the sportfishers I would eventually charter. They would also have to be highly patient individuals, especially when working with first-time fishermen.

A small group of local experts, many of whom I had featured in my previous books and articles, were invited to participate. Each pro has a particular specialty that added to the technical aspects of the school. Some are live bait specialists; others are experts at "throwing the iron" (cast-metal jigs). Some are bottom fishing veterans while others are best at offshore trolling.

Many of these instructors are involved with fishing on a full-time basis. Some are outdoor writers; others are lure manufacturers and tackle sales representatives interested in field testing their products as well as teaching fellow fishers how to best use them. The schools provide valuable immediate, on-the-spot feedback to these professionals on product performance.

The Sponsors

The final segment necessary to maintain a program such as this is sponsorship. In order to keep prices down, and still provide the best schools possible, I sought the assistance of a variety of tackle companies.

Wright & McGill, makers of Eagle Claw Hooks, was the first manufacturer to embrace the school concept. They became the primary patron, helping to provide students with the opportunity to fish with a variety of Eagle Claw hooks.

Next, Penn voiced an interest in supplying a collection of casting and spinning rods and reels for students to try out at the school. Instead of borrowing or renting an outfit, fishermen would be able to learn using some of the highest quality spinning tackle available. Penn, in return, receives feedback from instructors and students in an informal field-testing situation. Tackle used in the schools is routinely updated as new models are introduced so students are always fishing with state-of-the-art technology.

The Berkley Company signed on to provide line for the schools. As a veteran saltwater angler, I can attest that more fish are lost due to old worn monofilament than for any other reason. All students are provided with spools of top quality Berkley Big Game monofilament. Instruction is provided on how to tie proper knots.

Finally, a number of lure manufacturers signed on to provide their product to the school. Many also sent their own representatives to provide instruction to students on the best ways to use their lures. Students are given samples from a variety of companies including Luhr Jensen, U.F.O. Jigs, Haddock, Rapala, Advanced Angler Technology, A.A. Worms, and Braid Products.

The Results

After the first school sold out in October 1989, we scheduled four additional trips through June 1990. The demand was much greater than expected and soon we were offering 6, then 12, and finally 16 schools through October to accommodate strong angler interest. We advertised the trips in local papers, but most students signed up for the schools on the basis of word-of-mouth advertising. Many students were repeat clients who discovered that, in addition to a learning experience, the schools also provide a high-quality fishing environment. Fellow fishers are serious about their pursuit, and the problems too often encountered on party boats are non-existent. As interest spread up the coast from San Diego, schools we added to target fisheries at Catalina, San Clemente, Santa Barbara, and San Nicholas Islands.

As the season unfolded, I was surprised to see how many students signed up for a variety of schools. Trips targeted yellowtail one month, shallow water ling cod the next, and albacore and tuna the later in the year. Many accomplished anglers began to sign up for the schools as they discovered these trips provided an ideal environment for a great day on the water. The crew works extra hard to locate fish, and the problems often encountered on party boats, including overcrowding, deadheads, and fishermen who are uncooperative or less than interested in fishing, are avoided. Instructors are readily available to help the novice with the basics but they are equally able to provide the more advanced fisherman with an opportunity to learn to refine his techniques.

Ronnie Kovach's Eagle Claw Fishing Schools have continued to expand with over 30 programs annually, providing year-round, limited load trips for beginners and veterans alike. These are excellent charters for anyone to get more involved in the sport. We provide plenty of help from the instructors and crew tailored to individual needs.

The schools are filling an important need for fishermen on the West Coast. The success of these schools is the result of a high level of commitment by the instructors, captains and crews, as well as tackle representatives and manufacturers. In addition, local experts share both their knowledge and love of fishing with others. That they are meeting their goals is indicated by the overall positive feedback from students and the high proportion of repeat sign-ups and word-of-mouth referrals.

Party Boat Lessons

The sportfishing fleets found from San Diego, California to Port Angeles, Washington comprise some of the most competitive recreational industries in the West. Boat captains must not only compete against nature, but against the rest of the fleet as well. Despite the camaraderie shared by many skippers, the bottom line is that each is vying for customers to patronize their vessels.

Pick the Right Boat

What makes one boat better than another? How does the recreational angler decide which sportfisher to select? To begin with, it is important to inspect the operation first hand if possible. Go down to the dock on a day you're not fishing. Check out the boat. Is it clean? Does it seem to be maintained properly? What about safety equipment—is it visible and accessible?

Ask the skipper or crew if you can board and look around. Does it have a galley in which you would want to eat? Does it have a posted menu of the food it serves?

Go below deck. If the boat has bunks for overnight sleeping, what are they like? Is there proper ventilation, clean sheets, pillows and adequate lighting? All of these facets of the vessel will contribute to your overall comfort and safety on a future trip. For many anglers, these amenities are ultimately more important than the number of fish caught.

On that note, there are other performance elements you can examine to evaluate the success of a given boat operation. For example, monitor fish counts. Although some sportfishers may "fudge" these dock totals from time to time, the fish count can give you some idea of just who the real "fish hunters" are. Talk to other anglers. When fishermen have a good experience with a particular boat and crew, they want to communicate that to fellow enthusiasts. Similarly, if there is a "bad rap" on a boat, other anglers will frequently relay that information. Ask pertinent questions such as "does the crew fish?"

Does the captain allow "deadheads" to hog the stern and the best baits? Is the crew ready, willing, and able when it comes to getting fish? Does the skipper seem to have solid control over his vessel and crew?

Be aware of cut rate prices and special deals that are advertised over and over for certain boats. Usually, but not always, the better operations aren't going to "give it away." They don't have to. A crew works hard to build up a reputation. Much of it is predicated on word-of-mouth testimonials among fellow anglers. Boats of this caliber will routinely carry more people because the fisherman will often return to a sportfisher that has had a successful outing.

The bottom line is that you get what you pay for—or at least you should. Be selective and careful to link up with the best operators you can. Then stay loyal to these guys, pass the word along about their boat, and tip generously!

Learn to Ask More Questions!

How can you insure that you are getting a fair shake from the captain, crew, and landing operators? The answer is simple: ask more questions. For example, inquire as to who will be running the vessel. Is the skipper the owner? Does he actually pilot the boat anymore, or does he primarily stay home to collect the checks?

Are you getting a veteran captain? What is his reputation like—surly, cantankerous, polite, laid back, aggressive? More importantly, with what type of personality do *you* feel most comfortable for a long day on the water? Understand that some of the best skippers who seem to always find fish are some of the worst when it comes to public relations. Others are great public relations people but lousy fish hunters. Try to find the best of both worlds—a good fisherman who also cares about his passengers.

As I mentioned, some boat owners have become absentee skippers. Either their business is too diverse with multiple boat ownership, or they have become lazy, or both. In either case, the vessel's reputation might be based more on past glory than how it is run today. Check it out—who is running the boat and what are his credentials? Do this *before* you charter the sportfisher or sign up for an open-party trip.

Too many skippers have taken the public for granted. Business is never "too good" in a down economy, even if the tuna or salmon show up in bountiful numbers. A shrewd party boat operator realizes that he is in the entertainment business as much as the fishing business. Customers should be treated properly to insure that they will return when the bite slows down and conditions get tough. This is when the better operations shine with loyal passengers showing up at the dock.

As a party boat passenger, voice your complaints to either the charter master, boat captain, or landing operator if you feel that something is wrong with the trip. Corrections can't be made unless the problem is addressed to the appropriate people. You wouldn't expect poor medical treatment from your doctor; a faulty job from your auto mechanic; or a lousy meal served at your favorite restaurant. There is no reason to accept poor skippering or crew work from your sport boat operator. Speak up!

Skippers on the Cutting Edge

Let's face it, there are good skippers and bad skippers, and some that fall somewhere between the two extremes. As director of the Eagle Claw Fishing Schools, I am in the business of chartering top-of-the-line sportfishing vessels. I must have those captains in the first category— the good ones—if I am to operate a prestigious on-the-water seminar program.

Did you ever wonder what separates the cream of the crop from the rest of the many people running sport boats along the West Coast? What distinguishes one skipper from being on that "cutting edge" of success while others are resigned to simply running adequate boats at best?

Here are some impressions which seem to clearly represent some of the things the best captains routinely do time after time which raises them to the top of the class.

Boat Handling

Invariably skippers must rest and let the back-up captain or first mate operate the vessel. This is an issue of crew discipline and recruitment that I'll talk about shortly. What I want to focus on, instead, is how the better captains seem to maintain an articulate control of their sportfishers.

For example, the real pro generally sets up his boat on a pinnacle or high spot after considerable monitoring of the ship's electronics. In many cases, such as shallow water rockfishing or working rock piles for calico bass, it is critical to get a pinpoint anchor set. Although the passengers often grow impatient, the shrewd skipper must frequently make many trial runs over a particular hot spot before he can position the boat properly while at anchor. Nothing short of precise accuracy will do for the captain on that cutting edge.

Similarly, when offshore tuna fishing, watch how the better skippers always seem to have a routine. They position their boats so the anglers quickly know that the drift will always start on either the starboard or port side of the vessel. There is often so much confusion when the fishermen hear the cry "JIG STRIKE," that anglers will often scramble from side to side in the stern as they jockey for position.

A captain who announces this simple routine of designating one side as the singular area to start fishing minimizes chaos and greatly improves the catch ratio. Rather than stopping and letting the passengers fish anywhere, helter-skelter, the smart skipper maintains control of the boat and establishes a sense of order for the trip.

Controlling the Crew

The best party boat operations typically involve a well-disciplined crew, carrying out the orders and representing the skipper in their on-deck behavior. I have seen many times in which a captain barely moves out from behind the shelter of the wheel house to scrutinize what his crew is doing on the deck.

Paying customers do not, for the most part, want to see deckhands fishing; nor do they want to shout for a gaff much more than that first request. The captains who pilot the better boats seem to always get personally involved with their crews when it comes to running the deck.

I have seen skippers like Buzz Brizendine of the "Prowler," Nick Cates of the "New Lo Ann," Steve Giffen of the "Holiday," or Jim Peterson of the "First String" routinely walk the deck. They frequently jump up on the bait tank to supervise the chumming first hand. It seems that these guys always know what their crews are doing and keep an eye out for those passengers who need help.

Better operators also seem to keep their crews together for a long time. Passengers like to feel a sense of community if not "family" between the skippers, the deckhands, and even the galley cook. Usually, when you encounter an operation that seems to regularly rotate through crew members, beware that this may reflect problems with the captain and his ability to run a tight organization.

Innovation

Those skippers on that cutting edge also seem to be some of the most innovative fishermen in the West. You will find that many boat operators are simply "me too" type captains. Their daily runs, whether for tuna or sand bass, simply amount to a "same time-same place" approach. Those on that cutting edge are willing to break from the "pack" and try to pioneer some new territory or a new plan of attack on their own.

I recall a classic example of this recently while fishing with Captain "Cookie" Cook on the Sport King out of L.A. Harbor Sportfishing. For days the Huntington Flats and the Horseshoe Kelp had been pounded by every small yacht and party boat alike during the annual sand bass migration in the late spring. The bite was primarily concentrated in 90 to 120 feet of water on a hard bottom. Well, as luck would have it, we started out at this depth along with an awesome armada of over 150 other boats. By 10:00 a.m. it had become clear that something had changed and the bite was off.

Cook decided to bolt away from the fleet, heading south to the shallow waters off Huntington Beach. With decades of boat operating experience behind him, he explained how sometimes smaller schools of sand bass travel away from the mass and head into the shallow confines, not too far beyond the surf line.

Working in 30-40 foot depths, Cook found that "mother lode" of shallow biters. There were no other boats within five miles of us. By 1:00 p.m. we had all 30 anglers limited out with sand bass and a bonus round of keeper-size barracuda. Captain Cook radioed for the other boats to later join us and share in this new honey hole.

Captains like Billy Stevens, formerly of the "Cherokee Geisha," similarly demonstrate that innovative bend when it comes to locating hard-to-find offshore yellowtail and tuna. Stevens—a veteran airplane pilot—might actually fly his small plane looking for floating kelp paddies. He then radios the information to a small group of other boats. Amazingly, only a few shrewd captains are willing to share in Stevens' flying expenses, in exchange for receiving valuable coordinates for finding these floating "yellowtail motels."

Innovation also takes the form of making radical changes in tackle and lure presentation. The pioneering of San Diego's famous long-range skippers in developing an approach utilizing big surface plugs for tuna is a key example of this type of innovation. Up until recently, surface plugs were used primarily in Hawaii and for coastal striped bass fishing. Now, this obscure tactic produces some of the most spectacular tuna and dorado fishing on our local waters because the long-range operators had the vision to try these new baits deep into Mexican waters.

A Demand for Precision

The better skippers are adamant when it comes to precise presentation of lures or bait. Watch these guys carefully when they come down from the wheel house to put on a casting demonstration. Their tackle might look beat up at times, but I'll bet the rod, reel and line are precisely balanced for what they are doing. You won't see excellent anglers like these men casting a metal jig with a live bait stick, nor will you see them fooling around.

One of the most articulate captains to ever fish the Southern California scene is now-turned tackle manufacturer Russ Izor. A passenger on Captain Izor's "First String" would invariably receive a lecture on proper tackle selection from hook, line and sinker to rod and reel.

Many times Izor was confronted with horrible, weak puny anchovies while trying to fish Catalina Island in the summer months. His solution was simple: switch to an 8 foot spinning rod, lighter 12 to 15 pound test mono, and a smaller hook. Now the angler can more easily cast tiny pinhead 'chovies, with the little baits swimming better dragging against the fine diameter line. I might add that Izor's concern for precision tackle left a lasting impression with me and is a major point of emphasis on my Eagle Claw Saltwater Fishing Schools.

The Gambler Aspect

Sometimes it takes more than a concern for precision combined with innovation to find fish. Some of the best trips I recall occurred as a result of a skipper parlaying a long shot into a bonanza.

Captain Irv Grisbeck on the "Trilene Big Game" played the high-stakes game on a 3 1/2 day school I chartered during midsummer tuna season. After the first day, in rough seas out 90 miles, it was clear that the bite had fizzled and we were in store for two more days of scratch fishing at best.

Grisbeck discussed the situation candidly with my instructors and myself. One option—a calculated long shot—would be to motor south another 12 to 14 hours to the Benitos Island chain. Although we would be essentially sacrificing about one whole day of fishing time, in exchange for only about one solid day of fishing, we all agreed the risk was worth it.

As it turned out, we encountered some of the most unexpected, big 25 to 35 pound class yellowtail fishing of the season at Benitos. Our students got the trip of a lifetime, in much calmer seas, although they lost one day of fishing. Grisbeck's gamble–including absorbing the extra fuel costs—paid off in spades.

Other skippers like Brizendine, Cates and Giffen are legendary in their commitment to push the time to its maximum limit. These captains depend extensively upon solid one-day yellowtail or tuna action during the height of the season. One-day boats also have an optimal range of about 90 to 110 miles maximum, if they are to turn around and get back to port the same day.

Often it comes down to "no guts—no glory" for the one-day fleet. The skippers must shoot craps and make the longest possible run in order to find new schools of fish. In addition to checking the fish count at the dock, consider asking when the day-boat operators usually return to the dock. The skippers who stay out the longest are usually the ones with the best scores of yellowtail and tuna.

Patience and Perseverance

The captains who are on this cutting edge of angling and fish-finding professionalism also demonstrate the highest degree of patience and perseverance. In a nutshell, they don't panic, and they don't give up.

Skippers of this caliber have been there before when it comes to piloting the boat on your particular outing. They have fished in full moon conditions, green water, cold water, and the roughest seas. They have had to work with poor bait, small bait and even no bait. Their wealth of experience combined with a gutsy approach to their profession gives them the edge over adversity compared to most private boaters and less accomplished captains.

You have to understand that these are truly "men of the sea." Without creating an excessively romantic portrait of these top sportfishing skippers, the fact remains that they are running their boats because they love what they do. Most likely they can find better paying jobs with more reasonable hours. They entered this profession because of their passion for both catching and finding fish. Unlike the less-pressured locales like Hawaii or Florida, these skippers on the West Coast really have to be with the "program" if they are to tally fish in our local waters.

Lessons to be Learned

I'm not trying to simply glorify these party boat captains. This portrait of the top skippers of this particular fleet should give the recreational angler a better idea of what to look for when selecting a first class, well-run party or charter boat anywhere along the Pacific Coast.

There are valuable lessons to be learned from the attributes of these premier skippers. The values, attitudes, and approaches they internalize are certainly worthwhile for the recreational angler to emulate. These are the individuals who routinely catch the most and largest fish year after year. Their success, like that of any angler, is more a result of hard work than pure dumb luck.

Study these captains carefully. There is room for more fishermen on that cutting edge!

More Party Boat Strategy

The San Diego fleet of sportfishers is widely recognized as one of the premier operations for this type of marine angling. Invariably, saltwater buffs from beginner to expert alike from virtually all over the West venture south to San Diego to chase yellowtail, albacore, and tuna. These are some of the most valued species caught by sportfishing boats along the Pacific Coast.

The landings that operate out of San Diego collectively offer the widest range of sportfishing boats from which to choose. These landings can accommodate you, whether you prefer a half, three-quarters, full, or multi-day trip. San Diego party boat skippers realize that their job is easier when the passengers have some basic knowledge of the inside secrets of fishing the South Coast waters. A customer who has had a successful trip is more likely to enjoy himself and therefore more likely to book additional trips.

Here then are some of the insiders' tips from six of San Diego's finest sportfishing skippers. These tips might help you to dramatically improve your catch whether you are on a party boat or your own private vessel from San Diego to Coos Bay, irrespective of the species you are attempting to catch.

Come Prepared!

Captain Billy Stephens, a veteran charter boat and open party boat captain, states that many passengers have little notion as to what to bring out on an all-day trip fishing the Pacific.

"Check the dock counts," notes Stephens, "particularly in the prime summer months. See what we are catching. The kind of fish that show up in the counts tells the angler something about the test line he should have on his reels, the lures to use, the hook size, and the type of bait to select." Stephens emphasizes that veteran party boat anglers carefully monitor the dock totals, then gear up with an array of rods and reels so they can handle almost any contingency. Scrutinize these reports from Seattle to Cabo San Lucas, utilizing local sports pages or weekly outdoor tabloids.

Develop Rapport

Veteran skipper Nick Cates of Point Loma's "New Lo Ann" firmly believes that this communication skill is vital in becoming an accomplished party boater. "Find a crew you really like," stresses Cates, "develop rapport with them, and stay with that boat. These guys will then give you the inside scoop once you develop that rapport." Captain Cates notes that the crew often reserves the better baits in the tank for customers they feel have shown a sincere interest in wanting to learn and who are willing to follow instructions.

Ralph Botticelli pilots Point Loma's half-day boat, the "Daily Double." He, too, encourages his passengers to immediately introduce themselves to his crew to set up a learning situation for the day's outing. "Also," says Botticelli, "talk to other successful anglers. Don't be afraid to ask for tips and help."

Hooking Live Baits

The party boat fisherman can also learn how to properly hook a bait from a veteran crew member. "Collar a deckhand," suggests Captain Cates, "and have him show you how to hook the baits. This is the most important thing to live bait fishing. If you learn this, you will have a better chance of catching a fish on a slow day."

Veteran skippers emphasize that the angler must closely scale the size of the hook to the test line he is casting. "An extremely small hook on 30 pound line makes no sense at all," claims Captain Irv Grisbeck of the "Trilene Big Game." "If you fish 30 to 40 pound mono, you have to use a larger hook that can withstand the pressure when you set up with the heavy line."

Captain Donny Boulette is a recognized big fish expert. "When you are chasing big fish like tuna with heavy line," notes Boulette, "don't make the mistake of using a hook that is too small. The hook size must be matched with the bait and fish. People fail to realize that a big tuna will hit a large #7/0 hook with a tiny pinhead anchovy on it."

Fish the Bow

Party boats are sometimes difficult to fish in a wide-open bite with novice anglers all bunched up in the stern. Many fishermen prefer to stay planted in the rear of the boat—often becoming so-called "stern hogs"—because this is where all the chumming occurs.

Interestingly enough, one of the most productive yet generally unfished areas of the boat is at the other end in the bow. According to Captain Grisbeck, "there comes a point where you can't get beyond the upwind corner of the stern. When this happens, consider moving to the bow. The chum from the stern gets pushed up the boat's keel and, on many boats, ends up swirling in the bow."

This explains why many shrewd party boat fishermen often relocate from the stern to the bow after that first flurry of activity, following, for example, a jig stop on tuna. There is less chance of becoming broken off by a mass of converging lines. There is also less frenzy and confusion with fewer anglers working the bow and, as Grisbeck observes, a migration of chum bait that may actually end up in the front portion of the vessel.

Understand Kelp Paddies

When the action gets really heated up in the southernmost waters, it usually coincides with the appearance of floating offshore kelp paddies. These clumps of broken kelp can become a virtual "oasis" in a wide area of otherwise "dead" water. They are sometimes affectionately referred to as "yellowtail hotels," since these fish and members of the tuna family will frequently gravitate to the schools of bait found under the floating kelp stringers. Interestingly, floating kelp paddies like these can also "hitchhike" on a warm current and travel all the way to San Francisco Bay.

One of the most critical mistakes the neophyte makes is casting too soon as the sportfisher approaches the kelp paddy. "It is important not to cast too early," observes Captain Stephens. "Give the boat a chance to stop. Wait for the skipper to give the 'okay' over the P.A. system. The fish—particularly yellowtail—will usually charge the boat once it stops." Thus, by waiting to cast, the lines will be more spread out, keeping tangles and lost fish to a minimum.

Another often overlooked dimension to working the paddies is to fish considerably deeper than is typically done on most party boats. Captain Buzz Brizendine of the "Prowler" has put on some convincing demonstrations using heavier sinkers to catch not only more but also larger 'tails and tuna by getting the bait into deeper strike zones.

"It's just Greek to most anglers," explains Brizendine. "They just don't realize how much more effective it is to use a fairly heavy sinker on kelp paddy fish. Most of the yellowtail and tuna found under paddies are at 10 to 15 fathoms, not near the surface. It's like freshwater bass fishing—if you monitor fish at 50 feet, you wouldn't throw a surface plug at them. The same goes for paddy fishing. Use a sinker—you have to get the bait to where the fish are!" (More on kelp paddies and sinker usage later.)

Another Tip—Throw Plastics!

Too many anglers are remiss in not utilizing the wealth of soft plastic lures now on the market when they fish the Pacific. Captain Buzz Brizendine of the "Prowler" observes: "Many anglers clearly overlook the seasonal versatility of soft plastic lures, particularly in colder water conditions. For example, on our trips to the Punta Mesquite reefs south of San Diego, we consistently take some of the largest shallow water rockfish, ling cod, as well as sand and calico bass on plastic baits like Caba Caba Tubes, Scampies, Mojos, Lunker Thumpers, and Salty Magics."

Lures in this genre are available in an awesome array of colors and designs. Keep a wide selection in your tackle box to try when live bait and the "iron" fail to get bit. Brizendine suggests adding a small 1x3 inch strip of dead squid to the hook on any of these plastic baits. This will provide supplemental taste and scent for the bass and bottom fish.

Longer Rods for Live Baits

For many years, Southern Californians preferred short, powerful, 5 to 6 foot rods that allowed them to quickly "short pump" or stroke the fish quickly back to the boat. Although rods of this design are indeed strong enough to turn a big yellowtail or tuna, they are often impractical for throwing tiny anchovies with the stiffer fiberglass blanks. In contrast, anglers from San Francisco to Port Angeles, Washington have often utilized softer tip, longer rods on local trips.

Captain Ralph Botticelli of the "Daily Double" says, "It really helps to have a good bait stick, preferably 8 foot long with a good backbone and a medium light tip for throwing live baits." Botticelli notes that when the angler fishes the local kelp beds, especially for calico bass, he must be able to cast an anchovy or sardine a considerable distance. "Use the longer rod when fishing the kelp beds," says Botticelli. "Those people who can cast a live bait far away from the boat with the right rod will also have the power to pull calico bass out of the kelp. These are our most successful half-day anglers."

Remain Flexible!

One thing that all these longtime San Diego skippers recommend is for the party boat angler to remain highly flexible when fishing in this part of the south coast. The major migratory species that frequent these waters can be highly temperamental at times. One day, for instance, the yellowtails might annihilate the "iron," cast-metal jigs yo-yoed under kelp paddies. The next day the same group of fish may show no interest in artificial lures eating only a lively 'chovy on 12 to 15 pound string.

So the best advice may be to simply ask, then look and listen. Ask the skippers and crew what's happening. Look at the daily fish reports put out by these landings and watch what the successful party boat buffs are doing. Finally, listen to the deckhands and skippers when they talk about what is working for them. Each day the "program" can change. Develop a congenial rapport with the crew, learn from them, then implement the inside secrets!

The Pros' Hot Tips!

As you can see, learning to become an accomplished angler on a crowded party boat is no easy feat. Fishermen who ride these vessels frequently year after year often wonder why their success rate fails to improve. To understand this problem a little better, we must first look at the typical party boat environment. Unlike private yachts or chartered boats, a large sportfisher running an "open party" operation simply lets anyone on until they reach a full load. Passengers come from all walks of life and often range from first-time novices to longtime "regulars" who may assume more expert status.

On the better run sportfishers the captain and crew actively participate in helping their passengers both prepare for and then execute procedures during the day's outing. Unfortunately, a lot of people either fail to take advantage of a veteran crew's knowledge and assistance, or the crew itself becomes lax in assisting the passengers.

So what can you do? The single best piece of advice is to at least minimally watch what the more successful anglers do to beat the "party boat blues." Learn to adapt some of their integral "tricks of the trade" to maximize your chances on the water. Here then are some succinct tips commonly practiced by the shrewd veteran anglers. (In upcoming chapters I will elaborate more on some of these tricks as they apply to specific species.)

The Night Bite

Many three-quarter or full-day trips depart in darkness in order to reach the prime fishing grounds by daybreak. Typically, many passengers nestle into the bunks once the boat gets out of the harbor, ready to awaken at the smell of the morning bacon frying in the galley.

This is a practical approach if the vessel will still be running at dawn. Invariably with trips to the Farallons, San Clemente Island, the Los Coronados, or even the Mexican outer tuna banks, the skipper may shut the engines down in total darkness and either anchor or drift until daylight.

The smart angler will head out onto the deck when most of the remaining passengers are still down in their bunks. At the islands, this is an excellent time to target barracuda, calico, as well as sand and white sea bass in the dark! It is not uncommon for even the beginning angler to put some nice rockfish or ling cod in the sack by working in the wee, quiet hours of the morning.

These surface species usually hold at deeper depths during the night bite. This is why many anglers who take advantage of the uncrowded night bite will frequently fish live or dead bait with heavier than normal sinkers. They might also throw a soft plastic lure laced on a lead head to tap into these schools of sub-surface fish.

Many fishermen, including some die-hard veterans, firmly believe that it's not worth getting up to fish at night 70 miles out on a tuna run. Gamefish like yellowfin and bluefin tuna and albacore will definitely bite in total darkness—not just the early morning "gray" period, but even in TOTAL DARKNESS! Again, this can be a great opportunity to fish an uncrowded deck that might be in chaos later in the day.

Select Primo Baits

If you watch closely, you will note that some anglers seem to take a long time to pick a live anchovy or sardine from the bait tank. It's as if they are actually "studying" the bait. The accomplished party boater selects his baits very carefully. Put simply, not all baits are alike. This is particularly true with anchovies—the most popular live bait found on sportfishers. If you look carefully in the live

wells, you will see that some 'chovies are clearly friskier than others. Avoid selecting a large sluggish bait if a smaller more energetic specimen is available.

Next, examine the color of the anchovy's back. A majority of these baitfish will have a dark black dorsal coloration. However, a small percentage of the 'chovy population in a bait tank may have a distinctive greenish tint along the backbone instead. "Greenies" like these seem to be stronger baits than black-back 'chovies and, hence, get bit better.

Avoid picking a sardine, smelt, or anchovy that has a prominent red nose, patches of skin missing, or is wallowing from side to side on the surface of the bait well. These are usually weak baits. They won't swim well or for very long. Pass on this weak stock and look for a healthier model.

Fish Big Baits!

Although he may not catch the most fish, invariably the expert party boat angler who uses big baits will bring in the larger jackpot contenders. Let's say, for example, you are fishing calico bass primarily with anchovies. Quite frequently, a smaller population of "brown baits" consisting of tom cod, queenfish, herring, and perch is mixed in with the 'chovies.

While other passengers are culling through sub-12 inch bass trying to find a keeper fish, throw out a brown bait. The larger "bull" calicos will single out this offering while passing on the smaller anchovies that are being put in front of them. The same holds true for ling cod with voracious appetites. Other larger baits may be found mixed in with the 'chovies. Spanish and greenback mackerel, sardines, or smelt are all excellent alternatives for other species when anchovies seem to produce only smaller class fish.

Feather Your Bait!

Quite often the overwhelming majority of bait in the tanks are in a weak condition. It's tough to get gamefish to strike bait that won't swim much after they are cast. The veteran saltwater pro compensates for this situation by "feathering" the bait. Leave the reel in free spool and move the spool so slightly with your thumbs or fingertips to pull the bait back. A similar procedure can be practiced with a spinning reel. Leave the bail open and gently pull the slack line in a few inches, then manually wrap it around the spool.

This is what is meant by "feathering" the bait. The key is to pull the line in, using quick little spurts so that the bait kind of twitches and jerks on the retrieve. Frequently, inducing this erratic swimming action from an otherwise weak bait is just enough to trigger a strike from a wary surface fish.

Fish Deep!

As I mentioned with the night bite, there are times when it is better to fish deep. For example, on my Eagle Claw Fishing Schools during the summer months in southern waters my instructors work with the students to "wean" them away from the popular fly-line strategy.

Most of us learned that the best way to get bit with pelagic species is to cast an anchovy or other bait out, practically weightless, and let it peel out line near the surface. There are two problems with totally embracing the fly-line technique at the expense of a deeper approach.

1. Sometimes both the school of bait and the gamefish themselves may be significantly below the surface chum that is being thrown off the stern.

2. Some of the larger fish in the school may situate themselves below the smaller specimens and lazily pick off the weaker or crippled baitfish.

By adding a significantly larger sinker above the bait–perhaps as much as a 2 ounce ringed sinker—you may be able to tap into more and larger fish.

On our summer Eagle Claw Schools, many of the albacore in the 25 to 35 pound range were caught fishing deep bait like this. Small 8 to 12 pound yellowfin tuna provided most of the top fly-line activity.

Vary Retrieves

Too many saltwater anglers make the mistake of throwing out an artificial lure and cranking it in at the same speed, cast after cast, regardless of what species or time of year they are fishing. Some gamefish such as yellowtail or bonito prefer a cast-metal jig, for example, retrieved at a fairly high speed. The accomplished yellowtail hunter will use a reel with nothing less than a 5:1 gear ratio if the 'tails are on the surface iron or a yo-yo grind.

In contrast, barracuda typically key in on a much slower retrieve. This is true whether you are casting a candy bar style jig, a metal spoon, feather, or even a soft plastic lure for 'cuda—you have to "slow it down." Sometimes barries in particular will strike a lure on a stop-and-go retrieve. After making the cast, let the spoon or jig sink for a few seconds. Start to wind, but intermittently completely stop to let the lure sink. Invariably, the fish will attack the spoon or jig on the fall in this stop-and-go retrieve.

Other species like calico bass, stripers, or salmon will also home in on a slow-moving jig, spoon, or soft plastic bait. This is especially the case in colder water where the metabolism of the fish is slowed down and it simply won't move fast enough to attack anything.

Study the successful party boat anglers. Observe the lures they are using, as well as how they are *retrieving* them on a given day. If the bite is sporadic at best, it may pay to be experimental and mix up your retrieves until you find the pattern the fish prefer.

Checking Line and Knots

Another mistake beginners often make involves not re-currently checking line for nicks and frays. The most minuscule fracture in monofilament can result in a lost fish when you have to put pressure on the line. Veteran pros get into the habit of running their fingers over the 18 to 24 inches of mono above the hook to check for knocks and excessive kinking. If it is less than perfectly smooth—re-tie your hook and lure. Don't take a chance on a lost fish.

Equally important is to learn to tie a few good knots for saltwater trips. Not only do you need to tie the knot properly, it must be carefully cinched down or drawn tight against the lure's split ring or hook eyelet.

Too often I have seen novice anglers tie a seemingly correct knot but forget to draw it tight to prevent inadvertent slipping or even cutting which breaks the line at the knot. A handy little tip is to carefully moisten the knot with saliva before you draw the line down tight. This moisture minimizes friction and keeps the strands of monofilament from cutting into each other.

Use Your Drag

The drag mechanism on either a baitcaster or spinning reel is what you need to rely upon to tire out the fish. It is important to pre-set the drag prior to making your initial casts. My instructors and I have found that it helps to have the drag set somewhat loose for the beginning angler. Too often the novice fisher reaches for the drag knob or star wheel to tighten the drag while the fish is making a scorching run. A moderate drag setting to begin with prevents overtightening and, possibly, a broken line.

Better yet, try to keep your hands off the drag as much as possible. Ask the deckhands to pre-set it for you. They know where it should be set for the best chance of bringing in the fish.

Keep your thumb off that baitcasting spool! Sometimes there may be a tendency to use your thumb to slow the spool down when a fish is making a run. *Don't do it!* You can quickly blister your thumb from the friction generated by the line moving off the reel. Also, let your reel drag do the work. It has greater precision than your thumb. Persisting in "thumbing" the spool inevitably accounts for many lost fish by beginning anglers.

On another note, remember that saltwater live bait reels also do not have level wind mechanisms as do freshwater bass-casting models. So you should level wind the monofilament onto the spool yourself by guiding it between your thumb and index finger as you reel in.

Avoid letting the line build up on either the sides or the middle of the baitcasting reel. If a fish decides to make a fast run with the line bunched up in one spot, either the drag will fail to respond or the mono will cut into itself as gaps are formed on the spool. In either case, you will most likely lose the fish.

Follow Your Line!

On our schools, my instructors have a saying they frequently repeat on the deck: "No angles, no tangles." What this means is that it is important to keep your line in front of you at all times. This is true whether you are fly-lining on the surface, bottom-fishing, or drifting. You have optimal control over your bait or lure when you're "squared off" directly in front of the line. This also allows for a better swing and set of the fish with minimal line stretch.

This strategy also applies to playing out a fish. Once you hook up, you must *follow your fish!* This holds true for pelagic species like tuna and yellowtail, coastal predators like salmon and striped bass, as well as bottom grabbers like sharks and ling cod. All of these fish will pull you around the boat! This cannot be stressed enough for proper party boat etiquette. By following your fish, you not only keep the line in front of you at all times, but you also avoid crossing lines and tangling up with fellow passengers. If you don't move with your fish, you may lose it. When lines cross, it doesn't take much time or pressure to have the fish "sawed" off when the lines cut into each other. Move quickly and deftly to follow your fish!

Light-Lining

On our Eagle Claw Saltwater Schools we strongly encourage our passengers to use lighter tackle. Our instructors try to get party boat fishermen to move away from that 25 to 40 pound gear and scale down to 12 to 20 pound test line. This means using smaller reels, lighter action rods, and fine diameter monofilament. Anglers soon discover

that they clearly get bit more with the light tackle than other passengers using the heavier gear. Why is this so?

1. The fishery all along the West Coast tends to receive a lot of angling pressure especially on weekends. The various gamefish species are hammered with a barrage of live bait and lures. The fine diameter monofilament is simply more difficult for hook-shy gamefish to see, particularly when there is a lot of boat traffic in the area.

2. Light line makes the live bait swim more freely. A small pinhead anchovy is too tiny, for example, to be dragging out 30 pound string. This same bait on 12 pound mono becomes transformed into a highly active little dynamo palatable to even the most skittish gamefish.

Twelve to 20 pound test mono also allows smaller lures such as fathers, spoons, soft plastics, and compact cast-metal jigs to "swim" better. The light line creates less drag and resistance, with minimal impairment to the specific action of a given lure.

Multiple Outfits

On this note, the accomplished party boat pro begins to develop an arsenal of gear that can accommodate any situation encountered on a particular outing. As much as light gear has been emphasized here, there is a time and place for heavier tackle. For instance, you wouldn't want to be fishing heavy-duty freshwater bass tackle on 30 to 40 pound yellowfin tuna on a crowded party boat. In this situation, it is necessary to upscale your gear using 20 to 40 pound test mono and heavier spinning or baitcasting reels.

Similarly, even fishing for shallow water rockfish off San Simeon, for example, the angler might want to switch from standard 20 to 30 pound gear to lighter freshwater bass combos, tossing lures with 10 to 12 pound string. This can become a viable option if the rockfish are real finicky.

If you watch a longtime party boat angler, you will probably see him switching off, using light, medium and heavy outfits throughout the day. The light rig is for spooky fish, tiny baits, and small artificials. Use it with 10 to 15 pound line. The medium outfit features 20 pound string for most live bait fishing. The heavy gear relies on 25 to 40 pound line for throwing jumbo baits and larger artificial lures as well as for big fish ready to bite. As you develop more confidence in fishing party boats, carefully invest in a systematic approach with your gear, developing a tackle repertoire of light, medium, and heavy outfits.

Pros Love Lures!

I cannot emphasize enough how important it is to expand your options in becoming a better party boat angler. This translates into moving away from simply using live bait all the time and into trying an array of artificial lures.

As I noted, fishing the Pacific Coast can often be a tough proposition. The successful party boat fisherman realizes that he is in competition with the other anglers on the vessel and has live bait soaking all around him. Hence, selecting a lure to use under certain situations gives the fish something different to see besides the armada of live 'chovies commonly used on these trips.

A cast-metal jig, spoon, feather, plug, or soft plastic lure often provides the various gamefish with a different silhouette and action, which may trigger a strike in otherwise disinterested species. Sometimes more fish can also be tallied using artificials simply because the angler is able to canvass more water with more casts. This is true for salmon, striped bass, tuna, yellowtail, and the glamorous billfish species as well as bottom denizens including ling cod, flounder, halibut, and rockfish.

Similarly, artificial lures frequently account for the larger fish sacked each trip. In contrast to live bait, the expert lure fishermen will often work the artificials through deeper strike zones looking for larger specimens holding beneath the rest of the school.

The prominent profile of a jig, spoon, soft plastic, or plug offers the larger gamefish a more substantial morsel on which to focus compared to the smaller live baits used by the rest of the passengers.

Dump the Chutes!

Finally, here is a little tip worth noting to conclude these pro tips: be ready when the deckhands "dump the chutes." This is towards the end of the day when the crew calls it quits and empties the bait tanks.

This sudden commotion often creates one last feeding frenzy with the additional bait dumped off the stern. Always move to the back of the boat and try to fire off a few final casts. The sudden influx and noise of the flushing of the bait tanks can sometimes stimulate a larger fish holding far back in the outside chum line to move up to the stern for a final foray. Many jackpot winners come when the deckhands decide to "dump the chutes"!

Along this same line, don't hesitate to make a quick final cast just before the skipper moves the boat to a new spot. As he begins to pull up the anchor and move the boat forward, a lot of bait that was finding sanctuary under the hull now becomes exposed off the stern. Here again, there is a prime opportunity to nail the lone jackpot fish as the bigger specimens make a final charge at the exposed bait.

Again—Learn to Be Adaptable!

These basic tips will help you in becoming a more effective party boat angler. Above and beyond all the tricks with tackle, bait, and on-deck maneuvering, your greatest resource will be your ability to adapt quickly. Even the most accomplished saltwater buffs routinely stop to observe what is going on around them. If they are not getting bit and someone else is, they carefully analyze what the person is doing to enhance success. Novice party boaters should routinely stop and take a moment to make such observations. Then, adjust your "program," adapting to the strategies that are producing results at that time. Remember, conditions may change dramatically on a given trip from hour to hour so adaptation is an on-going process.

Do this and I guarantee you will beat the party boat blues!

How to Win Jackpots

One of the routine rituals of party boat fishing is competing in the jackpot. This is the modest cash pool anglers voluntarily contribute to prior to departure. The cost to participate usually ranges between two and five dollars per person. At the end of the trip, the deckhand will ask all anglers to bring their largest fish back to the stern, where they will be weighed on a balance bar against the other passengers' trophies.

A lot of jackpot fishing depends upon luck. Then again, it is often the shrewd veteran who knows the inside tricks and invariably takes home the "J.P." If you want to play in this low-level tournament, let me share with you some basic tips that might help produce the biggest fish of the day.

First of all, the adage "BIG BAITS CATCH BIG FISH" is definitely applicable for these party boat trips. Rather than tossing the routine menu of pinhead anchovies on a local sand bass or calico bite, be selective and look for a large "brown bait" in the tank. This collection of herring, tom cod, small shiner perch or queenfish is a favorite of big "bull" calicos, lunker-class ling cod or "barn door" halibut.

Similarly, on an offshore bite, consider fly-lining the larger sardines or mackerel instead of the standard anchovy fare. Bigger tuna, dorado and maybe even a striped marlin will home in on the larger baitfish which will stand out in a chum line of 'chovies'.

Trophy pelagic species such as bonito, salmon, stripers, barracuda, bass, yellowtail and tuna will also attack a well-presented artificial lure. Again, the cast-iron jig, soft plastic tail-swimming bait, or highly polished spoon may present a larger, more dramatic silhouette to surface-feeding gamefish on the prowl for a big morsel.

Larger gamefish will also frequently be found at deeper strike zones than the rest of the school. On our Eagle Claw Saltwater Seminars, my instructors routinely lecture the students to fish deep! While working the deck on our special charters, we will often go around from angler to angler and add larger, heavier sinkers to their setups to get them out of the strict fly-line mode. Veteran party boat skippers frequently mention, for example, that some of the largest specimens in both tuna and yellowtail tallied each season are caught in the deeper 15 fathom range. Fish deep!

Finally, steadfast perseverance may be the single most important ingredient to becoming a perennial jackpot contender. So often, the winning "J.P." fish is caught by the angler who was rigged properly and ready to cast when the captain gave the word. On the other hand, I've seen my share of jackpot fish weighed in by an angler who has confidence in what he is doing and sticking with that program until the skipper starts the engines and heads back home.

If you are fortunate to win that jackpot, also remember to share in the wealth with the crew. These past seasons have been pretty lean years financially speaking for the West Coast sportfishing industry. For you, the lucky angler, this is a form of recreation. For the crew, this is their livelihood. Give them a share of your "J.P." cash—they'll remember you the next time!

The Hidden Essentials

Many anglers who fish the Pacific Coast often overlook some of the "hidden essentials" that can make their outings even more pleasurable. Besides the basic array of reels, rods, and terminal tackle, there are several other things you might consider taking along on a sportfishing boat.

If you are packing sea sickness medication with the idea of taking it only if you start to feel ill, be aware that once you start feeling bad, it is usually too late for the medication to help. Follow directions precisely and consult your physician if necessary. Above all, if you think

you may become seasick, start your medication before you leave the dock (check the box for the suggested time span).

Another preventative worth packing is sunscreen. Even on hazy, overcast days it is possible to get a nasty burn in a relatively short span of time. Dermatologists inform us that the frequency of skin cancer is on the rise, especially on the West Coast. Consider applying sunscreen before the bite heats up, since it is tough to take a break from the action.

If the bite gets red hot, plan on getting your feet wet as you move around the deck. Although boat shoes, sneakers, or sandals are more fashionable, a better long-term investment might be a pair of rubber deck boots.

On cold mornings, keep your hands warm with either mittens or gloves. You can purchase wool mittens especially designed for fishermen with the finger tips cut out to allow for a better feel. Try a pair of the new neoprene gloves like those used in scuba diving.

A hat will keep the sun from frying your head as well as keeping the anchovy scales out of your hair as the deckhands chum in the stern. Don't expect the ship's galley to have amenities like these for sale. Do your shopping before you board the boat.

Water is another overlooked essential. Some boats have water readily available in the galley, while on others it is hard to find. If you are going to need water for thirst or dehydration, consider bringing your own plastic bottle along to play it safe.

Finally, if you are taking an overnight trip, you might want to bring along some extra warm clothing to wear down in the bunks. Most sportfishers will provide you with a blanket and a pillow when you get your bunk assignment. If you have any tendency to get cold at night, bring some extra clothes for sleeping. You can strip away the layers in the morning as the weather warms. On multi-day trips where showers are available, plan on bringing your own towel.

Polarized Eyewear

One of the most overlooked pieces of equipment in the serious bass fisherman's repertoire is superior sunglasses. Over the years we have talked about the need for anglers to invest in good sunglasses as perhaps the ultimate fish-finding device. Above and beyond this, keep in mind that eyes also need the protection from ultraviolet (UV) light quality sunglasses can provide. Not all sunglasses provide these features.

We have looked at many different sunglasses in search of the ultimate product that would feature the following characteristics: 1) superior polarization, 2) light weight, 3) scratch resistance, and 4) affordablity. After considerable experimentation, we believe we have found the ultimate fishing sunglasses in the product line made by Costa Del Mar of Florida. Saltwater anglers need to have superior polarization in a lens. Polarization blocks the nasty horizontal reflected light we call glare. This greatly increases your ability to see below the surface of the water and thus to spot key targets.

So, check out the sunglasses you own now. If they are not polarized—no matter how expensive or fashionable they are—they aren't what you need for fishing. Pick a pair that will help you on the water. Polarization is the only effective method for removing dangerous and irritating glare.

We like Costa Del Mar because it specializes in polarized protective eyewear specifically designed for fishermen. The lenses are optically correct, hard coated for scratch resistance, and provide the ultimate in glare reduction. In addition to being fashionable, these models are also exceptionally lightweight, durable and suitable for serious tournament angling and guiding where sunglasses may be worn from 10 to 18 hours per day.

These sunglasses also come in a variety of lens colors which filter out varying amounts of glare and light for a variety of situations. Select the color that works best under the conditions you will be fishing.

Color	Percent Light Transmitted	Fishing Conditions
light gray	21 %	maximum glare moderate sunlight
dark gray	10%	maximum glare intense sunlight
light amber	29%	maximum glare sight fishing low light, haze or fog
dark amber	12%	(same as light amber)
light vermilion	21%	under maximum glare provides visual acuity enhances color
dark vermilion	10%	(same as light vermilion)

Think about how many times you have tried to follow your cast, pick up your jig as it hits the water, or tried to "sight" fish while casting to tuna boiling on the corner? If you take this sport seriously, then consider developing a repertoire of lens colors for such critical conditions as low light, intense sun, glare, fog or haze.

Quality *polarized* sunglasses are an essential addition to your saltwater tackle collection. These glasses also help to protect your eyes under extreme climatic conditions. The investment is well worth it!

Small Craft Lessons

For many saltwater anglers, the ultimate dream is to own their own boat. In contrast to open party boats or charter vessels, smaller craft permit fishermen to come and go as they please without being tied to a specific landing's schedule. Also, to some degree, there is nothing like being your own captain, facing the challenge of making your own decisions and designing your own strategies for a given day on the water.

Basic Tactics

Smaller craft—although usually faster than large scale sportfishers—nevertheless have two key problems that may inhibit their success: 1) lack of range and 2) limited bait supply.

Still the shrewd private boater can make some specific adjustments that will diminish the potential impact of limited range and bait. Let's look at both of these issues and some of the strategies small craft owners can implement to improve their chances.

Limited Range

For the most part, few private vessels under 40 feet in length are going to have the fuel capacity to travel much more than 200 miles total distance. This puts most West Coast based boats well within the various zones for finding substantial numbers of fish.

The most obvious spots are offshore islands. Santa Catalina, San Clemente, the Farallons and the Channel Islands are all within a one-day trip range for the properly equipped private boat. Similarly, the Los Coronados Islands are only 14 miles south of San Diego Harbor again offering a potential target for even the smaller 17 to 25 foot craft.

What the novice boater often overlooks are the tremendous inshore possibilities that are so close to a variety of local landings or public launch ramps. The following are some classic examples.

The Horseshoe Kelp is a matter of a 30 to 60 minute run out of L.A. Harbor. The "Shoe" persists in providing some of the best opportunities to nail bonito, bass, barracuda, and yellowtail anywhere in the Southland. The famous Huntington Flats area, also less than an hour from L.A. Harbor, provides another haven in the late spring and summer for the small boater. Here there are a lot of sand bass and 'cuda close to shore.

Similarly, the oil rigs situated a few miles off Huntington Beach and the Barn Kelp near Oceanside are also one-day trips requiring minimal navigational skills. These spots are easy to find because invariably there are usually a few sport boats working the area. Small boat owners often pass up some of the best saltwater light tackle sport by not familiarizing themselves with our harbors and bays. Further north Morro, Avila, San Francisco, Coos, Winchester, Yaquina, and Tillamook Bays, to name only a few, are popular haunts for private boaters.

Professional saltwater guides like Mike Gardner have become legends for their prowess at working Newport and Los Alamitos Bays, using light tackle from small aluminum boats. Gardner's clients routinely tally big scores of sand and spotted bay bass along with a smattering of halibut, croaker, and corbina.

Bob Suekawa, the owner of Haddock Lures, has put on convincing demonstrations at the Long Beach Federal Breakwall tossing soft-plastic lures from freshwater bass boats in the middle of the night. Suekawa's "moonlight madness" from small boats outfitted with quiet electric trolling motors results in many big nocturnal calico bass that hunker in tight to the "wall's" rocky boulders.

On their days off, one of the most popular places to find San Diego's top deckhands is drifting San Diego or Mission Bay from small outboard skiffs. Here again, a lot of private boaters fail to realize that they might concentrate their efforts *inside* the harbor before they venture outside to test the bite.

Interestingly, party boats will seldom ever fish these harbors and bays. For one thing, skippers feel that the passengers have paid top dollar for the true "deep sea" experience. Hence, they motor outside the harbor to more scenic grounds when in reality some of the best bass and halibut fishing may be near the fuel docks, pilings, and bait receivers inside the landing basin! Further north, salmon and ling cod can be a reality in these sheltered areas, along with rockfish, greenling, turbot, and flounder. It is also often possible to find fish either in between our off islands in the prominent channel waters or at much shorter distances than the party boat fleet is targeting.

For example, it is rare to see sportfishers troll between the mainland and Catalina. Often the vessels are committed to specific offshore locales such as Catalina and San Clemente Islands. The sooner they get there, the sooner the customers get what they signed up for. For this same reason, the sportfishing fleet may be billing a trip as a serious "offshore" expedition where the anglers are pre-conditioned to look for a 70 to 100 mile boat ride— one way. Fish that are "short"—say 20 to 30 miles offshore—are often missed by the larger boats because of the way the landing is promoting longer offshore trips. Thus, the small craft owner can benefit simply by striking out on his own to explore waters—usually via trolling—that the larger vessels pass by.

Another situation that actually favors the small boat skipper is fishing the "high spots" that dot our coastal waters from the mid-Baja Peninsula to the Canadian border. Charts and books are available that clearly demarcate these rock piles, reefs, and wrecks using precise Loran readings.

For many years, my father and I fished these high spots in the Dana/Laguna area by looking for the black buoys that commercial lobster fishermen set out. These buoys invariably mark a rocky pinnacle that frequently are loaded with big "grumper" sand bass and some toad "bull" calicos along with lings and a myriad of rockfish.

Why wouldn't the larger sport vessels fish these high spots? There are easily enough fish on this structure to sustain action for 2 to 3 anglers in a small boat. There aren't enough fish to warrant a 60 to 80 foot party boat taking the time to anchor with a full load of passengers.

The issue of fuel capacity and boat range can be of paramount importance on some offshore trips—especially during tuna season. The fact remains that there is considerable water left unexplored by the large sportfishers that small craft owners can readily investigate.

Keep in mind that the faster you go, the more fuel you burn. I have fished on private boats on overnight sojourns, where the neophyte captain tries to run at nearly full throttle to get to the fishing grounds. Not only is this dangerous in the dark, but "fuel-ish." It is no coincidence that party boats average 10 to 13 knots cruising to the fishing grounds for both safety's sake and to conserve on fuel consumption. The trick is to leave earlier, run slower, and thus have more fuel left to chase down the fish.

Limited Bait

Next to fuel capacity, the issue of having a limited bait supply is crucial for the small boater to effectively strategize the outing. Without a doubt, the big 60 to 80 foot sportfishers will always have some advantage here due to giant bait tanks and massive chum power. The smart private boater can take action to offset this condition.

Don't underestimate the effectiveness of those awkward-looking canvas "diaper bags" that many boat owners hang over the stern on 17 to 40 foot craft. You can't keep many scoops of bait in these contraptions, but what you do put in usually stays fresh. Consider, however, adding a second bag to your boat. This modest addition will enhance your chumming potential dramatically. For example, you can have one diaper bag filled with smaller pinhead 'chovies which are perfect for chumming. In the other bag, you put your "hook bait" comprised of sardines, larger anchovies, live squid, or mackerel.

In harbors and bays that have a source of live baitfish, don't overlook what is in the bait receiver. Tell the attendant that you want the hot little pinheads for chum. Then ask him what else he has in the way of live squid, sardines, mackerel, or assorted "brown baits" (tom cod, herring, and shiner perch) to put in your other tank. The private boater may assume that the bait receiver only has the tiny pinhead anchovies the attendant proposes to give him when he first pulls alongside the dock.

It is also quite common for the smart private boater to "grease" the bait receiver attendant beforehand. As you pull up, tender a modest offering to insure that you get the primo baits. I've seen yacht owners offer additional cash, a fifth of liquor, a dozen donuts or even an assortment of lures to encourage the attendant to give them the best bait possible. This is no different from slipping the maitre'd at the restaurant a 20 dollar bill for a good table. Believe me—this little ploy is done all the time at the receiver by those private boaters who know how to routinely secure the best live bait.

After receiving the bait, make certain not to overcrowd it in your tank. The attendant at the bait receiver usually has a pretty good idea when you've filled the tank if you don't. The bait will often prematurely suffocate or seriously injure each other if overcrowded.

If you don't have a live bait tank on your boat, can you still compete utilizing other types of bait? The answer is emphatically *yes*! To some degree, we become spoiled out here in Southern California with fresh bait readily available and vessels equipped with aerated tanks to keep it alive. In other parts of the state and outside California, live bait becomes more problematic so alternative offerings are made.

Frozen anchovies—not salted, but instead freshly dead frozen 'chovies—often perform quite well when live ones aren't available. You can chum with the frozen baitfish either whole or cut into chunks. At times, pelagic species such as barracuda and bass will attack frozen 'chovy fly-lined or drifted among a chum line of chunked bait.

On an Eagle Claw Saltwater School to Kauai, the charter boat captain routinely relied upon fresh, dead anchovies to bring up the yellowfin tuna—both as chum and fly-line bait. Similarly, in Cabo San Lucas charter boat crews cut chunks of fresh-dead mackerel and pin them on hooks to lure dorado to the boat following a trolling jig strike. This type of chunkin' will also work for gamefish in the Southland, especially if there is no supply of live fresh chum with which to compete. Private boaters rarely try this tactic, however. (More on this later.)

Longtime party boat skipper and local expert, Captain Russ Izor, put a meat grinder on the stern of his sportfisher. Izor grinds up dead mackerel, 'chovies, squid, or sardines, and lets the "meat" drift behind the stern forming its own unique chum line. On many occasions, I have seen this trick neatly spice up the bass and barracuda action when only weak puny pinhead 'chovies were left for chumming.

When chumming, one of the best substitutes for fresh anchovies is frozen squid. Small craft operators should always carry a few one pound trays of frozen "squirts" on ice. You never know when this bait will come in handy.

You can use the squid whole, bounced off the bottom or fly-lined near the surface. I have personally caught everything from halibut to yellowtail on whole frozen squid. You can also dice it up to form a chum for perch, whitefish, sheepshead, and especially sand bass. Use a 1x3 inch strip of squid as a tippet for swimming or bottom bouncin' soft plastic lures. (I'll elaborate on these tricks with squid in future chapters.)

Although few party boat skippers ever use this tactic anymore, the private boater might consider stripping a fresh bonito or mackerel for bait. Either fly-lined or drifted along the bottom on a sliding sinker rig, the strip mackerel or bonito can be a big fish killer. Keep in mind that strip bait like this often brings in the sharks. Yellowtail, white sea bass, big calicos and sand bass frequently attack a big 8 to 10 inch long strip like this when chum is limited to small 'chovies or entirely absent.

Small Craft Trolling

As for actual boat operation, trolling and drifting allow the small bait owner the best opportunity to compete with the sportfishers in open sea. Many of the party boats won't begin to set up a trolling pattern until they are in the vicinity of their scheduled destination. Without a doubt, go ahead and try your luck at trolling if there are pelagic gamefish in your locale that are known to strike a lure presented in this fashion.

Feathers, spoons, cast-metal jigs, and especially minnow-shaped saltwater plugs make excellent trolling fare. Trolling allows the small boater to run and hunt down a quality fish here and there with almost no chum power. In contrast, the larger sportfisher has to look for a "mother lode" population of fish to accommodate greater numbers of passengers.

Soft plastic lures like the Mojo, Scampi, Lunker Thumper, and Salty Magic, however, are tough to match when it comes to lazily drifting along kelp beds, sandy bottoms, and key high spots. Keep experimenting with shapes, colors and actions of the lures until you find the pattern the fish want while drifting these baits. Keep a good supply of soft plastics in root beer/flake, lime green, and smoke glitter as the basic colors most of the major gamefish seem to prefer.

Lots of Pluses!

Private boaters have a distinct advantage going for them over the larger sportfishing vessels. For one thing, a competent skipper can put a small boat in places where the party boats won't normally venture. You can fish the inside of the kelp beds working isolated potholes in the kelp with a smaller boat. Party boats also won't usually take time to throw at the "boiler" rocks that protrude above the surface with waves crashing over them. The white water around the "boilers" can provide sanctuary for lunker calicos and monster ling cod or trophy rockfish.

Big sportfishers won't always maneuver too close to the shore to work the surf line or next to the rocky structure of an offshore island. A skilled small craft operator can carefully explore these seldom fished areas. Finally, private boaters can fully experience the benefits of using light line and sporting tackle on major gamefish. This is usually a problem on a crowded party boat. The light gear will often get bit better, particularly in highly pressured waters.

Drift Fishing Basics

Drifting allows the small craft owner to cover more territory. Some sportfishing captains rarely use this tactic. Frequently the larger party boats will drift for rock cod, since deep water anchoring is nearly impossible at 300 foot depths. Except for rock codding, salmon mooching, and occasionally halibut or striped bass drifting, most sportfishing operators prefer to have their customers fishing from an anchored vessel. It is easier to monitor the passengers with regard to where their lines are and to make sure they are on the bottom if necessary while the party boat sits still at anchor. Long stretches of prime fish-holding water can in turn be explored by small boaters setting up drift patterns.

Drifting also permits the small boaters to work their baits closer to the beach and, again, over long spans of viable water. Along the southern coast, thick kelp beds and rocky outcroppings are primary areas to find calico and white sea bass, yellowtail, bonito, and barracuda. These are excellent places to drift. The similar terrain in the northern environment can host rockfish, ling cod, turbot, flounder, greenling and possibly salmon and stripers.

Barred sand bass typically stage their annual spawning migration over expanses of hard muddy bottom. Halibut orchestrate a similar ritual on sandy stretches. Drifting enables the angler to move through this kind of area fairly rapidly, eliminating major portions of otherwise "dead" water.

Drift Baits

The most popular lures used for drifting are soft plastic grubs and tail-swimming baits. These come in a variety of shapes and colors. This kind of lure is threaded onto a basic lead head jig and allowed to drift and bob along the bottom.

Double-tail swimming "plastics" such as the Scampi, Mojo, and Haddock's Lunker Thumper have enjoyed considerable success as a multiple-species bait among party boaters for years. When the fish want a fairly active lure, it is hard to beat one of the double-tail models. Proven colors include root beer flake, lime green, silver flake, fluorescent pink, solid white, yellow, and black.

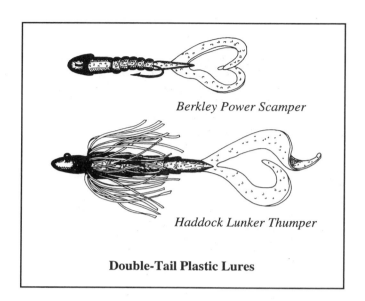

Berkley Power Scamper

Haddock Lunker Thumper

Double-Tail Plastic Lures

However, there are some occasions when the drift is slow with little current. In this situation, it is possible to garner more strikes from a soft plastic bait with less tail action. Lures like Advanced Angler Technology's (A.A.T.'s) Salty Magic are similar to the popular Scampi design, but with a flagellating single tail. Another option is to switch to a large 5 inch whip-tail grub such as those used in freshwater bass circles. The Mr. Twister model or Kalin's Salty Lunker Grub will perform quite well as a drift bait.

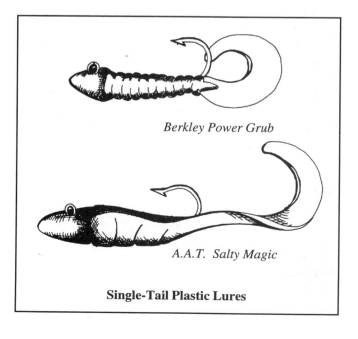

Berkley Power Grub

A.A.T. Salty Magic

Single-Tail Plastic Lures

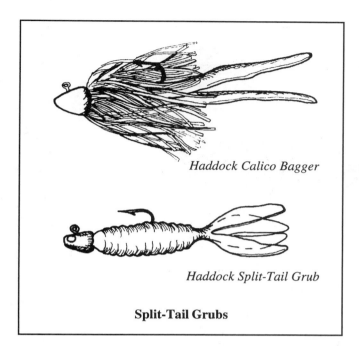

Haddock Calico Bagger

Haddock Split-Tail Grub

Split-Tail Grubs

Another essential strategy to utilize in drifting soft plastic lures is to add a small strip of frozen squid as a trailer. There are some situations when the bass will only attack the baits if they are tipped with squid. Use thin 1x3 inch strips hooked on top of the plastic lure. The small strip will not impede the action of the bait as it drifts.

A variation on the soft plastics is to drift lead heads by themselves with a whole frozen squid trailer. A favorite combination has been to use a Bomber Gumpy Jig in green scale with the nylon bristles. Many anglers aren't so fancy and simply pin the squid onto a bare lead head.

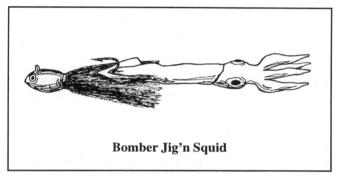

Bomber Jig'n Squid

There are times when the fish, particularly the calicos and sandies, want a maximum slow-down lure. Fat, simple paddle-tail grubs such as Haddock's Split Tail or Mann's Sting Ray can prove to be a surprising "secret weapon" when a super slow-moving bait is preferred.

Keep an adequate assortment of lead heads on board ranging from 1/2 to 1 1/4 ounces, depending upon the speed of the drift and the depth you are fishing. Some of the plastic lures such as the single-tail grubs will "swim" better with the lighter head. It is usually important to maintain good bottom contact with the bait that requires a heavier head. It is not that critical to invest time or money into painted lead heads for this type of fishing. You will lose quite a few jigs while they are bouncing through rocks and kelp.

Many veteran drift fishermen prefer to use lead heads with strong cadmium-plated hooks. These hooks won't rust and are strong enough to handle a 20 pound white sea bass. Instead I prefer jigs with bronze wire hooks. These hooks will rust and are not as strong as the cadmium versions. However, they are much sharper, offering excellent penetration especially with light mono.

The wire hooks may often bend out as pressure is applied when the jig becomes stuck. Beware if you reuse the lure by re-bending the hook—most likely the hook will be fatigued. It will probably be all right for smaller fish, but it may bend out on a big "grumper" sand bass or bull calico.

This "squid'n jig" combo produces some of the larger calicos, sandies, a variety of rockfish, and even white sea bass. Be prepared to get a lot of "short strikes" from tom cod, lizard fish, and smaller bass. Sharks are also a possibility. When a big fish decides to eat this combination, wait until you feel solid pressure on the end of the line. You have to make certain they have eaten this lengthy offering and are not just holding onto the tail end of the squid.

Surprisingly, you can also drift with lightweight spoons. The rocking motion of the boat often imparts a sensational, erratic fluttering action from these lures as they bob up and down with the rod in the rod holder or over the gunwale. Models such as Haddock's Jig'n Spoon, the Crippled Herring, Nordic, Dungeness Stinger and the Krocadile can account for some unexpected catches on the drift. Along with the bass species, mackerel, bonito, and barracuda will often nail one of these spoons as it lazily bobs along the bottom.

One other method is worth mentioning. It is possible to work drift patterns over hard mud or sandy bottoms with saltwater minnow imitations. These lures can also be

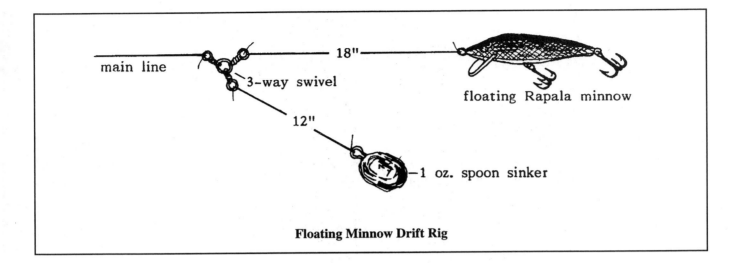

main line

18"

3-way swivel

12"

floating Rapala minnow

—1 oz. spoon sinker

Floating Minnow Drift Rig

drifted over pinnacles and along kelp lines if the trebles are replaced with single Siwash hooks.

The way to use these minnows is to construct a dropper rig. Tie your mainline to a three-way swivel. Next, add a 12 inch length of leader tied to a 1 to 3 ounce flat spoon sinker. Tie a 18 to 24 inch length of 10 to 12 pound test mono with a floating Rapala minnow attached to the other remaining eyelet of the swivel.

You need to have a moderately fast drift with this tactic to generate enough action from the lures. It is best to use the floating models in the minnows, since they have more action than the sinking versions. Also a floating lure in this genre will appear to be a wayward anchovy or smelt slowly swimming above the bottom. Stay with predominately chrome patterns with blue or black backs. Halibut, stripers, rockfish, and sand bass will annihilate these baits drifted over sandy beaches or hard bottoms.

Almost any type of saltwater spinning or conventional outfit can be used for working the various soft plastic lures, spoons, or minnow plugs on the drift. However, the baits will have better action fished with lighter 10 to 15 pound test monofilament. Many "drifters" prefer a heavy-duty freshwater popping or bass rod in 6 to 7 foot lengths teamed with a level wind baitcasting reel. Premium grade mono with high abrasion resistance and minimal stretch is also a necessity.

Setting a Drift Pattern

The direction the wind is blowing is obviously critical in setting up a drift pattern. From personal experience, I have found that a wind blowing out of the west pushing the boat towards the beach is usually best. There have been days

when winds from the opposite direction have produced equally well. A mild blow coming from out of the west, however, keeps the boat near the beach where a lot of the kelp and rocky structure is located.

Try to work about two rods per passenger if space permits. You may find that for some species such as calico, rockfish, ling cod, halibut, flounder, turbot, sand and white sea bass, you may actually get bit better drifting artificials instead of live or dead baits. The trick is to mix up the menu until you hit upon the right combination that the fish seem to prefer.

For example, if three persons are fishing out of a 14 foot aluminum skiff, set up 6 outfits. One rod can have a grub; a second, a grub in a different color with a lighter lead head. The third and fourth rigs could have twin-tail swimming baits like a Scampi or Mojo. One can have a twin tail with a skirt, the other, no skirt. The final set of outfits might consist of a rod with one of the new hollow tube baits while the other might be set up with a light fluttering spoon.

The anglers let out enough line on the six different lures bouncing along at varying depths. Once the fish start keying in on one particular offering over the others, switch the baits on the remaining outfits to create a barrage of the "hot" lure at the proper depth.

Fishing multiple outfits in this manner is perfect for saltwater drifting. The anglers can work together to present the maximum array of baits at different depths in an effort to quickly determine the feeding pattern of the fish. The beauty of this is that it is possible to isolate this feeding preference without the availability of live bait for chum.

One of the most obvious places to try to drift is along the outside kelp line. Be prepared to lose some lures here. The bass species and shallow rockfish such as cabezon, sheepshead, johnny bass, and sculpin can be scattered through the thick kelp along with ling cod. As the boat is moving, invariably an open-hook lead head jig will snag a kelp stringer. It usually isn't worth the effort to start the motor to head up-swell to free the jig. Usually the speed of the drift will serve to embed the hook deep into the kelp. Break off the lure, re-tie, and continue the drift.

Always look for visible rocky outcroppings. Locals sometimes refer to these as "boilers." The swells crash over the exposed tips creating a frothy mass of white water and foam. You can spot-cast into the turbulence as you drift by. Frequently a big bull calico or ling cod will be waiting right in the foam. Definitely drift your baits along the outer edges of these boiler rocks. Quite often the rocky structure extends considerably out from what you see on the surface. Gamefish will congregate where the edge of the rocks meets the hard sandy bottom.

If you have a simple electronic depth finder on board, look for the stretches of hard bottom. Circle around in an area and determine if there are any rocky pinnacles jutting up from the bottom worth exploring. If you have a set of buoy markers, drop one over to mark a pinnacle. Sand bass gravitate to the hard bottom; calicos sometimes stack up on the rocky pinnacles. Set buoys on the rock piles that look good, motor up-swell and begin a drift that puts your lures over the pinnacle. Repeat this procedure as long as the structure continues to produce strikes.

In the wintertime, as I mentioned previously, commercial lobster fishermen can also be helpful as you look for the pinnacles. These underwater rock piles are usually too small for party boats. If you look carefully, frequently the lobster trap buoys will be directly above the pinnacle. Set your drift pattern so the boat moves along the outside edge of as many of these markers as possible. Take care not to come too close to the buoy lines. It is important not to interfere with the lobster fisherman's traps. He found the pinnacle and is basically letting you work his spot as long as the trap is left alone.

The actual "strike" that occurs while drifting can range from a gentle "tap tap" to a vicious grab that will nearly yank the rod out of the boat. Rod holders are recommended for this type of fishing. If you lay the rods over the gunwale while drifting, keep an eye on them at all times. Swing hard on the fish when you feel solid pressure on the end of the line. Avoid "short-pumping" the fish to the surface. Many species that are caught on the drift are taken between 45 and 90 foot depths. Maintain constant tension on the line following a solid hook set. This will minimize the chances of the fish throwing a hook from deep water.

Be Experimental

Drift fishing along the Pacific Coast can be an exciting and highly productive adventure. You can never really know what species will attack a lure with this presentation. It is imperative to stay alert for the strike. *Be experimental!* Without the availability of live bait and a supply of chum, it may take some innovation to fool the various gamefish into hitting the artificials.

Mix up your assortment of offerings. Keep switching baits until you discover the particular pattern the fish are keying on. Vary the depths through which the different lures are drifting. Work all types of structure from kelp and rocks to sandy and hard mud bottoms. A virtual potpourri of species await the accomplished drift fisher.

Tackle Lessons

Often the most overlooked piece of equipment in the saltwater angler's tackle box is the hook. As simple as this may sound, many fishermen working from the surf, piers, jetties, harbors, party boats or private yachts fail to put much thought into proper hook selection. Whether you are using bait or fishing with an artificial lure, the precise type of hook matched to your strategy is extremely integral to your success. Put simply, the hook is the first—and last—part of your terminal tackle with which the fish comes into contact.

Use the Right Hook

A hook that is too small can result in poor penetration, while a hook that is too large can restrict the proper swimming action of the bait. A frail hook may break on a strong gamefish, while a heavy-duty hook may alter the action of a particular lure.

Let's review some aspects of proper hook selection for saltwater angling along the West Coast.

Live Bait Hooks

The Eagle Claw #318-N short-shank live bait style hook is used extensively in the Pacific. With this type of hook, it is important to properly match hook size with live bait size rather than the size of the species sought. For example, I have seen many anglers select a size 4 live bait hook from their boxes when rigging up at the start of the trip. This size hook is popularly used with live anchovies.

The problem arises when you go to the bait tank to select a 'chovy and find that all the skipper was able to secure were tiny pinheads. If you fail to account for the small size of the anchovies and persist in using the size 4 hook, you may seriously injure the tiny baitfish. In this situation, reevaluate your hook selection and scale down to either a size 6 to 8 in this sort of hook.

Conversely, while you are using the size 4 hook with medium size 'chovies, you might spot a small tom cod in the tank. The tendency might be to continue fishing as you were, simply pinning the brown bait onto the same hook. Once again problems may arise when using a hook that is much too small for such a prominent offering. In this case, when you go to set up on the fish, use a larger hook with a fairly wide gap so it will readily tear out of the tom cod. Your best strategy here would be to either switch to another outfit with a larger hook or re-tie with your existing rig, scaling up to either an Eagle Claw #118 (bronze) or 318-N (nickel) Eagle Claw hook in #2/0 to #4/0 sizes. However, there are occasions when matching the hook to the size of the bait is totally immaterial. For instance, on a "wide open" albacore, yellowfin, or big eye tuna bite, I have seen bruiser-class fish eat pinhead 'chovies impaled on a #6/0 Eagle Claw #118MG (Magnum) live bait hook.

Thus, as a rough rule of thumb, try to match the hook to the size of the live bait. If you sense that you are in the midst of a feeding frenzy—throw out the book and select the largest hook you think you can get away with!

The actual construction of the live bait hook is another dimension to consider. Some hooks in this design are made from a thin wire construction. These are excellent on light lines, especially with a fragile bait. Although a wire hook generally provides excellent penetration, it may fatigue on a big fish. Examples include Eagle Claw's #L112, L118, L212, and L318N models.

Other hooks are made with heavy gauge wire. They are fairly strong for almost all situations. These are thicker "magnum" versions made for the toughest pelagic species such as the Eagle Claw #318-N or 118 Magnum series. Magnum class live bait hooks typically require at least 20 pound test mono to minimize line stretch. It takes somewhat more power on the set to garner adequate penetration with the magnum-style live bait hook.

Bait	Hook Size
Small, med. anchovies	4, 2
Large anchovies	1, 1/0
Sardines	1/0, 2/0
Smelt	1/0, 2/0
Mackerel	4/0
Squid	4/0
Tom cod ("brown baits")	2/0, 4/0

Eagle Claw Hooks

What about hook color? Well, this may be one of the truly overrated concerns among saltwater fishing buffs. Some veteran anglers, skippers, and deckhands firmly believe that a bronze live bait hook will overwhelmingly get bit better than a nickel-plated version. They theorize that the dull bronze finish is more difficult for the fish to detect and it won't reflect light unnaturally under water.

On the other hand, a majority of fishermen prefer the nickel-plated live bait hooks. These are usually more expensive than their bronze counterparts. In addition, these chrome-colored hooks won't rust as fast as the bronze models. The bottom line? Fish whichever color hook *you* have the most confidence in.

A recent innovation is to fish a unique live bait model with a larger soldered ring that slides through the eye of the hook. This is the Eagle Claw #1080G "Lazer Ringer." This hook is expensive because of increased manufacturing costs. After tying your line to the ring instead of directly to the eyelet, the hook will swivel quite freely. Some hard-core tuna fishermen adamantly feel that a bait will swim dramatically better using a ringed live bait hook. For them, the extra cost is well worth it.

Baitholder Hooks

Anglers working the surf line, break walls, and harbors commonly use a diverse menu of baits ranging from sand crabs and mussels, to cut anchovies and strips of frozen squid. The hook that is best suited for this array of offerings is a long-shank baitholder model such as the Eagle Claw #181-A series. Baitholders are usually sold in the flat bronze finish. They are characterized by one to two extra barbs found on the shaft of the hook. As you thread the bait onto the hook, it is essential to cover up not only the point but as much of the shaft as possible. The extra barbs on the shaft help to secure the upper portion of the bait so it won't slide down the hook.

It is usually more important with baitholders to match the size of the hook to the quarry you are seeking as well as to your choice of baits. When fishing at night, for example, I stalk big bull calico bass near the beach, along the surf line, and on the rocks using heavy-duty baitcasting rods and reels, 4 ounce sinkers, and 25 pound test line. My favorite offerings for calicos near the surf line or kelp bed are whole frozen squid or grunion. With bass that can easily top the 5 pound mark, I use a long-shank Eagle Claw #181-A baitholder in the #2/0 to #4/0 range.

In contrast, I switch to a light freshwater spinning outfit spooled with 6 pound mono when working from smaller yachts or uncrowded party boats. My choice of baits for smaller gamesters such as calicos, sand bass, bonito, barracuda or rockfish might be only tiny "pinhead" anchovies. In this case, I use an ultrasmall #6 or #8 live bait hook to match with the bait, the quarry, and the light spinning line. Here again, I switch back to the popular Eagle Claw #318-N model.

Wire octopus-style hooks can also be used in place of the bronze long-shank models with a similar mix of baits. These wire versions offer excellent penetration but may

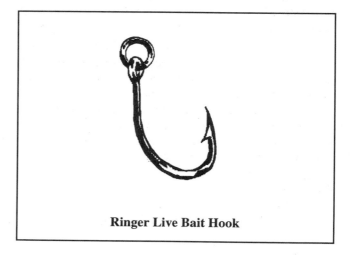

Ringer Live Bait Hook

not be as strong for bottom scratching among the rocks and coral. An example is the Eagle Claw #L226-N Octopus hook.

I might add that a large octopus-style hook performs especially well with certain live baits such as mudsuckers or sculpin. The hook has a wide gap, pulls through tough-skinned baitfish fairly easily, and allows for good penetration. This has been a longtime staple, for example, for soaking mudsuckers while fishing for double-digit stripers in San Francisco Bay.

Lead Head Hooks

Soft plastic lures like the Mojo, Scampi, Lunker Thumper, and Caba Caba Tube are now used extensively on the West Coast. Plastic baits of this genre are usually fished behind a lead jig head. As with baitholder style and live bait hooks, it is equally important to scrutinize the hook molded into the lead head. It is critical to use a jig head with a hook that is both long enough and has an adequate gap to match with the plastic tail section.

For example, the 3/4 to 1 ounce lead head used with a medium-size 4 inch Haddock Lunker Thumper would be too small to fish with the larger 6 inch long Thumper. The hook shaft of this lead head is too short for the longer bait. If you use it with the larger Thumper, the hook will ride too close to the head. You will miss many fish that may strike the lure more towards the mid-section. In addition, the gap—that space between the point of the hook and the shaft—will be too narrow to use the small lead head with the magnum plastic tail. You thus will need to switch to another leadhead, either the same weight or heavier, but with a bigger hook and wider gap.

Most jig heads feature a strong cadmium hook. These hooks are made to withstand considerable pressure. They are terrific when you are fishing a lead head lure around rocky structure as is found around jetties and break walls. Cadmium hooks also resist rusting to a great degree.

There are times, however, particularly when fishing soft plastics with light line, that it may be better to use a jig head molded around a bronze wire hook. This type of hook is somewhat weaker than the cadmium style and will rust more easily. The lead head with the wire hook offers superb penetration, especially when teamed with light mono. These hooks are much sharper than cadmium and can be used right from the package.

Jig Hooks

Cast-metal jigs or "iron" usually have a specific hook affixed to the split ring. Presumably, this factory stocked hook offers the best combination of balance and "swimming" ability with the jig. Still most of these lures are sold with treble hooks and there are occasions where you may want to change them. Frequently, the manufacturer makes the mistake of using a treble hook that is too small for a particular type of "iron." If you are casting jigs for large gamefish like yellowtail or tuna, you may want to replace some of the smaller trebles with the next size up.

Similarly, the treble hooks used for jig fishing are also sold in graduated strengths, designated by an "X," Greater strength is indicated by higher numbers (i.e. 2X, 4X, 6X). When throwing the "iron" on 25 to 100 pound class fish, you might consider replacing weaker treble hooks with the stronger versions. Some manufacturers such as Tady and U.F.O. also market their jigs with single hooks. A single hook can offer a distinct advantage over the treble.

A jig with a single hook can be fished easily through kelp stringers so it will hang up less than the "iron" with a conventional treble hook. Some pros also feel that you can get better leverage and penetration with a single hook, since twisting and torquing is more likely with a treble. Ironically, fewer fish might be lost using a jig with a single hook compared to models with the standard trebles. However, most anglers are convinced that three points are better than one and thus usually opt for the jig with the treble hook.

The single hooks on the jigs themselves can either be fixed to the lure with screws or allowed to swivel freely on a soldered ring. Manufacturers like U.F.O. and Tady decide which single-hooking method allows their jigs to swim best and sell them accordingly.

Spoon Hooks

Much of what was said about cast-metal jig hooks applies to spoons. Don't overestimate the propensity of these lures to nail big fish. Be aware that you may have to replace the stock treble hooks with a larger size. Some spoons like the Crippled Herring, Krocadile, and Dungeness Stinger are sold with a large single Siwash hook. With light monofilament, this long-shank, single Siwash with extrawide gap makes hook penetration quick, deep, and effective.

In a pinch you can use a more compact #2/0 to #6/0 short-shank live bait Eagle Claw #318-N hook in place of a Siwash style. The split rings on most spoons can be opened easily to replaced the factory treble with a live bait hook. Although this short-shank hook is not as effective as the long-shank Siwash style, it still features a fairly wide gap to enhance hook sets.

Plug Hooks

Minnow-shaped plugs are underrated lures for West Coast marine angling. Models such as the Rapala and Jensen Minnow will at times catch everything from bonito and barracuda to yellowtail and tuna. These lures require a delicate balance when it comes to hooks. The heavy-duty models usually are stocked with strong cadmium trebles. Smaller plugs like those used in freshwater will frequently feature needle-sharp bronze trebles. These are more suitable when fishing with lighter tackle.

Frequently, deckhands or skippers on party boats will request, for safety reasons, that you replace treble hooks on plugs with stainless double hooks. They feel that the double hooks are safer for their crew to handle than the 6 points on a set of trebles coming over the rail.

Be careful when replacing treble hooks on minnow-shaped plugs. Often you may inadvertently alter the balance and swimming action of the lure by switching to a set of different trebles. If possible, "tank-test" the plug after you change treble hooks by trying it in a swimming pool. Make a number of practice casts before actually using it in the field. To be sure, the treble hooks on many plugs used in saltwater, especially the bronze finish, will have to be routinely checked for excessive rusting and eventually replaced.

As a final option, you might want to replace all the treble hooks on your saltwater plugs with single Siwash models. Usually, these extra-long hooks won't significantly alter the action of the lure. Again, "tank test" the modified plug to be sure. The single hooks can be a real

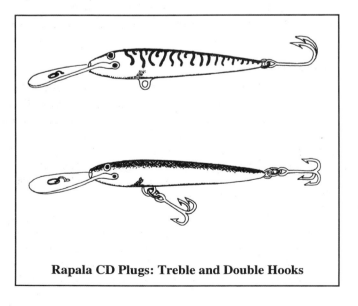

Rapala CD Plugs: Treble and Double Hooks

boon, particularly when fishing bonito or barracuda and other species with prominent teeth.

Worth the Effort!

Whether you fish with natural bait or artificial lures, avoid becoming lazy when selecting the right combination of hooks to use during your outing. Take the extra effort to properly match the hook to the baits and lures you are using as well as to the query you are seeking.

Hooks are the least expensive item in the saltwater angler's tackle box. They should be regularly sharpened and re-sharpened. Invest in a simple and widely used Luhr Jensen hook file. Keep it in your tackle box—and use it!

Rusting, rocks, kelp, and toothy gamefish can significantly reduce the strength, sharpness, and overall effectiveness of all your various hooks. Inspect them throughout the trip and, if in doubt, always replace them with new hooks. The extra effort is definitely worth it!

Hooking Strategies

An angler may own the finest tackle in the world yet not have productive days on the Pacific because he does not know proper hooking methods for presenting his baits. Let's then review the assorted baits used for fishing the Pacific Coast and the ways the pros hook these different offerings.

Anchovies

These small baitfish remain the staple option for most small craft and party boat fishing along the coast. There are basically three ways to hook a 'chovy. For fly-lining the bait totally weightless without a sinker, it is best to gently run a short-shank live bait hook under the skin directly behind the gill cover. It is important not to actually penetrate the hard gill cover itself. This might quickly drown the anchovy if the gills fail to operate. This technique is termed "gill-hooking" even though the gills of the tiny baitfish remain unimpaired. You can continue to use this gill-hooking tactic as you add no more than 1/4 ounce of weight. This allows the 'chovy to suspend slightly below the surface.

As you begin to use a heavier sinker, you will have to take measures to keep the anchovy from prematurely drowning or having its swimming ability severely impaired. A gill-hook strategy might not be the best option in this situation. Instead, carefully run the short-shank Eagle Claw #318-N hook through first the lower and then the upper lip of the bait. This serves to keep the mouth of the anchovy pinned shut so that an inordinate amount of water is not pushed through its gills.

This lip-hooking technique is suitable for fishing an anchovy directly on the bottom, while drifting for halibut, for example. It can be used in deep open water when you want to "plunk" a bait 50 to 150 feet deep on an offshore kelp paddy for albacore, yellowtail, or tuna.

A final, though seldom-used option is to carefully run your hook across the narrow body section of the 'chovy directly ahead or behind its anal pore. This kind of "butt hooking" is highly suitable for fly-lining. In this situation, you may want to get the bait to swim down below the surface but you don't want to add any unnatural resistance with even the smallest sinker.

Anal-hooking an anchovy with a fly-line presentation can be quite effective in getting the bait below pesky small school fish such as mackerel in order to reach bigger prey like yellowtail or calico bass.

One final point is worth mentioning when it comes to hooking anchovies. We instruct our students in our Eagle Claw Saltwater Schools to routinely check their hands, rod butts, and reel seats for loose scales. This is usually the telltale sign that the novice is grasping the anchovy too firmly which may quickly injure the small baitfish. Be "kinder and gentler" with these little baits when handling them in the hooking process. "Cradle" the 'chovy in your hand as you walk from the bait well to your rod at the rail. Apply minimum pressure in grasping the bait as you proceed to hook it.

Sardines

The proliferation of this larger baitfish has been an absolute boon to the West Coast party boat fleets these past years, after a prolonged period of near extinction in our waters. Much of what I discussed about properly hooking anchovies will apply to sardines.

If the 'dine is only 3 or 4 inches long, gill-hook the bait for fly-lining as you would a small 'chovy. You can also use butt hooking to make the sardine swim deeper without the addition of extraneous weight.

Employ a lip-hooking strategy on the smaller 'dines. If you want to fish these baits down deep, try "plunking" with a heavier sinker. However, this technique has to be modified in the case of casting magnum-size sardines between 7 and 10 inches in length. In this situation, it is more effective to run the short-shank live bait hook through the nostril pores on the bridge of the 'dines snout.

This is called nose-hooking. Care must be taken not to break through the thin gristle that forms a bridge between the nostril pores. The sardine must be gently lob-cast with this method to insure that the hook does not pull through the gristle. 'Dines are stellar baits for everything from ling cod and halibut to salmon and striped bass to yellowtail and tuna. Handle them with care, keeping your hands wet when you bait your hooks.

Mackerel

Both Spanish (brown) and the greenback mackerel can be cast with the nose-hooking technique mentioned above for large sardines. Of course, with bigger baitfish in this genre, you will have to dramatically scale up in hook size. Many anglers make the mistake of not using a large enough hook with the "mack." When a big calico, yellowtail, or tuna decides to eat the mackerel, it will typically attack the baitfish at the head with some viciousness. When they decide to eat this kind of bait, they eat it hard! Hook size is not as restrictive as it is with more delicate baits like pinhead anchovies.

In recent years, deckhands and party boat skippers have been encouraging their passengers to fish small nickel or cadmium-plated treble hooks for mackerel. Use the treble in place of a short-shank baitholder. However, be certain to insert only one of the three points into the nostril-pores when nose-hooking a mackerel with a treble hook. At first glance it may appear rather strange to have two remaining totally exposed points left outside the "mack's" nose portion. When yellowtail are "on" mackerel, the treble hooks won't deter the strike and may actually increase catch-to-strike ratios.

Occasionally, both types of mackerel may also be hooked behind the anal fin. Sometimes when fishing thick kelp stringers for bull calicos, it helps to hook the "macks" in this manner to force them to dive deeper into the kelp beds where the big bass live.

Brown Baits

This collection of small baitfish includes tom cod, herring, queenfish, 7-11 perch, and baby pompanos. The brown coloration comes from the hues surrounding many of the dorsal, caudal, and anal fins of this array of baits. Brown baits hooked across the snout through the nostrils can be fished quite effectively weightless. You can also cross-hook them above or behind the anal fin if more depth is desired on the fly-line.

Frequently, however, the best bite with these fairly large baits occurs at 60 to 120 foot depths, particularly when probing for big calicos over submerged rock piles, reefs, and underwater wrecks. You can fish the brown baits, lip-hooked, on a "plunker" rig ahead of a large split-shot or a rubber-core sinker. There are some other hooking possibilities worth exploring.

First, run your line through a 1/2 to 2 ounce sliding egg sinker so it rests directly above your hook. Now, hook the brown bait through the lower and upper lips and let the sinker take the baitfish deep, possibly to the bottom. Instead of using a sliding egg sinker, try a variation on this theme. Take a 1 to 3 ounce lead head—painted or unpainted (whichever you have confidence in)—and lip-hook the brown bait with the jig. This is another example of a rather strange hooking procedure, but it really works when fishing deep structure!

The calicos do not seem to be bothered by the exposed lead head or the large hook. The long-shank cadmium hooks commonly molded into the lead head also provide the angler with an extraordinarily strong hook with a large gap to generate maximum penetration at depths over 60 feet. (More on this when I talk about "bull" bass fishing in upcoming chapters.)

This "jig-and-brownie" combo has personally produced some stellar catches for this author in both sand bass and big bull calicos while fishing the high spots in the Horseshoe Kelp region.

Squid

Live, fresh-dead, and frozen squid can be hooked in identical fashion. The simplest and most widely used procedure is to run an Eagle Claw #118, #118MG, or #318-N hook in sizes #2/0 to #4/0 short-shank live bait hook once through the tail portion of the squid. The bait can be fly-lined with this hooking. Either a big split-shot or rubber-core sinker may also be added 12 to 18 inches above the hook for greater depth.

The little ploy mentioned utilizing a sliding-egg sinker resting against the hook also works super for fishing a live or frozen squid deep. The fish typically eat the squid head first. As they pull and tug on the bait, the squid moves freely through the sliding egg sinker with the yellowtail, sea bass, halibut, or rockfish feeling minimal resistance.

Squid can also be bounced on the bottom pinned behind a jig head. Here again, the lead head can be bare, painted, with or without feathers or a vinyl skirt. This setup is known as the "jig-and-squid." It has been highly effective on the various bass species, especially when you need to get the squid to penetrate through a mat of thick kelp.

Give the fish some time to eat this jig-and-squid combo before setting up on the initial strike. The overall rig is fairly long and the bass may not always strike near the tail portion where the lead head and the hook are situated.

Strip Baits

Saltwater buffs in Southern California may often be remiss in not trying more strip baits. Their north Pacific counterparts recognize the merit of strip baits well. There are situations when gamefish simply want a more prominent offering and/or live bait is not available. Here is where the shrewd angler might consider cutting a small filet of mackerel or bonito as a strip bait. I like to actually cut the filet into somewhat of a triangular, wedge-like shape, wide at the top, tapering nearly to a point at the bottom.

Then simply run a fairly large Eagle Claw #118, #118MG, or #318-N 2/0 to 5/0 short-shank live bait hook, a longer Eagle Claw O'Shaughnessy model #254-N hook, or a lead head once and through the wider portion of the filet strip. The strip can be fished on the surface as it drifts back into the current. It can also be allowed to sink by adding either the lead head or a sinker and then S-L-O-W-L-Y "pumped" back to the boat following the cast. As you lift-and-drop the rod tip "pumping" the strip back in, it will undulate in the water as if it is alive.

In warm water years, you can also strip giant squid into foot long pieces. These should be cut from the main body of the squid and would not include the tentacles. This bait can be terrific fly-lined or "plunked" below the surface for yellowtail at a time when smaller squid would normally not be available. The hooking of the giant squid strip would be similar to that of mackerel or bonito filets— once through the head portion of the lengthy squid strip.

'Dads

Finally, some coastal fishermen have found that freshwater crawdads are excellent for shallow water rockfish, sheepshead, and even calicos along the break walls or on outside reefs and pinnacles. When fishing 'dads, I recommend a thinner, long-shank baitholder hook such as the Eagle Claw #181-A. Surprisingly, the best place to hook these little crustaceans are not through the tail but rather between the eyes through the gristle bridge that forms a point. Hooked like this, the crayfish will be able to propel itself more freely than if its movement was restricted with a tail-hooking ploy.

Match the Hook!

It is imperative to routinely check the hook you are using to match up with the available size bait. For example, you may need to fish tiny pinhead anchovies on a #6 live bait

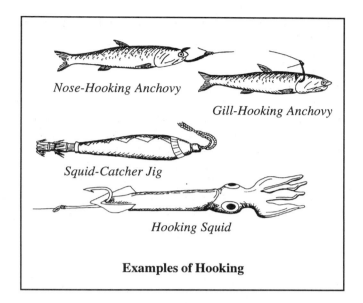

Nose-Hooking Anchovy

Gill-Hooking Anchovy

Squid-Catcher Jig

Hooking Squid

Examples of Hooking

hook. When you grab a small Spanish mackerel out of the bottom of the same tank, you will have to switch to a larger Eagle Claw #118 or #318-N (regular or magnum) 2/0 to 4/0 hook. Also, be prepared to switch from finer wire hooks with small baits and/or light line, to heavier gauge "magnum" hooks for big baits and 25 to 50 pound mono.

Too often I have watched novice anglers make the same mistake over and over of thinking that one size hook will be suitable for all the different baits available for the day's fishing. Study the diverse menu that is on deck that day—'chovies, 'dines, "macks," squid, brown baits. How about the more exotic offerings such as frozen squid, strip filets, or even freshwater crawdads?

Whatever your selection, make sure to match your hook to the particular bait so that you are able to present your offerings in the most lifelike manner.

Use Good Line!

I am always amazed at how otherwise dedicated anglers seem to treat monofilament line as a secondary piece of equipment and feel my advice applies to everything but line. Even with a new high-speed baitcasting reel and custom-wrapped rod, the most important link between you and the fish is your line. After spending upwards of over 200 dollars on a first class outfit, the last thing you want to do is scrimp on your monofilament.

Premium grade line has a number of distinct advantages over the "cheaper spread" usually sold at discount on large bulk spools. A quality monofilament made by a name-brand manufacturer will usually demonstrate three

significant qualities: 1) uniformity, 2) abrasion-resistance, and 3) knot strength.

Although the big bulk spool of discount mono may seem on the surface to be a good deal, in reality you are probably purchasing line of varying diameters and breaking strengths. The test strength marked on the spool is the average for the entire run. This number varies little with quality line, but inexpensive mono may demonstrate wide variations with weak spots or differences in diameter between the beginning and end of the spool.

Second, a premium grade monofilament exemplifies a relatively uniform diameter and breaking strength, while maintaining a measure of abrasion resistance. If you cast where the fish live, then invariably your monofilament will be subject to the nicks and fractures caused by making contact with rocks, kelp, and the toothy critters themselves. A premium grade mono can withstand considerable abrasion before it weakens; the cheaper grades will not.

Finally, whenever you tie a knot in the monofilament, it will weaken to some degree. This occurs as the mono cuts into itself as the knot is drawn. As with abrasion resistance, a better grade line suffers minimal reduction in knot strength when it is pulled against itself and the metal of the hook eyelet or lure split ring.

What about line color? I personally believe that this is one of the most overrated concerns confronting the saltwater buff. Speaking from personal experience on both coasts, I think line color is more a matter of personal preference and confidence than "scientific fact." Fish clear, blue, green, or even pink—as long as you feel confident with your choice.

I will say, however, that when it comes to "serious fishin'" for pelagic species such as yellowtail, tuna, salmon, and marlin, I prefer not to use any monofilament with a fluorescent hue. There have been too many times when anglers using a mono that "glows" have been thoroughly stymied on yellowtail, while those fishermen who got bit used the flat-colored lines. On the other hand, don't overlook the fluorescent mono for surf-fishing, trolling, and bottom bouncin'.

Light-Line Fever

"Light-liners" are usually into a world of their own. They won't always gravitate to the stern of a crowded party boat, especially with everyone else fishing 30 to 40 pound string. They can't afford to get "sawed off." They aren't the back-breakin', stand-up strokers either who like to tackle tuna "mano-a-mano" with locked down drags and 50 to 80 pound gear.

Light-liners represent more of the "finesse" dimension of the sport. We like to use smaller reels, longer, softer, more parabolic rods, scaled-down lures and, of course, fine-diameter monofilament. Granted, light-liners lose their share of fish, but they may also get bit more often and frequently land jackpot winners.

There are a number of reasons why light-liners get bit so well these days. To begin with, the live bait situation in many locales up and down the coast is a "hit or miss" proposition. One day you find "race horse" size anchovies at the bait receiver; the very next day the live wells are loaded with tiny pinheads.

Smaller and, for that matter, weaker bait swims with less drag and resistance when hooked on lighter 10 to 15 pound test monofilament. Pinhead 'chovies and even larger specimens cast more easily using lighter line, especially when you need to fly-line the bait without the use of a sinker.

Lighter monofilament also permits certain saltwater lures to "swim" better than if you were throwing them on heavier string. Spoons, minnow-shaped plugs, bonito and 'cuda feathers, as well as a parade of soft plastic baits move through the water better if they are retrieved with lighter line and, thus, with less resistance.

There is also the simple fact that it is more difficult for the fish to see finer diameter monofilament. A good example of this is when it comes to stalking bluefin tuna on an inshore bite. In contrast to those found on the outer banks, it can be a real test of skill to persuade fish near the coastline to eat a live bait.

Invariably you will see veteran bluefin tuna experts scaling all the way down to 10 to 12 pound mono to get these finicky tuna to bite. Some reels become spooled and some bluefin are lost on the spider web-like line. The point is by light-lining these fish you do get bit. (More on this strategy later.)

Keeping your tackle in perfect working condition is imperative for successful light-lining. Reel drags must be perfectly smooth and the same holds true for rod line guides. The slightest rough spot on a guide can nick the thin diameter mono and then you have problems. Buy only premium grade monofilament in the smaller breaking test. Re-tie knots and change line often. Light-line fever—catch it!

No Dinkers with Sinkers

For some reason, many recreational anglers fail to realize the importance of selecting the right sinker for the precise conditions encountered. In southern waters, for example,

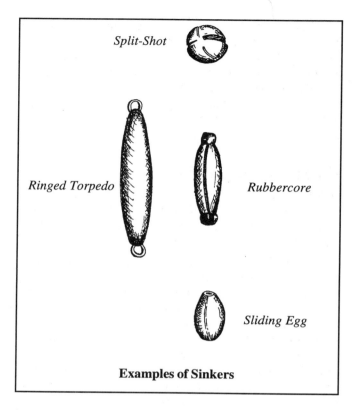

Examples of Sinkers

Split-Shot

Ringed Torpedo

Rubbercore

Sliding Egg

it seems that we are drilled from the start by deckhands, skippers and veterans alike, to "Fly Line That Bait"!

Without a doubt, there are many occasions when an anchovy, sardine, mackerel, or live squid performs best when frantically swimming on the surface unencumbered by any weight. Shrewd pros realize that this is the time to select a sinker to probe the mid-depths to the bottom for not only more but larger fish once the surface action begins to fizzle.

For example, it is common to see many novice fishermen fly-line anchovies at the beginning of the yearly sand bass migration into 30 to 120 depths in Southern California. Let the truth be known, however, that those bigger 6-8 pound "grumper" sandies are going to be laying on or near the bottom and sometimes at that 90-120 foot range. If you want these trophy sand bass, you will have to use anything from a large split-shot, rubber-core, or sliding-egg sinker, somewhere between 3/4 to 1 1/2 ounces in weight.

Similarly, it is common knowledge among longtime tuna skippers that some of the best meter marks found on offshore trips are at 15 fathoms. Most anglers cast fly-lined baits following the initial jig stop or sliding onto a kelp paddy. The smart veteran might start by "plunkin'" that 90 foot range with a heavy 1 to 2 ounce sinker for the larger yellowfin, bluefin, and even that rare albacore!

These same sinker strategies work for bonito, calico bass, barracuda and yellowtail. So often, the smaller, more aggressive members of the schools are found crashing on the chum near the surface. Forget these "dinkers"— be smart and work your sinkers for those better fish, lazily swimming at the greater depths. In later chapters I'll review specific rigs and the precise sinkers that should be used to complete these key terminal setups.

When Equipment Fails

Did you ever wonder how much luck truly plays in becoming a successful saltwater angler? During our schools, my instructors and I routinely hear students comment that the angler with the big fish "sure is lucky."

The truth of the matter is that luck probably has a minor roll in a successful day on the water. If you really scrutinize what the apparently "lucky" anglers are doing, you will soon find that they minimize the chances that something might go wrong. Without question, proper hook, line, sinker, and bait selection is integral for putting together your successful "program" for a day on the water. There are other factors that may contribute to a lack of success on the water. Here are some core issues that we have isolated in our schools which deal with proper equipment. We teach our students the importance of handling each one as essential to becoming an accomplished Pacific fisherman.

Spooling

As simple as this sounds, many novice anglers fail to sufficiently fill their reels with enough line. As you get further and further down into the spool, casting distance becomes more difficult to obtain. This is particularly the case with spinning reels. Many times when the fish are boiling on the far outside chum, a long cast is imperative to getting bit. If you fail to fill your reel with enough line, you may miss out on the action.

In addition, it is important to keep your thumbs off the spool when a fish starts to take line from a casting reel. Many neophyte anglers panic when they encounter the first surge of line from a big fish. They quickly put thumb pressure on the spool, thinking that if they don't, the fish will run out all the line. Let your drag do its job! The chances of becoming spooled are rare, especially if you took the time to fill your reel to capacity.

Finally, don't forget that with casting reels, you have to level wind the line yourself. Move the monofilament from side to side on the spool using your thumb and index finger. If you fail to do this rudimentary procedure, the line will invariably build up in one area of the spool. When a big fish tries to take out drag, the uneven line on the spool digs and cuts into itself rather than smoothly paying out from side to side. This may cause the monofilament to quickly break.

Extraneous Hardware

If you need to use hardware such as snaps, swivels, or snap-swivel combinations, *keep it simple*. A snap-swivel, in particular, is very tempting to use, especially when it comes to conveniently changing jigs, spoons, or plugs. However, this little device usually dramatically kills the action of the saltwater lures. Most lure manufacturers market their baits with the appropriate snaps or split rings that have been pre-tested to insure that the lure will generate the best action.

If when trolling, for instance, you need to use hardware, invest in quality goods. When it comes to swivels, split rings, or snap-swivel combos, the cheap varieties won't usually hold up on a big fish. Invest in quality terminal tackle, perhaps even ball-bearing swivels if necessary.

Wrong Lure—Wrong Time

It is a mistake to fish the same diameter monofilament over and over based on past successes. The same holds true for lure fishing. Just because a particular jig worked one week doesn't mean it will be equally effective at the same spot the next week.

Water clarity, prevalence of specific natural baits, and overhead sunlight can affect the role color plays in selecting a particular lure. A white jig might have been dynamite last week when the white sea bass were in the area feeding on squid. Next week, the best pattern might be the same jig in blue and white as the sea bass shift to feeding on 'chovies or sardines.

It pays to be equally flexible when it comes to selecting size and action of soft plastic lures, spoons, and plugs. Don't take anything for granted based on prior success. Today is a new day—give the fish what they want.

Advanced Species Lessons: Inshore Fish

Working with the notion that 10 percent of the anglers are catching 90 percent of the fish, Eagle Claw Fishing School instructors continually look for methods above and beyond traditional strategies to fool the myriad of species we target. In the next three chapters I will take the reader beyond the routines most commonly utilized to catch the different Pacific species. We will look at some of the highly specialized and "secret" tactics that the pros use to catch these diverse saltwater fish. I've divided the different species into inshore, offshore, and bottom fish.

Bull Bass!

The calico or kelp bass, along with its cousin the sand bass, constitute with bonito and barracuda, the "three B's" of Southern California sportfishing. Although the calico bass fishery is not what it once was, this gamefish still remains high on the list for both sport and table fare. The problem facing the serious Pacific angler is how to locate and catch those bigger 4 to 10 pound "bull" calicos. The number of trophy fish in this category are definitely on the decline. Here are some of the most effective strategies we have found for catching "bull" bass. Please practice "catch and release" on these great gamefish keeping few or none of these prize specimens. If you want a souvenir of the day's catch, bring your camera for a permanent record and have a fiberglass reproduction made for a wall mount.

Big Baits = Big Calicos!

How many times have you heard this adage repeated? Freshwater bass fishermen surely recognize it as a fact. The same holds true for the saltwater basser. If you fish for the bigger calico specimens, you have to be willing to fish the BIG baits. These include green and Spanish mackerel, smelt, sardines, squid, and the full gamut of "brown baits" (tom cod, herring, queenfish, baby pompano, and shiner perch).

Bull bass fishing also requires stout tackle. Too often novice students try to fish a 1 1/2 pound tom cod for calicos using a 7 foot, light action live bait rod, 15 pound test, and a spinning reel. This simply isn't tough enough gear to pull these stubborn gamesters from thick cover such as rock piles, submerged wrecks, and kelp forests.

Dedicated "bull" bassers typically fish longer 8 to 10 foot jig sticks, conventional reels spooled with 30 pound test, big Eagle Claw #118 MG (magnum) 4/0 to 6/0 hooks, a tight drag, and large baits. The longer rod helps in three ways:

1. It allows the angler to gently lob a big baitfish using a lengthy leader, without tearing out the hook.

2. Longer rods make for longer casts to those hard-to-reach "pot holes" deep inside a kelp bed.

3. With the 8 to 10 foot blank, the calico fisherman is able to really pick up a lot of slack line quickly and to swing and set with maximum leverage.

Bull bass root tight into cover. In this weight class they tend to be solitary predators and are fairly territorial. It takes precision casting with powerful precision tackle to yank the trophy bass from this kind of structure. More often than not, the best way to present a large bait into these hard-to-reach haunts is to simply fly-line it without any weight at all. On most casts, if the baitfish lands near the target, it will also find the opening in the kelp bed, the major rocky pinnacle, or the submerged structure of an old shipwreck.

If you want the bait to stay near the surface, either cross-hook the two nostril openings or lip-hook it through the upper and lower lip. Invariably the "bull" bass seem to be caught more and more in a sub-surface mode. This is where butt-hooking is critical.

Here is a great trick we ourselves learned from the crew of the Sportfisher Holiday while fishing "bull" calicos off the Ensenada, Mexico kelp beds. Most anglers simply run their bait hooks (Eagle Claw #318N-4/0) across the anal fin of a sardine, mackerel, or tom cod in and out so the hook point penetrates outside the flesh. The deckhands showed me their secret trick. Instead of running the point of the hook in and out through the flesh behind the anal fin, they actually *inserted* the hook point into the baitfish's anal pore. They then keep carefully pushing the shaft of the short-shank baitholder hook further and further up into the baitfish body cavity until the eye of the hook actually rests up against the anal pore. (They also use the heavy-duty Eagle Claw #118MG Magnum hooks.)

It might seem that the hook will easily slide back out even though it is smoothly inserted into the anal pore. In reality, it appears that the barb of the hook grabs just enough "meat" deep inside the pore to snag itself with hardly any further motion from the hook. The beauty of this setup is that it allows the baitfish to swim down without a sinker to restrict it. In addition, because the hook point remains *embedded* in the baitfish's body cavity, the bait is almost 100 percent weedless! This is very critical especially when fishing "bull" bass in thick kelp beds. Invariably with the traditional butt-hooking going across the baitfish's lower fin area, the hook point remains exposed and susceptible to becoming hung up as the bait swims among the kelp stringers. This newer, subtle hooking method is absolutely terrific for hauling big bull calicos out of the kelp!

At other times you will want your baitfish to get to the bottom more quickly, especially while looking for the trophy calicos on rocky pinnacles or submerged wrecks. A 3/4 to 1 1/2 ounce sliding egg sinker butted right up against the eye of the short-shank baitholder hook will do the trick (Eagle Claw #118MG or #318N 2/0 to 4/0). Although always an awkward looking rig, this basic slider combo allows the baitfish to actually swim fairly unencumbered, particularly once the sinker hits the bottom. Be sure to hook the bait with the mouth sealed shut. Run the hook through the upper and lower lip when you use the sliding-egg sinker.

Another strategy that will take the baitfish deep fairly fast is to pin it onto a 1 to 3 ounce lead head jig with a large wide gap hook. This is really a horrible looking combo from an "aesthetic standpoint." It is a bare, plain lead head jig with a big baitfish pinned on through the upper and lower lips. It is truly amazing that a "bull" bass would be fooled by such an obvious not-so-subtle setup, but they are!

The open hook provides for optimal penetration. Remember this is a big fish rig requiring a stiff rod and heavy string to pull the lead head hook out of the mackerel, tom cod, herring, or smelt. The leadhead itself functions as nothing more than a simple sinker, taking a reluctant baitfish down towards the bottom quickly. Quite frequently, you will get bit using the leadhead as it is sinking through the mid-depth strike zones. This is also an excellent strategy to employ when the current is ripping and it seems difficult to maintain control over your setup using conventional sinkers.

A word of caution: remember with this open-hook lead head you will have a tendency to hang up more especially with a wide gap hook. When you do get bit, let the bass run with the bait a little. These are big baits and it may take even the largest "bull" calicos some time to crunch it.

'Chovies and Squid for Calicos

Rarely will we resort to anchovies if we are looking for trophy bass. Sometimes even with the best "hook bait" 'chovies in the tank you can't keep the smaller 10 to 13 inch calicos from nailing your bait. Still I want to point out that there are definite situations in which big bull bass lazily roll and boil on the far outside chum. They are extremely boat shy and wait for the current to funnel the anchovy chum to them, sometimes 50 to 70 yards behind the stern.

In this situation, you can sometimes tally a lunker calico by selecting the best-looking *green back* anchovy in the bait tank. The secret is twofold: 1) hook the 'chovy gently with a smaller #4 to #6 Eagle Claw 318-N live bait hook underneath the gills; and 2) fly-line the "hot" bait with a freshwater bass outfit spooled with 10 to 12 pound test monofilament. This combination is the ultimate finesse setup for getting highly temperamental bull bass to eat on the outside chum.

Day in and day out, however, probably more calicos over 4 pounds are scored on live squid than any other bait. Bull bass love the "candy"! Fish the sliding-egg sinker rig, or fly-line the squid weightless. Use a rubber-core sinker, split-shot or lead head to probe different depths where the big calicos might be stalking.

Another seldom-used calico rig for squid is to tie a 1 to 2 ounce *chrome* torpedo sinker to the end of the line.

Next, add an 18 to 24 inch length of leader with an Eagle Claw #318-N 2/0 to 4/0 live bait hook. This is a potent bottom-scratchin' rig for bull bass, particularly in the colder months.

As the chrome sinker lays on the bottom, its shiny finish refracts light, giving it the illusion of a wounded squid or baitfish. With either a whole live or dead squid trailing behind it, the trophy calico may not be able to refuse the offering! Slowly "pump" this rig back to the boat following your cast using a gentle lift-and-drop motion with the rod. When a big bass strikes the squid with this rig, *leave the reel in gear.* Point the rod tip towards the fish as you give it some time and line to swallow the bait, then swing and set! "Pump" rigs like this will also account for mixed bags of sand bass, barracuda, halibut, white sea bass, and even salmon along with the calicos. Don't forget to use a *chrome* torpedo sinker for the best effect.

"Bulls" on the Iron!

There are a number of anglers from Santa Barbara to San Diego who specialize in fishing for big calicos with cast-metal jigs. To see a bull bass practically explode upon a well-retrieved jig is a heart-stopping sight! The fish are mean and tough, especially if you fish the iron in and around the kelp.

How the kelp stringers are lying can be a critical feature in the proper selection of a jig to be used for "bull" calicos. For example, if the kelp is down with few signs of the plant on the surface, then your best choice might be a medium size—medium weight jig to keep your lure below the surface. The U.F.O. #2 and #4, Tady 6xJR, Yo Ho Ho #1 to #3, and Salas Christy 2 are perfect for the sub-surface calico action. Best colors are green/yellow, blue/white, and solid chrome.

If the kelp is "up" with stringers showing, then most likely the bull bass will be on or near the surface. Here is where you want to throw a large but "light" alloy jig for maximum swimming action and minimal sinking effect. Models like the U.F.O. "P.O.S.," Tady 45, and Salas 7x light are bona fide bull bass killers. In contrast to the faster sinking sub-surface jigs listed above, the larger "lights" should be tried in a different mix of colors. These include flat General Motors green, sardine, brown/purple/blue squid, and blue/white with black belly.

If you're lucky, you might also be able to find some of the Tady 45s in a "light" version but with a large *single* fixed hook instead of the treble. Veteran bull bass fishermen recognized these single-hook Tady 45s as secret weapons for hauling big calicos out of dense kelp pockets.

The single hook rides upright and is practically weedless, rarely snagging up on the kelp stringers. The single hook configuration also seems to allow the jig to swim more erratically with more side-to-side "kick." The large prominent single hook is also designed for excellent penetration and "bite," allowing for a solid hook-set to pull these brutes from the kelp beds.

Fishing "bulls" on the iron requires patience and perseverance. Often you won't see signs of surface activity, making nine casts in a row when all of a sudden a big calico juts up from below to annihilate the surface iron on your tenth cast. Other times you may be slowly winding the smaller heavier jig through submerged kelp stringers. Suddenly, out of the blue, you feel a powerful strike and a big bull bass tries to take you far into the deeper kelp.

Not many saltwater fishermen have the patience to fish trophy calicos with the iron. Those who stick with the jigs are often rewarded with the magnificent trophy of an 8 to 10 pound bull bass caught on the iron. Use the same basic 8 to 10 foot jig sticks, conventional reels, 30 pound test line, and hammered drags as the standard tackle for fishing big calicos on the iron as you would for throwing big baits.

Trophy Calicos on Plastics!

When times get really tough and the better quality calicos shut off on live bait and turn away from jigs, switch to your arsenal of soft plastics. Historically, a lot of lunker calicos have been caught on the basic fork-tail design lure. The famous Scampi, Mojo, and Haddock Lunker Thumper all produce an occasional wall hanger calico.

The newer Berkley Power Scamper and Power Grub should also be given a serious try, especially during those seemingly ultra-finicky feeding periods when a lure with some scent in it just might start the action.

Two other tail configurations are essential to experiment with when stalking bull bass: large sickle tails and shad-style knob-tails. The A.A.T. Salty Magic has scored many big calicos on our Eagle Claw Fishing Schools to remote Mexican islands like Benitos, Cedros, and San Martin. There are occasions when the prominent sickle-tail lure either cast or drifted generates a different vibration pattern in contrast to the common fork-tail models that often trigger strikes from big calico bass.

Similarly A.A. Worm's Shad-Tails, with their peculiar looking knobby tail design, have been spectacular bull bass killers in cold water and in thick kelp. Interestingly, with the fork-tail and sickle-tail models, we encourage our students to always use the lead head/plastic bodies with a 1x3 inch piece of squid or mackerel as a trailer to spice up the lure. It is best to fish the A.A. Shads without any trailer so as to not inhibit the fast vibrating action generated by the knob-tail.

The latest design in soft plastics are Pacific eels marketed by A.A.T. and A.A. Worms. You won't catch many calicos with these eels but when you do get bit it is typically a real keeper. The plastic eels work especially well at 60 to 120 foot depths nailing ling cod, sand and white sea bass, rockfish, or even halibut, in addition to deep-water bull bass. (More on eels in other sections.)

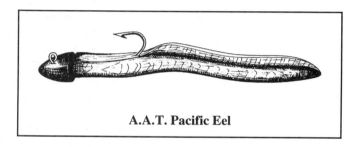

A.A.T. Pacific Eel

I recommend to my students three things when it comes to fishing for the big bull calicos with soft plastics:

1. If you can get away with it, use lighter 10 to 12 pound test and freshwater bass gear. The plastic baits swim better with the fine diameter mono, and big calicos are *old* calicos. They are wary and smart. It is easier to fool them with light line.

2. Swim your plastics S-L-O-W-L-Y. For the most part, the bull bass will usually strike the soft plastics with a steady methodical retrieve. Occasionally stop and pause letting the lure glide towards the bottom. Be prepared for strikes on the sink. No strikes? Continue to wind.

3. If you do get bit on the soft plastics with light gear, *wind fast* to turn a big bull bass away from heavy cover. It takes a long time for a calico bass to reach trophy size. I stress again that these are very smart gamefish and, unless you take control quickly, they'll bust you off in the rocks, kelp, or underwater wreckage.

Bulls on Plugs!

Big bull calicos will definitely strike a slow-trolled Rapala CD-14 or CD-18 Magnum plug. As I've mentioned with other species, the best strategy is to troll the large minnow-shaped plug behind the stern as chum is being tossed out. When the bull bass want a BIG bait like a green or Spanish mackerel and, if they are not available, the magnum-size Rapala plugs will often do the trick.

Trolling the large Rapalas parallel to offshore kelp beds can also be productive. Consider replacing the factory treble hooks with double hooks to minimize the plugs fouling up on the kelp stringers.

The best colors to use with the Rapalas when pluggin' for bull bass are as follows: green/mackerel, silver foil/black back, and fluorescent "fire tiger."

Grumper Sand Bass

Unlike the more glamorous species such as yellowtail, albacore, and white sea bass, "sandies" can be found in the fish sacks on practically a year-round basis from San Diego to Monterey. Both party boat skippers and small boaters depend upon sand bass to comprise an integral portion of their fish counts during the height of the late spring and midsummer months. Shrewd anglers have also found that this species can be taken in the dead of winter all the way down to 150 foot depths. Sand bass are depicted as a relatively easy fish to catch. However, there are some interesting strategies the veteran anglers use to key in on the larger 4 to 8 pound "grumper" specimens. Let's examine some of the insider's tips to catch not only more sand bass, but the larger "grumper" class fish as well.

Yo-yo Spoons

One of the most overlooked methods for catching these fish is to vertically spoon for sandies. This can be practiced on either party boats or smaller, private craft. Often sand bass cluster in large schools suspended off the bottom. Typically most fishermen lower their baited anchovy rigs all the way to the bottom and wait for a strike. By vertically jigging a spoon directly above, below, and through these suspended bass, a wider portion of the strike zone is covered.

Frequently, the larger "grumpers" will key in on the erratic flash and vibration generated from a spoon yo-yoed straight up and down in this fashion. Stay with lighter 10 to 15 pound test line. The spoon will dart and dance more, simulating a frantic 'chovy with the light mono. Try the Haddock Jig'n Spoon or the old standbys, a chrome Krocadile or Crippled Herring in 1 to 2 ounce versions.

Grind a Jig for Sandies

Saltwater anglers are sometimes remiss in not throwing the "iron" on sand bass. A heavier medium-size jig can often produce that larger "grumper" fish to round out your limit. Jigs in the medium-size range such as the U.F.O. #2, #3 and #4, Yo Ho Ho #1 to #3, or the Salas Christy #1 and

#2 are perfect for this kind of fishing. Like the spoons mentioned above, these can also be yo-yoed with the basic lift-and-drop rod motion directly off the bottom or above it for suspended sandies.

Don't overlook actually casting these heavier jigs out some distance from the boat to target marauding schools of sand bass lying outside a chum line. Although sandies are typically not as skittish as calico bass, they will often hesitate to school up tight near the boat. After casting the jig out, let it sink. Count it down to different depths until you find where the fish are holding. Maintain a steady wind—not too fast—and occasionally pause intermittently throughout the retrieve. This stop-and-go tactic will also prove effective on the larger grumpers. Be prepared for strikes to occur as the retrieve is halted and the jig begins to sink.

You don't need to be too particular when it comes to selecting which color of iron to throw to the sand bass. The basic menu of blue/white, green/yellow, and brown and yellow (scrambled egg) works well. You might also try a solid chrome or white jig in this genre, particularly when using the vertical yo-yoing technique. You might also consider adding either a whole frozen squid or a strip of cut bonito or mackerel to one of the jig's treble hooks. Frequently, the addition of a chunk of "meat" combined with the "iron" produces some of the larger sandies holding deep near the bottom.

Fork-Tail Plastics Catch Grumpers

A large portion of the sandies caught each year on artificial lures are taken on some sort of soft plastic fork-tail lure. Popular models include the Scampi, Mojo, Lunker Thumper, Kreepy Krawler, Berkley Power Scamper, and Shabby Shrimp. The most effective sand bass colors year after year are root beer flake, lime green, chartreuse, and fluorescent pink. Here are a couple of other pointers to enhance these baits which may yield some of the larger "grumper" fish.

Keep a tray of frozen squid handy. Cut the squid into 1x3 inch strips. Add this behind one of the plastic fork-tails as a trailer. This added attractant can really spice up the lure, especially when the sandies are not aggressively feeding. Don't hesitate to throw the larger models in these baits. The more prominent 6 to 8 inch long versions are normally associated with deep-water bottom fishing. They will also account for some of the jackpot "grumpers" tallied each year.

If the sandies seem to prefer an ultraslow moving lure, lace on a vinyl skirt above the front of the plastic tail. The skirt flares out on the sink, allowing the bait to glide slowly to the bottom. The extra bulk from the skirting material also creates more resistance so that a slower retrieve is easier to maintain with a fork-tail rigged in this manner.

Single Tails Work Too

Another often overlooked bait is a variation of the double or fork-tail lure, composed of a larger, single sickle-like tail. Lures such as A.A.T.'s Salty Magic and A.A. Worm's Single Tails are molded in this design. These are terrific slow-moving pulsating baits for colder water conditions. There are times when the sand bass are simply not interested in the "tighter" vibration generated by a fork-tail. The larger, more prominent single-tail lures like the Salty Magic displace a considerable amount of water on the slow retrieve. This type of lure seems to be particularly appealing to the larger sand bass found in the school. These baits should also be tipped with a small piece of frozen squid.

Another interesting ploy is to construct a "school of Magics." Tie your main line to a three-way swivel. Attach a 24 to 30 inch length of leader with a large 7 inch Salty Magic attached to the other end. Add a shorter 12 to 18 inch length of leader to the remaining swivel eyelet and a more compact 4 inch Magic. Don't be surprised if you nail two bass on one drop with this tandem rig. The bigger female "grumpers" will often attack the larger lure after a smaller male has hit the little Magic. This combination can be either cast-and-retrieved or slowly drifted along the bottom.

Grubs for Sand Bass

In some situations, sand bass prefer a soft plastic lure with practically no tail motion at all. Classic straight-tail grubs such as the Haddock Split-Tail and Four-Tail series as well as the Bagley Salty Dog are perfect for this kind of presentation. In my personal experience, I have found that grubs excel under low light conditions such as early dawn, on super-slow drifts, and in colder water. Always use a piece of squid as a trailer, plus a few drops of fish attractant to provide extra "flavor." Also, these baits can be customized to look more appealing by adding a colorful vinyl skirt. Don't forget to stock up on Berkley Power Grubs when the sandies seem to be a little sluggish The built-in scent really works.

When the bite is really a "pick" and the sandies are in a semi-lethargic state, switch to one of these bottom-plodding grubs. Big "grumpers" will sometimes jump on one of these rather simple lures when other offerings fail to get bit.

Knob-Tails Nail Grumpers

Soft plastic knob-tails have gained considerable popularity in recent years among calico bass fishermen. The same baits will also work on sand bass, once again, in colder water. The secret is not to retrieve these lures too quickly. The Mr. Twister Sassy Shad, A.A. Worm's Super Shad, and the Kalin Salty Lunker Shad are made to replicate so-called small "brown baits" like queenfish or tom cod. Darker color schemes featuring brown, green, black, and chartreuse will also be effective on sand bass.

Fish the knob-tails on light mono to maximize the tight swimming action of the distinctive paddle-tail. This can be a "sleeper" lure on the slow-grind through schools of suspended sandies. Use the larger models in these baits to home in on the grumpers.

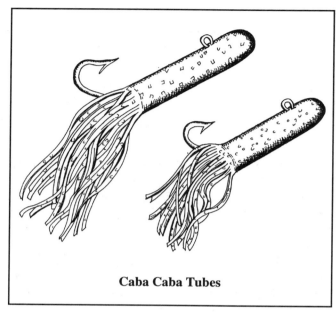

Caba Caba Tubes

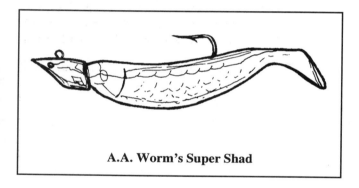

A.A. Worm's Super Shad

Tube Baits for Sandies

One of the more recent innovations in saltwater lures has been the application of soft hollow-bodied plastic "tubes" for pelagic species. These lures have their origins among freshwater bass buffs. Tube bait design and rigging is uncomplicated. Some models like A.A.T.'s Caba Caba Tube have specially engineered heads that are made to slide up into the hollow portion of the tube. This gives the Caba Caba the appearance of a "soft-headed" bait similar to a live squid or baby octopus.

The "tubes" fish well in a variety of capacities when you are in sand bass territory. They are excellent drift baits all through the year. You can also cast and retrieve the "tube" slowly "pumping" it back to the boat as you would a live squid. By gently lowering and raising your rod tip to create the "pumping" action, the miniature tentacles on these "tubes" will open and flair as the lure sashays through the water.

Tube baits can also be used in a more vertical presentation when you are metering fish directly below the boat. Be prepared for a big "grumper" to practically "inhale" this lure as it sinks to the bottom.

For extra effect, squirt a considerable amount of liquid fish scent up into the hollow body. As the tube darts back and forth in the water, the attractant is emitted leaving a virtual chum slick around the bait. All of the popular colors used with other soft plastic lures will perform equally well in tube baits. However, the best choices are milky glow, root beer flake, and lime with black glitter flake for grumpers.

Deep-Troll Rapalas for Sand Bass

Small craft owners may find it difficult to keep a school of hungry sandies around the boat with limited chum power. One of the ways to maximize your chances of staying with schools of cruising bass is to slow-troll a plug that replicates an anchovy.

The Rapala CD-13 or CD-14 Magnum plugs are the perfect choice for this strategy. However, if the sand bass are feeding well below 15 feet, you will have to find ways to get the lure down to these fish. A sophisticated downrigger system is obviously one choice. A less expensive and remarkably effective method is to use a large torpedo sinker to drag the Rapala down deeper.

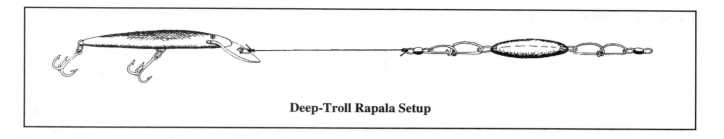

Deep-Troll Rapala Setup

Select a ringed torpedo weight in the 4 to 12 ounce range, depending upon how deep the sand bass are holding. Tie your main line to one eye of the sinker. To the other, tie on about 5 feet of the leader with the CD-13 sinking Rapala plug attached.

You will need to use a fairly stiff conventional rod and a reel filled with 20 pound test for this trolling setup. The heavy weight, combined with the drag from the lure, puts a strain on light tackle. Use a 12 to 15 pound test leader line with this rig. The lighter mono for the leader will allow the lure to swim with less restriction than it would if tied directly to 20 pound line. Big sand bass eat these plugs!

Shiny Sinker Slider Rigs

If the action is hot and heavy, here is another double rig that is worth trying. Slide your main line through a 1 to 4 ounce chrome ring sinker. Tie it off to a swivel. Add an 18 to 24 inch length of leader with a live bait hook. Pin an anchovy onto this basic slider rig to be fished off the bottom. Before you make that cast, add a split-ring and a small treble hook to the other end of the shiny sinker.

As you cast, the 'chovy and weight sink to the bottom. Sometimes, a big "grumper" will bushwhack the chrome sinker on the fall while ignoring the anchovy. Other times, after hooking a smaller bass on the 'chovy, a group of larger free swimmers will start to follow the hooked fish as you retrieve. The chrome weight is often too much for the other members of the school to pass up, and you now find yourself with two sandies on the end of the line!

Using Big Baits for Grumpers

As a final ploy, think about trying some alternatives to the standard menu of anchovies if you want to tempt sand bass with bait. Filet a small mackerel. Either a greenback or Spanish model will be fine. Use about half of the filet, sliced diagonally to form a triangular-shaped wedge.

Pin the wider end of this half filet onto an Eagle Claw #118MG or #318-N size 4/0 live bait hook. Pinch on a large lead split-shot marketed for saltwater live bait fish-

ing. Cast the "slab" of mackerel out, let it go to the bottom and begin to work it back to the boat. The trick is to "feather" the spool of the conventional reel. This is done by rolling the spool S-L-O-W-L-Y with your index and middle finger to pick up line. This is done instead of using the reel handle.

By feathering the mackerel back to the boat, you will make the filet dart and dip through the water, mimicking a frantic "mack" under attack. Don't expect the sand bass to initially annihilate the slab. Typically, they will pick it up, mouth it, tug on it, or shake it back and forth like a dog

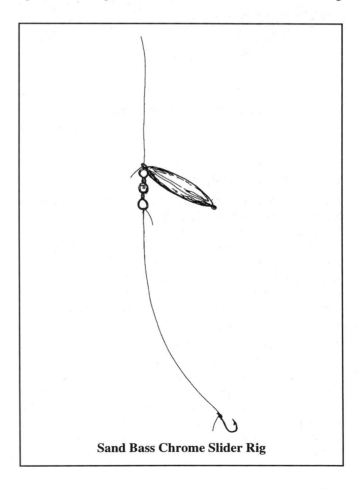

Sand Bass Chrome Slider Rig

feasting on a bone. The feathering allows you to tempt, tease, and finally coax the bass into thoroughly eating the bait.

When the tension on the line increases and the fish starts to run, free-spool the slab. Swing and set hard after a few seconds. Big "grumper" sandies will occasionally be fooled by this mackerel filet after being hammered by the standard parade of popular offerings. If you let the mackerel filet simply rest on the bottom, you may not be able to get by the sharks.

Another tactic I mentioned earlier was popularized years ago with the calico bass fraternity, yet still works today on grumper sandies. Tie on a Bomber Gumpy Jig. This is basically a fancy lead head with either nylon bristles or bucktail for the tail. Then pin on a whole frozen squid to the Bomber. Soak the bristles in a generous dose of liquid fish attractant and you are ready for action. This "squid'n jig" combo also requires a slow pumping action with the rod to generate strikes. Be ready to let the sand bass run with this large offering a little before you swing and set. This is definitely a "big fish" bait.

Be Innovative!

Don't take these fish for granted. There are many instances when sand bass can become highly selective feeders as the bite "shuts off." On the other hand, sandies are accessible all year long for the skippers who want to look for them. The tips outlined above will provide you with some additional ammunition to use, especially when the action seems to go into a stall. These tricks will work not only on school fish, but may also help you tally that jackpot winning "grumper."

Striped Bass

Striped bass are the primary gamefish sought by Northern California saltwater sportsmen although they are found all the way to the Canadian border. There has probably been more written about this North Coast fish than all other species combined. The information in this section should get you started as a "striper sniper." There is a wealth of other resources available that will provide you with even more sophisticated tools to track these intriguing fish.

Begin to monitor accounts published in weekly outdoor newspaper columns. These seasonal reports are essential to follow in order to get a general idea of where the stripers are schooling. I emphasize schooling—this gamefish can suddenly appear in hordes and you need to respond on short notice. Next, visit area tackle stores.

Develop a rapport with the proprietor. Try to buy your bait and at least some portion of your terminal gear from these shops. In exchange, the sales personnel may turn you on to valuable insiders' tips of "where, when, and how" to fish stripers. Definitely check out local sportfishing landings to determine where and when the boats are running for striped bass.

Working the Surf Line for Stripers

Usually by early June, huge schools of line sides will cruise within the breakers south of the Golden Gate, herding masses of anchovies or any other available baitfish. These stripers can be smaller 8 to 10 pound school fish, on up to 20 to 30 pound class brutes. They can become easy targets for the small craft owner. Keep an eye open for telltale signs of nearby striper activity. This can be signaled by sea birds dipping into the water, visual sightings of "dark water" (meatballs of bait), or surface boils.

If you are lucky enough to first see an indication of surface-feeding fish, definitely take a shot at them with artificial lures. Top-water plugs in larger freshwater or saltwater sizes such as the Arbogast Dasher, Heddon Lucky 13, Bomber Model Long-A, magnum class Rapalas and Rebels, or the Cordell Pencil Popper are time-proven striper killers. These are the same lures surf fishermen actually throw from the beach when trying to reach the bass cruising the surf line.

Expect to make a fairly long cast, keeping the boat some distance from the surface frenzy and of course the breaking surf. A medium-action 8 to 9 foot saltwater spinning rod and a spinner filled with 20 pound mono should do the trick. Heavy-duty freshwater popping rods will also work for this type of casting. However, novice striper fishermen will probably find the spinning combos easier to cast when using these large bulky plugs, especially in the wind. The fish can pop up on either side of the breakers.

Other lure possibilities should also be explored when the stripers are near the beach. Spoons such as the ever popular Krocadile, Tony Acetta Pet, and the Kastmaster are excellent choices under these conditions. The traditional solid chrome, chrome and blue, or chrome and red color schemes produce annually for fan-casting for stripers from the boat. Slab-shaped crankplugs in beefier sizes are similarly effective. The Cordell Spot is a standout lure for plugs in this genre along with the Rattlin' Rapala and Rat-L-Trap.

One of the simplest lures to use for stripers near the surf line is the hair jig. Models enjoying great popularity

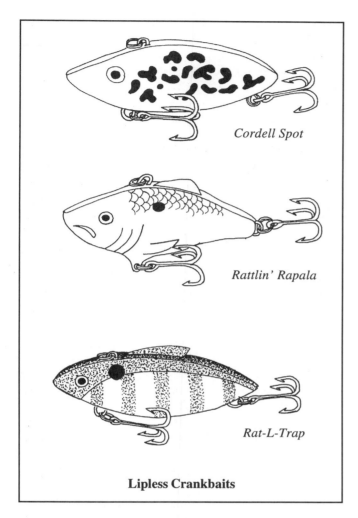

Cordell Spot

Rattlin' Rapala

Rat-L-Trap

Lipless Crankbaits

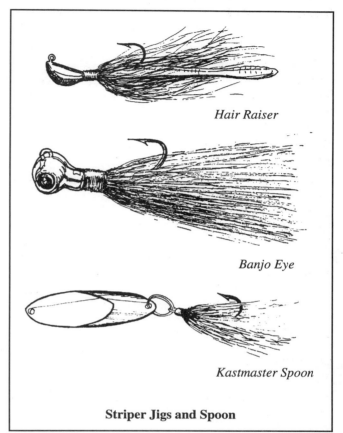

Hair Raiser

Banjo Eye

Kastmaster Spoon

Striper Jigs and Spoon

over past seasons are the Hair Raiser, the Banjo Eye, and the Worm Tail. The latter is a hair jig featuring a long, white plastic curly tail worm as a trailer. On this note, include soft plastic jigs such as the Scrounger, Salty Magic, and Kalin Lunker Grub in your striper arsenal.

Here are a couple of fairly basic rules of thumb to observe when tossing lures on striped bass. These guidelines are appropriate whether you are spot-casting outside the surf line or inside the more sheltered bays.

1. Learn to vary your retrieve to key in on the pace at which the stripers appear to be feeding. For example, if the fish are in a wild surface-feeding frenzy, then consider ripping that crank plug, surface lure, spoon, or jig back to the boat fairly rapidly. If they seem touchy, slow down the retrieve.

2. If the stripers become skittish, or if the water clarity is high, or the bite simply appears to have ground down, then switch to smaller lures and lighter monofilament.

3. Mix up your presentations as conditions change throughout the day. For instance, when the line sides are "hot" a swimming jig with a curl-tail may be the ticket. When the action cools, it might be better to use a slow sashaying jig with minimal tail movement.

If fan-casting from the boat this close to the beach isn't your fancy, slow-trolling is a good alternative. Spoons, jigs, and crankplugs are adaptable to this method. Sometimes the lure will have to be pulled through a specific fish-holding strata some distance above the bottom. Other times the stripers may be sulking near the bottom and a deep diving lure will work better.

Party boats often chum with live bait in the surf line. If you have this kind of fire power at your disposal, then live bait drifting or fly-lining a 'chovy, smelt, herring, or sardine will produce. A nose or gill-hooked anchovy with a small 1/4 to 3/8 ounce rubber-core sinker or a larger split-shot crimped above the bait will get bit when gently drifted behind the boat. If more weight is needed to fight the current or wave action, then a sliding sinker rig or a three-way swivel setup will be necessary. The sinkers can vary from 1 to 4 ounces in weight.

Stripers chase baitfish along the beach from late June through early September. Boat positioning is critical with this approach. To be effective, the boater will frequently have to pilot his craft perilously close to the beach. The stripers will gravitate to the sandy or rocky points, as well as narrow creases where the shoreline takes a turn forming a feeding funnel for trapped baitfish.

Fishing spots like this require considerable boat handling skill and full attention to the surf conditions. Many veteran private boaters recommend fishing the surf line in teamwork fashion. One person should be responsible for staying on the wheel while the others fish. Then rotate that responsibility. Someone has to maintain control of the boat at all times when working this close to the shore.

Line Sides in the Bay

By late summer, stripers should start migrating into the San Francisco Bay. After gorging themselves on ocean-bred anchovies for the past months along the Pacifica, Rockaway, and Lindeman beaches, the big line sides follow the schools of bait inland. Activity now begins to heat up in such legendary striper haunts as Candlestick Park, Hunter's Point, and the San Mateo Bridge in the southwest bay, and the Alameda Rocks, the Berkeley Flats, and the Oakland Estuary in the northeast section. Schools of stripers also inhabit San Francisco Bay from mid-May through early fall. These fish come down from the Delta in late spring.

Party boat skippers will run so-called "potluck" trips on which they drift for stripers, salmon, or halibut in the expanses of the Bay. The object of most Bay drifting is to keep the bait roughly 3 feet above the bottom. Mudsuckers are considered the primo bait for stripers. Live shiner perch, bullheads, anchovies, squid, grass shrimp, herring, and smelt are also on the seasonal menu for these northern gamefish.

Let's elaborate on some of these baits for a moment. The mudsuckers are sold at area bait shops. They are

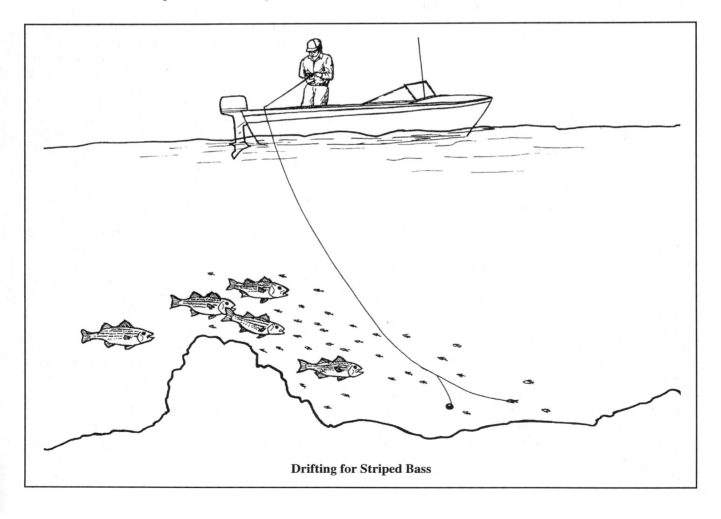

Drifting for Striped Bass

usually fished live on the drift, hooked through both lips with either a long-shank baitholder or short-shank live bait hook. Shiner perch can be caught around the pilings in the Bay using pieces of pile worm or shrimp on a tiny #10 to #14 baitholder hook. They can then be placed in aerated live wells or bait buckets. Hook the shiners as you would a "brown bait" to fly-line it either behind the dorsal fin, under the anal fin, or through the nose.

Anchovies and smelt of course produce best when alive. Standard live bait hooking procedures previously discussed are appropriate. Frozen versions of these baitfish, as well as herring, also work. Whole baitfish, halves, or chunks can be tried. Here is another little tip. Take a frozen anchovy or herring and cut it in half. Next, slice each section about two-thirds of the way into the bait.

A halved 'chovy or herring cut part way up the center creates a scissors effect with the flaps of meat. These sliced half-sections give the illusion of a baitfish floundering on the bottom with the two flaps moving in the current. This helps to lure stripers to this bait. Locals also like to make an incision in the whole dead baitfish, again primarily to emit scent and fish oils to attract the striped bass.

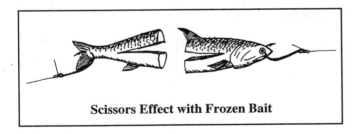

Scissors Effect with Frozen Bait

Veteran striper snipers will disagree among themselves as to whether it is best to fish bullheads alive or dead. One theory recommends drifting a live bullhead available from area bait vendors. This lively sculpin-like baitfish is a tantalizing morsel for a hungry striper slowly drifted along the bottom. Another school of thought suggests drifting only dead bullheads. The reason is that live bullheads have a tendency to burrow into the mud.

Some experts prefer to take live bullheads, kill them first, then use them for bait. You can, however, purchase frozen bullheads at the bait shops. If you do this, always make sure there is a lot of slime coating left on the bait as you look through the packaging. This slime layer dissipates an apparent odor in the water that attracts the snipers. The slime also has luminescent properties that make the bullhead practically glow in the Bay's cloudy water.

A variety of routine drifting rigs will be suitable with the above-mentioned baits. The basic sliding egg sinker setup, a three-way swivel combo, a split-shot rig—all of these will produce when drifting for stripers in San Francisco Bay. Sinker size will vary depending upon currents, tidal conditions, and the bottom topography.

Many of the area's regular anglers also recommend using a double hook trap setup when drifting these different baits, especially with bullheads, cut 'chovies, smelt, or herring. Consider using a large chunk of styrofoam tied above the bait as a drift bobber. A favorite tactic is to fish a live shiner perch 5 to 8 feet underneath the float and let it drift in the current. You will also often hear longtime striper fishermen talk about "walking" their baits off the bottom. This is an important technique, requiring some finessing with, again, the object being to keep the bait from hanging up on the bottom terrain.

One strategy is to use a three-way swivel combination. Tie your sinker onto a lighter, 8 to 12 inch leader. A very soft flexible pencil lead can be used in this situation. This kind of sinker hangs up less than conventional weights. Tie your bait onto a heavier, 18 to 36 inch leader. The trick is to kind of "pump" the rod tip as you either drift or cast-and-retrieve, easing the bait above the rocks and along the ledges. If the weight is hung up or if the fish heads for the rocks, the lighter leader with the sinker may break off first either saving the bait, or allowing you to play the striper without any further hang-ups. In many ways, this is quite similar to mooching for salmon.

A variation on this theme is to "chrome" the stripers. Tie a 1 to 4 ounce shiny chrome ringed torpedo sinker to your main line. Run an 18 to 36 inch leader with your bait on the other end of the weight. After you cast, be prepared for strikes on the fall, as the shiny sinker creates a lot of "flash" on the way down. The torpedo weight can then be either bounced along the bottom or "pumped" and retrieved above it through shallower strike zones.

Here are a couple of other pointers to keep in mind for fishing stripers in the Bay with live bait. First, if you feel uncomfortable working drift patterns, consider fishing the line sides at anchor. This is a particularly good tactic if you want to zero in on a lunker using bullheads for bait. Try to fish at the peak of high tide if possible.

Second, give these fish plenty of time to eat the larger offerings such as mudsuckers or bullheads. Leave the reel in free-spool, allowing the bass to mouth the big bait with minimal resistance. Don't underestimate the magnitude

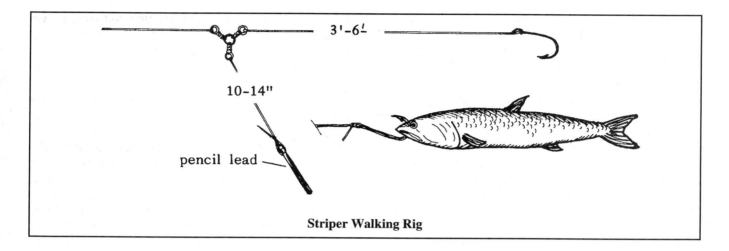

Striper Walking Rig

of the initial strike. It may take the form of nothing more than a subtle "tick" in the line. In sum, it pays to be patient when still-fishing or drifting for striped bass.

Lures for Stripers

Many of the lures mentioned in the earlier discussion of stripers from the surf line will be effective in the quieter waters of the San Francisco Bay. Also consider using both the large and more compact plugs associated with freshwater bassin'. Long distance casting may not always be that critical. Both medium saltwater spinning and freshwater popping outfits are perfect for bay striper snipin'.

When you switch to artificials, there are a couple of things to look for to enhance your chances. Always keep your eyes peeled for surface activity: birds picking at bait, swirls, boiling fish. Fire casts wherever you can find moving currents. Toss your lures up-current. The stripers will be facing into the current, waiting for wayward bait to flow down to them.

Next, seek out structure in the Bay. Striped bass will establish ambush points on all types of obstructions. Boat docks, rock piles, riprap, bridge pilings, channel markers, chunks of broken asphalt or concrete, old duck blinds, broken pipe, rock jetties, and piers, all constitute prime structure for striped bass.

Stripers "wolf pack" in schools trying to herd the bait into pockets created by the structure. As aggressive as the fish can become, they also spook easily. The best way to

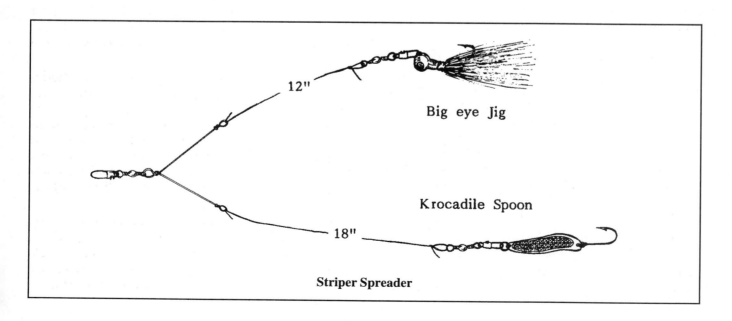

Big eye Jig

Krocadile Spoon

Striper Spreader

stalk those gamefish in the shallow waters is to use an electric trolling motor quietly coming up behind the stripers when possible. You can actually follow the schools with the trolling motor as they migrate over the shallow flats.

There are regional favorites that Bay Area locals like to toss when a lure bite materializes. Large freshwater plugs such as the Cordell Spot, Rebels, and Rapalas persist at nailing Bay stripers. A black or white Hair Raiser jig is another killer. Other banana-head jigs with a red head and white skirt, or red head with orange skirt are equally productive. The Worm-Tail models are also frequently used, commonly in white, for both drifting or spot-casting towards structure. More traditional freshwater bassin' jigs such as the Brawley Bass Bug are equally worth trying. If the water is real dirty, select a jig with a relatively bulky skirt like the Bass Bug. This lure will displace more water and the bulky body will show up better under murky conditions. Spoons of practically any shape are possible striper catchers. It is hard to beat the Kastmaster and Krocadile series in chrome. These will cast well, with minimal wind resistance.

Another interesting option is to present two lures at one time. You can buy a wire spreader rig at local tackle dealers. The spreader frame allows you to tie two different leaders with diverse baits for real variety when drifting or slow-trolling. A popular combination is a Tony Acetta Pet Spoon teamed with a hair jig on separate leaders.

Some anglers also use Pink Ladies or similar planers to take spoons or plugs down deeper in the bay while trolling for stripers. The basic setup and principles outlined for using these planing devices for salmon are pretty much applicable for striper deep-trolling.

Read the Water!

Striped bass are both excellent sport and fine eating. When the fish are concentrated, the bite can go "wide open" for both bait soakers and lure fishermen. Learn to "read" the water when you fish for stripers. There are vast expanses of "dead" water found along stretches of beach-front access or the quiet water in San Francisco Bay. Learn to rely upon your "eyeballs" and instincts to home in on these northern gamefish. Be on the constant lookout for any indication of striper activity and then be prepared to move quickly to follow the fish.

Mystic Whites

None of the gamefish found along the Pacific Coast are more mystical than the white sea bass. Not really a "bass" but rather a giant croaker, whites are commonly caught from Monterey south to about midway down the Baja peninsula. They reach gargantuan weights of over 60 pounds but remain one of the most difficult species to catch.

Every spring I conduct Eagle Claw Fishing Schools targeting these giant croaker. We usually travel to Catalina Island, one of the prime hot spot for white sea bass. The best months are typically February through May. The single most critical ingredient to locating whites is to find areas where live squid are concentrated. In most years, during the spring the squid come up from deep water and may be either netted or jigged by party boats and smaller charter operators. I cannot emphasize enough: find the squid—the sea bass will be nearby!

Here are some of the time-proven methods we teach in our seminars to fool these wily croaker.

Live Bait for White Sea Bass

As you might expect, nothing works better on white sea bass than a fresh, live squid. The typical live bait outfit consists of a baitcasting reel, 20 pound monofilament, and a medium action 7 to 8 foot rod. I should point out that in recent years there has been a tendency, however, to challenge these whites with heavy-duty freshwater gear. The hot setup is a level wind freshwater bass reel spooled with 10 to 15 pound string, matched with a 7 to 7 1/2 foot, trigger grip, poppin' rod or flippin' stick.

Many veteran charter boat skippers emphasize how wary whites can become. This is especially true on a crowded weekend at some place like Catalina with an armada of over 200 boats working the island. The lighter monofilament can thus be more effective. Its thinner diameter more easily fools heavily pressured schools of sea bass.

The simplest rigging is a sliding egg sinker butted directly against an Eagle Claw #318N size 2/0 to 4/0 live bait hook. Although this particular rigging looks rather awkward (with the sinker riding against the eye of the hook) it is really quite effective. Pin the squid onto the hook once through the tail then back inside the body once again. The squid is now pretty much free to float, swim or dive as it pleases, pulling out line through the sliding egg sinker.

Now then, here is an important point. Over the years in these sea bass schools we have fished in 30 to 90 foot depths with the live squid. Novice anglers often falsely assume that whites are primarily bottom feeders and hence overweight the squid. The trick is instead of using heavier 3/4 to 2 ounce sliding-egg sinkers to get your squid to the bottom quickly switch to lighter 1/8 to 1/4 ounce sliders. (These smaller egg sinkers are more akin to what you would expect to find in your trout tackle box—but they do work!) The tiny egg sinkers permit the maximum motion from the live squid, short of fly-lining it weightless. So often we found the sea bass to be suspended at mid-depths, in which case a slow-sinking squid would be much more potent than one soaking on the bottom.

There are times, however, when the whites are indeed lying on the bottom. Here is where the heavier 3/4 to 2 ounce slider is most effective. Similarly, if the big croaker actually start to boil in the chum line on the surface, then certainly switch to a fly-line rig without any weight at all.

Two other strategies will also work with live squid:

1. If the sea bass are in deeper water, say 90 to 150 feet, then try fishing them on a dropper loop rig. Set up with a 4 to 10 ounce torpedo sinker. Use the bigger weights if the current is ripping. Next, add a dropper loop and hitch on an Eagle Claw #318-N size 4/0 hook. (I like the bigger hooks fishing at greater depths for maximum penetration.) The live squid will swim around in a circle while the torpedo sinker rests on the bottom or even the rocks.

2. Pin a whole live squid tail-first onto a large lead head. This squid'n jig combo is so basic, it is sometimes hard to imagine that the croaker would be fooled by it. When you sense that the white sea bass are in an exceptional feeding mode, use the big 1 to 3 ounce lead with the live squid. An unpainted version is just fine. Occasionally when these fish school, they will go on a feeding binge that will rival the best tuna bites! When the whites are in this mode, we teach our students to fish the lead head since the open hook generates the maximum strike-to-catch ratios.

Sea bass will also strike fresh dead or frozen squid. The strategies I outlined for working live squid will perform with frozen or fresh dead bait. The secret will be to S-L-O-W-L-Y "pump" the dead squid back to the boat. Pumpin' squid in this manner is simple. Just slowly lift the rod tip from 3 o'clock to 12 o'clock then gently drop it back down again. This gives the dead squid the illusion of gliding casually up and down as it might if it where alive.

If you fly-line fresh dead or frozen squid, be sure to let out enough line to allow the bait to drift back into the current. With your reel in free-spool, occasionally pause and "feather" the spool by giving it a couple of quick flicks with the index and middle fingers pulling in a few inches of line. "Feathering" the dead squid in this manner

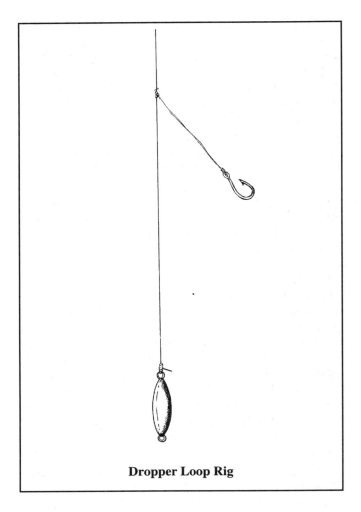

Dropper Loop Rig

is a dynamite secret for fooling big white sea bass when the live squid isn't available. As you "flick" the spool suddenly the dead squid darts and dances from side to side as if it sensed it was under attack.

If you want to try a bizarre technique, here is one final trick for using dead or frozen squid: carefully pin a large anchovy or sardine *inside the belly of the squid*. The squid is basically wrapped around the live baitfish. As you fly-line this weird setup, the baitfish kicks from side to side really giving the dead squid an eerie lifelike appearance!

White sea bass will also strike other live or cut bait offerings if the live squid is in short supply. The key is usually to *think BIG*. Select the large anchovies, a sardine, smelt, green or Spanish mackerel, or even a so-called brown bait like a tom cod or herring.

The squid rigs will work for these large baitfish as well. I particularly like to use a big lead head with a mackerel or brown bait laced on and hooked through the upper and lower lip. In contrast to squid, give the sea bass somewhat more time to really munch on these magnum-size baitfish. Use the larger Eagle Claw #4/0 318-N hooks and *swing hard* to drive the point home. These giant croaker have fairly hard mouths so a good hook set is imperative. You may also want to try an anal-hooking strategy to get the big baits to dive downward in a steady pace. Again, white sea bass frequently suspend and a slow-diving baitfish might become a prime target as it swims through the mid-depth feeding zones.

Cut baits such as a slab of bonito or mackerel, or an elongated strip of the same, will also sometimes nail whites when squid is scarce. The sliding egg sinker butted up against a large 4/0 live bait hook is the best option when fishing either a slab or strip for sea bass.

"Doink" the Iron!

Sea bass will also attack a well-bounced cast-iron jig. The technique is termed the "doink." The "doink" requires a long 8 to 10 foot jig stick, a conventional reel filled with 30 to 40 pound test mono, and at least a 4:1 gear ratio for picking up slack line quickly. As for jigs, a solid white candy bar style in the lightweight alloy is the prime favorite. Other optional colors for doing the "doink" with the iron include solid chrome, blue/white, or scrambled egg (brown/white/yellow). Popular model jigs to use with this interesting ploy are the original Candy Bar, Salas 7x or 6x, Tady 45, and the U.F.O. Pacific Offshore series.

Make a long cast with the big light jig and let it sink to the bottom. Occasionally, you might get lucky and have one of the "toad-size" croaker snap it up on the sink. Once the jig hits the bottom, throw the reel into gear and make a long sweep of the rod from the 3 o'clock to 12 o'clock position. This is the same rod motion I spoke about in pumpin' the squid. The difference, however, is that you want to make a quick, sharp lifting sweep in doing the "doink" instead of the S-L-O-W-E-R motion involved in pumpin' a bait.

As the rod tip reaches the 12 o'clock position, begin to reel back now, picking up some of the slack with the jig fluttering erratically towards the bottom. Once the iron hits the bottom again, make another quick sweep with the long rod. Repeat the sequence basically all the way back to the boat.

"Doinkin'" like this allows you to "walk" the jig off the bottom at roughly a 45 degree angle over a long stretch of terrain. It is clearly distinctively different from the more stationary lift-and-drop strategy of yo-yoing or bouncin' a jig. As you might expect, most of the strikes occur as the sea bass practically inhales the big lure as it slowly flutters on the sink. You need to have a modestly tight line in order to set the treble hooks. This is why you must reel back up much of the slack from the 12 o'clock position while doing the "doink."

As an added treat, pin on one to two dead or live squid to the cast-metal jig, hooking the bait twice through the tail with one of the treble hook points. This creates a massive offering underwater—but it really takes its share of lunker sea bass. Presumably the complete squid and jig gives the illusion of a "meatball" of bait, so the whites key in on what they think is a pod of squid.

Normal yo-yoing will also take a share of sea bass each season. In this situation, scale down somewhat in jig selection. More compact models such as the U.F.O. #2, #3 and #5, Salas 6xJR and CP-105, or the Tady A1 are excellent choices. Again, a solid white pattern is overwhelmingly my first choice, followed by blue/chrome, blue/white, and "scrambled egg" in the smaller class of iron. Instead of a whole squid, add a strip or two about 1x3 inches in length.

Sea bass will also eat the iron on a slow surface grind. Look for signs of the fish coming up and boilin' on the chum. The tip is to retrieve lighter surface jigs at a modest pace—not ultra fast as you might for yellowtail or bonito. Pick a good large light swimming jig such as the U.F.O. "P.O.S.," Tady 45, or Salas 7X.

Spoon the Sea Bass!

One of the most underrated strategies for white sea bass is vertical spoonin'. These fish often really key in on any erratic slow-falling, fluttering lure. This perfectly describes a full arsenal of saltwater spoons. Large 1 to 3 ounce polished chrome wobblers like the Krocadile are excellent for the slow-paced lift-and-drop sequence of vertical spoonin'.

More distinctively slab-shaped spoons such as the Crippled Herring, Nordic, or Haddock Jig'n Spoon will also catch the monster croaker on the lift-and-drop. Here too, it helps to add either a whole squid or a strip of squid or mackerel as a tantalizer. Be prepared for most strikes to occur while the spoon flutters down on the sink.

On many of our Eagle Claw Fishing Schools we have found that white sea bass will often gravitate to some of the murkiest water found on the coast. A highly polished spoon in bright chrome, chrome/blue, or prism scale finish will cut through the dark water, generating a brilliant erratic flash on which the sea bass will focus. This is the main reason why spoons can be so effective on the big croakers!

Whites on Plastic

One of my favorite tactics for hunting this elusive game-fish is fishing them with soft plastic lures using heavy freshwater bass tackle. There are some situations where the "whites" simply don't want to chase a jig or a spoon too fast or too far. Squid is not available in the live variety and they won't eat a big baitfish either. This is the perfect time to try an ultra slow-moving soft plastic lure. The traditional fork-tail models such as the Scampi and the Mojo will work. You might also try the more radical A.A.T. Salty Magic with the prominent single sickle tail. The A.A. Worm's Super Shad series, with the distinctive knobby, fish-like tail, will also nail white sea bass, especially in cold water and if they are on or near the surface.

Another option is the A.A.T. Caba Caba Tube. The magnum-size, hollow-bodied tube baits have been the rage among bottom fishermen from Vancouver to Cabo San Lucas. Their squid-like appearance with multiple tentacles is an absolute dead ringer for the real McCoy. The Caba Caba Tubes are often a stellar lure when fishing for lethargic whites.

A final sea bass killer in the parade of soft plastic baits are the saltwater eels made by Advanced Angler Technology (A.A.T.) and A.A. Worms. These plastic eels fished on a lead head are real sleepers on the West Coast but they catch quality fish. At the greater 90 to 120 foot depths, a slowly pumped eel can be deadly on the sea bass.

Usually anglers tossing the soft plastics work their baits from the surface all the way to the bottom while exploring potential white sea bass haunts. This is usually done with a basic cast-and-wind approach. However, on some occasions it pays to slow-drift these lures through sea bass territory in numbers. For example, I have seen many multiple hook-ups on the soft plastics as marauding schools of the big croaker simultaneously attacked a "school" of soft plastic lures drifting behind the boat. It is as if the colorful glow of the various plastic baits trigger dramatic interest in the whites as they lazily pass through the school. Almost without exception, definitely trim your soft plastics with a strip of cut bait or squid. White sea bass appear to have an excellent sense of smell, so the trailer can only help.

As for color selection, the ever-popular root beer flake pattern in all the styles mentioned would have to be first choice. Lime green, milky glow, clear, solid black, and purple are other colors options worth trying on the croakers.

White Sea Bass on Plugs

Although it is an unusual situation, it is worth noting that white sea bass will sometimes hit a slow-trolled plug. The secret is to try to drag a large CD-14 or CD-18 Magnum Rapala plug through the chum line. Once in a while a solitary sea bass—or even a small school—may pop up in the chum for a split second. Pulling one of these big Rapala minnows through the chum line may result in the strike of a lifetime as a giant croaker bushwhacks the sardine or mackerel imitation. Slow-trolling through the chum circle will also work with cast-metal jigs, spoons, or even soft plastics. Make sure you throttle down and keep it S-L-O-W when it comes to white sea bass.

More White Sea Bass Tips

Here are a couple more tips that might help you catch one of the granddaddy croakers. These fish are near-nocturnal feeders. Some of the best fishing we encounter on our sea bass schools is right before dawn in the "gray period." Don't sleep through what may possibly be the best action of the day.

White sea bass will also feed in the shallows. We have caught them just outside the surf lines, in the white water off Catalina Island, and in the shallow bull kelp of Baja, California. I have never found water either too dirty or too shallow to host these croaker. Novices may avoid this kind of water, thinking it is uninhabitable. Don't make that mistake.

Finally, keep in mind that whites are usually school fish. Find one and you'll most likely find more. Catch one and you should catch more! The sport is first in finding them, then getting them to bite. Good luck!

North Coast Salmon

North Coasters react to the first reports of salmon activity in the same way Southlanders become excited about tuna. The feisty chinook, or king salmon, and their smaller cousins the silver or cohos are some of the premium saltwater gamefish caught off the central and northern coastlines.

In this section, I want to carefully review the primary techniques West Coasters use to catch these fish. Salmon can be exceptionally aggressive biters at times, then all of a sudden "shut off" with a serious case of marine lockjaw. The accomplished salmon fisherman has to develop an array of specialized tactics. Let's focus first on some of the rudimentary trolling methods.

Trolling for Salmon

During a typical season salmon can be taken from mid-February through the first part of November. In the early part of the run, veteran salmon experts rely upon trolling to find the fish scattered over a large area.

Most salmon trolling is done at depths around 20 to 60 feet. Popular trolling areas are in San Francisco Bay outside the Golden Gate Bridge between Duxbury Point and the Farallon Islands, Pillar Point, Monterey, and Humboldt Bays, Pacifica, Muir Beach, Half Moon Bay, Rock Point, Stinson Beach, and Bolinas Point in Northern California. Prime points for the salmon sportfishing fleets from Oregon to the Canadian border include Coos Bay, Newport, Tillamook Bay, Westport and Port Angeles. Salmon trolling is best at 2 to 4 miles per hour. There are a variety of trolling tactics that will work. All are worth trying.

Perhaps the simplest is to set up a sinker release system. The release mechanism itself is nothing more than a spring loaded device that is used to hold a fairly heavy 1 to 3 pound ball weight down until the chinook strikes. Your main line is attached to one end of the sinker release. The cast-iron weight is snapped into the release bar and your leader with either a natural bait or a lure is tied to the rear eye of the sinker release. Sometimes a flasher or dodger is also used as an attractor.

When a salmon hits the trolled lure or bait, the pressure from the strike pulls the spring on the release device, opening the clip that holds the cast-iron weight. The sinker is automatically released and falls to the bottom. The cast-iron weights are comparatively inexpensive in contrast to smooth, slick sinkers poured from quality lead. The cast-iron ball looks crude; but, remember, it sinks to the bottom and is totally disposable.

Many anglers are adamant that they will receive more strikes trolling for salmon if they use large metal attractors.

Dodgers are made to rotate through the water in a side-to-side motion. This slow wobble effect can be maintained only at modest speeds. Flashers, on the other hand, actually rotate on a 360° plane. This spinning effect allows the fisherman to troll somewhat faster using the flasher.

The most popular dodger and flasher colors for salmon trolling are nickel, prism, or a hammered brass and chrome 50/50 combination. Some local experts recommend a precise length of 14 inches of leader between the attractor and the lure or trolled bait. Planing devices can also be used to take either bait or lures to the proper depths where salmon are holding. Planers have been popular in certain inland trout circles for many years.

Interestingly, the unit itself is quite simple to understand. The planer is akin to the diving lip of a crankplug. The lip is weighted so it will go deeper. Tie your main line to the front or lip portion of the planer. Then tie a leader with either bait or a lure (with or without a flasher or dodger in between) to the rear of the unit. As you let out line, the diving plane cocks itself into position to dig in and takes the offering down. When the salmon strikes the lure or bait, the planer trips into a neutral plane. The lip no longer digs in and the device can be retrieved with minimal resistance.

Some of the popular diving planes sold for salmon fishing along the Pacific Coast are the Deep Six, Pink Lady, Depth Glider, and Fish Seeker. Read the instructions carefully with each model. Some will clearly dive deeper than others. Try to obtain reports from local sources as to what depths the salmon are cruising and use planers with corresponding diving capabilities.

Both sinker release and diving plane systems for trolling require fairly stout tackle and heavier monofilament lines. With diving planes, 12 to 15 pound test for your main line would be the bare minimum. For sinker release outfits dragging 1 to 3 pounds of cast iron requires at least 20 pound string.

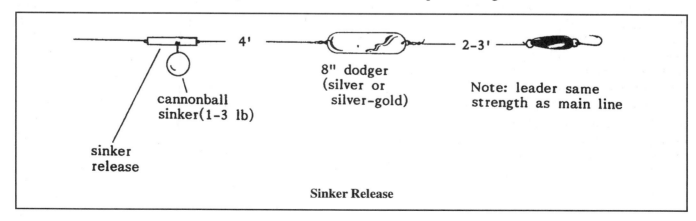

Sinker Release

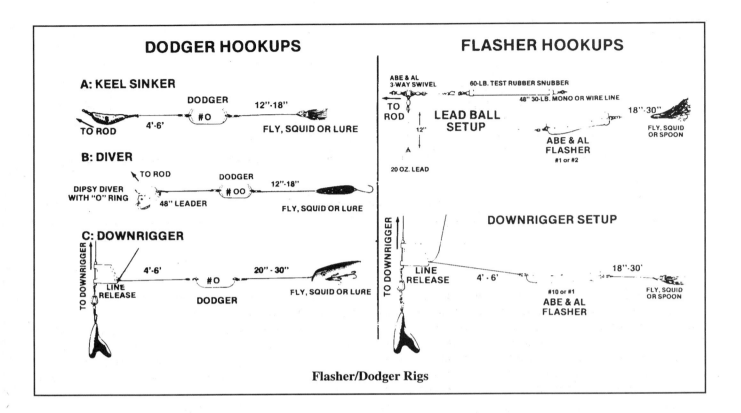

Flasher/Dodger Rigs

An alternative method which allows the angler to troll much lighter line with the optimal depth control is to use a downrigger. The downrigger can accommodate anywhere from the lightest to the heaviest monofilament permitting the angler to play the salmon up from deep water without any major encumbrances. A large weight suspended on an extended boom or downrigger arm can take the lure down to depths over 200 feet. When the salmon strikes the deep-trolled bait, it jerks the line away from the heavy sinker in a smooth release so the weight remains vertical below the boat. Then the angler is free to fight the salmon on solely the monofilament main line without any cumbersome sinkers. The heavy weight is usually reeled up back to the boat while the fisherman is playing out the coho or king.

Anchovies are the principle natural bait used for salmon trolling. They are typically threaded onto either a crowbar hook harness or a plastic baitholder rig. The crowbar hook is the more traditional setup. More and more salmon slammers now prefer one of the popular plastic baitholders. These are sold as Rotary Salmon Killers or Herring Aids. They help to provide a more natural spinning and wobbling motion when the frozen 'chovy is dragged through the water.

The anchovies can be trolled behind any one of three primary setups: 1) a cannonball sinker release system, 2) a diving plane, or 3) a downrigger. The first two methods also commonly involved adding a dodger to the leader to generate greater flash and attraction.

Numerous lures can be slow-trolled for kings. The "hoochie" is a generic term used to describe the popular plastic squid-like jig dragged behind any of the basic trolling combinations. Shiny spoons such as the Krocadile and Apex will also produce on the slow troll. The key to remember is to throttle down when you pull lures in this genre. These fish are somewhat cautious in their feeding habits when it comes to trolled offerings. They won't usually annihilate a fast-moving lure as will tuna or yellowtail.

The deep trolling approach is essential when the chinooks or silvers are disbursed, or when the sea is rough with a lot of chop and swells. If you are a private boater, try to be a little imaginative when you drag the lures or bait behind the boat. You will find that your success ratio at salmon trolling will improve dramatically if you are more creative with your trolling patterns. How is this done?

To begin with, vary your line of direction. Instead of trolling in a routine straight line, pull your lures or bait in

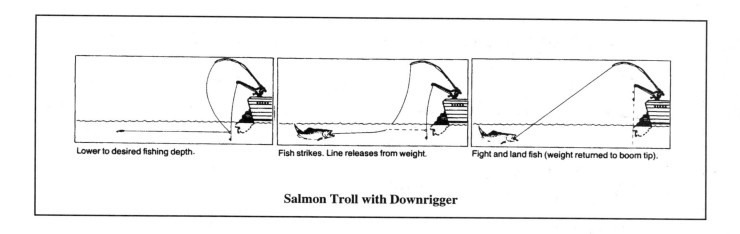

Lower to desired fishing depth.

Fish strikes. Line releases from weight.

Fight and land fish (weight returned to boom tip).

Salmon Troll with Downrigger

an "S" pattern. As the line swings through the different curves in this trolling sequence, the lures or bait will increase then decrease in action. This appears much more lifelike to the salmon. Natural baitfish don't swim in straight lines, at the same pace, in the same manner all the time. By varying the boat's direction, this more natural erratic movement is imparted into your trolled offerings.

Here's another trick that private boaters can try to generate a similar effect. As you are trolling along, intermittently throw your motor into neutral, then back into gear again. As you put the boat into the neutral position, your trolled bait or lures will start to flutter to the bottom. Putting the boat back into gear starts the bait or lures moving quicker along the normal plane. This subtle "go-and-stop-and-go" procedure gives the trolled offerings the illusion of dying, wounded baitfish—a natural target for finicky salmon.

Finally, there seems to be some evidence that quite frequently the largest kings are caught at greater depths. Try letting out more line to get the trolled bait or lure down deeper. This can be especially effective on a party boat if you troll slightly deeper than the other passengers. You may end up with the jackpot king!

More Trolling Secrets for Salmon

Many experts believe that the single most important variable to address when trolling for chinooks and cohos is tidal condition. Salmon feeding activity is generally at its most intense one hour before and one hour after a major tide change. If tide fluctuation is minimal between high and low periods, for example, between 3 and 8 feet, then both salmon and baitfish will be found feeding along tidal rips, eddies, and in open water.

The period before a slack tide, during the slack and immediately after it, will also generate a lot of salmon action because the fish won't have to exhaust their energy fighting current. Familiarize yourself with tidal conditions using a tide chart for your local area and try to plan your trips around prime periods.

Both chinook and silvers feed aggressively during low light conditions at dawn and dusk. Salmon are very light sensitive and can be found closer to the surface when overhead light is minimal. Veteran salmon trollers concur that a low light condition combined with a major tidal change is the maximum situation to get their gamefish to bite.

Always be on the lookout for marine birds picking at baitfish as a sign that kings or silvers are nearby. Interestingly, if you carefully monitor which birds are actually working the baitfish, you may be able to pinpoint precisely the level at which the salmon are located. For example, sea gulls are typically surface feeders. If you observe gulls working the "meatballs" of bait then most likely look for chinooks or coho in the first 20 feet of water. On the other hand, the sight of birds like deeper-diving cormorants may signal that the salmon are stratified all the way down at the 40 foot range.

Both cohos and kings always face the current to feed so troll with the current rather then against it. In places like Puget Sound, for instance, the tide may be very strong between changes. Look for salmon off points in the eddies, actually avoiding trolling with the tide which may move too fast to effectively work your lures.

As for selecting the right color in a spoon or plug for salmon trolling a rough rule of thumb would be as follows:

Color	Depth
red or metallic finish	surface feeders (up to 30 feet)
yellow, chartreuse, Prism-Lite	medium depths (30 to 60 feet)
green or blue	deep (beyond 60 feet)

Coho generally are located at depths less than 50 feet and usually at the surface to 30 foot range. These speedy salmon prefer faster-moving lures. Chinook, in contrast, prefer deeper water, larger spoons and plugs, and slower attractor blades, dodgers, etc. The most popular color finishes in trolling spoons used for these two species over the years have been:

Best Colors for Trolling Spoons

Coho (Silver)	Chinook (King)
chartreuse/ fire dot	chartreuse/ fire dot
fire	mother of pearl
50-50 green/chartreuse combo	Glo/green stripe
solid brass	solid chrome
solid chrome	50/50 brass/chrome
50/50 brass/chrome	chrome/neon blue stripe
chrome/blue	chrome/neon green stripe
Prism-Lite silver	Prism-Lite chrome/ blue
Prism-Lite gold	Prism-Lite chrome/ chartreuse
Prism-Lite green/blue/red combos	

Troll the J-Plug!

The Luhr Jensen J-Plug is perhaps one of the most deadly lures ever designed for West Coast salmon fishing. It resembles a frantic wounded baitfish darting from side to side as it is trolled. The lure itself has a rather intricate design. A bead chain slides through the nose and out through the bottom of the plug where it is connected to one to two treble hooks. When a salmon becomes hooked, the trebles actually pull away from the base of the plug on the small bead chain, allowing the angler to fight the coho or king with minimal interference from the J-Plug itself. The plug body actually slides up the line free of the chain and treble hook assembly and away from the salmon. As the fish shakes its head, leverage cannot thus be exerted against the plug body which is far removed from the hooks. This specialized J-Plug rigging dramatically increases salmon strike-to-catch ratios.

J-Plugs can be trolled by themselves on a sub-surface flat-line program tied directly to 12 to 20 pound mono. Let out about 50 to 100 feet of line behind the boat. You can also add a 1 to 8 ounce beaded keel sinker on a 4 to 6 foot length of leader connected to the J-Plug to pull the lure down to more medium depths. Use 12 to 30 pound monofilament with the keel sinker addition.

You can also deep-troll J-Plugs on either downriggers or utilizing diving planes, sometimes in combination with metallic dodger attractors. Gear up with heavy 20 to 30 pound test line if you decide to troll the J-Plugs at greater depths to minimize excessive stretch and to maximize solid hook penetration.

As for selecting the right color finish for trolling J-Plugs, you have a wide range of options. The silver, gold, and copper metallic finish match indigenous baitfish. The various "glow in the dark" (GLO) finishes available in this key lure are designed specifically for deep trolling.

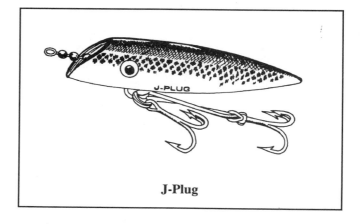

J-Plug

The commercial salmon fishing fleet also uses J-Plugs extensively and now some of their core colors are available to the sport fisherman. The Commercial Royal Blue, Commercial Royal Green, Commercial Royal White, Commercial Surf Green, and Commercial Squid are now marketed to the salmon angler. These finishes in the J-Plug come especially close to replicating the natural tones of north coast Pacific baitfish.

Mooching

Veteran party boat and private boat captains will use both their electronics and their "eyeballs," as they say, to pinpoint concentrations of bait. Once the "meatballs" of bait are located, the marauding schools of salmon should be nearby. Skippers will often try to make a visual sighting of "dark water." This distinctive patch of discoloration indicates a ball of bait—anchovies, smelt, or even squid or shrimp. Sometimes you can literally see a fish oil slick and smell the aroma of live bait that has been slashed by cruising schools of salmon. Be on the lookout for signs of boiling silvers or kings on the surface. Stretches of ocean where currents converge are similarly observable with the naked eye and are potentially good bait-holding areas.

Without visual sightings, your chart recorder or liquid crystal unit is your next best tool to use to locate the bait. As I noted, many salmon experts feel that the first two hours of daylight and twilight are the best times to find these gamefish along with the schools of bait. Definitely plan to start early and stay out late with a potential lull in the midday action.

Once the baitfish are located, it's time to start "mooching." This tactic is a patented drifting method for nailing the kings. Mooching is excellent, especially inside the more quiet waters of the northern and central bays. It is usually a better strategy to use for salmon when you pinpoint concentrations of the fish. Mooching also seems to account for the larger chinooks weighed in annually in Central and Northern California, Oregon and Washington.

Mooching doesn't require the heavier gear associated with sinker releases or planers. Most salmon buffs prefer a longer, whippier, parabolic rod in 8 to 9 foot lengths for this particular line of attack. In addition to the more sensitive lengthy rods, moochers like to use lighter 10 to 15 pound mono with heavy freshwater class baitcasting reels.

The fine diameter line gets bit more, the parabolic rods telegraph the super touchy strike better, and there isn't much worry about playing a 20 to 30 pound king on light string in open water. Mooching is really the "hot ticket" when it comes to both sport and greater action with this delicate fishery.

The object of moochin' is to drift live or dead baits across schools of baitfish and hopefully pursuing salmon. You must pay out line as the boat drifts to keep the bait near the bottom. Usually a live anchovy is mooched best with the nose-hooking technique previously discussed. A #2 to #3/0 live bait hook is the standard combo, depending upon the size of the anchovy. Herring can also be mooched. With larger baitfish, consider using a double-hook trap setup.

The terminal rigs utilized with the mooching approach can vary a lot, depending upon personal preference. The basic sliding-egg sinker system works fine with the nose-hooked 'chovy or for trap-hooked baitfish drifted along the bottom. Another option is to use a 1/2 to 4 ounce crescent weight for this kind of salmon drifting. The keel-shape design evident with this type of sinker rides particularly well on a slow drift in more turbulent current.

A favorite setup among local salmon anglers is the sliding sleeve with a dipsey sinker. The sliding sleeve is constructed from rubber tubing with the weight clipped to the middle of the sleeve. The nice thing about the design of this mooching rig is that you can quickly change weights depending upon conditions by easily snapping on different sinkers to the sleeve.

Once you get your bait down to the bottom, an integral trick to the mooching program is to gently "pump" the rod every so often. By lifting and dropping the rod in this manner much more tantalizing action is given to the bait. Salmon seem to really prefer a slow-fluttering offering.

As you drift along, the rod is usually placed in a rod holder, taken out for intermittent pumping action. The drift of the boat down swell also instills a lot of action as the bait bounces along. But keep in mind that even the biggest kings will often strike in the most nerve-wracking, "picky" way. This is where some skillful, patient rod handling comes into play.

The soft-tipped, parabolic rods will telegraph the telltale "tick" of the initial strike. Immediately drop the rod and give the fish some slack to further mouth the bait. When you feel the gentle resistance or pulling on the line on the second tap, swing and set. Sometimes you will have to feather the spool, rolling it with your finger tips or continue to lift and drop the rod in a gentle pumping motion. You may have to engage in a war of nerves as you

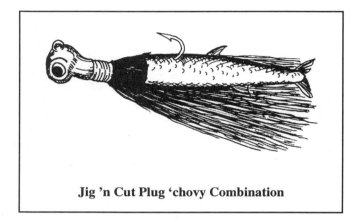

Jig 'n Cut Plug 'chovy Combination

coax the chinook to really eat the bait. This is all part of the challenge with the mooching strategy—but it does result in many trophy kings in the ice chest.

It is also possible to mooch with either artificial lures or a cut plug of bait as a trailer to a salmon jig. Abe Cuanang is one of Northern California's foremost salmon experts. Using basic 8 to 9 foot steelhead rods, with freshwater-sized baitcasting creels, Cuanang will mooch many lunker kings with jigs. He likes to work 4 to 5 outfits

at one time, letting out line to cover 10, 15, 20, and 25 foot depths. The rods remain on holders or along the boat railing. Cuanang's trick is to use a strip of anchovy teamed with a white banana-head jig (for example, the popular Hair Raiser model).

This jig'n plug bait combo is deadly in the warmer summer months on the chinooks. Cuanang recommends drifting a jig in 1/4 to 1 ounce patterns. The lighter heads will generate more action, but the heavier models are needed in rough seas. He will also let out more line with his assorted outfits as the day evolves, probing deeper strike zones.

I should note that this tactic is akin to the drifting that Southland anglers do using soft plastic baits along off-shore kelp beds and reefs. With both methods, the waves and current help to make the jigs bob and dart like an errant baitfish. Cuanang also suggests that the small craft owner invests in a sea anchor for successful mooching. This parachute-like anchor will slow the drift down significantly, letting hook-shy salmon catch up with the bouncing jigs.

These basic mooching strategies can also be tried in Southern California. Salmon are sometimes found—al-

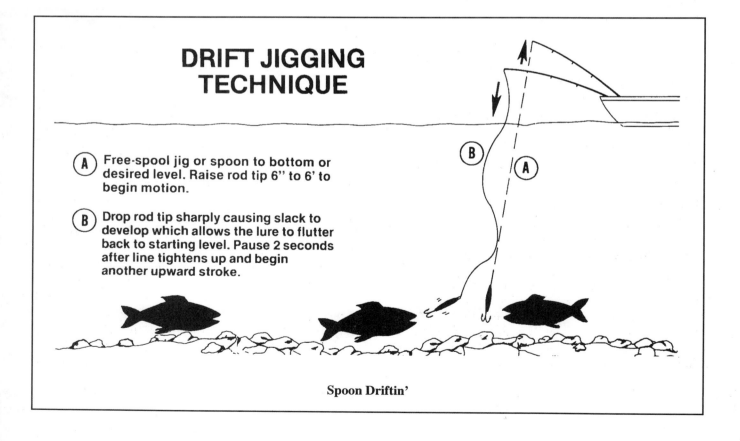

DRIFT JIGGING TECHNIQUE

(A) **Free-spool jig or spoon to bottom or desired level. Raise rod tip 6" to 6' to begin motion.**

(B) **Drop rod tip sharply causing slack to develop which allows the lure to flutter back to starting level. Pause 2 seconds after line tightens up and begin another upward stroke.**

Spoon Driftin'

beit rarely—as far south as Newport Beach. Local tackle expert, Mike Callan, has employed the standard sliding sinker setup and a live anchovy to boat some hefty double-digit kings in the Southland. Callan observes that the salmon are usually found less than a mile offshore, making them easily accessible to the small boat owners.

Spoon Drifting for Salmon

Abe Cuanang has also perfected another interesting ploy for coastal salmon fishing. Instead of using jigs or bait in a mooching program, he will yo-yo a spoon in a vertical presentation as the boat drifts along. The key is to home in on the meatballs of bait. Once in the vicinity of the bait concentrations, Cuanang likes to yo-yo a brightly polished spoon for school salmon. The versatile Haddock Jig'n Spoon, Krocadile, Nordic, and Dungeness Stinger and Crippled Herring models in chrome finishes are perfect for this vertical spoonin' method. As with all spoonin', be prepared for strikes on the fall following the lifting action. Soft plastics can also be worked vertically along a drift pattern. Giant tube baits like the Caba Caba Tube have also been racking up some impressive tallies on the kings and silvers. Both single and double-tail grubs are also worth experimenting with for salmon. Try them when a slow-swimming lure is needed. Definitely explore these different possibilities to expand your repertoire of king salmon tricks.

Salmon are terrific sport, especially on light tackle. These fish have excellent eyesight and they can be exceptionally spooky at times. You will get bit more if you stay with lighter lines, fresher bait—even if it's dead—and careful rigging of the lures and baitfish. If you decide to mooch for salmon, keep your hooks extremely sharp. Be prepared to spend some time "teasing" this gamefish into eating your bait. The effort spent will be well worth it!

Bonito—Inshore Tuna

Bonito are, without a doubt, one of the real treasures of the Pacific Coast. These diminutive members of the tuna family are legendary fighters. Pound for pound, it would be hard to find many species—salt or freshwater—that compare with the bonito's spectacular power. "Bongos" or "boneheads"—as they are called by deckhands—are reasonably easy to catch. They have an affinity to both live bait and artificial lures. Most bonito are caught in Southern California, but they will travel all the way above Monterey in some warm current years.

Bongos on Bait

A fly-lined anchovy is without question numero uno as far as bonito baits are concerned. The fish will, on occasion, strike sardines, smelt, or even whole squid, but 'chovies are the preferred choice. Light to medium-weight spinning or casting gear will handle most school bonies in the 1 to 4 pound range. Lighter 10 to 12 pound test mono will get bit better and naturally provides greater sport with these small tuna. These are times, however, when you may run into a school of 8 to 12 pound bonito. Bongos in this class will be sheer terror on the light gear. A conventional outfit spooled with 20 pound string would be more appropriate on bruisers this size.

Live bait hooks range in size from an Eagle Claw 318-N in #1 to #6 depending upon the quality of the anchovies. Use a split-shot or a small rubber-core sinker if you need to get the bait down below the surface. If you are careful, there is another trick you can try on both party and private boats when you are confronted with a tank of small pinhead anchovies. Using spinning tackle, and preferably an 8 to 8 1/2 foot rod, run your line through a large, clear Cast-a-Bubble float and fill it about half way with water. (To fill the bubble submerge it in the bait tank.) Butt the sliding float with a snap-swivel and add a 5 to 7 foot length of leader with a #6 bait hook. Nose- or gill-hook the tiny 'chovy and make your cast with this bait'n bubble combo. You have to watch behind you when using the super-long leader so as to not hook other anglers.

The weighted bobber provides you with considerable extra distance when other fly-liners are fighting the size of the fly-weight pinheads. The bubble will ride on the surface, but so will your bait. When the bonies hit the small 'chovy, they will feel no resistance on the initial run, pulling the bait and leader through the sliding float.

Bonies on Spoons and Iron

Bonito will usually strike a shiny artificial without much hesitation. Small boaters working inshore harbors and bays will find that the smaller Krocadile spoons used for trout fishing are dynamite bonito lures. Fish them on 8 to 12 pound test line. Other spoons such as the Nordic, Crippled Herring, Dungeness Stinger, and Haddock Jig'n Spoon are also excellent for school bonito in the quiet water.

Outside along the kelp lines, on the flats, or at the islands, I prefer to throw cast-metal jigs. The U.F.O. #1, #2, or #4 in blue/white, blue/chrome, or solid chrome have been excellent "iron" for the bongos. The Yo Ho Ho #1 to #3 are strong backup models. Solid chrome, chrome and blue, sardine, mackerel, and green and yellow are also effective bonito colors in larger jigs such as the U.F.O. #3, Yo Ho Ho #4, Tady A-1, or Salas Christy 2. These will work perfectly on a yo-yo grind if the bonito are holding deep. Occasionally bongos eat the big surface iron. A Tady 45, Salas 6 or 7x, or U.F.O. "P.O.S." in blue/white, sardine, solid chrome, or solid white are my choices. Usually it is larger 8 to 15 pound bonito that chase down large jigs like these.

I should add that although they are dwindling in numbers, veteran feather fishermen will also hammer the bonito, stroking and pumping single-hook chrome heads. Blue/white, solid white, green/yellow, and red/white will all produce.

Pluggin' for Bonito

This smaller member of the tuna family provides some of the most spectacular light-line action found from coast to coast. Although most bonito are caught on live anchovies, plug-casting sometimes takes the largest specimens. Frequently, you may be in a situation where you do not have any live bait, for example, when fishing on a small yacht or from a landing that doesn't stock live 'chovies. Here is when a good plug caster can really put on a show.

A variety of freshwater bass or trout plugs can be effective for bonito when teamed with light 10 to 12 pound monofilament. The fine diameter line allows you to make longer casts, and it also lets the lure "swim" more naturally. On that note, do not add a snap-swivel to any of these plugs I'm about to mention. The snap-swivel combination has a tendency to deaden the action of the lure. For most of these plugs, I recommend tying directly to the knot eyelet.

Without question, the Rapala CD-9, 11, or 13 series are perfectly matched with light mono. Be certain to purchase the heavy-duty "magnum" series in the Rapala. These have strong saltwater cadmium hooks and are "wired." The plugs have a wire connecting both front and real trebles in case a large fish pulls the hooks from the body of the lure. These are sinking minnows and can be retrieved fairly fast. The best Rapala colors for "bongos" are silver foil with either blue or black backs.

A plug in this genre swims well, but expect them to really get somewhat torn up by this toothy gamefish over a period of time. A hard plastic lure like the Jensen Minnow is another option. This is a floater-diver made to swim less deeply than the sinking Rapalas, but it is equally effective on sub-surface bonies. Toss the Jensen Minnow in solid chrome or mackerel patterns.

Regardless of which plug you decide to use, when it comes to getting bit, the key may often be the retrieve. Although a straight grind often produces, try a stop-and-go sequence. Wind the plug fast—then pause for a second. Start the retrieve again, stopping about ten yards later. Usually the bonito will practically bump into the plug on the "stop" phase of the retrieve, angrily striking it as you commence to wind again.

Pluggin' for bonito with light gear is terrific sport. You can fan-cast to open water standing on docks and rocky jetties, or while maneuvering a private boat into schools of feeding fish. During certain times of the year when party boat crowd are light, don't hesitate to whip out the light baitcasting or spinning gear and toss plugs for "bongos." Often when chum and hook bait are poor you might catch the only bonito on board wing these plugs!

Try trolling these minnow-shaped plugs from small craft. Let out enough line to keep the lure riding well below the surface. Without live bait or with minimal chum power, you can cover a lot of territory trolling for these little tuna with these anchovy-like plugs, often scoring limits and trophy-size fish!

Incredible Sport

Bonito are incredible fighters and comprise a major portion of the sport catch of the Southern California fleet. They are excellent gamefish for the novice saltwater buff to hone his skills on. Many anglers discard bonito as "trash fish" as far as culinary value is concerned. I, too, was of that opinion until Captain Russ Izor shared some of his secrets for preparing bongos with me.

The trick is to cut off the head, let the fish bleed, and ice it as soon as possible. This can be tough to do on a party boat, so the next best thing is to keep the bonies wet in the gunny sack. When you get home, filet the fish and trim around the black dorsal vein. Remove the meat and place it in a frying pan filled with about 1.2 inches of beer. Poach the filet on both sides in the a warm beer. Let the fish cool. Mash it up with a fork, add mayonnaise, a dash of mustard or relish, and you have an incredibly taste tuna ready for salad!

You can freeze down the filets for future cooking as you need them. The beer removes the "fishiness" from the filets and the final result is on par with store-bought tuna. Bonito are also fantastic smoked. For those who own smokers, simply leave the skin on the filets and smoke the bonito for a moderate length of time. The result is good eating!

"Hot 'cuda Secrets"

As a popular gamefish, barracuda seem to receive everything from praise to condemnation—all depending upon how tough the bite is. During so-called "scratch" fishing when few surface species are active, barries are a welcome sight. This is especially true as both anglers and fish emerge out of the cold water, winter doldrums with the start of the spring surface action.

On the other hand, I've seen veteran saltwater fishermen curse the "slime" as they invade the chum line during a yellowtail or white sea bass flurry. Love 'em or hate 'em, the bottom line is that 'cuda are excellent fighters on light tackle and are highly cooperative in attacking artificial lures. You can find them from mid-Baja all the way up to San Francisco Bay during warm water years.

Over the years, barracuda have been a staple catch on many of the Eagle Claw Saltwater Fishing Schools I conduct. They are always an integral component of the surface bite at Catalina Island, the Coronados, Huntington Flats or the Horseshoe Kelp. Scooters also show up quite routinely on our long-range programs from Punta Colonet to Benitos Islands, close to 300 miles south of the border.

You can't take barracuda for granted. Even when they "show," they won't always eat. There are, however, a few key tricks worth noting that will result in not only limits of barries but scores on the larger "log" size fish as well. Here's 10 hot tips to try the next time you are in 'cuda territory.

Splicing Leaders

For decades, one of the problems anglers faced when casting for barracuda has been how to keep the fish from biting through the monofilament. Over 20 years ago when I started working in tackle stores, I can remember selling thousands of 6 to 10 inch long plastic coated wire leaders when the local 'cuda bite heated up.

Nowadays, the barrie population simply isn't what it was in the past. There is also considerable more angling pressure, and the fish are quite spooky at times. Thus, wire leaders usually won't be effective for today's action.

You might consider scaling up in line size, say 20-30 pound test. However, this usually isn't too effective either. For one thing, the finer diameter 10 to 15 pound mono is harder for the fish to see. Also, with live anchovies often ranging from small and weak to fair condition at best, a lighter line will allow the bait to swim better with less drag in the water.

The solution is to splice a smaller strand of heavier monofilament to your lighter line coming off your reel. You can do this by joining 10 to 15 pound test line tied to a small barrel swivel, with a short 18 to 30 inch length of 20 to 30 pound mono as a leader.

Understand that if it's a real touchy bite, the scooters may still not hit the heavier monofilament leader. Thus, you may have to take your chances with the 10 to 15 pound string with your hook tied directly to the line. Usually, this little piece of 20 to 30 pound mono will do the trick. The anchovy still encounters minimal resistance with most of the line in the water being your 10 to 15 pound test coming off the reel. The short monofilament leader may restrict the bait slightly, but it is still a superior alternative to using the wire version.

Shiny Pump Sinkers for Barracuda

Quite often you may encounter solid barracuda action, yet all the fish seem to be either sub-legal or on the small side. How do you get the larger "stove pipe" class 'cuda in the 6-8 pound range to bite? Well, the secret may be that the larger "log" barries are lazily swimming below the smaller school fish. As the school crashes through the chum, the bigger 'cuda remain deeper picking off the cripples as the wounded baitfish flutter to the bottom. One excellent way to search out these larger barracuda is to get your live bait down to deeper strike zones. To do this, you will need a 1 to 2 ounce chrome torpedo sinker.

Tie your line to one of the rings on each end of this sinker. Next, tie an 18-30 inch length of monofilament leader to the other end with your hook. To effectively fish this awkward-looking combination, cast out and let the rig sink to about mid-depth from the bottom. Throw your reel into gear and slowly "pump" the shiny sinker back in.

To properly "pump" the rig, lift your rod tip from the 3 to the 12 o'clock position. Reel up the slack. Then drop the rod back down to 3 o'clock. This "pumping" sequence makes the sinker sort of rise and fall as it is slowly retrieved back to the boat. You need 1 to 2 ounces in this type of program to get the bait quickly past the pesky, smaller 'cuda. The chrome surface of the sinker also generates considerable erratic flash underwater. This provides the illusion of bait being in a panic and highly vulnerable to larger barries. Make sure your live anchovy is pinned on with the hook running through both the upper and lower lip. This will keep the bait from drowning or being dragged by the gills with the heavy chromed sinker.

Soft Plastics at Night

One of the more interesting ways to fish for barracuda is in total darkness. Some of the largest specimens tallied each season in southern waters are caught on twilight trips. It appears that when the sun goes down, the bigger "logs" are less twitchy and easier to fool.

Strangely enough, one of the best ways to get midnight 'cudas to bite is to slowly wind a soft plastic fork-tail lure across the bottom. Calico bass enthusiasts will quickly recognize the Scampi, Mojo, Lunker Thumper, Berkley Power Scamper, and Shabby Shrimp as staples in their arsenal of soft plastics. Well, these are also terrific on barries at night—the key is to pick the right color.

Everyone knows that root beer flake is the hottest pattern when it comes to using these soft plastic fork-tails on saltwater bass. The counterpart color for nighttime 'cuda is, of all things, lime green. Who can explain why these fish home in on this color scheme primarily in the dark? Trip after trip on these twilight runs, I have seen the lime green fork-tails outfish almost any other type of artificial lure, accounting for many "stove pipe" class barracuda.

Pump the Tubes!

Like the fork-tail lures, hollow-bodied tube baits have also been the recent rage in the saltwater soft plastics' sweepstakes. Here, too, color can be critical. On many occasions a Caba Caba Tube rigged on a 1 to 3 ounce lead head will often nail limits of barries in practically any color combination. However, on many trips when the bite has been especially tough, I have watched my Eagle Claw students score some big numbers on the "slime" pumping a tube bait in blue flake color.

"Pumping the tube" is exactly the same procedure I outlined for fishing the shiny sinker. This is a deadly tactic, particularly when the barracuda are holding deep and seem lethargic or when there is a poor selection of live bait in the tank.

The Jig 'n Spoon for 'cuda

As you must have gathered by now, I am a strong proponent of fishing deep and with light line when it comes to 'cuda. Another relatively seldom practiced ploy is to work a narrow-bodied spoon for the "slime." This type of lure is truly a "no brainer." Even the most outright neophyte can catch barracuda jigging this type of artificial on or near the bottom. Spoons such as the Haddock Jig 'n Spoon, Luhr Jensen Crippled Herring and Dungeness Stinger, or the Nordic are perfect for this approach in 1 to 4 ounce sizes.

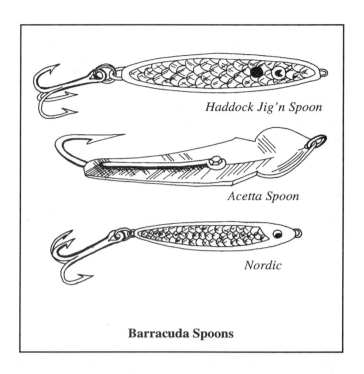

Haddock Jig'n Spoon

Acetta Spoon

Nordic

Barracuda Spoons

Simply drop the spoon over the side of the rail, and let it sink to the bottom. Watch your line closely. If you experience a sudden slack or "jump" in the line, quickly throw the reel into gear, pick up the slack and set the hook! Strikes are quite common on the fall with this type of lure.

Once on the bottom, jig the spoon by lifting your rod tip from 3 to 12 o'clock again, using a quick, pronounced lift-and-drop motion. The object is to make the spoon look like an anchovy that is frantically swimming near the bottom. As you would expect, many times the 'cuda hit the spoon in the flutter phase, as it is sinking back to the bottom.

Slow-Spoonin' for Barries

In contrast to the slim profile of the jigging spoon, a variation of this type of metal lure is the wide-bodied model. Popular spoons like the Krocodile, Hot Shot, Tony Acetta Pet, and Kastmaster exemplify this type of lure. The highly polished metallic surface of these wide-bodied models produce dramatic flash as the spoon is retrieved. Not many of today's anglers fish these barracuda killers, but they are still as potent as they were decades ago.

One of the best situations in which to throw a spoon in this genre is again when the barries seem especially slow and sluggish. Sometimes that slow, rolling motion of the spoon lazily flashing from side to side under the surface is just enough to trigger strikes from otherwise disinterested 'cuda. Be sure that you tie directly to the split rings on any spoon. If you add a snap-swivel, more than likely you will damper the swimming action of the lure.

The Stop 'n Go 'cuda Trick

Barracuda love the iron. Jig fishermen will typically rise to the occasion when a school of barries moves in. More compact jigs such as the Yo Ho Ho #1 to #3, U.F.O. #2 and #4, Tady AA or Salas Christy #1, #2 are perfect for this type of fishing. Usually I prefer to fish a "light" version of these lures if the barracuda are right on the surface. Other times, however, I'll switch to a heavier model if I need more distance or if the fish appear to be deep. One surefire technique I would like to pass along is simply termed the "stop-and-go". Most anglers in the Southland are taught to wind a jig in with a moderate-to-fast retrieve. With yellowtail, tuna and bonito, the best strategy is to maintain a steady wind without pausing.

With barracuda—and especially when the fish seem reluctant to really eat the bait—try a slow retrieve with intermittent pauses. This stop-and-go procedure can be sensational on big "log" size fish. The trick is to have the patience of letting the jig sink for a few seconds following the pause. Invariably, the barries seem to casually follow the slow-moving iron, only to strike it when you come to a complete halt in the retrieve. I have literally seen the "slime" follow the jig closely, then viciously attack it after bumping into the iron as I abruptly stopped my retrieve.

The Big Iron for Barracuda

Most of the barracuda fishing done with iron is practiced with the smaller, more compact jigs I listed above. On some occasions, interestingly, I have seen the jackpot 'cuda nailed on a large yellowtail-size jig. Look through your tackle box the next time you're out for barracuda. Select a large "light" surface iron such as a Tady 45 or Salas 6X-7X series. Try throwing this kind of lure on an 8 to 10 foot long jig stick and a conventional reel spooled with 30 pound string. No need for wire leaders here either. Tie direct to the big jig and engage in a moderately slow retrieve back to the boat.

Be prepared for big 'cuda when tossing the big iron! Strikes may not be frequent compared to other methods, but the barries that do eat these big jigs are typically jackpot contenders! The best retrieve is a slow grind, intermittently pausing to let the big surface iron flutter on the sink for a few feet. Two specialized colors for this type of 'cuda surface iron are solid white and, interestingly,

white/black combination. Round out your selection with standard blue/white and blue/chrome models.

Slow-Trollin' Plugs

There is an array of Rapala saltwater minnow-shaped plugs that produce sensational results at times when trolled slowly for barracuda. The CD-9, 11, 13 and 14 in the saltwater Magnum series are perfect, particularly when dragged with 12 to 15 pound test mono. The diving models generate a lot of side-to-side wobble and will troll effectively through deeper strike zones. These sinking plugs work especially well when the barries are at depths of between 5 and 15 feet.

Another option is to use a jointed minnow as a compromise. The Rapala "Sliver" Series, for example, is deadly on big 'cuda. Plugs in this genre feature a metal diving lip with a jointed body. They pull fairly deep without losing much of the wobble. Do not add any snap-swivels to the split ring on these plugs. Tie direct to the lure's split ring, with 10-20 pound test mono, depending upon the size of the plug. Keep your speed down so the lure doesn't start to plane to the surface. Strikes are vicious when barracuda eat these plugs!

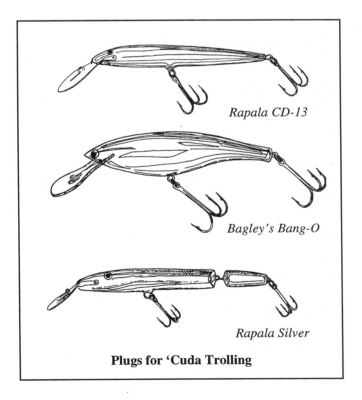

Rapala CD-13

Bagley's Bang-O

Rapala Silver

Plugs for 'Cuda Trolling

Feathers and Barracuda

The old fashion feather, with a chrome head, red eye, and single hook, remains a 'cuda killer in the hands of a pro. The trick is to learn how to "pump" the feather in the same fashion I mentioned for both the shiny sinker rig and the

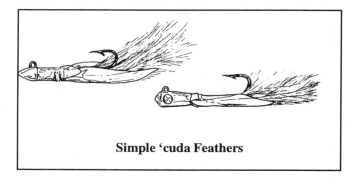

Simple 'cuda Feathers

tube baits. Hard-core feather specialists like to pump a white model, in a size that most closely replicates the length of the anchovies in the bait tank. You preferably need to use a long, 8 to 8 1/2 rod, so you can make prominent rhythmic sweeps with the tip. This "pumping action" gives the illusion of the feather looking like a frantic anchovy darting and pausing while under attack. Barries will also attack this lure with a vengeance!

Keep It Slow

For the most part, perhaps the best single piece of advice is to work your barracuda strategies S-L-O-W-L-Y. Unlike bonito, tuna, or yellowtail, 'cuda seem to prefer slower moving prey.

Monitor your retrieve constantly. When you finally get bit, remember the pace that the barries preferred. Invariably, this will be the basic pattern for the retrieve for that particular day. More 'cuda will follow!

Advanced Species Lessons: Offshore Fish

For all the years I have been writing about the migratory pelagic gamefish of the Pacific, I never thought I would be talking about albacore as a Northern California/Pacific Northwest species. For the last few years, however, the best longfin tuna fishing has been in these areas.

Albacore!

Some marine biologists theorize that the migration patterns of the albies for the most part stay the same over long periods of time. Others speculate that once a new pattern is established it remains in tact unless there are dramatic climatic changes. Whatever the case, albacore off the Southern California coast are practically a distant memory.

Occasionally the longfins show up near Morro Bay, Avila Beach, or even Monterey, but they are more likely to be found further north, even as far as Port Angeles, Washington. Still there are core strategies for catching these prize chicken-of-the-sea regardless of where you encounter them.

Troll the Tuna

Trolling persists as one of the staple strategies to locate and catch albacore. The standard 15 mm tuna feather rigged with the sliding double hook trolled with 50 to 60 pound gear is the ideal setup. Recently on our Eagle Claw Schools, we found another technique using trolling feathers to be highly effective on tuna and we even catch a few stray albies on it. This technique, called the "daisy chain," had its origins on the Eastern Seaboard among world-class bluefin tuna specialists.

It is easy to construct a "Daisy chain." You need vinyl squid or hoochies that are commonly used for North Coast salmon fishing. We thread one of the hoochies about 24 inches above the end of the line. Then we thread on a small metal sleeve and carefully crimp it down. This keeps the squid from sliding any further down the line.

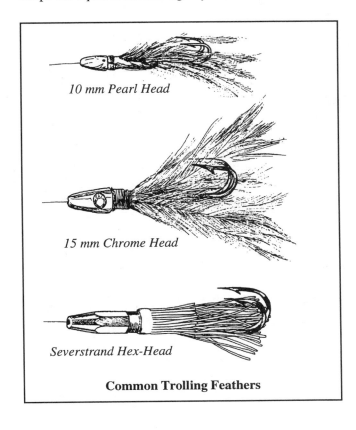

10 mm Pearl Head

15 mm Chrome Head

Severstrand Hex-Head

Common Trolling Feathers

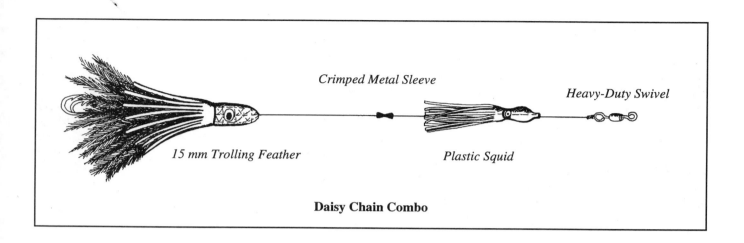

Crimped Metal Sleeve

Heavy-Duty Swivel

15 mm Trolling Feather

Plastic Squid

Daisy Chain Combo

Next run the end of the line through your favorite 15 mm tuna feather and tie on the double hook. This is a simple daisy chain rig. This setup is much more effective than a basic tuna feather because it gives the illusion of a medium-size baitfish—the feather—chasing a small squid or an even smaller baitfish (the vinyl squid). There is absolutely no doubt that, based on extensive observations, this daisy chain rig will outfish the traditional single feather dramatically—sometimes 3 to 1!

It seems that the albacore become more interested when they see all the commotion and flash of what appears to be a larger baitfish apparently in pursuit of smaller prey. The daisy chain trolling combo definitely has a tendency to generate strikes when conventional offerings seem useless.

As for color selection, the basic rule of dark feathers for overcast skies and bright feathers for a bright day seems to usually work. We start with black/purple, black/green, and green/blue feathers in the morning then switch to red/white, blue/white, green/yellow, "Mexican flag," or zucchini by midday. I try to match the vinyl squid with the colors of the main trolling feather.

I always tell our students not to overlook a *solid white* tuna feather as a viable option. For years this simple color has been the secret of the commercial tuna fleet. Pull the bland solid white model with confidence—it almost always gets bit! The commercial boys obviously knew what they were doing when they marketed the all white feather.

Albacore will also eat a big plug. There are not a lot of options here—the CD-18 Magnum Rapala minnow is the staple for longfin. In contrast to yellowtail fishing where the best colors in the CD-18 are green mackerel and fire tiger, switch to blue mackerel, or silver foil/black

back when trolling for albies. Frequently the longfins will nail a trolled Rapala and pass on any other options. Never tie the CD-18 with wire leaders or extra snap-swivels. The big plugs are made to swim right out of the box with your monofilament tied directly to the eyelet.

Albies on Bait

Sportfishers catch the majority of albacore on live bait. Usually an anchovy or sardine fly-lined on the surface with 20 to 30 pound test casting outfits is preferred. You can butt hook the 'chovies or 'dines to make them swim deeper. If extra depth is needed, use a 1/2 to 2 ounce sliding egg sinker or an 18 to 24 inch leader connected to a chrome 2 ounce torpedo sinker.

I might add that even on off days with few albacore around, quite frequently our students have tallied some incidental catches of the longfins by fishing *deep*—at least 90 feet. Rather than fly-lining after a jig strike while trolling for yellowfin tuna, try either the slider sinker or chrome torpedo (plunker) rig to get down to the 15 fathom range. Strangely enough, this is where some of the few albacore catches have been made as the longfins suspend deep beneath schools of yellowfin tuna.

Longfins on the Iron!

Along a similar vein, albacore will attack a deep yo-yo jig or a jig dropped back on the slide as the boat glides to a stop following a trolling strike. Pick your iron carefully for albies. Some historically proven models in heavy versions are Salas Yo-Yo 4 and CP-105, Tady A1 and A2, and U.F.O. #3 and #5. The best colors are blue/white, blue/chrome, scrambled egg, and surprisingly red/white. As when fishing the iron for other tuna species, you have to wind fast on the yo-yo retrieve when you jig for albacore. You simply can't reel too fast—keep winding!

I wouldn't recommend throwing the iron on the longfins with anything less than 30 pound string. You get a lot of line stretch at 90 to 180 foot depths so heavier mono is best. Reels should have close to 4:1 gear ratios or better to retrieve the jig fast. My preference is the Penn 500 Jigmaster (4:1) or 505 Jigmaster Hi-Speed (5:1).

Another Albacore Trick

Here is an interesting little ploy I learned first hand when chasing albacore with a commercial fisherman. Working from a small yacht with minimal chum bait we set out two trolling rods for each of us to watch. Besides the trolling outfits, we had 6 additional live bait rigs set up within an arm's length of the stern. As the trolling outfits got bit, we quickly reeled in the lead longfins. Then we quickly baited with anchovies and tossed out our bait outfits. When the albies bit the bait hooks, we set up on the fish then put the rod back into a rod holder with the tuna on the end of the line!

We would then grab a second or third outfit, bait up, cast out, set the hook, and place each rod back in the rod holder with the reel in gear. It is quite a sight, I might add, to see 5 or 6 rods semi-bent, all sitting in rod holders with an albacore sulking below! We then reeled in each fish one at a time rarely losing a tuna.

This little strategy allowed us to hook as many fish as we could, using little chum without letting the bulk of the school swim away as might have occurred if we had taken the time to fight only the first hooked tuna. Surprisingly, as long as the albacore don't feel any major resistance from the rod tip, they will pretty much swim in a circle, taking minimal drag, waiting for you to reel in the fish one at a time.

Yellowfin in the Dark!

I rarely write about a particular fishing trip. I try to avoid romanticizing about a day on the water and instead focus on the core techniques used by expert anglers to catch the fish. I want to modify that position by relating perhaps the most phenomenal saltwater adventure I have ever experienced on the Pacific Coast. I also want to specifically share with you some of the key lessons I learned from this trip.

It all started in mid-November. I had scheduled a 2 1/2 day, mini long-range trip for one of my Eagle Claw Fishing Schools. Our destination was San Martin Island, about 155 miles south of San Diego. After an outstanding tuna season, I figured by mid-November the offshore bite would wind down and we would target the shallow water rockfish and ling cod that abound in this area in the late fall and early winter.

As we boarded the Holiday, an 85 foot sportfisher out of Point Loma Sportfishing in San Diego, I could see many of the top boats in the fleet still sitting in their slips. It was obvious that the local offshore season had indeed come to an end. While the students were loading their gear, I met with the Holiday's well-known skipper, Steve Giffin. I Iearned he was interested in taking a shot at an offshore bite.

Giffin is a true "man of the sea." His prowess is legendary especially as a premier tuna fisherman. There are only a handful of skippers who have the experience, the boat, and the crew to find marauding schools of offshore tuna, yellowtail, and dorado the way Giffin does. On this particular evening, Giffin explained to my instructors and me that there was a strong possibility the yellowfin tuna and yellowtail might still be within striking distance.

Giffin theorized that the tuna might remain in the area since the water temperature was still in the mid-60 degree range—as a result of the El Niño. Finally, the most compelling argument for taking a shot at the offshore bite was simply that no local 1 to 1 1/2 day boats had sampled this band of warm water for almost two weeks. There was minimal passenger interest in tuna fishing once November rolled around.

So the plan was to put the trolling feathers out at first light about 75 miles down the line and keep heading south until we got bit. As it turned out, it didn't take long to find new groups of local fish, but it wasn't exactly what I had planned. We immediately encountered hordes of baby 1 to 3 pound yellowtail on floating kelp paddies at the 75 mile mark. The students quickly tossed their cast-metal jigs, spoons, and live sardines as they had been shown in the seminars we had conducted the night before. After everyone had caught a few fish, we encouraged the students to practice catch'n release, returning the smaller 'tails back to their paddies to grow and mature for next season's action.

It was now 4:00 in the afternoon and we had motored almost 100 miles south of San Diego. We had found numerous kelp paddies laden with more small yellows. Except for one 120 pound striped marlin caught by one of the students, the action was on the immature 'tails. This was becoming too boring for my tastes.

Suddenly we had a triple jig strike in open water. All through the season, most of the trolling strikes we had on our Eagle Claw charters occurred after Giffin found one of three conditions: 1) metered, deep schools of tuna; 2) fish crashing on the water with birds picking at the surface boils; or 3) floating kelp paddies. This jig strike was different. We were out in the middle of nowhere, with no signs of life evident for the past hour or so. This was a classic "blind" jig strike!

At first there were three nice 18 to 25 pound yellowfin coming into the stern nailed with the feathers on heavy trolling gear. Then almost immediately the corner exploded and I watched as 35 pound class yellowfin slashed through the sardine chum.

Chaos, pandemonium, then near-hysteria broke out as 26 anglers and rods went into instant b-e-n-d-o mode! There were tuna everywhere! All the students were bit so I quickly grabbed a 60 pound trolling outfit, hammered the drag shut tight, and cut off the tuna feathers. I tied on a 5 ounce Crippled Herring spoon with a single large Siwash hook. I figured there might be some bigger tuna below the school fish. I stripped out 5 feet of line, lowered the spoon in the corner, and a 35 pound tuna arched its back out of the water and inhaled the lure. I reared back and swung and a 35 pound yellowfin came hurtling over the rail in true "jack pole" fashion.

Now, inspired by images of great tuna fishermen of the past, I immediately put my improvised jack-pole outfit to use again. I flipped the big spoon on the surface with the short 5 foot length of line. BAM! Instantly another 35 pounder was flung over the rail like an incoming artillery shell. I repeated this scenario four more times until the last fish turned its head the opposite direction and hot-railed me all the way to the bow before I broke it off.

By six o'clock, the sun was sinking and there were well over 100 yellowfin and a nice smattering of dorado lying all over the deck. Giffin took command of the bait tank, directing the crew while nursing the chum like a field general in the heat of battle.

At sundown, things really started to heat up. There were more dorado and more tuna. They struck our baits with total aggression. We moved the students up from 20 to 30 pound gear. It didn't make any difference. The bigger fish ate the heavier string and the action became even more intense as dusk settled.

Giffin, in turn, sensing that this might develop into a stage beyond "wide open," set out his parachute-like sea anchor so that the Holiday would drift slowly in the dark. I watched as raw first timers staggered into the galley to take a breather after catching their twentieth or thirtieth fish. Legs and arms were shaking as if infected by a mysterious palsy. For sure no one leaving San Diego the night before expected to get a workout like this one the next day.

I began to feel the effect of lack of food and sleep, and the stress of constant winding, but I couldn't resist the bite and stayed on the deck. I started with 60 pound outfits, went down to 30, 20 and finally 12 pound test line. I watched as a 25 pound bull dorado jumped on the light 12 pound string silhouetted in the moonlight at 1:00 in the morning. By 2:00 a.m., I realized I was starting to experience some form of sensory deprivation. I have fished the coast for over 40 years, and in all that time I never imagined I would one day willingly put my rod in the rack during a wide-open bite. I had had enough! I simply couldn't fish any more.

I remember going slowly down the stairs to the bunks just as 5 to 8 pound giant squid started coming around the boat, swimming under the light Giffin hung over this side. By now, there were only a handful of students left on deck with one of the instructors standing watch. As I looked over my shoulder, I saw three rods bent over with 35 pound yellowfin on the other end of the line. Would this bite ever end?

By 6:00 a.m., another wave of 25 to 35 pound yellowfin mixed with solid 18 to 25 pound dorado charged the boat. At 10:00 a.m., with over 800 fish caught—and I might add, the vast majority released—we started back from the fisherman's heaven we had discovered 125 miles below the border. We had experienced an absolute "adventure of a lifetime" in local waters and had gained a wealth of insights from this expedition.

The following is a summary of what I learned about offshore fishing from this trip.

Moon Phase. This trip occurred during a full moon with no cloud cover. Many anglers firmly believe that the offshore fish won't bite in a full moon. Yet three of the best schools we have ever had occurred precisely on the full moon, while some of the fewest productive trips have been during a new moon. Unlike inshore species, offshore pelagic fish such as tuna, yellowtail, and dorado do not seem to be governed by tidal flows. These offshore cruisers have to feed constantly to supply their high metabolisms.

Kelp Paddies. Don't get too concerned if you aren't seeing a lot of kelp paddies on a tuna trip. Schools of marauding fish can attack from the sides out of the range of a depth finder creating a spectacular "blind-strike" situation.

Night Bite. Tuna and dorado will definitely bite in the dark, not just in the long range water further south, but up in the local waters, too.

Fishing the Iron. These species will voraciously eat the iron in the middle of the night. We found solid white, white/black, and white/brown/yellow heavy jigs like the Salas CP105, U.F.O. #5 and #6, and Tady AA produced outstanding catches in the dark. Models with chrome surfaces didn't get bit nearly as well. It seems the dull white finish was the key.

Useful Equipment. A sea anchor combined with a light suspended over the rail facilitated this spectacular night bite. The combination of the quartz lamp and the sea anchor helped to create the illusion that a big 85 foot boat was really an artificial kelp paddy. The bright light attracted baitfish along with the jumbo squid as the sportfisher drifted lazily in the night.

Don't Give Up! Never say it's over 'til it's over! Captain Steve Giffin had the foresight to access the situation in mid-November and predict that we might still find some tuna based on the variables at hand. Another less-seasoned skipper might well have dismissed the offshore option and instead we would have been fishing rockfish at San Martin!

Bluefin Blues

Like the white sea bass, the bluefin tuna is one of the toughest and more unpredictable species found along the Pacific Coast. For one thing, as with albacore, you can never tell where or when bluefin will show up. You might find them nearly 260 miles south of San Diego near Guadalupe Island or north towards Morro Bay. One thing for certain, however, when you find bluefin tuna you will be in for some of the meanest action you have ever encountered!

Bluefin Strategy

These are not excessively complicated fish to understand. There seems to be two types of behavior evidenced by bluefin and for some reason it appears to be based on where they are found. If these tuna come close to the beach, they seem to be incredibly finicky feeders. They will typically "show" generating huge surface boils from 30 to 60 pound class specimens but rarely eating any hooked baits. If, however, you encounter bluefin tuna offshore along the deep outer banks, you have a much better chance of getting these schools of fish to bite. Let me elaborate on how to approach these spectacular battlers again based on primarily where you find them.

Inshore Bluefin

During certain years and on a highly sporadic basis, I might add, marauding schools of bluefin will "show" in local waters. Catalina, San Clemente, the Coronados, and San Nicholas Islands will sometimes host these tuna. They might also make a spectacular appearance in the shallow waters of Santa Monica Bay.

When these tuna "show" in this part of the country it is usually time to catch that "light line fever" I talked about earlier. Here is where you need those compact Penn 140, 146, 506, and 501 baitcasting reels, spooled with 12 to 15 pound *premium* monofilament. These smaller Penn baitcasters will hold well over 300 yards of 12 pound test string—and you may need all of that to land a 30 to 40 pound inshore bluefin. Match with 7 foot light/medium action Penn Sabre rods.

As for hooks and sinkers, usually forget the sinkers. These are primarily fly-line fish. Hooks are another story You will need to scale way down to between #6 and #8 Eagle Claw #118 *bronze* live bait hooks. I emphasize *bronze* instead of nickel-plated models. Many skippers and deckhands adamantly concur that these coastal tuna are very smart and can pick up any subtle unnatural flash from a nickel-plated hook. We might be over-estimating the bluefin's intelligence level. Nevertheless, I know the tiny bronze hooks will get bit under extremely tough conditions.

Usually you will be stuck with small anchovies for bait from the coastal landings. This is another reason for light line, whippier rods, and smaller hooks. A basic—but very gentle—gill-hooking will work best with the 'chovies. Reel drags must be in absolutely perfect condition to sustain the scorching runs of these inshore bluefin.

When you fish for coastal bluefin, the catch ratio is very low, even with precision tackle. You are saddled with a tiny hook, fine diameter monofilament that will stretch, and sometimes over an hour to land the fish. Remember, the longer you pull on the bluefin, the greater the chance for the little hook to wear a hole in the fish's mouth and come free. Good luck!

Offshore Bluefin

Unlike their coastal brethren, bluefin found on the outer banks behave more closely to yellowfin, big eye, and albacore. They are just stronger, meaner fish.

Occasionally you may locate schools of offshore bluefin as they chase bait to the surface evidenced by diving sea birds or on a jig strike. Even here, bluefin do not seem to strike traditional trolled tuna feathers as well as they will a plug. Give the CD-18 Magnum Rapala a serious try. Instead, most bluefin schools are located on the outer banks. Skippers look for sonar readings or "meter marks" of deep marauding fish. It is not uncommon to meter bluefin at depths of 150 to 250 foot depths. Getting them to bite at these depths is another story.

A basic fly-line program will work using larger Penn 500, 505, 25GLS, 45GLS, 113HL, and International 12T and 30T reels. You should fish at least 300 yards of 30 pound test and have backup reels spooled with 50 pound string. When these fish do come up near the surface, it is not uncommon to see them devour a large sardine or mackerel fly-lined with 50 pound test line.

If the bluefin are stratified in midstrike zones of 30 to 90 feet, then fish either a sliding egg sinker butted up against the hook, a large split-shot, or a 3/4 to 1 1/2 ounce rubber-core sinker. When the tuna are beyond 15 fathoms, we like to have our students fish a 2 to 4 ounce chrome torpedo sinker tied about 18 to 24 inches above the hook. This "plunker" rig is a key technique for getting big baits like sardines or mackerel down deep to big bluefin. Live bait should be hooked either across the nostril openings or through the upper and lower lips. An Eagle Claw #118 Magnum hook in 3/0 to 6/0 sizes is recommended.

Offshore bluefin will also eat the iron occasionally but you have to have a lot of perseverance and *fish deep*. The U.F.O. #3 and #5, the heavy Tady A-1 and Salas CP-105 are my personal favorites for the deep bluefin yo-yo bite. Don't wind these jigs on anything less than 40 pound line. Bluefin well over 120 pounds have been landed on iron jigs so pull hard with heavy string!

Unlike the finesse light line program used for coastal bluefin, the offshore marauders will really hurt you if you don't have the right equipment. You might be fishing in over 6000 feet of water and a big 60 to 80 pound bluefin can sulk a long time at these depths.

We encourage all of our students in the Eagle Claw bluefin seminars to invest in quality Braid stand-up tuna support gear. A simple rod butt belt *will not suffice*. You need a larger rod butt support with a gimble bar to keep your rod from twisting and torquing on big bluefin. (You can have tackle shops add a gimble rod butt fixture if your rod did not come with one.)

Next, you should augment the larger butt belt with a kidney back support. Check out the Braid product line designed especially for big Pacific Coast tuna. Braid's butt belt and back brace combos are the staple gear for a

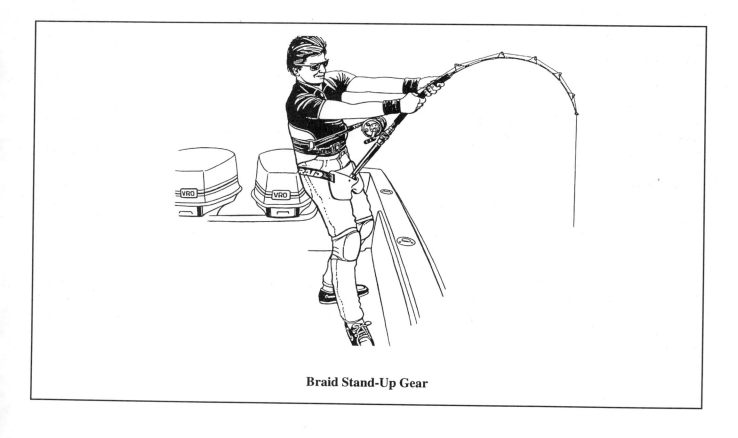

Braid Stand-Up Gear

trip like this. They provide back safety and support and the reel can actually be clipped to a special harness setup so you can take your hands off the reel when you need to rest. Braid's system also allows you to fight the bluefin with your knees instead of your back.

I also suggest soft leather batter's gloves and knee pads for maximum comfort. Remember, you most likely won't encounter these fish fighting them in a fighting chair. Rather, you will be going "mano-a-mano" with bluefin tuna as you are pinned up against the railing of the boat sometimes spending well over an hour to bring up a "smaller" 40 to 50 pounder!

Big Eye Tuna

If there is one single gamefish that can generate an overnight frenzy of angler excitement with its appearance off the Southern California coast, it is the big eye tuna. Albacore may be the "chicken of the sea," and bonito the feistiest tuna pound for pound, but the big eye is the one that puts the fisherman to the most severe physical test.

Upon first appearance, big eye look identical to yellowfin tuna. After closer inspection, they still look like yellowfin. The biologists claim that the only precise way to differentiate a big eye from a yellowfin is to do a dissection of the two species. The liver striations of each species is different. Most party boat skippers simply designate any yellowfin-like tuna over 50 pounds as "big eye" in their fish counts.

Local Big Eye

Many articles have been written about fishing big eye tuna, primarily from a long range perspective. These stories focus on catching 150 to 300 pounders or the so-called "gorilla" class fish from such faraway places as Clarion and Socorro Islands on multi-day long-range trips deep into Mexican waters.

I want to take a somewhat different approach. Frequently—and especially in a warm water El Niño year—there will be accounts of big eye tuna being caught within one-day range of the Southern California private and party boat fleet. Many anglers are caught off guard and may be unprepared for an encounter with these pelagic brutes on overnight albacore, yellowfin, or kelp patty-hopping yellowtail runs.

So here are the basics—when, where, and how to fish big eye tuna on a local trip.

When and Where

Most veteran party boat skippers agree that the period from late August through mid-November is the best time to encounter big eye off our coast.

A multitude of popular offshore banks have been known to host these tuna during this time of the year. For one-day outings, big eye territory ranges from Santa Barbara Island in the North to 100 to 120 miles south of San Diego. Some of the popular fish-holding areas include the Cortez, Osborne, Cherry, Tanner, and Sixty Mile Banks, along with the 43, 181, 209, 273, and 395 spots.

Many of the good local skippers feel that the big eye will gravitate to the ledges and the underwater sea mounts and not necessarily the highest spots found on these banks. As a rough rule of thumb, anytime you find clean, 68 degree water or better, you have a good chance of running into big eye tuna.

Big Eye Tackle

To begin with, it is important to be equipped properly to handle tuna in the 50 to 200 pound class. If you are on a typical offshore yellowtail, albacore, or yellowfin trip, it might be wise to always carry at least one heavier outfit if there is the possibility of finding some big eye. The optimal reel for these jumbo tuna fish would be in the 4/0 size, with enough spool capacity to hold 300 yards of 50 pound test monofilament such as the Penn 113-HL 4/0 Senator. Other models such as the Penn 45GLS and International 30 are higher quality reels perfect for big eye in this size range. These reels feature precision lever drags instead of the star system. They are designed especially to withstand blistering runs from trophy-class fish.

Captain Buzz Brizendine of the sportfisher Prowler out of Fisherman's Landing in San Diego encourages his passengers to bring out their highest quality gear if there is an opportunity for big eye. "If the people own a high-tech reel like the Penn 2-speed Internationals, I tell them it's entirely appropriate equipment on our boat if the big eye tuna are around."

The popular short 5 1/2 to 6 1/2 foot long stand-up Penn Sabre tuna rods used on long-range trips will work fine for the one-day encounter. The Penn 865XH or the Penn Stand-Up System series of rods exemplify this kind of heavy-duty blank. It is preferable to use a rod with a gimble butt.

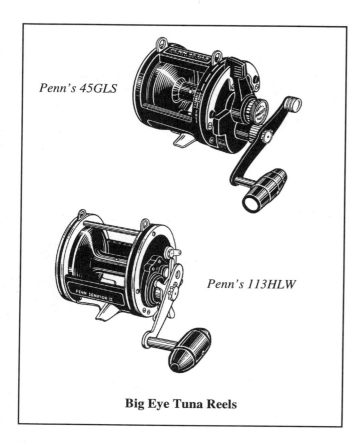

Penn's 45GLS

Penn's 113HLW

Big Eye Tuna Reels

Captain Irv Grisbeck of the sportfisher Berkley Trilene Big Game out of H&M Landing in San Diego tallied 238 big eye tuna on one stop within one day of the dock. "Don't over-gun yourself," warns Grisbeck, "when it comes to big eye gear. You can have the best tuna rod in the world matched with a big Penn 50-Wide class reel, but this outfit may be too much for some people to handle. In this case you may be better off scaling down to a lighter rig than an outfit that overwhelms you."

Longtime tackle dealer Ron De La Mare recommends that you always carry a fairly heavy 50 to 60 pound outfit when venturing into local big eye territory. "The big boys," notes De La Mare, "can show up at anytime on one of these local offshore trips. You don't want to leave this kind of rig at home gathering dust in the garage, when you wish you had it when the big tuna show."

The bottom line? It is definitely wise to carry a heavy rig with you on the autumn offshore trips. Instead of trying to fish the big eye on strictly 100 pound mono, consider a rod and reel that will hold 50 to 60 pound string but won't stress you out when fighting the fish. Don't forget your

Braid stand-up gear either. Big eye over 60 pounds can be mean, back-breaking brutes. Invest in quality stand-up gear—you'll need it!

As far as line is concerned, De La Mare has set up many anglers for big eye and he adamantly says, "good premium mono is your best investment. Don't' scrimp on line! You can use clear, pink, or blue monofilament for big eye, but make sure it is premium grade quality."

De La Mare also talks about the importance of good "knotsmanship" when it comes to fishing big eye. "Make sure all your knots are tied perfectly," stresses De La Mare. "If you tied the knot on your big eye outfit the night before you got to the spot and your rod was left in the rack overnight, definitely re-check your knot even if you haven't used the outfit before you encounter the fish."

As a final comment with regard to line, most big eye experts recommend using a 4 to 6 foot length of leader attached to your main monofilament, if you are spooled with less than 80 pound test. The leader should be 100 to 125 pound test and connected to your main line with a good quality ball-bearing swivel. There are many times when the mono will either rub against the big tuna's back or be bumped by marauding pesky skipjack during a long battle. The heavy length of leader will minimize excessive chaffing and will result in more fish landed.

Big Eye Tactics

For local fishing, big eye tuna can be caught on three basic methods: 1) trolling, 2) live bait, and 3) cast-iron jigs.

Trolling. Not only party boats but also smaller charter vessels and private yachts can improve their odds by trolling for these magnum tuna. If you are carrying minimal chum, then trolling is definitely the name of the game. Regardless of chum power, pulling lures in the wake allows the skipper the greatest opportunity to cover immense spans of open water most effectively.

When trolling, boat operators should be alert for numerous signs of potential big eye activity. A wayward kelp patty always presents a possible "oasis in the desert" for a school of these tuna. These floating patties are always worth dragging some jigs by.

You may be lucky enough to see more visible signs of the big tuna such as schools of boiling fish or sea birds swarming on bait pushed towards the surface. You may even spot actual "jumpers" as large tuna arch their backs and "hump" over the surface.

In recent years, shrewd skippers have invested in the finest electronic sonar devices which may become a potent weapon in the hunt for schools of big eye. It is now quite common for sportfishing captains, for example, to leave their meters on at all times once they reach the outer banks. Frequently they will receive "meter marks" from schools of tuna holding at deeper strike zones. A trolling pattern may then be set up to circumscribe the general area of the readings in an attempt to bring the school up to the surface to strike the lures.

It pays to troll a somewhat larger than normal tuna feather when searching for big eye. "This is the one situation," comments Captain Brizendine, "when most party boat skippers allow you—and encourage you—to troll a larger lure." A feathered jig in 20 to 25 mm head size is perfect for this kind of tuna trolling. These are rigged with a standard, double tuna hook. The California Lure's IKKA is an example of this larger trolling feather.

Smaller 15 mm albacore feathers will also work at times for big eye. One trick is to stack 2 or 3 of these compact jigs on top of each other by simply threading them onto the line before tying the double hook. The stacking technique creates a longer lure, but with a relatively small head and a slim profile in the water. With one feather stacked on top of another, the lure also has somewhat of a hinged effect when it swims in the water, similar to a jointed plug.

Stacking jigs also allows you to come up with a variety of custom color combinations when you put 2 to 3 feathers in tandem. The traditional albacore color patterns perform equally well for big eye tuna. These include red/white, blue/white, green/yellow, zucchini, Mexican Flag, and purple/black. Don't forget the "sleeper" jig sometimes used by commercial tuna fishermen in a solid white feather. Not surprisingly, small marlin jigs will also take their share of big eye in local waters. The miniature Door Knob, 3.5 Zucker, small California Lure Runner, and the Seven Strand Clones all can be pulled for big eye.

As an added option, consider dragging a large, saltwater plug. The CD-18 Magnum Rapala minnows are also big eye killers. Make sure that if you are trolling with mono heavier than 30 pounds, you use heavy-duty double hooks with these plugs. Smaller treble hooks will likely straighten out when heavier mono is used for trolling the plugs. Consider switching to stainless steel double hooks. The Braid "speedster" series—a unique lipless plug—is another option. The "Speedster" trolls fairly fast, comes rigged with two large single tuna hooks, and tallies a lot of trophy big eye each season. A variation on the lipless design is Braid's other big eye killer, the solid metal Reflecta plug. This lure also can be trolled at higher speeds.

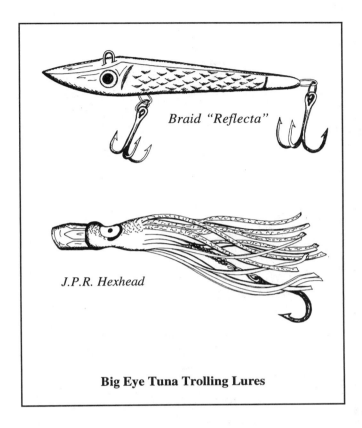

Braid "Reflecta"

J.P.R. Hexhead

Big Eye Tuna Trolling Lures

Most party boats pull their big eye lures at somewhere between 5 and 7 knots, while smaller yachts troll at 5 to 10 knots. Tom Schlauch, the captain of the charter boat Dreamer out of L.A. Harbor Sportfishing, states that there may be nothing too big or too fast for big eye. "The best tuna weighed-in in past seasons was a 135 pound fish that ate a Doorknob marlin jig on a full-bore troll at 13 knots!" According to Captain Schlauch always be prepared for "blind" strikes on big eye when you least expect it, trolling over larger stretches of seemingly barren ocean.

Live Bait. Big eye, like yellowfin, bluefin, and albacore will readily eat live bait—and big offerings at that. Don't ever be intimidated, for example, to throw out the biggest mackerel or sardine you can find in the tank if you think big eye tuna are nearby. When using anchovies, you may want to use a slightly larger hook size than you might otherwise use with an individual bait. In contrast to bluefin tuna, the big eye are usually less fussy when it comes to a precise match between hook and bait.

The standard gill collar, nose, or anal hooking techniques used for 'chovies or sardines will work for big eye. Avoid using treble hooks with live bait. Instead, switch to heavy-duty hooks like the Eagle Claw #118 Magnum, or #318 Magnum models to help withstand the tremendous pressure exerted by these fish. You may need to fish all the way up to a size 8/0 to handle tuna of this magnitude.

If you get a deep meter reading of fish, then add either a large 1 to 2 ounce rubber-core sinker, Izorline Big Shot, or sliding egg sinker above the bait to get it down to the 15 fathom range (90 feet). I personally like to use a 2 ounce chrome-plated torpedo sinker with my hook attached to the 18 inch length of leader that is tied to a shiny sinker. The chrome creates added "flash" or attraction as you slowly "pump" the bait back from the deeper strike zones.

The experts recommend at least 30 pound test for live bait action and preferably 50 pound mono to turn the powerful big eye. There are times, however, when you may catch these fish on lighter gear. On one of the Eagle Claw Saltwater Schools on the Prowler, we tallied 66 big eye tuna from 55 to 115 pounds. A majority of these fish were caught on 20 pound string including the jackpot tuna! Not one of the students on this charter were ever spooled because the fish seemed to be remarkably "boat happy." Rarely did any of the tuna run off more than 200 yards of line, with most staying near the stern.

Keep in mind that this was an extraordinary situation. Normally a large 75 to 100 pound tuna can tear off 300 yards of 20 pound mono in a few quick seconds. Remember the longer you pull on these fish, the greater the chances are that you will inadvertently wear a hole in the tuna's mouth where the point is buried. Then the hook will eventually pull loose.

On the Iron! Big eye, like other tunas, will also attack a cast-metal jig. During that same school I mentioned, I personally had a 150 pounder readily eat the "iron" on straight 80 pound test line on a trolling rod while yo-yoing a U.F.O. #3 jig. Unfortunately, the treble hook on the jig straightened out just before we could get three gaffs into the monster! I had inadvertently over-scaled the lure with the 80 pound test mono.

As you would do with albacore, fish the iron on the "slide" as the boat glides to a stop following a jig strike on the troll. The fish may attack the iron on either a sub-surface retrieve or a fast yo-yo wind coming up from deeper water. Throw heavy cast metal jigs with strong treble hooks on 30 to 50 pound string. You might also consider switching the trebles to an even stronger, single Siwash-style, free-swinging hook for extra leverage. Try the U.F.O. #3 or #5, Tady T.L.C. or A-1 heavy, or Salas 6xJR, Yo-Yo 4 or CP-105 also in heavy models. Popular colors are solid chrome, blue/chrome, blue/white, and scrambled egg. Tie a good knot!

Well, there you have it—a fairly concise tackle program for stalking big eye tuna while on a local one day trip. The Boy Scout motto is highly appropriate when it comes to this species: be prepared! The drag on your reel, the line guides on your rod, the monofilament and knots must be in perfect condition to harness the incredible energy of these tuna when you are fighting them from the rail, standing up. Again, I emphasize these fish can really hurt you if your not using proper stand-up gear.

Captain Grisbeck sums it up best when he observed that "big eye are not a finesse style fight. You just have to beat them into submission—the sooner you pull hard on them, the greater your chances are of landing one."

El Dorado!

In the Florida Keys they call them "dolphin fish," and in Hawaii they are known as "mahi mahi." Along the Pacific Coastline from Baja to Catalina Island, angler's excitement levels sizzle with the mention of "dorado." These golden speedsters are frequently found in local southern California waters in late summer and fall, particularly in an El Niño warm-water year. When tropical storms in Cabo San Lucas push warm 68 to 75 degree water northward, look for dorado to hitchhike on the tropical currents.

Dorado are without a doubt one of the most spectacular gamefish of the Pacific. Once hooked—especially on light tackle—dorado will often stage an incredibly exciting aerial show. When they feel the point of the hook, expect these fish to become airborne, frequently engaging in a series of multiple leaps, stretching over 100 yards.

There are some highly specialized tactics we have found during our late summer and fall programs to catch dorado in solid numbers. This species can basically be caught by: 1) live bait casting, 2) "chunkin', 3) trolling, 4) jigging, 5) pluggin', and 6) spoonin'. Let's look closely at each of these methods for nailing dorado.

Live Bait for Dorados

Count on most dorado to be caught on live bait. Basic 20 to 30 pound conventional outfits or 15 to 20 spinning gear is perfect for these fish, whose average size range is 8 to 15 pounds. The standard fly-line setup, a shiny torpedo weight "plunker" rig, a sliding egg sinker butted against the hook, or a simple rubber core or split-shot placed 12 to 24 inches above the hook are live bait options for the mahi mahi. Sometimes the fish will start out eating the baits deep, up to about 15 fathoms. Here is where the split-shot, rubber-core, sliding-egg, or shiny torpedo sinker combos should be tried. If the action heats up, forget the weights and work live bait right on the surface carefully fly-lining.

Dorado, surprisingly for such a prized species, are really not that particular when it comes to live bait preferences. Big anchovies, sardines, and both greenback and Spanish mackerel will all get bit when the mahi turn on. In fact, there are occasions when the bigger the bait, the bigger the dorado. I've caught 45 pounders on the biggest mackerel I could find in the tank.

Expect a scorching run of line when the dorado first picks up the bait. Keep your thumb out of the way—these fish can really peel out line quickly when you set up on the mahi mahi. Expect the fish to launch itself into that series of jumps I talked about. It is thus important to both keep your line tight and to follow the hooked fish. Dorado travel so fast you may experience the initial hook-up on the stern and 10 seconds later you are in the bow section of an 85 foot sportfisher!

Chunkin'

It has only been in recent years that party and charter boat skippers have started to "chunk" for dorado. This method of dead bait fishing is practiced extensively in Hawaii and the Florida Keys where live bait is at a premium—if you can find it.

The trick is to cut up chunks—say about 2 to 4 inches square—of fresh dead or frozen baitfish such as mackerel or even bonito or small yelllowfin tuna and skipjack. You can also "sacrifice" a small dorado and "chunk" it. It doesn't seem to make much difference. The mahi mahi are not too picky when they decide to eat chunk baits. For chunkin', as odd as this sounds, fly-lining without any weight appears to work best. The key is to try to get the "chunk" to drift away from the boat in the current. As for hooking the "chunk," the traditional 2/0 to 4/0 #181 Eagle Claw hook has two additional mini baitholder barbs on the shank. This allows it to grab into the "meatier" portion of the chunk and keep it from slipping. If you tie into a school of big "bull" (male) dorado then consider switching to the Eagle Claw #318-N or even 118 MG Magnum short-shank live bait hooks to use with the chunks.

Always try to leave on at least some of the skin when cutting the chunks—the oilier the better. The dorado will really home in on the flash and taste of the oily skin portion as the chunk drifts away from the stern. Chunkin' is an important strategy for the small craft owner caught in a wide-open mahi mahi bite with little or no live bait.

Trolling for Mahi

Many dorado are sacked each year utilizing basic offshore trolling strategies. The simple tuna feather with a double-hook is a solid producer. Almost any color will work for the mahi at one time or another. On our Eagle Claw Schools, we run dark patterns (e.g., purple, black, green) combinations in the overcast mornings, switching to brighter tuna feathers (white, "Mexican Flag," "zucchini," green/yellow, blue/white, red/white) during midday.

However, traveling further south into Mexican waters, we have found the dorado to have a special preference for "hot pink," when it comes to trolling feathers. More importantly, the further south you go, it seems the bigger the trolling jig the dorado will attack. On numerous trips to Cabo San Lucas, big bull dorado annihilated our large marlin jigs rigged on 250 pound test monofilament.

Another rather bizarre trolling lure that really nails some of the biggest specimens each season is the Braid "Ten Pin." This single-hook lure actually looks like a miniature bowling pin. It wobbles back and forth on the troll and can be pulled quite "short" even in the boat's prop wash. Big bull mahi really clobber this esoteric plug on the troll along with yellowfin tuna that might be mixed in with the dorado or vice versa.

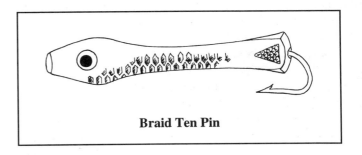

Braid Ten Pin

The ever-popular CD-18 Magnum Rapala also takes its share of dorado slow-trolled offshore. If they are running in small school size weights of 6 to 8 pounds, switch to trolling a more compact CD-14 Magnum Rapala. I might add that almost any color in either the Rapalas or the Ten Pin will catch mahi. Pick your favorite and try it!

Dorado on the Iron!

Many novice anglers falsely assume that dorado won't eat the iron. This is entirely incorrect. Not only will they eat jigs, they will inhale them during a red hot bite. The problem becomes that with all their leaping and head-shaking only about 30 to 40 percent of the mahi hooked on the iron are ever landed.

There is, however, a simple remedy for this problem. Switch to single tuna hooks replacing the treble on your favorite jigs. This little adjustment will elevate your catch-to-hook ratio well above 70 percent of the dorado. Small to medium size jigs are perfect, primarily in the heavy versions. The Salas CP105, Tady A1, and U.F.O. #3 and #5 are proven winners. Blue and white, "scrambled egg," solid chrome and "dorado" (green/yellow/white/blue) patterns are best.

You can either grind the iron across the surface, especially on the "slide" following a trolling hook-up or use a deep yo-yo wind starting at roughly 90 foot depths. Retrieve the yo-yo jig *fast* all the way back to the boat. Don't worry, you won't outrun these fish with the jig.

Mahi Eat Surface Plugs!

That's right. Mahi mahi will eat a surface plug! Large saltwater poppers like the Yozuri Hydro Tiger, Pele Plug, or Cordell Pencil Popper will catch dorado—and the big bulls at that. You can "twitch" the plug using a "hi-stick" tactic, keeping the rod tip high quickly retrieving the lure all the way back to the boat. The object is to twitch the rod tip while reeling in the slack as quickly as possible. This makes the surface plug "spit" water from the front cupped portion of the lure.

The other variation is to "low-stick" the surface plug pointing the rod tip toward the water and "pulling" the lure casually back to the boat. Both hi- and low-sticking techniques often produce spectacular strikes as the dorado boil to eat the big surface plug. A word of caution here: do not swing when you see the splash and commotion as the

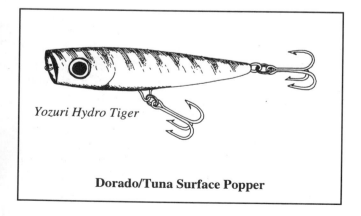

Yozuri Hydro Tiger

Dorado/Tuna Surface Popper

mahi hit the plug. Wait until you feel *distinct tight pressure* on the line, then swing and set hard. Many times the dorado will make a pass at the surface plug, blow up on it, but never becoming hooked. When you feel that tight pressure following the visual fireworks then you know that the mahi has pulled the plug under water and it is solidly hooked in the fish's mouth. Yellowfin tuna, often mixed in with the dorado and vice versa, will also jump on these saltwater surface poppers!

Spoon the Dorados!

Because these fish are so difficult to land at times with all their acrobatics, we like to have our students try to nail the dorado on basic spoons. The Haddock Jig'n Spoon, Krocadile, and Crippled Herring are excellent spoons for mahi mahi. However, make sure all these models are rigged with a long-shank single hook instead of trebles.

As I noted with dorado on the "iron," the single-hook lure will give you greater leverage and more control over hyperactive species like mahi mahi. Usually the single-hook spoon also features a much wider hook gap, allowing for better penetration and holding power set in the dorado's bony mouth structure. Practically any color spoon will catch mahi mahi. We like solid chrome, chrome/blue, or any prism scale-like finish. A 1 to 3 ounce model is perfect.

A Final Mahi Mahi Tip

One intriguing observation veteran captains have made while watching a dorado bite build up is that these fish are incredibly gregarious. They seem to be playing "follow the leader." Here is the hot inside scoop: Once you hook that first dorado, try to keep it near the boat after you have exhausted the fight. If you have to slow-drag it while the boat drifts, do it! What happens is that other mahi in the school become super curious and gravitate to their "captured brother." Out of nowhere, an entire school of dorado can show up. A feeding frenzy usually follows!

Trophy Yellowtail!

Much has been written about the basic techniques for catching yellowtail—one of the most coveted gamefish in the Pacific. Less has been written, however, on how to catch the better quality trophy 'tails in that 20 to 40 pound range. Yellowtail are found from Cabo San Lucas to Morro Bay. Each year they seem to get smaller and smaller. Catalina Island, once an absolute mecca for these gamesters, now hosts sparse schools of yellows and usually those are 5 to 8 pound "firecracker" class fish. The same holds true for the Los Coronados Islands—once heralded as the yellowtail capitol of the world in the 1960s and 1970s.

However, there are still some big yellowtail to be found in Southern California waters. San Clemente, Catalina, San Nicholas, and the Coronados Islands have modest populations of home guard yellows. These fish take up year-round residence at these offshore islands, migrating only a short way. Similarly, the Cortez Bank, 95 miles west of San Pedro, has its share of lunker 'tails, many in the 30 to 40 pound class. If you want to catch one of these bigger yellows, then you must think about using some BIG FISH strategy. The basic fly-line tactic with small pinhead anchovies just won't cut it if you're hunting these jumbo members of the jack family.

Some of the methods I discuss here for catching big yellowtail were pioneered in Mexican waters. At locations like San Martin, Cedros, Benitos, and Guadalupe Islands—all two or three days travel by boat from San Diego—yellowtail still flourish with 30 pounders quite common. I'll share some of these Baja strategies with you and, hopefully, you will nail one of these stellar fighters!

Fish the Macks!

You are going to need to become an accomplished mackerel fisherman if you're looking for trophy-size tails With these big fish, there is really no bait—up to about two pounds–that will intimidate them. Usually a Spanish or greenback mackerel fly-lined with 30 pound test mono on stout baitcasting combos will be the major program to try first.

The macks should be hooked across the nostril pores if the fish are on the surface. Use the butt-hooking method if you want the mackerel to dive deeper with the fly-line approach. Select larger #4/0 to #6/0 Eagle Claw #118 MG Magnum live bait hooks. Give the 'tails a considerable amount of time to thoroughly eat the big bait.

Dropper Loop Yellows

It is amazing how infrequently Southern California anglers fail to utilize this simple terminal rig, particularly when fishing for yellowtail. Further south in the waters off Baja, the dropper loop setup probably accounts for over 80 percent of the yellowtail scored each year. The rig is so simple. Tie on a 4 to 8 one torpedo sinker to the end of the line. Affix a dropper loop about 6 inches in length, about 12 to 18 inches above the sinker. Hitch on a #4/0 to #6/0 Eagle Claw #118MG or #318-N Magnum live bait hooks.

The beauty of the dropper loop setup is that the big baits—like mackerel or sardines—are allowed to swim above the rocky bottom and pivoting around the main, 30 to 50 pound test line. If a big 'tail begins to back you off into the rocks, if you are lucky, the sinker will break off, but you will still have the yellow hooked safely above on the dropper-loop. Interestingly, during the wintertime period at many of Southern California's offshore islands, home guard 'tails are found deep all the way to 240 foot depths. Fly-lining baits won't even begin to tap into this winter population. A torpedo sinker in the 4 to 8 ounce range combined with a dropper loop will! If live squid is available, it is even better for the cold weather bite. Yellowtail will sometimes go crazy at depths of 15 to 40 fathoms as they attack the live "squirt" fished on a deep-water dropper loop!

Slabs and Strips

Big mackerel are not always available. However, you might have some fairly fresh macks frozen down in you freezer or maybe a small bonito you would like to strip for yellowtail. Like the dropper loop strategy, not enough Southland anglers utilize cut baits like mackerel or bonito to catch lunker-class yellows. You can either use thin elongated strips about 1x10 inches in length or rectangular slabs. The secret is to leave as much skin on as possible. The oily iridescent skin of the mackerel or the bonito creates a lot of flash and smell in the water.

You can fish slabs or strips for 'tails in a number of ways. Conventional fly-lining works especially well if you have a good current to take the meat away from the stern and let it flutter imitating a live baitfish. Strips and slabs also can be used in conjunction with a dropper loop rig. Just make sure to pin the meat on carefully, hooking it once then back thorough. You don't want to create a ball of meat, but rather a slab or strip that flutters as it extends away from the main line.

Strips and slabs also catch yellowtail fished on a simple sliding egg sinker setup. In this situation I am usually targeting 'tails at mid-depth range, not on the surface or the bottom, but somewhere in between. Use a 2 to 5 ounce egg weight and let it butt directly up against the hook.

As with any big bait, let the yellows really munch on the slab or strip before you set up on the fish. You will find that 'tails will sometimes playfully tug or pull on the meat without really chomping on the bait. When this happens, coax them into eating the slab or strip by reeling in 6 to 12 inches of line. Twitch the rod tip a little then throw the reel back into free spool. This little ploy gives the illusion that the baitfish—the slab or strip—suddenly became frantic and is starting to swim away. This will often trigger the final definite bite from the yellowtail and allow you to set up on the fish.

'Tails on the Iron

As a rough rule of thumb, the further south you venture, the better the jig fishing for yellows. Years ago it was not uncommon to see a competent iron chucker nail a limit of 10 yellows in the 20 to 25 pound class working his jig from the bow of the boat. Those days are just about history, at least in Southern California waters.

Still, from the Coronado Islands south, it is imperative to be ready to throw the iron particularly if you run across a school of marauding breezers. Yellowtail moving like this are difficult to fish with live bait. They are moving fast and don't seem to want to settle down and are usually chasing a pod of baitfish. This is where either a long cast with a surface jig or a deeper yo-yo retrieve with a heavy model can be deadly.

Many times, the breezing 'tails are out of range for even the best live bait casters. If the fish are up and boiling on the surface, try throwing a large, light Salas 6x, 7x, Tady 45, or U.F.O./ P.O.S. model. These are dynamite surface jigs for big yellowtail. The best colors are scrambled egg, blue/white, solid white, solid chrome, sardine, and brown/purple (squid).

If the breezers come up, then are metered down, switch to a medium-size heavy jig and drop it to 60 to 90 foot depths. Wind as fast as you can back to the boat—don't even stop. If you get bit and the fish misses the treble hook—*keep winding!* An unexpected pause in the deep yo-yo retrieve breaks up the swimming action of the jig and no longer fools the yellowtail. Keep in mind that you cannot reel line in too quickly for these gamefish. You can't outrun them with your iron! Favorite yellowtail yo-yo iron? Try U.F.O. #3, #5, Tady A1, and Salas CP-105 in blue/white, scrambled egg, dorado, or sardine patterns.

'Tails on Tubes!

As strange as this sounds, on many of our Eagle Claw schools we have found that the new hollow-bodied Caba Caba Tubes actually catch yellowtail. It makes sense when you think about it. The tube bait is designed to replicate live squid. It is fished fairly deep and swims in a circle. In many ways it resembles a live squid on a dropper loop.

Tube baits for yellowtail may raise some eyebrows, but I can attest they do work at times when good bait is scarce and traditional iron isn't producing. I always like to add a small 1x3 inch strip of frozen squid or cut mackerel to make the Caba Caba Tube even more appealing.

Yellows on Spoons!

Another one of the most overlooked methods to catch quality yellows is to spoon them. Again, learning a lesson from our yellowtail seminars, there are definitely times when the 'tails turn their noses up to everything from live bait to cast-metal jigs. This is where a subtle lure like a spoon can be a real sleeper.

The Haddock Jig'n Spoon with its simple slab-shaped design often gets bit as it sinks to the bottom while chasing breezing yellows. The "brown bait" prism scale finish has been a hot yellowtail color in this model spoon along with "staple anchovy" and "sardine prism" in the 2 1/8 ounce size.

The other option is to fish the larger 2 to 5 ounce Krocadile spoons. Don't leave home without them when you are looking for big yellows in a sub-surface or deep in a lethargic feeding mode. The big chrome or prism scale Krocs really do the job at times on trophy 'tails as they lazily flutter on the sink. Krocadile spoons give off considerable flash that is distinctively different from what the yellowtail see from a jig. Definitely give the big Krocs a try when you're in yellowtail territory.

Yellowtail Nail Rapalas!

On many of our Eagle Claw Schools we encounter breezing schools of yellowtail that are moving quickly over great expanses of water. The way we target these fish best is to troll large CD-18 Magnum Rapala plugs in and around the general area.

An example of this occurred one early spring at San Martin Island about 155 miles south of San Diego. The breezing 'tails would pop up then quickly dive deep and keep moving. It was very frustrating as we tossed the yo-yo jigs and fly-lined the sardines. But there were no strikes.

After about an hour of this run-and-gun approach, I tied on a big CD-18 Magnum Rapala and trolled it behind the stern. Almost instantly a 20 pound yellowtail nailed the plug. I quickly set out another rod with a CD-18. An instant double-hook up followed. Then I went for broke and put out four trolling outfits loaded with the jumbo Rapala minnows. You guessed it—a quadruple hook-up!

The rest was easy. We had found the main concentration of the breezing school of yellows loaded the stern with live chum and in less than two hours hauled almost 200 yellowtail onto the boat! The big Rapalas saved the day. This scenario has been repeated many times, whenever we have difficulty getting the breezers to settle down or even find the heart of the school. Drag those CD-18s!

Advanced Species Lessons: Bottom Fish

Ling cod are one of the most misunderstood and under-rated species anglers may encounter while fishing off the Pacific Coast. To begin with, "lings" are not true cod. They are members of the greenling family of fishes, which includes several other smaller varieties that are often caught in Western kelp beds.

Love Those Lings!

Ling cod are not necessarily a deep-water species as is sometimes incorrectly assumed. These fish are frequently caught on so-called rock cod trips by anglers working 250 to 300 foot depths. However, substantial numbers of these bottom dwellers found at the 30 to 180 foot range.

You can fish for lings all through the year in Southern California although interest is greatest in the colder winter months. In Northern California and the Pacific Northwest, lings can become a daily pursuit, weather permitting. In contrast to other rockfish species such as salmon grouper, chuckleheads, and reds, ling cod put up a fight all the way to the surface. These fish are voracious feeders. They prey upon everything from squid, anchovies and sardines to smaller rockfish.

More and more saltwater buffs are discovering that this gruesome-looking bottom fish offers some terrific action on medium weight gear using both bait and artificials. Lings ranging from 7 to 15 pounds show up in sport catches annually along the coast from Southern California to Ensenada, Mexico. Further north, look for some monster 40 to 60 pound ling cod from the Farallon Islands to Vancouver.

The Tackle

When a ling eats the bait or lure along the shallow offshore ledges, expect the fish to instantly back into the rocks. For this reason, a powerful rod and reel are necessary in order to apply leverage adequate to move the fish out of the structure. Without a doubt, there may be many times during a shallow water trip when you will have to lean into the rod and apply maximum pressure on 20 to 30 pound test mono in order to turn the ling away from the rocky bottom. Consider a Penn 500 or 505, Jigmaster, 506 Jigmaster Jr., or a 25GLS.

Thus, a fairly strong, single piece, 6 to 7 foot long rod blank is recommended, teamed with a conventional reel with either a star or lever drag mechanism. In a pinch, a heavy-duty spinning reel will work, matched with a heavy action, 6 to 7 foot rod. Fill the reels with 20 to 30 pound test monofilament.

Ling Cod on Bait

A variety of ploys work for fishing ling cod with bait at 6 to 25 fathoms. Novice anglers usually simply twist on a 1 to 1 1/2 ounce rubber-core sinker about 12 to 18 inches above an Eagle Claw #318-N or 118-MG live bait hook in sizes #1 to #2 with an anchovy pinned through the nose. This basic live bait rig works only if the boat is anchored and the current is minimal.

An alternate strategy is to use a 4 to 12 ounce torpedo sinker fixed below a dropper loop. As you peel the loose mono from the reel, add a short dropper loop about 18 to 24 inches above the end of the line. Next, tie on a torpedo sinker weighing 4 to 12 ounces, depending upon the prevailing current and depth. To complete the dropper rig, take the loop you formed and run the two strands of line through the eye of a short-shank #4/0 Eagle Claw #118 magnum or #318-N live bait hook.

Now, when you hook a live 'chovy, sardine, or squid onto the dropper hook, the bait will swim in a tight circle a good 18 to 24 inches suspended off the bottom. Snags are also minimized with the dropper loop rig since the narrow torpedo sinker slides more easily in and out of the rocks.

There are a few more tips worth mentioning in regard to using bait on the dropper setup.

1. If the 'chovies are primarily small pinheads, try putting 2 to 4 of them on a single hook. This gives your overall offering a much larger silhouette for the lings to key in on. It also deters, to some degree, the smaller rockfish from striking the anchovy cluster.

2. Frozen squid works almost as well as live or fresh-dead squid. Often, sportfishing boats have only small anchovies on board for a shallow water trip. Always check before you leave the dock. If the boat doesn't have squid, buy a tray for your own personal use.

3. Consider using a strip bait—a small, 1x3 inch long filet of freshly caught rockfish. The strip stays on the hook remarkably well, making it difficult for pesky smaller rockfish to steal. Lings are especially aggressive feeders and quite frequently attack the small rockfish strip over any other baits. Be sure to leave the colorful, mottled red skin on the rockfish filet for added attraction. Cut eel, herring, smelt, mackerel, bonito, and sardines are equally good strip bait options.

4. There are also times when you can fish a whole mackerel or small rockfish right on the bottom using a large 5 ounce sliding egg sinker. Thread the baitfish onto a #4/0 to #6/0 short-shank live bait hook with the sliding egg sinker resting snug against the eye of the hook. This forms a heavy makeshift lead head jig of sorts which keeps the larger offerings near the bottom. When a ling cod strikes the bait, the egg sinker slides up the line out of the way of the hook.

Finally, there are many instances, while fishing for lings and most rockfish for that matter, that the action will intensify if you *drift* rather than fish at anchor with bait. On many trips larger rockfish and ling cod seem more interested in biting if dropper loop rigs are slow drifted rather than fished vertically in a relatively stationary fashion.

Interestingly, I have found that multiple-hook gangion rigs normally used for deep-water rock codding do not produce as well for most ling cod fishing as do either the dropper or slide-sinker setups.

Lings on the Iron

Shallow water ling cod are excellent targets for the serious jig fisherman. The main concern is to select a cast-metal jig with enough weight to maintain constant contact with the bottom. Too often, I have seen anglers using the smaller jigs identical to the ones they threw on bonito or barracuda on shallow water lings. If there is significant current and/or you are drifting, you need larger, heavier "iron."

The U.F.O. #5 and #6 and Salas 6xJR, 6X, and 7X models in "heavy" are perfect for yo-yoing ling cod along the shallow ledges. Use these jigs with either 30 or 40 pound test line. Lower the jig to the bottom and be prepared for strikes to occur as the lure is sinking. If there is a sudden slack in your line, then a ling cod or other rockfish has inhaled the jig.

Once on the bottom, "jerk" the rod from the 3 o'clock position to 12 o'clock. Then lower the rod, allowing the lure to sink. As you might expect, many lings are nailed on the iron on the "fall" as the jig slowly flutters following the lift sequence with the rod. You must set up hard with these fish! They have bony mouth structures, so keep your jig hooks sharp for this style of yo-yo fishing.

The favored colors for taking lings on the "iron" are solid chrome, blue and white, and solid white. An alternative jig is the old-fashioned diamond style in silver-chrome finish, in 8 to 16 ounce models for the shallow bite.

If you initially fail to get bit on the iron, try this simple tactic: add a whole or large piece of squid or a chunk or strip of filet to the jig hooks. Many times I have seen this little ploy yield stellar catches of ling cod by spicing up the lure with a natural bait trailer.

Another intriguing strategy is to add a dropper loop and a 4/0 bait hook about 18 to 24 inches above the "iron." But instead of pinning a piece of squid or anchovy onto the hook, thread on a 4 to 6 inch long *black* plastic worm! As bizarre as this may sound, the plastic worm normally associated with freshwater bass fishing apparently generates some extremely sensuous movements above the jig during the vertical yo-yo motion. The black coloration in the plastic worm shows up well in this deeper water.

A variation on this theme is to add a single colorful shrimp fly to the dropper loop, above either the diamond or candy bar style jig. We have also experienced phenomenal luck with ling cod on our shallow water schools fishing the dropper loop and "iron" combo but adding a Berkley Power Grub on the dropper hook. We are not certain why this specific combination is so deadly on these fish though we suspect the scented grub might increase their curiosity. Sometimes you will get bit on the Power Grub by a smaller rockfish and then the ling strikes the cast-metal jig as you are reeling up. Again, these are excitable, aggressive, voracious fish!

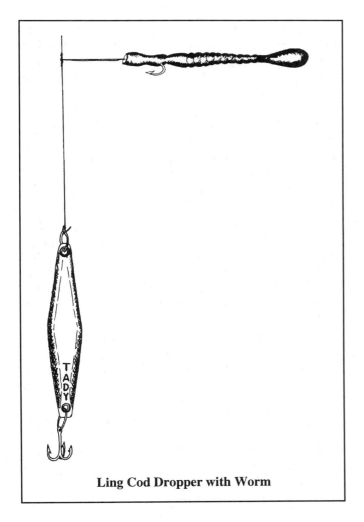

Ling Cod Dropper with Worm

Your chances of tallying a big ling on this tube bait are also enhanced by making a few additions to the lure. If the fish seem to be uninterested in the tube, add a small strip of squid or rockfish filet to the single hook. You might also inject the hollow cavity of the Caba Caba Tube with Berkley Strike. As the lure swims and sashays in the water, a vapor trail of fish attractant is emitted out of the tail often calling in hungry lings to investigate the odor.

The Caba Caba is the perfect lure for the shallow water action. You can fish them from 3 to 8 ounces in weight, depending upon current and depth. The best colors for fishing shallow water ling cod are white glow, root beer flake, motor oil, and black with red or orange tentacles. It seems, however, that as you fish these tubes further north, the darker color patterns produce the best results. The single hook molded into the lead head also permits excellent penetration and leverage on the set at great depths compared to lures with treble hooks.

Curl-Tails for Ling Cod

Other soft plastic lures also work quite well on shallow water ling cod. The secret is to dramatically scale up in size compared to the soft plastics you might normally use for, say, calico bassin'. The basic Scampi or Haddock Lunker Thumper with the twin fork-tails combined with the larger 4 to 16 ounce lead heads are longtime ling cod favorites in fluorescent pink or root beer flake patterns.

A.A.T.'s single-tail Salty Magic is another option. This hand-poured bait has a distinctive elongated single curl-tail made from soft plastic. Teamed with a 4 ounce lead head, the Magic is an excellent choice for tempting ling cod on a slow retrieve, methodically bumping the lure across the bottom. The best colors in this new bait are black molly, motor oil, watermelon green, root beer flake and the fluorescent pink "bubble gum" pattern. Here again, the addition of a strip trailer in either squid or rockfish filet significantly enhances any of these soft plastics utilized in 30 to 125 foot depths.

Some rather inventive anglers like to fish the shallow lings with a "school of plastics." Tie off your main line to a larger soft plastic curl-tail. Then add a dropper loop about 18 to 24 inches above the main lure. Tie a shorter 12 inch length of mono to the dropper loop and add a smaller curl-tail bait to the end of this leader.

You can either cast this tandem rig out or lower it straight down on a vertical drop. As aggressive as the ling cod are, the sight of two swimming tails nearby is sometimes enough to trigger strikes when single plastic lures fail to generate any interest. I should caution—it is also

Caba Caba Lings

A recent innovation has been the Caba Caba Tube designed by longtime lure manufacturer, Leonard Hashimoto. This hollow-bodied tube bait is manufactured from soft plastic and is sold in either 6 or 8 inch lengths under the A.A.T. label. The unique shape of the lead head inserted directly into the hollow-portion of the lure allows the Caba Caba to swim in a circle on the drop. Once it hits the bottom, a sharp twitch of the rod tip forces the lure to sort of "jump" off the bottom and start swimming in a circle.

Both the current and the action imparted by the angler fishing the Caba Caba Tube allows the mass of soft plastic tentacles in the tail portion of the bait to pulsate rhythmically. This is an amazing replica of a live squid swimming while under attack.

possible to nail two lings at one time with this trick rig if the fish are schooled together.

Heavy Spoons

Ling cod are also prone to hit a shiny polished chrome spoon fished with a vertical yo-yo presentation on the shallow rocky ledges. The Crippled Herring, Haddock Jig'n Spoon, and Luhr Jensen Dungeness Stinger in 2 to 4 ounce models are perfect for these conditions. If the spoon fails to get bit, add some strip bait to one of the points on the treble or single hook to spice up this relatively simple lure.

Consider trying the larger 3 to 5 ounce Krocadile spoons. These magnificent wobblers generate considerable "flash" as they seductively sink on a lift-and-drop sequence with the rod tip. The "Krocs" definitely catch some real "toad" lings each year along the Pacific using both the smooth and hammered chrome finishes on 20 to 30 pound mono.

More Ling Cod Tips

Fishing ling cod in shallow water can be spectacular sport, especially if the fish are eating artificial lures. However, it is imperative to routinely check your first few feet of monofilament for nicks or cracks as a result of bouncing your offerings in the rocks where these fish live. On this note, it is critical to get a solid hook-set into the fish and to pull *hard* instantly! You must turn the fish away from its rocky domain quickly or it will snag your lure or bait into the structure.

Finally, be flexible in challenging this species. The tactic you used to nail some nice lings today may not work tomorrow. This is a temperamental species. Be prepared to try a variety of approaches. Add squid or fresh strip bait when action dwindles and keep your hooks honed to needle sharpness.

Ling cod are not only terrific fighters but sensational table fare as well. Sometimes the flesh of the fish will take on an eerie bluish tint. This coloration does not affect the flesh or impair the culinary quality of these fish. The flesh turns white when cooked.

So, whenever you venture into cold Pacific water take a shot at this sensational bottom fishing, especially when there are big ling cod at 30 to 90 foot depths.

Shallow-Water Rockfish

Not all parts of the Pacific Coast are blessed with reel-smokin' migratory warm water gamefish. Once you ven-

ture above Morro Bay, most of the angling focuses on an absolute smorgasbord of shallow-water rockfish. The menu is extensive and indeed tasty table fare. Interestingly, many of these species are found not only in Wilapa Bay outside Seattle but all the way down the coast into Mexican waters near San Martin Island.

There are many tactics you can use for rockfish whether you are fishing the northern or southern sector. Popular rockfish species include blue, black, copper, olive, yellowtail, china, starry, and vermilion. Along with whitefish, salmon grouper, cabazon, and the voracious ling cod, rockfish will all be tempted by a multitude of special techniques, some of which were pioneered on the Eagle Claw Fishing Schools.

In separate sections I focus on catching lings and deepwater cow cod. Here I want to share some of the inside tips and tricks that will really fill your sacks up with shallow-water rockfish.

The Dropper Loop

Without a doubt, the most versatile rig for fishing the rockfish at 90 to 120 foot depths is the dropper loop setup. By tying 1 to 3 six inch long loops off your main line about 12 to 18 inches apart, you allow the cut or live bait to lazily pivot around the main line in the current. A torpedo sinker, 2 to 12 ounces in weight, depending upon the current, is tied to the very end of the line.

The dropper loop rig is not quite the same as a deepwater rock cod gangion. For one thing, many anglers fish the dropper loop with only one hook—preferably an Eagle Claw #318-N in size 2/0 to 4/0. A rock cod gangion features 4 to 10 hooks, usually ranging from 4/0 to 8/0 Sealy or tuna-circle style and extra hardware such as swivels, snaps, and split rings. The dropper loop rig is very clean, without all the extraneous hardware.

The torpedo sinker is a subtle but important component for this shallow-water rockfish setup. It is designed to slide in between the rocks and crevices without becoming hung up as much as a ball, pyramid, spoon, or triangle weight.

Secret Power Grubs

Many years ago, the research people at Berkley sent us some of their freshwater Power Grubs to experiment with in our saltwater schools. These curl-tail lures are impregnated with a fish attractant and were marketed for freshwater bass fishing.

Lacing the Power Grubs onto Eagle Claw #318-N 4/0 hooks affixed to dropper loops caused the rockfish to go absolutely nuts for these new baits. We tried white, black, chartreuse, and yellow—color never seems to matter—they all work! The trick was to add a sliver of cut squid, mackerel or a small anchovy hooked with the Power Grub. We find that not only do the rockfish really clobber this grub/bait combo, but we caught the bigger rockfish as well.

Berkley utilized many of the field reports generated from the shallow-water rockfish seminars we conducted to modify the Power Grubs. They added more specific saltwater scents including an entirely new collection of these baits for coastal fishing.

The Grub and Jig Combo

One combination that we found to work especially well on big red rockfish, "johnny bass" (olive rockfish), salmon grouper, and chuckleheads is a heavy jig with a Berkley Power Grub fished 18 to 24 inches above it on a dropper loop.

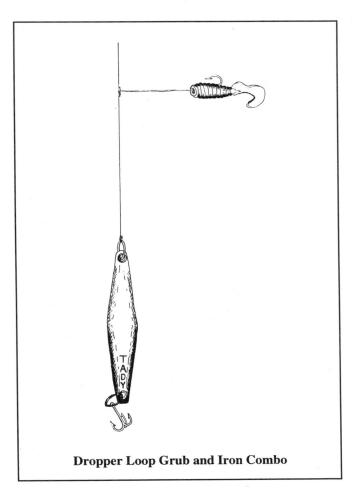

Dropper Loop Grub and Iron Combo

Heavy iron like a U.F.O. #5 or #6, Tady 45, or Salas 6x or 7x in scrambled egg, solid white, solid chrome, or blue/chrome patterns are tied to your 25 to 30 pound mono. Above it, add the dropper loop, the Eagle Claw #318-N 4/0 hook, with a Power Grub threaded on the hook.

As you bounce the jig off the bottom, invariably you either get bit on the iron or the dropper loop grub—or both! Many times we have seen smaller rockfish caught on the grub, while reeling a larger fish such as a ling cod attacks the jig. This is a potent combination that will work from Baja to Seattle!

Rockfish Love Plastics!

Throughout this book you will see multiple references to using soft plastic lures on a large array of species. These inexpensive baits are also important options for the serious shallow-water rockfish hunter. In locales like San Simeon, Santa Cruz, the Farallon Islands, and Coos Bay, anglers working from small skiffs to party boats can partake in some of the most spectacular light-line action using freshwater bass gear, 10 to 12 pound mono, and an armada of soft plastic lures to probe the rocky coastal reefs and inshore kelp beds.

Fork-tail models such as the Mojo, Scampi, and Lunker Thumper, sickle-tails like the Salty Magic, soft plastic eels, Caba Caba Tubes, and, of course, curl-tail grubs will all catch their share of shallow-water rockfish in these areas. Some sport fishing landings even have special tournaments or charters that permit only light line, scaled-down rods and reels and soft plastics in staging major rockfish safaris. Much of the rock fishing occurs in less than 50 foot depths.

It is important to remain highly open-minded in your choice of soft plastics. For example, there are times when the rockfish will annihilate a basic fork-tail lure. Then the next day, the same species will be keying in on large prominent sickle-tail baits. Perhaps the current picked up on the second day and the sickle-tail design generates maximum vibration, triggering strikes from the now-aggressive rockfish.

Similarly ultracold water may move into the shallow reefs and kelp beds creating a near lockjaw effect from these bottom dwellers. Here is a good situation to try a maximum "slow-down" lure methodically pumped along the bottom like a Caba Caba Tube or a soft plastic eel. Again, the emphasis is on remaining flexible and realizing that you can't take these rockfish species for granted. Their feeding behavior and lure or bait preferences can fluctuate on a day-to-day basis is much as any pelagic species.

Spoon the Rockfish!

Another tip I want to encourage you to try is a vertical spoonin' strategy on the rockfish population. Underrated and infrequently used, slab-style spoons (Crippled Herring, Dungeness Stinger, Nordic, Haddock Jig'n Spoon) and wobblers (Krocadile) all work on shallow water rockfish.

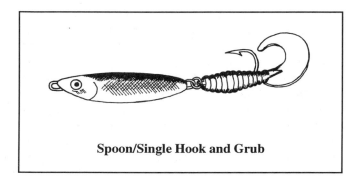

Spoon/Single Hook and Grub

A simple lift-and-drop sequence is all that is needed in 36 to 180 foot depths. Many strikes occur on the sink as the spoon flutters to the bottom. It is important for the spoon to establish good bottom contact at times as you make it flip-flop off the bottom with short rod twitches.

You can also add a dropper loop and a Berkley Power Grub above a bottom bouncin' spoon. At times this combo will fish with lighter 10 to 20 pound test line compared to the 25 to 30 pound mono needed to work the jig and grub combinations.

If you are fishing in particularly rocky terrain you might consider replacing the treble hooks on your spoons with either single Siwash models or large Eagle Claw #318-N hooks in 2/0 to 6/0 sizes. Then thread a Power Grub onto the single hook and you have a unique highly potent lure for shallow-water rockfish!

Sculpin Clackers

One other shallow-water rockfish tactic is worth noting—sculpin clackers. Originally this little trick was designed to get sculpin, one of the finest tasting rockfish in the Pacific, to get out of their lethargic mood and bite. It is a simple ploy to master.

Select your favorite spoon or heavy jig. Before you tie it onto your line, thread on one to two sliding egg sinkers so they ride above the lure. Use larger sinkers with bigger jigs and spoons and lighter eggs with smaller lures.

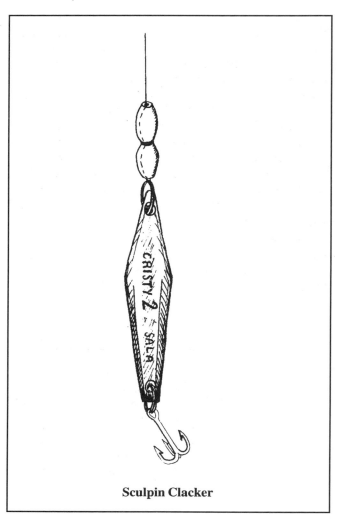

Sculpin Clacker

Once the jig or spoon hits the bottom, bounce the lure with your rod tip using short strokes. As you do this, the sliding egg sinkers make a "clacking" noise as they bang into each other and the lure's eyelet or ring. It is this clacking noise that often triggers strikes from otherwise finicky rockfish. As a teaser, add a strip of cut squid or mackerel to the spoon or cast-metal jig.

Deep-Water Rock Cod

Usually "rock codding" is identified with bazooka-like rods, wench-like reels, heavy line, and back-breaking work. Well, to some degree this depiction isn't too far off base. But with proper tackle selection, there are ways to minimize the physical strain that can be generated from dragging up 600 to 800 feet of line from the bottom. The prime cod themselves are "cow cod" with weights of up to 28 pounds along with a collection of smaller deep-water rockfish including chili peppers, bank perch, barber poles, starries, and salmon grouper. It is important to purchase a high quality reel in the Penn 4/0 to 6/0 range. The reel has to hold at least 300 yards of 50 pound class Dacron. Don't try to cut corners and opt for a smaller baitcasting model for this style of fishing. Next, add a power handle to enhance your leverage when reeling. These are sold as accessory items at most tackle stores. The oversized handle will make reeling a lot easier, providing considerable leverage for grinding in a full gangion of fish.

The deep-water rock cod rod should definitely have at least a roller tip-top. Better models have roller guides the full length of the blank. The more rollers, the less line friction and the easier it is to wind up the heavy sinkers and full gangions.

A rock cod plate or "rail board" is another necessary piece of equipment for the deep-water bite. The plate bolts onto the lower portion of the rod blank. It allows the angler to brace the heavy rod and reel against the boat railing. This serves to reduce a lot of the twisting and turning that would otherwise be inherent in trying to handle such heavy-duty gear.

The reels can be filled with either economically priced Dacron or Micron line. The Micron is considerably more expensive than Dacron. It has a finer diameter for comparable breaking tests, allowing the angler to fill the reel with more line. Most veteran rock codders recommend against using monofilament at these depths. There is too much stretch with the mono and the fabric lines usually have greater abrasion resistance.

An alternative to consider is wire line. The wire line has hardly any stretch. I have fished it down to 600 feet for rock cod and it is amazing stuff. The "strike" is so pronounced even at these great depths that it is as if the

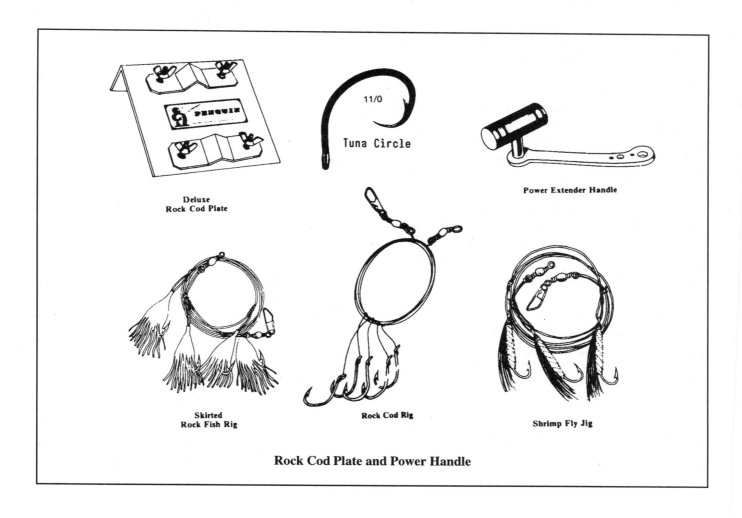

Rock Cod Plate and Power Handle

fish is only a few feet below the surface. The angler is thus able to set the hook quickly and to get strong penetration into the rockfish due to minimal line stretch. Wire is expensive to use and highly temperamental. It can often practically break in half if there is a bend formed in the strand. It takes some skill and expertise to fish this material but the results can be worth the extra investment and effort.

Now that we're set up for the deep-water action, we'll be looking for chili peppers, salmon grouper, starries, reds, goldeneyes, barber poles, bank perch, canaries, and larger cow cod. We need to use anywhere from 1 to 6 pounds of lead.

The configuration of the gangion hooks themselves is worth commenting upon. Most fishermen purchase their gangions with thin wire Sealy-type hooks tied to 50 to 80 pound mono. This style hook can be sharpened fairly easily. But as you drop deeper and deeper, it is easier for the rockfish to steal the bait.

An alternative is to use heavier gangions with the rather strange-looking tuna-circle hooks. These thick, cadmium-plated models, actually have the points turned inward toward the center of the hook. Upon first glance, it seems impossible for a fish to impale itself on the barb with this unique design. But the tuna-circle hooks really do work—especially for deep-water rock codding. The rockfish can't steal the bait easily with this circular hook design. They will continue to eat the bait eventually swallowing it deep.

I learned a trick from some of the shrewd sportfisher deckhands who moonlight at fishing rock cod commercially. What they do is to put the tuna-circle hook in a vice and carefully open up the gap between the point and the rest of the hook. Use pliers to grasp the point portion and gently bend it outward. By doing this, there is slightly more exposed point. Although this increases the potential for bait stealing a little, it also enhances hook penetration. It is critical with this trick then to take a file to the tuna-circle hooks and hone the points to needle sharpness.

Another deep-water strategy is to join gangions together, increasing your offerings from 5 to 10 or 15 baits. Simply clip the gangions together with the snap-swivels. I recommend using pliers however to crimp the swivels shut tight so that they won't inadvertently open up with the weight of additional fish.

There are commercially made gangions sometimes sold at tackle stores and at landings that feature a greater number of hooks on a wire leader. These are worth the extra money for fishing beyond that 300 foot range. The wire leaders won't fray or stretch. The hooks on the gangions in this class tend to be spaced perfectly, allowing the bait to stand apart from the main leader in a natural fashion.

The same baits itemized for the shallow approach will work with the deep-water attack. Also consider using strips of other gamefish as an added bonus. Mackerel filets or strips of smaller rockfish can be sensational at times. These offerings will catch larger rockfish. If you have ample supplies of whole squid, pin these onto a gangion. The "cods" will eat the big bait.

Large brightly colored shrimp fly rigs also take their share of rockfish. Sometimes it is better to add a whole anchovy, a chunk of squid, or a strip of mackerel as a trailer to the shrimp fly gangion.

Instead of using a shrimp fly setup, there are other little tricks you can employ to dress up the basic gangion. Fasten on strips of brightly colored cloth, colorful (deflated) balloons, or strands of fluorescent yarn. These can be fished either by themselves or with a natural bait as a trailer.

Another option is to add soft plastic trailers to the gangion hooks. Single- or double-tail grubs, tube lures, chunks of plastic worms—they'll all work at times laced onto gangions. The brighter, more opulent fluorescent colors seem to give the best results at these depths.

Another recent innovation has been to add a chemical luminescent light tube to the bottom of the gangion, usually tied above the rock cod weight. The light emitted from this chemical tube illuminates the gangion and the multiple offerings tied above it. Many anglers firmly believe the light draws rockfish into the area.

It is important to maintain contact with the bottom during a rock cod drift. Although you may be working at 300 foot depths, you may have to let out 450 feet of line to stay on the bottom. This is because of the drift of the boat. It is usually difficult due to wind and current to fish straight up and down while rock codding beyond 150 feet. So pay out line as needed to stay near the bottom with your bait.

Rock codders have also found that heavy 15 to 32 ounce jigs will often produce spectacular results, especially on bigger fish. The larger Salas, Tady, and U.F.O. models, along with DiClad, Hexbar, and Diamond Jigs are popular favorites up and down the coast. Chrome and white are preferred colors once you hit that 300 foot mark. Another tip is to add a piece of strip bait or a whole squid to the "iron" and yo-yo it off the bottom. This method also accounts for trophy bottom fish.

Be prepared to work either the gangions or the heavy jig slightly above the bottom at times. On party boats, the skipper may tell the passengers to take a few "turns" on the reel to take the bait up off the bottom. This is because the fish are being metered above the ocean floor. Private boaters should also rely upon their electronics to pinpoint similar concentrations of rockfish suspended off the ocean floor.

Fishing deep for cow cod and rockfish can be an exciting adventure. There is no telling what species lurk in these deeper environments. It can be a true potpourri for the taking. It also doesn't have to be strictly a "meat trip." These bottom dwellers are prone to eat an artificial lure. With this kind of fishing it pays to be experimental. Use quality lines and take extra care to pre-sharpen all your hooks on both the lures and the gangions. It is a long way up to the surface on some of the drops you will make. Don't give that fish a chance to throw the hook or break the line. Make no doubt about it, this will indeed be some of the best eatin' fish you will find in the Pacific!

Halibut and Other Flatfish

Halibut, both the California and Pacific varieties, are some of the toughest species to fool along our coastline. These toothy flatfish reach weights of over 40 pounds for the California halibut and hundreds of pounds for the Pacific variety. They put up a respectable fight on medium-weight gear. The challenge to halibut fishing however is less in the actual playing of the fish, but more in finding them and getting them to eat a lure or bait.

I want to highlight some of the different techniques used both in the South and in the North to take halibut. Southern Californians prospecting the bottom in Santa Monica, Newport, Mission, and San Diego Bays, the backside of Catalina Island, the Huntington Flats, and South Island at the Coronados have their favorite tactics. Halibut anglers in the San Francisco Bay Area drag the bottoms around Angel, Alcatraz, and Treasure Islands, Deep Hole, Raccoon Straits, the International Airport, and off of Candlestick Park. They too have their patented methods for nailing flatties. Further north into Oregon and Washington locations like Tillamook and Coos Bay or Port Angeles will kick out their share of big flatfish combined with a sampling of smaller relatives like the starry flounder and petrale sole.

As I delineate these regional differences, keep in mind that it pays to be experimental in this sport. South Coasters can learn from Northern fishermen and vice versa.

Evaluate all these methods and try them in your particular locale. The flatfish may be surprised to see something new!

Finding Halibut

Halibut are most active between the months of March and October, with summer being the best overall season. These fish can be taken from the surf line, beyond it, around the kelp beds, on the flats, around offshore islands, and in secluded harbors and bays.

Halibut fishing is best with a major interchange of tidal flow. A high tide is usually better than low tide for working outside waters. Experts agree that two hours before the turning tide is the best time to try for halibut.

In the bays and estuaries, the incoming tide with its exchange of clearer water is the optimum condition. High tide, slightly beyond the surf line, is similarly the prime time to look for halibut along this 6 to 10 foot depth. (In fact, it is not uncommon to see anglers on surfboards, drifting bait or lures, off the Southern beaches a few yards off the breakers!)

Halibut can be found on sandy beaches of offshore islands. Inside harbors, look for flatties around the floating bait receivers. In the winter months, head to the back beaches of quiet bays—halibut will gravitate to the warmer shallow water.

Barn Doors on Bait

Halibut typically lie semi-submerged into the sand, lazily waiting for an errant baitfish or other marine creature to pass nearby. There are occasions when these fish will suspend or even take a bait fly-lined on the surface. But, for the most part, count on finding 'buts near the bottom.

Anchovies are probably the principle bait used to fool halibut all along the coast. Sometimes live squid are also used in Southern California, along with smelt, grunion, or sardines. Northerners prefer live mudsuckers along with the 'chovy offerings. (Keep in mind that some bait shops in Southern California also sporadically keep stocks of mudsuckers on hand.)

In both regions, "brown baits" are also often used by the pros to score on the bigger "barn door" class fish topping the 20 pound mark. Tomcod, herring, queenfish, and shiner perch—fished whole and alive—are excellent baits for trophy flatties.

The slider rig is used in both areas. South Coasters usually prefer a 1/2 to 2 ounce sliding egg sinker. Northerners, because of the rushing currents, opt for sliding

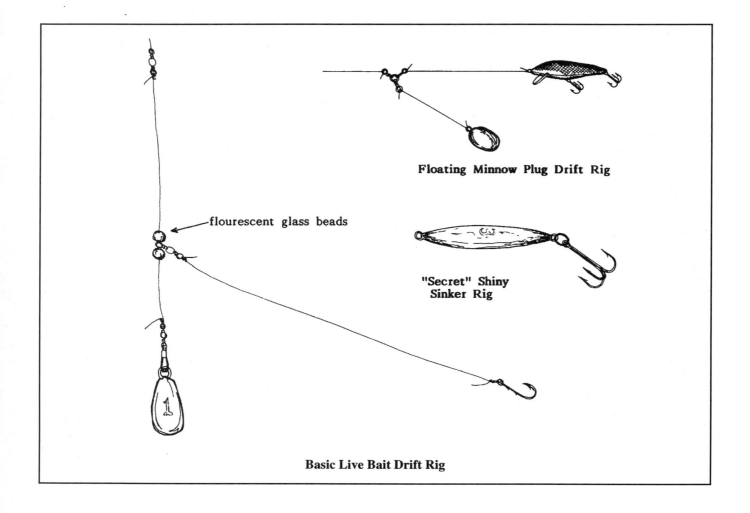

Floating Minnow Plug Drift Rig

"Secret" Shiny Sinker Rig

flourescent glass beads

Basic Live Bait Drift Rig

weights up to 12 ounces. The leader can be anywhere from 10 to 20 pound mono with a short-shank, live bait hook.

If you are using anchovies or sardines, a #1 to #4 hook should be adequate. With squid or larger brown baits, a #3/0 to #4/0 short shank live bait hook is necessary.

Southern Californians also like to fish halibut with a dropper rig basically like the one described for white sea bass fishing. A 1 to 4 ounce sinker is attached to the bottom of the rig. The sinker can be either a chrome or plain ringed model, or a spoon shape designed for easy drifting.

On this note, most of the time the halibut want a slow-moving bait. When fishing from a boat, set up slow drift patterns for the 'buts. Remember, these fish characteristically will not move too far to attack a bait. You have to bring it to them. Smaller flatfish like sand dabs, petrale sole, starry flounder, rex sole and diamond turbot also respond well to a slow-drift program.

In the northern coast, another preferred rig for halibut is the standard three-way swivel setup. But instead of using lighter 10 to 20 pound test mono leaders, Northern anglers attach a 50 pound test piece of line with a #3/0 hook. This is the patented configuration for drifting a live shiner perch for barn door halibut. Due to ripping currents in locations like San Francisco Bay, for example, be prepared to use a heavier 10 to 12 ounce torpedo or spoon sinker on a short leader to complete the three-way swivel rig.

There are a few modifications that you can make to these basic halibut rigs. First, instead of using a short-shank bait hook, substitute it with a #8 or #10 treble hook for anchovies, a #4 to #6 treble for bigger baits. Hook the baitfish through the nose or under the anal fin. The nose-hooking, I might mention, is probably best for slow-drifting, since it keeps the bait swimming fairly naturally through the water.

The treble hook may get snagged a little more frequently. But it will also provide an extra amount of insurance when setting the hook on these touchy feeders. The treble hooks should be bronze. Their color blends in better with the bait and are sharper than nickel or cadmium plated trebles.

Another secret tip is to hook two modest-sized 'chovies onto a treble hook, each on a separate barb. The commotion and flash created by two live baitfish being drifted along the bottom may be too much for even the laziest halibut to resist.

The actual "bite" itself can be perplexing and nerve-racking when a halibut decides to eat the bait. I prefer fishing the 'buts with conventional tackle, since it often helps to keep the reel in free spool following that initial "tick" or "tug" on the line. Don't overlook strip baits (frozen mackerel, squid, bonito, smelt, herring, eel, etc.). Halibut and its flatfish relatives at times will eat strip when other offerings are scarce. The same holds true for the smaller sole, turbot, and flounder species.

The trick is to be *patient.* You almost have to coax the halibut into swallowing the bait. One way to do this is to fish them with the reel out of gear. As the halibut hits the bait, start to use your fingertips and gently "roll" the spool of your reel, taking in a small portion of line. As you nudge the bait slowly away from the 'but expect the fish to pull back. Again, "roll" the spool to tease the bait away from the fish. Eventually, the halibut will mouth the bait with more aggressiveness and hopefully you will feel dull resistance on the end of the line. Now is the moment of glory! Go ahead and set, but do it in a rather cautious, "mushy" manner. Don't try to swing hard on the halibut—you may pull the bait away.

This give-and-take ritual may last well over 30 seconds from the initial "tap tap" you feel. It's a real art to entice these fish by free-spooling and "rolling" the line, but the results may be worth the patience. This technique is very much akin to "mooching" for salmon, popularized in the Pacific Northwest.

A final tip to consider is adding a trap hook to the live bait offering. Simply tie a dropper loop above the bait with a short 6 to 8 inch length of leader. Tie a small treble hook to the leader. Embed the treble into the other end of the bait away from the main hook. Although the trap setup may impede the overall lively action of the bait, better catch-to-strike ratios might result.

Flatties on Artificials

Halibut and the smaller flatfish will definitely strike an artificial lure. Here, as with bait drifting, there are Northern and Southern approaches to this dimension of the sport.

To begin with, slow-trolling at 4 to 5 knots is the name of the game. Don't expect these bottom-dwelling flatfish to swim after a lure trolled much faster than this.

Next, the object is to get the lure down so it plods along the bottom. South Coast fishermen look for smooth sandy bottoms to troll their lure. Anglers working the Central Coast from Cayucos to San Simeon look for similar sandy stretches. Northern aficionados exploring San Francisco Bay and northernmost environs prefer broken bottoms with clay and sand as prime halibut territory.

Long minnow-shaped plugs can be trolled for halibut. The Bagley Bang-O in 'chovy and mackerel finishes has been a favorite in the Bay Area, slow-trolled and bounced along the bottom. South Coast fishermen have had similar success with deeper diving spoon- billed models made by Rebel and Rapala. The slow-troll speed will be adequate to get these plugs down into the shallow flats of harbors and bays or in the 6 to 10 foot depths along the surf line.

Another interesting method is to use a three-way swivel rig to get a lightweight floating minnow plug to suspend just above the bottom on a slow-troll. Take a 2 to 4 ounce flat spoon sinker and tie it to one eye of the three-way swivel with 6 to 8 inches of leader line. On a longer length (24 to 30 inches) of 10 to 12 pound test leader, tie a floating #9 or #11-FS Rapala in silver finish. The floating plug will wiggle slightly above the bottom as the sinker drags along in the sand. This setup is terrific for working outside the surf lines or in sheltered bays and harbors.

Plastic tail-swimming lures can be similarly bottom-bounced for halibut. Here a drift usually is more effective than a slow-troll. Lunker Thumpers, Salty Magics, Mojos, Scampis, Salty Lunker Grubs, and the Scrounger will work. The squid tippet should also be used to spice up these plastic baits in a bottom-bouncing capacity. These are excellent combos to toss on light line for turbot, flounder and sole as well as the bigger halibut.

Northern anglers have also had some excellent results working the popular bucktail Hair Raiser Jigs along the bottom for halibut. South Coasters have been reluctant to use hair jigs for marine species. This is really an oversight. The slow sashaying of the deer hair in the water can be exceptionally tantalizing to finicky feeders. Hair Raisers in yellow, white, or red are proven winners for halibut.

I might add that I like to have jigs in this design for another reason. I am a strong proponent of using fish scents in the marine environment to attract saltwater species. A deer hair jig like the Hair Raiser saturated in

Berkley Strike, for instance, can be a "hot" enticement for hook-shy halibut.

Shiny spoons can also be slowly trolled along the bottom or fan-casted from an anchored or drifting boat for halibut. The Kastmaster, Krocadile, Diamond Jig, Nordic, Crippled Herring, and smaller Hexbar designs account for many legal-sized flatties during the season. The important thing is to keep the lure slowly plodding along the bottom where the halibut are lurking. Use the smaller spoons for turbot, sole, and flounder.

Finesse Flatfish!

Halibut and the related smaller flatfish are one of the truly fine-eating fish that you can seek along the Pacific Coast. They are very touchy feeders and require much finessing especially if you are using bait. Don't force these fish to bite. They have a tendency to "mouth" the bait and must often be teased or coaxed to more aggressively eat the offering. Once hooked, take your time playing in the fish. Don't try to initiate some quick, spectacular short pumps in an effort to "stroke" the flatfish right in. Instead, maintain constant even pressure allowing the fish to fight the drag. Always gaff halibut and larger sole, turbot, or flounder broadside against the flat surface.

Shark!

For a long time sharks and rays were generally relegated to the category of "trash fish" as far as marine anglers were concerned. In recent years, an increasing number of saltwater enthusiasts have experienced the thrill and excitement of fishing these toothy gamefish. More and more anglers are looking to sharks and rays as an alternative to other types of big game fishing.

Not all sharks are sought by the weekend fishermen. Some, like the shovel nose, are basically nuisances. Others, such as the leopard and the thresher, are not only fished for their fighting qualities but for culinary reasons as well. Broiled, barbecued, and smoked shark meat, from some of the prime species, is often compared to such fine table fare as broadbill swordfish. As more anglers come into contact with these predators and try shark meat, fishing for these gamefish will continue to grow in popularity.

Some of the sharks I'll discuss in this chapter such as the thresher and the leopard range from the Mexican to the Canadian borders. Others, like the mako, are primarily found in the South, while the six and seven gill variety are found in colder Northern waters.

There are basically three dominant ways to fish shark: 1) still-fishing at anchor; 2) trolling; or 3) chum-slick drifting. The first strategy is most commonly practiced in San Francisco Bay. The latter two tactics work on a variety of species when you hunt sharks in open sea.

Bay Area Sharkin'

Anglers in the San Francisco Bay Area set their sights primarily on six and seven gills, soupfin, and leopard sharks. The "big boys" are the seven gills, also known as "cow sharks." These sharks can reach weights of over 200 pounds in the cold waters of the Bay. The "soupys" push close to 100 pounds while a big leopard tops out at about 40 pounds.

In contrast to shark fishing in the Southland, most Bay Area anglers prefer to fish them at anchor. It's possible to fish all the way down to 90 foot depths probing the deep channels around Marin, Angel Island, The Bay Bridge, Hunter's Point, and the Dumbarton Bridge. So, it is important for the private boaters to have a decent depth finder and carry plenty of anchor line. Most of the action, however, will occur in the 20 to 60 foot level in the channels. Occasionally it is also possible to catch sharks from the bank in the Bay, primarily leopards and small, less desirable dogfish.

Angelo Cuanang is considered a major authority on this Bay Area sharkin'. The six and seven gills will eat a large offering. He recommends using a chunk of tail section of a dogfish, a small shark locally called a stickle back. A strip of striper belly or actual salmon stomach is another prime bait for these "big boys." If you want to really get elaborate, try a combination of a strip of fish topped with fresh dead squid. It will take anywhere from 1 to 3 pounds of sinker to keep the bait on the bottom if the deep currents are ripping.

Cuanang notes that it is important to match your tackle to the size of your quarry. When it comes to 100 to 300 pound seven gills, it's time to bring out the "artillery." His basic rig consists of a reel in the Penn 4/0 class size. He fills it with 200 yards of .025 diameter single strand stainless steel wire backed with heavy Dacron line. His typical rod for monster bay sharks like this is a 20 pound IGFA big game rod.

The best time to fish the "big boys" according to Cuanang is in that 1 to 2 hour span at the height or the bottom of the tidal flow. Occasionally the six and seven gills will hit a chunk of bait on the drift. But most Bay Area shark specialists feel that better catches result from anchoring on the edge of the deep channels. The best fishing

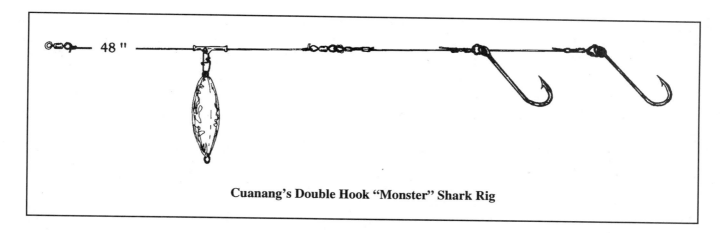

Cuanang's Double Hook "Monster" Shark Rig

for the larger seven gill sharks is during the spring and fall months. Soupfins are taken most frequently during the spring and on through summer.

As for the actual setup for hooking these larger offerings, Cuanang also has designed a rather specialized rig. He starts by tying a #3/0 swivel to a 4 foot length of 120 pound test monofilament. He then slips onto the large diameter mono a rubber sliding sinker sleeve. This allows the heavy sinker to easily slide up and down along the 4 foot leader. Next, Cuanang attaches a 24 to 30 inch length of 200 pound test piano or 49 strand braided wire to a lower swivel. (This swivel is also used to butt off the sliding sleeve.) Tied to the other end of this leader is a 10/0 to 13/0 Eagle Claw #LE9011 welded eye Titan Ocean hook.

Medium-range conventional reels that hold 300 yards of 25 to 30 pound test mono filled with aluminum spools are perfect on the smaller sharks. A medium to heavy 7 to 8 foot single-piece live bait rod is equally suitable for this kind of sharkin'.

The 10 to 40 pound sharks including the leopards, soupfins, and dogfish can be taken on more conventional, commercially made shark leaders consisting of sturdy 50 to 60 pound test wire and a single hook and swivel. A basic sliding sinker setup is perfect. Use frozen squid, smelt, anchovies, grunion, grass, or ghost shrimp, and mudsuckers. At certain times of the year, Bay Area bait vendors will also sell a slimy sculpin-like fish called a "midshipman" which makes an excellent shark tantalizer.

Trolling and Drifting for Sharks

Once out in open water, sharks can also be pursued in more traditional ways by either trolling or drifting through a chum slick. The trolling technique is used primarily for

100 to 300 pound makos or thresher sharks. Big game 50 to 80 pound class gear is necessary for this slow-down approach. Usually, the shark experts prefer to slow-troll a whole bonito, mackerel or squid. Fresh bonito or mackerel is the best ticket. If you have to rely upon frozen bonito or macks, try to remove the backbone of the fish before pinning it on a hook. This will make the bait more flexible and lifelike in the water.

These baits are often pinned onto a unique trolling feather combination. This is made by running a heavy wire leader through standard brightly colored 15 mm or larger tuna feather. An Eagle Claw #LE9011 or #LE9014 big game hook is attached to the wire. A double-trap effect is constructed by attaching a stronger hook of about equal size to a short wire cable to the rear. This stinger wire is then tied into the loop formed by the cable on the lead hook. Crimped metal sleeves secure the wire cables together. The mouth of the dead bonito or mackerel is stapled shut to keep the bait from spinning on a slow-troll.

Some shark fishermen also use a downrigger to drag their baits into deeper strike zones. Sharks will lie out in the deep canyons and sub-marine ledges. The downrigger gets a slowly trolled mackerel or bonito into this strata.

Makos will sometimes strike an artificial lure trolled at modest speeds of about seven knots. It is not uncommon to nail one of these missiles while trolling a large tuna or marlin jig. The super husky, #CD-18 sinking Rapala lure has also accounted for a few prominent mako tallies. Threshers will typically smack at the lure with their tails and get foul-hooked in the jig. A tail-wrapped thresher, even on heavy string, could provide the angler with a battle lasting many hours.

A highly efficient means to both locate and catch sharks is to use a controlled chumming program. East

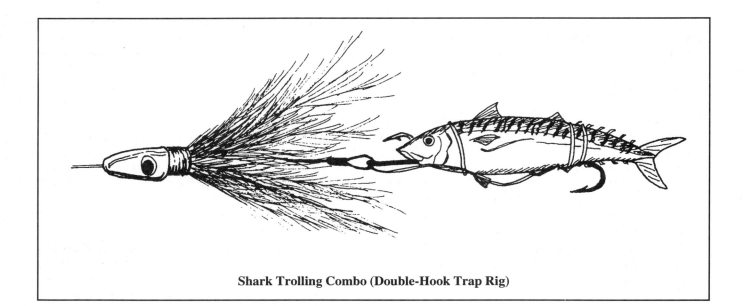

Shark Trolling Combo (Double-Hook Trap Rig)

Coast fishermen are frequently without the benefit of live bait. In its place, they grind up small bunker baitfish, place the ground meat into drums, and gradually disperse it over the side of the boat. This has the effect of leaving an aromatic chum slick on top of the water. The gamefish are attracted to the film and move up the line toward the anglers in the stern.

West Coast sharkers have implemented a similar procedure to lure makos, threshers, and blue sharks to the boat. Instead of using bunker minnows, take relatively fresh mackerel, bonito, brown baits, smelt, or squid—in any combination—and mash up the blend in a meat grinder. Freeze it down in a milk carton to form a block of chum.

Next, when you motor into prime open-water shark territory (e.g. the La Jolla Trench, Oceanside, or Monterey Bay) peel away the wax milk carton and place the block of ground chum in a wire fish basket. These are widely sold for storing your panfish catch. Tie a rope to the handle of the basket and drag it with the chum block behind the boat. The block will slowly defrost, leaving an oily slick behind it. As an added enticement, empty a bottle of saltwater Berkley Strike onto the frozen block. Also, every so often, toss out some larger pieces of squid, mackerel, 'chovy, or bonito to spice up the chum line.

As an alternative, many landings and bait stores sell a five pound block of frozen squid. You can place this in the basket. It will not work as well as the ground fish meat, but it might suffice in a pinch, especially if you pour on some of the Strike compound for extra effect.

Once a shark shows in the chum line, don't be surprised if others follow. It may seem like all of a sudden the ocean becomes "alive" with these denizens of the deep coming from out of nowhere. This provides additional excitement for the hunt.

You can use anything from 10 to 12 pound ultralight saltwater outfits on up to 50 to 80 pound string and marlin-style gear. But, you will need about 10 to 15 feet of 60 to 100 pound monofilament or heavy stainless steel wire for a leader. The Eagle Claw #LE9011, #LE9014, or #LE9015 big game hooks in #8/0 to #12/0 sizes are perfect for fly-lining a slab of bait back into the chum slick.

Sharks can be tough fighters. The makos (also termed bonito sharks) and the threshers with their sickle-like tails will sometimes put on some pretty spectacular surface fireworks. The makos will often skyrocket to the surface and turn a cartwheel in the air.

Handling Sharks

Let's never forget that these are potentially dangerous critters. This is true for even the smaller 20 pound leopards and blues. These fish have prominent teeth that can indeed inflict injury to the less-than-careful angler. Many anglers release sharks at boat side by cutting the wire leader.

If you want to land sharks, Angelo Cuanang recommends using a homemade bang stick to subdue these gamefish before they are brought on board. The 12 or 20 gauge shotgun charge is detonated against the shark while the fish is still in the water alongside the boat. The bang stick has been utilized for years by scuba divers who encounter sharks. They are usually homemade by the divers.

Instead of owning a bang stick, a fish billy and a gaff are your next best options. Saltwater pros recommend sticking the makos right behind the front dorsal fin. A similar swipe of the gaff works best with the threshers, but be careful of the tail. Thresher sharks can whip that awesome tail quickly with great force, slashing violently at would-be targets. It wouldn't be a bad idea to perhaps carry a flying gaff, to keep the shark some distance from the boat. If possible, avoid gaffing the shark on its side. The fish can put up a lot of twisting action, making it tough to handle in this position.

Most shark hunters recommend bleeding the catch almost immediately after the fish is boated. This serves to keep the meat from becoming tainted.

Bat Rays

There is a small fraternity of saltwater anglers who like to play tug-o-war with bruiser bat rays. San Diego and Newport Harbors, Mission Bay, Santa Barbara, the Elkhorn Slough at Moss Landing, and the Monterey Peninsula are only a few spots to fish for "mud marlin."

"Bats" can range up to well over 100 pounds in weight. They generate tremendous resistance in the water once they start flopping those wings. They will hang tight to the bottom, occasionally planing to the surface. It takes some stout gear, preferably 40 pound test mono or heavier, teamed with strong live bait rods.

Bat rays can be caught both from the bank and from boats. The channels leading into sheltered harbors are good areas to try as well as the territory around floating bait receivers. These fish are nocturnal feeders with much of the best action occurring after dark. They are frequently taken as incidental catches during the daylight hours by anglers still-fishing or drifting bait in these bays.

If I had to pick one setup to use for fishing big bat rays, it would be a sliding egg sinker. Use anywhere from 2 to 5 ounces of weight depending upon the current. Butt the sinker with a heavy-duty ball-bearing swivel. Clip on a 3 to 5 foot wire leader (60 to 80 pound test) with a single #6/0 to #10/0 hook. Double-hook a whole frozen squid onto the leader and wait for the ensuing battle.

Other options include a slab of cut mackerel or bonito. Clams, bloodworms, shrimp, and even bloody chicken livers will produce at times. To avoid bait-stealers, consider adding a rear booby trap hook, similar to the trolling rig I mentioned in the previous section.

Sharks and rays are terrific alternatives for the weekend angler wishing to experience the thrill of big game fishing at a fraction of the cost associated with bill fishing and other exotic species. Sharks can put up a respectable fight and their potential as a fine food fish is slowly being discovered.

Treat these marine predators with respect. Even the most seemingly innocuous species can inflict a serious wound or do damage to the inside of a boat. Be careful with "jaws," and pass the word along—shark fishing is great sport!

Big Game Fishing Lessons

From late July through mid November, private yacht owners and charter boat operators prospect the offshore waters of Southern California for striped marlin. Further south, in Mexican territory, striped marlin action intensifies from May through October. "Stripes," unlike their larger blue or black cousins, range somewhere between 100 and 175 pounds on the average off the West Coast. A 200 pound specimen is a real wall hanger, though catches have been recorded topping well over the 300 pound mark in this region.

Striped Marlin Basics

In Southern California, most of the striped marlin fishing occurs from San Diego to the far south, and northward around San Clemente and Catalina Islands, extending further north occasionally to the outside of the Channel Islands. In Baja, the resort town of Cabo San Lucas and the Buena Vista area are the centers of billfish activity along with numerous smaller fly-in "fish ranches" outside these two ports. There are basically two ways that West Coast anglers fish for marlin: 1) trolling and 2) live bait drifting or casting.

Stripers on the Troll

Perhaps the simplest strategy for the less experienced marlin fisherman to employ is a basic trolling program. You will need a quality reel in the 4/0 class. A Penn 113HL, 45GLS, or International 30T are perfect reels for stripers. It should hold 300 to 500 yards of 30 to 50 pound string. In recent years, most local pros have switched to premium grade mono in this line category. A smaller number of anglers still prefer the more expensive and less stretchable Micron fabric line. Either will suffice. The rod should be somewhere in an IGFA 20 to 50 pound range with roller guides and tip-top.

Many Southern California marlin hunters prefer to fight the fish standing at the rail instead of from a fighting chair. In contrast, Baja skippers almost invariably prefer to have their customers work from a chair. The lighter 30 pound outfits are perfect for this kind of "stand-up fishing" combined with either a reel harness or, minimally, a rod butt apron. Heavier gear in the 80 pound class will usually wear the angler down from a stand-up position. This more traditional magnum-sized outfit performs best from a fighting chair.

Years ago the common way to troll for stripes off the West Coast was to drag a bridled fresh or frozen flying fish. This tactic is practically extinct. It has been replaced with the so-called brightly colored "psychedelic" marlin jigs. These are really jumbo versions of big tuna feathers. But instead of having feathers, they have highly opulent plastic skirts laced over multi-colored faceted beads. Marlin jigs in this genre are sold commercially rigged with either a single- or double-hook trap setup on 100 to 200 pound test monofilament leader.

I might add that the size of the hooks and the diameter of the leaders may vary from model to model. This is because of the diverse swimming action that you can get from the different kinds of jigs. The object for the manufacturer is to create the best swimming jig possible combined with the right configuration of hooks and leader material.

Striped marlin jigs are commonly sold by such regionally favorite names as Sevenstrand, California Lures, Door Knobs, and Zucker. These are expensive lures, costing anywhere from $15 to $60 for a winning marlin jig. Many models have considerable handiwork involved in their construction. Also, without fail, take a file to the stock hooks and hone them to perfection.

The time-proven color schemes for jigs used by the best striped marlin skippers are as follows: green and yellow mackerel, green and yellow, black and green ("Mean Joe Green"), black and purple, red and yellow ("bleeding mackerel"), and red and black ("goat fish").

As you would with trolling feathers for tuna, plan on making changes in color patterns throughout the day. Consider starting with darker colors in the early morning (e.g. black and purple) and switching to more brilliant tones by midday (e.g. red and yellow). Don't become locked into one favorite pattern trip after trip. Stripes here on the West Coast are quite unpredictable. What works today may be totally "dead" tomorrow as far as jig color and models are concerned. (I'll elaborate further on jig color shortly.)

Most trolling is done behind the boat through the third and fifth wake. As strange as this may sound, each vessel seems to troll differently. Sometimes the prop wash is significantly unique from one style of craft to another. Hence, the same model jig will actually "swim" differently behind each type of boat. But staying within the third to fifth wake will probably be a safe distance of line to let out in dragging the marlin jig. Some boats are said to get bit "short" while others are known for getting bit "long." Charter boat skippers usually know precisely how much line to let out for the optimal trolling distance on their particular boat. Experiment to find out which style is best for you and your own vessel.

Many boats are equipped with outriggers. These long extension poles allow the angler to clip his line to the outrigger tip and thus troll to the outside of the boat's wake. This is helpful in setting up a diverse trolling pattern with three or more rods. The fisherman can then spread his or her jigs across the wake more evenly to cover wider strike territory. A common ploy is to run three lines off the stern in rod holders each at different lengths behind the boat, then have two additional outfits clipped to the outriggers. When a marlin strikes one of the outside lines, it will snap free from the outrigger pole, permitting the angler to set up on the fish.

In this part of the world, marlin trolling is usually done at 7 to 9 knots. The boat pilot has to "gun" the throttle for 4 to 5 seconds following the strike to more easily drive the hook home into the fish's hard mouth. It will also help at times to vary trolling directions while keeping your speed relatively constant. As with any type of trolling program, it pays to be a little experimental. Also, don't be surprised if a good-sized mako or thresher shark decides to beat a marlin to your jig!

Stripes on Bait

A more challenging approach to corralling one of these prized billfish is to try to bait a marlin. The trick is to "make" mackerel. You have to have either a "diaper bag" style bait tank or a built-in one with proper water circula-

tion. The mackerel—either Spanish or greenback—can be jigged from under floating kelp paddies, around oil platforms, or sometimes near the docks and bait receivers. A medium 3/4 to 1 1/2 pound mackerel is perfect for stripes. Save the larger "macks" in case you run across a broadbill swordfish.

The typical live bait outfit consists of a conventional like a Penn GLS25, 505, or International 12T filled with 30 to 40 pound test mono. The rod is usually a thick-walled 6 to 7 foot live bait action with a special marlin tip-top. (This is basically a modified roller guide capable of handling the big diameter monofilament used with live bait leaders.)

You can purchase commercially tied marlin live bait leaders. These are comprised of about an 8 foot length of 80 to 150 pound test monofilament. Tie on a heavy-duty ball bearing snap-swivel and clip the snap into the loop of the pre-tied leader. Or tie your main line only to a strong ball bearing swivel (without the snap) and hitch the entire 8 foot leader through the eyelet and the loop. (This is similar to hitching a simple snelled hook through a swivel eyelet without using any additional knots.)

Many experts such as longtime big game fisherman, Ron De La Mare, recommends another alternative. De La Mare prefers 30 pound mono for his primary line. Then using a nail knot to join two strands of monofilament, he splices on a 10 to 12 foot section of 80 pound mono. Next, he ties the 80 pound test to a sturdy ball bearing swivel (no snap). Then, to the other eye of the swivel he runs a 3 to 5 foot strand of 125 pound test monofilament.

The 80 pound test spliced to the 30 pound test main line serves as a shock leader. By using the nail knot, the 80 pound test mono is easily reeled up through the rod guides and is equally easy to cast. The 125 pound test connected to the swivel handles the abrasion against the marlin and its bill.

It is practically impossible to actually cast the commercially tied live bait leaders because of the extraordinarily long 8 foot piece of monofilament. The angler will have to gently strip off line as he lowers these long leaders with a baited mackerel into the water. With De La Mare's specialized leader, you can actually make an overhand cast on feeding fish. Skippers call this the "drop-back" strategy.

The mackerel themselves should be hooked through the nostrils. It is best to have a live bait outfit all set up and ready to go. Have a mackerel hooked and resting in the bait tank with the leader dangling over the side. You're now ready for action if you encounter a "feeder."

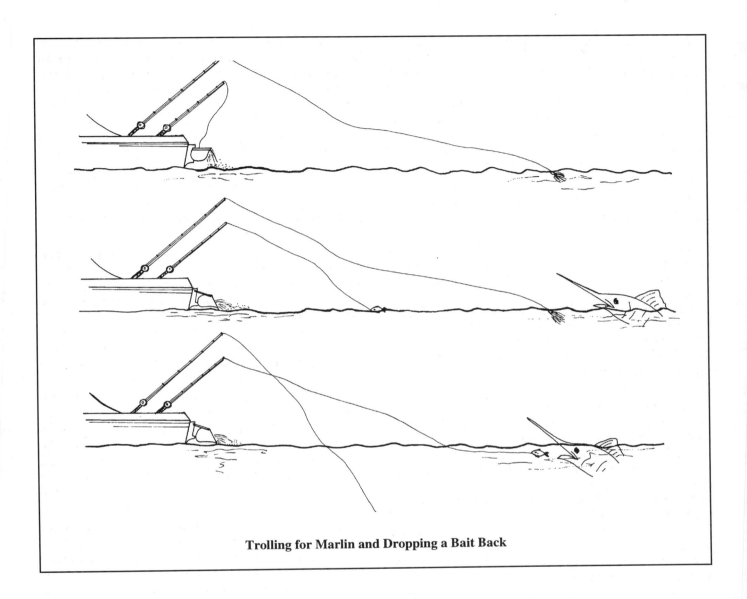

Trolling for Marlin and Dropping a Bait Back

Another option is to always have a live bait hooked and resting in the bait tank. As you troll with the jigs, stripes will frequently come up to the stern and slash at the lures without taking one. This is the perfect time to instantly drop a live mackerel over the stern to the feeding fish.

The jigs serve as a "teaser" of sorts to draw the interest of the marlin. The live mackerel dropped directly between the jigs is often too tempting for the stripes to pass up. Be prepared for a vicious strike with this strategy!

You can also slowly drift or slow-troll with a live mackerel with either the lighter bait outfit or the heavier trolling rod and reel. This is commonly done only in areas where the marlin are "showing." Throttle way down, dragging the mackerel at no more than 1 or 2 knots.

Use Your Eyeballs!

The most accomplished marlin fishermen in Southern California and Baja rely upon good binoculars more than their tackle. They are constantly on the lookout for any "signs of life." Working in 64(+) degree, clear, deep blue water, they will continually scan for birds on a "pick," i.e. dipping and diving on baitfish. This is a good sign that marlin are nearby, pushing meatballs of bait to the surface.

Veteran West Coast billfish skippers also use an interesting typology to identify the feeding mode of the striped marlin. Each classification requires a slightly different tactic.

1 *"Feeders"*: These are basically striped marlin thrashing through a school of bait. Birds will usually be in the vicinity picking at the baitfish. You can troll on the perimeter of the feeding activity or cast a live mackerel directly into the commotion. Some captains actually like to run over the top of the feeders and drop a live bait at the precise spot where the fish were last seen. Presumably the marlin have momentarily sounded but may still be directly under the bait.

2. *"Tailers"*: Skippers also call these "eyeball fish." They are usually seen down swell with their large tails sticking up. You must get down swell on a tailer and put the bait or trolled lure in front of the fish.

3 *"Sleepers"*: This is an interesting phenomena to witness firsthand. The marlin appear to be listless as if they are actually sleeping. You will typically spot the tail and sometimes the dorsal fin or the "hump" that the dorsal folds into. Cast live mackerel on the sleepers aiming close to the head of the fish. Pinpoint accuracy on the cast and skillful boat handling are critical when maneuvering on a "sleeper."

4. *"Jumpers"*: Marlin seen putting on a display of free-form aerial fireworks are not always in a feeding mode. These are termed "jumpers." Chasing after jumpers can often be a "sucker's bite," with the fish showing no interest in trolled lures or live bait. Many skippers refuse to run on a "jumper."

Mike Callan, a longtime tackle sales representative and renown tournament angler from Long Beach, California offers another perspective in regard to "jumpers." Callan notes that "often times a jumper is on a 'meatball' of bait, using its body and tail to create a concussion. This will scatter the tightly grouped anchovies which are herded by 3 to 6 striped marlin underwater. An angler should always run to the jumper, attempt to estimate the location of the fish from last appearance and troll the area with jigs or bait. The chances of getting a strike using this technique are significantly improved."

Precision Is Critical

You can experience big game fishing, West Coast style at its finest when you start chasing striped marlin. The fish are more readily available in Baja than in Southern California. It requires excellent boat handling as well as angling skill to land a marlin in these waters. Hooks must be perfectly honed. This is of paramount importance. The tackle and especially the reel drags must be in precise working order.

In Baja and Southern California, the Marlin fishing is not for small boats in the 16-20 foot class. It is not uncommon to be out well over 50 miles from the beach for striped marlin. Full navigational and electronic equipment is strongly recommended. The sea can be rough and unpredictable. Private yacht owners new to the sport may benefit by spending some time with a veteran skipper or fishing on a charter boat to become more familiar with striped marlin hunting, West Coast style.

Black and Blue Marlin: More Trolling Lessons

Besides striped marlin, their big brute cousins, the blacks and the blues, usually are caught by trolling large jigs. Blue and black marlin are much tougher than the smaller stripers, averaging anywhere from 200 to 600 pounds. Blues and blacks pushing the 1,000 pound mark—so called granders—have been caught in Baja waters.

Pulling lures of this genre can be more complicated than it seems. There is a definite rationale which underlies the "science" of selecting the right marlin jig the accomplished skipper, deckhand, or angler decides to troll behind the boat whether it is targeting stripers, blues, or blacks.

Let's examine some of the variables which experts consider when fishing for marlin off Southern California and Baja California, Mexico. Some of these men have also served as instructors on our Eagle Claw Big Game Schools.

Head Shapes

The design of the head portion of the marlin trolling lure is perhaps the most significant variable the experts evaluate when choosing which jig to troll. Head shapes can be basically divided into three major categories: 1) swimming; 2) straight-running; and 3) pusher designs.

Swimming Heads. The slight concave nose section of the swimming head helps this model to kind of sashay through the water. Popular West Coast manufacturers such as Seven Strand, Zucker, and California Lures market jigs in this style. "Swimmers" can be typically pulled at 4 to 15 knots. Most models will exhibit a 6 to 12 inch lateral action which gives the illusion that the lure is "swimming" from side to side.

Straight-Running Heads. These models exemplified by California Lures original Koga Head design have a flat nose combined with somewhat of a keel-shaped underbelly. These jigs are excellent for high-speed trolling in the 12 to 15 knot range.

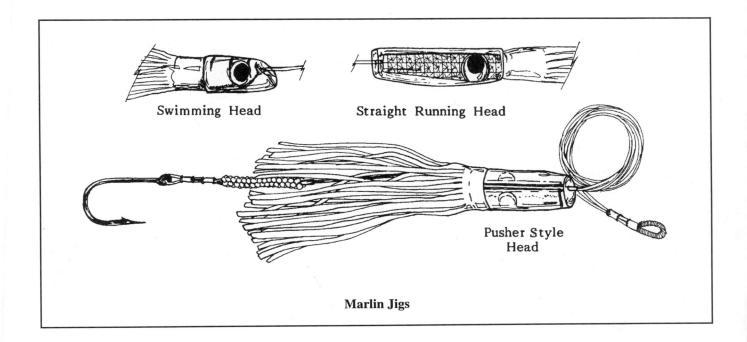

Swimming Head

Straight Running Head

Pusher Style Head

Marlin Jigs

Pusher-Style Heads. These jigs have enjoyed considerable popularity in the West in the past few years. Sevenstrand's Flathead Pusher series exemplifies this head design. As the "pusher" is dropped behind the stern, it will initially rise to the surface and grab some air then dive again. During this rise-and-sink process, the lure will leave a stream of bubbles, skippers refer to as a "smoke trail."

Most veteran charter boat captains, like Tom Schlauch of the Dreamer out of Long Beach, California, develop a particular preference for one head shape over another. This is usually based on the conditions they recurrently encounter year after year. "I like the pusher head," observes Schlauch. "I want a lot of air and bubbles in the wake when I pull a jig. If it doesn't leave a trail of bubbles as it goes down, I won't use it. I won't pull a 'clean' jig."

Much of Schlauch's preference for the pusher design is simply due to the fact that the marlin are not typically in overabundance in Southern California and Baja. Hence, it may take some minor commotion from the bait to attract and interest the fish.

However, this skipper is also quick to point out that other head designs have specific application and should not be overlooked. "For example," notes Schlauch, "too many of our West Coast marlin are 'eyeball' fish—that is, you have to be on the look out for them, then run hard at 15 knots to troll the jig by the fish. This is when you switch

to a straight-running head like the Koga to keep the lure in the water."

Similarly, longtime Southern California tackle dealer and big game specialist Ron De La Mare emphasizes that the angler must experiment with different jig head shapes as they are trolled behind a specific boat. "You must determine which jig pulls best on which boat," says De La Mare. "For instance, when I'm on someone else's boat, I always watch to see what jigs the skipper or crew put out so I can find out which head shape trolls best for that boat." Like Schlauch, De La Mare is also cautious not to get into a rut by employing only one style of jig on the troll. The signs of marine life are one of the things he will look for in deciding which lure to drag.

"The thing is, on days where there are no signs of tailers, feeders, birds, bait, or when there is general inactivity, you can use a fast-moving lure with a bubble stream to cover more territory, "claims De La Mare. "However, once I see some sign of activity and I feel I'm in the prime fish area, I then throttle down and switch to a slow-swimming jig to more thoroughly cover this zone."

Most West Coast skippers do not mix jig styles when trolling, because each of the major head shapes requires a particular boat speed for proper action. They will, however, often put out an array of "pushers" in a variety of sizes and lengths.

Size

The overall length of the marlin jig is another variable Western anglers consider in selecting the proper lure for the different marlin species. Most fishermen seem to agree that the smaller jigs in the 9 to 11 inch length range work best for stripes. Models such as the "3.5" Zucker, California Lure's "Runner" and Sevenstrand's 1200 to 1220 series are currently favorite West Coast models scaled down for stripes.

In contrast, anglers looking for bigger blues or the rarer black marlin commonly troll longer lures up to 16 inches with a larger bulkier head. The Zucker "5.5" and "7.5," California Lure's "Blue Runner", and Sevenstrand's "PR-7" are commonly dragged for blacks and blues.

But here again, as with most angling, nothing is etched in stone. "I've watched big blues come in and bite little jigs pulled down the center," relates Captain Schlauch. Similarly, in my own experience, I have had striped marlin readily attack two 15 mm tuna feathers stacked on top of each other.

There can also be variation between similar jig head shapes with regard to overall weight of the lure. Some models are made with a weighted head which forces the lure to stay under the surface longer. A typical weighted striped marlin jig weighs in at about 11 ounces. In contrast, an unweighted model in similar proportions may weigh only 5 ounces. The weighted jig creates more of a "smoke trail" behind the lure. The unweighted version allows the jig to "pop" more often, generating greater surface commotion.

Color

Jig color is sometimes felt to be as important as head design. Based on my informal survey of skippers, anglers, and manufacturers, there appears to be some consensus as to which color schemes work best in the West.

Noted author and manufacturer Charlie Davis of Sevenstrand reports that the most popular colors in marlin jigs used for Southern California and Baja are goatfish (pink-yellow), dorado (green-yellow), bleeding mackerel (red-yellow), and basic mackerel (yellow-dull green).

"In the past few years," says Davis, "we have also found marlin fishermen trolling two other more subtle colors. The "Mean Joe" (black-green) and sablefish (purple-black) seem to work especially well out here in the late afternoons."

Captain Schlauch is somewhat more emphatic with regard to which colors he recommends on his boat. "I'll put anything in the water as long as it's mackerel or dorado colored," observes Schlauch. "Dorado are found worldwide. It is an absolutely staple form of prey for all marlin species."

Ron De La Mare, on the other hand, feels that a predominance of reds and yellows in the complexion of a jig is essential for getting bit further south in Baja waters. "Red and red-yellow combinations," notes De La Mare," are the primary Baja marlin colors. It's what they seem to bite best. If I give a Mexican deckhand a number of jigs to put out, invariably they always select the ones with red or yellow in them."

Interestingly, the issue of bright versus overcast skies seems to be down-played by these experts. Most will try a darker color in the early dawn hours or under cloudy skies. However, they will similarly drag the identical patterns during the bright afternoon sun if the fish have any history of eating a certain color scheme at that time of day.

It would seem, then, that the "confidence factor" plays an important role in deciding which color marlin jig to select. "Quite often," comments De La Mare, "the hot jig color at the moment in Southern California is based more on the frequency that the lure is being dragged rather than its specific coloration. If two or three fish are caught in Southern California on one particular color jig, then every marlin fishermen in the area seems to troll that color."

Try Different Strategies!

It is evident that although there is a "science" of sorts in selecting the correct marlin jig, this is far from an "exact" science. Clearly it pays to be somewhat experimental in your selection process.

First, assess the prevailing water conditions. Is the water flat and calm, choppy, or with swells? Next, focus on your boat's particular wake and trolling speed. Then try to match the head shape of the marlin jig to these conditions so it drags properly in the water. If it's rough and windy, be prepared to switch to a heavier head to keep the lure down in the water longer.

Also, for West Coast trolling, the jig should be pulled through the third to fifth "hump" formed by the boat wake. The lure should plane in the bottom third of the "hump" for maximum effectiveness.

Next, at least initially match size of the jig to the size of the query—smaller models for stripes, larger versions for blues and blacks. But again, don't hesitate to scale up or down if you fail to get bit after a moderate amount of time.

Finally, work with the most popular color schemes as noted by the experts. However, be most flexible here, switching colors intermittently until some sort of pattern can be established.

If after assessing all these variables your jigs still fail to get bit, there is one more rather obscure option. Remove all the hooks from 3 or 4 of your lures and put them out across the stern. Although "teasers" are seldom used in the West, this "school of teasers" can often generate some terrific results if you are working an area where you are sighting marlin activity.

With this ploy, the trick is to have a live bait hooked and ready to throw. One person must keep a steady eye on the hookless jigs as the boat moves through the area. If a fish comes up to smack the lure, quickly shoot a bait down the stern and reel in the jigs.

Whatever effective trolling patterns you decipher, remember they may only apply for that particular trip. With marlin fishing, tomorrow is always another day.

Advanced Billfish Strategies

Checking the Jigs

Bill Miyagawa is the owner of Zucker Lures in Oceanside, California. He is a highly regarded angler specializing in trophy pelagic species. According to Miyagawa, as rudimentary as this seems, the weekend fisherman often fails to intermittently check his jigs when trolling for marlin. You must pull a jig that is not spinning," he emphasizes, "not fouled with grass, and not jumping out of the water." Miyagawa feels that any slight spin on the trolled jig will dramatically impair its effectiveness when it comes to getting bit.

He points out that subtle things can also generate a spinning effect with the lures if they are not frequently monitored. For example, a change in boat direction or an increase in wind and wave chop can all of a sudden make the jigs spin.

Besides making routine checks for proper alignment, Miyagawa recommends using a simple ball-bearing swivel to eliminate the potential for jig spin. "Always use a ball-bearing swivel," he notes. "Other swivels just bind too much, creating line twist. Invest in good ball bearing types. Check to make sure they are not binding due to rust. They might look great on the outside, but may foul up due to wear. Make sure the swivel turns well."

Two-Man Casting

The late Don McAdams is still the all-tackle world record holder for black sea bass. He was also an expert live bait fisherman when it came to catching striped marlin on the West Coast. McAdams liked to implement a two-man casting system, working from the bow, when a visual sighting of marlin occurs. His strategy is fairly simple to understand.

The first angler should cast a bait such as a mackerel or sardine underhand and on the inside of the fish as it swims parallel to the boat. If you envision the marlin's spike to be at the 12:00 position, the first man's cast should land at approximately 1:00.

The second angler in the bow is usually the better caster. He will make an overhand lob cast so that the bait lands further from the boat on the other side of the fish at the 10:00 position.

"The object then," according to McAdams, "is to cast about 10 feet in front of the marlin, because these fish are not able to see that well straight ahead." Then with two anglers casting in this manner, you will have a wide spread in the presentation with the fish looking in both lateral directions.

McAdams further explains that the livelier and faster baits swimming in the tanks will invariably get bit best with this method. "In fact," he relates, "one of the things we learned on the boat I fish was that it is best to leave one bait hooked and soaking in the bow tank at all times. I found out that the bait which remains hooked, swimming in the tank, would actually swim better when casted later on. This was perhaps due to the fact that this bait would not be in as much immediate shock as the one you randomly grab from the tank, hook, then cast."

A Basic Color Set

Curt Dills is a longtime fishing tackle sales representative and big game angler from Southern California. He is a firm believer in trolling a basic set of colors to maximize the opportunity for a jig strike. "The biggest thing that catches me more marlin," says Dills, "is proper color selection. The whole key to my success is using the same basic four-color lure set trip after trip."

Dills' recommends the following array of jig colors to cover most conditions encountered from Cabo San Lucas to Catalina Island: 1) green and yellow, 2) green and black, 3) orange, yellow and black; and 4) either red and white or black and purple.

"This is my basic set," says Dills. "If one or more of these jig colors gets bit more than the others, I'll pull more or all of that particular color." Interestingly, this marlin expert fishes this combination all through the season irrespective of species, climate, or water color.

"It amazing," notes Dills, "how the marlin can lock into one of the odd ball colors like orange, yellow and black, and that will be the only thing they'll hit. I've been in Cabo San Lucas for instance, where you put out all four colors and the fish will strike only one for the entire day."

Matching Jigs

Bill Beebe Jr. is the son of one of the foremost billfish photographers in the world and an excellent fisherman in his own right. Beebe's theory on trolling jigs varies somewhat from Dills' approach. He firmly believes that it is imperative that all the lures dragged behind the boat are nearly identical.

"For example, I'll routinely troll four Zucker #5.5 or #7 jigs," says Beebe. "You want to be trolling the same jigs by size, model, and brand so that the marlin think it's a school of identical baitfish. Generally, a school of baitfish will all swim the same."

Thus, Beebe is careful not to mix and match his jigs when setting up a trolling program. For this expert, pulling two different types of marlin jigs is like trying to convince the fish that there is a mixed smorgasbord of bait such as sardines and mackerel swimming together. As for lure color, he puts minimal emphasis here, again feeling that identical size and swimming action are more critical variables.

Beebe employs this strategy when fishing for both stripers and blues. "However, I feel blues are even more attuned and particular when it comes to matching jigs," he notes. "When I troll for blues, I especially want every lure to be the same. When one guy changes to a different model, everybody should change to that model."

Throwing on Meatballs

Bill Lescher has been skippering large sportfishing boats in Southern California on and off for nearly three decades. In recent years, he has shifted his focus to chasing striped marlin from his own yacht. Lescher's favorite tactic is throwing bait on stripers. He stresses that the average boater puts too much emphasis on having to see the fish before throwing on it. "Some people," claims Lescher, "won't throw a mackerel on a meatball of baitfish unless they actually see a marlin on it. But, you don't have to see a marlin on a meatball for it to hold fish."

Lescher points out that usually when a concentration or "meatball" of bait is near the surface, something in the way of larger prey is pushing it up toward the top. He backs this contention with the appearance of sea birds dipping on the meatball of bait. According to Lescher, "birds won't work anything unless there is something down below. Something has to push the bait upwards. The baitfish won't make themselves available prey unless something is pushing them up to the surface from down below."

Using similar logic, Lescher also encourages the private yacht owner to definitely make a cast or two on a meatball, even if a pesky seal is near the bait. "It requires a herd of seals to push the bait," he claims. "If there is one seal working a meatball along with birds, there is probably a marlin underneath. It is simply too difficult for a single seal to push all the bait. There have to be other critters around. They all eat from the same table."

Lescher also passes along another useful tip in visually sighting a meatball of bait. In calm seas, the presence of baitfish near the surface makes the water appear to be similar to a choppy windstreak. In contrast, a meatball occurring in choppier water actually seems to smooth out an area on the surface.

Patterning Billfish

Ron De La Mare believes that the average marlin fisherman is not analytical enough as to what's going on around him. "The thing to do," relates De La Mare, "is to notice your water temperature and your depth and this can possibly establish a pattern which you can use when fishing a bank. The bank may come up to 30 or 40 fathoms, but you're getting bit consistently on the edge in 100 fathoms. That's where you want to stay and fish. You must observe what's going on."

So, for this marlin fisherman, the accumulation of pertinent data is a necessity. De La Mare will, for example, closely scrutinize area depth charts to pinpoint potential underwater ledges or banks where the bait will concentrate with hopefully the marlin nearby.

Similarly, a degree difference in water temperature can equally affect the bite according to De La Mare. "The temperature break," he observes, "may establish where the bait is. The bait may be located on one side or the other of the break with the variation being as much as three or four degrees in some places. You have to watch while you fish to look at the temperature gauge."

Thus, De La Mare simply rarely leaves anything to sheer chance. He tries to isolate dead stretches of water by utilizing his depth chart, pathometer, and temperature gauge. And then, when he finds fish, he carefully makes a mental note of how all these variables come together so he can keep his boat in similar water throughout the day. Like freshwater bass pros, this marlin angler always attempts to "pattern the fish."

The Right Hook

Captain Tom Schlauch's specialty is baiting striped marlin on light tackle. Schlauch has some specific ideas when it comes to selecting the proper hook for tossing live mackerel or sardines on stripers.

"I think long-shank hooks tend to come back and foul into the bait, while it's hooked and swimming in the tank or when casted, compared to short-shank models," claims Schlauch. He elaborates that he does not like to have a swimming bait with a long-shank hook, since it has a tendency to swim back into itself forming a deadly loop.

Schlauch likes to bait stripers with the biggest hook they will bite—and, the hook preferably should be unsnelled. "Nowadays," he says, "I fish a simple Eagle Claw, short-shank #6/0 style 318 for marlin. I've never had any trouble with pulling hard on them."

Similarly, Captain Schlauch will use the biggest diameter leader he feels he can cast while baiting stripers. His typical live bait setup consists of three feet of 125 to 150 pound test leader, attached to a ball-bearing swivel, which in turn is attached to 80 pound test monofilament spliced to the 20 to 50 pound mono on the reel with a nail knot. Schlauch emphasizes that he uses a heavy-duty swivel but without a snap.

Thus, in contrast to other charter boat skippers, Schlauch dismisses the "finesse" approach when it comes to baiting striped marlin. His prescription: "Use the largest hook and leader you can get away with."

A Dynamic Group

As you can see, all of these men have a particular perspective when it comes to stalking striped and blue marlin. The one common thread that all these billfishermen seem to share is that they leave nothing to chance.

Each angler has put many hours on the water in his quest for stripes and blues. Fishermen of this caliber are not only meticulous in establishing their game plan, but also remain persistent and confident when the marlin are reluctant to bite.

Although not an "exact science" per se, marlin fishing requires an extremely high level of precision in contrast to other forms of angling. Try to implement some of the specialized techniques shared by this group of experts. The result may be the fish of a lifetime!

Advanced Lure Lessons

Over the years on our Eagle Claw Fishing Schools, we have discovered a wealth of new strategies. We have also refined older established methods for catching not only more but better quality fish ranging from bottom grabbers to pelagic gamesters. Here are some of the most potent technique we routinely utilize on our programs fishing exclusively with artificial lures.

Soft Plastics on Parade

It would be difficult to find a group of anglers who are as innovative as the ones who fish the Pacific Coast. Many of the major strategies for catching marine gamefish had their origins out West. This is certainly the case with the proliferation of soft plastic lures now widely used from coast to coast. Many of these unique baits were designed, tested, and perfected by Western saltwater buffs.

For years, the staple lures used for Pacific party boat fishing included a basic menu of spoons, feathers, cast metal jigs, and occasionally a handful of minnow-shaped plugs. Today, however, Western fishermen would be severely remiss if they didn't carry a complete array of "plastic," as the deckhands term these baits, on both offshore and coastal outings.

Let's briefly examine then the evolution of this family of soft plastic lures and the popular models used up and down the Pacific Coast today.

The History of Soft Plastics

Up until the mid-1970s, very few soft plastic lures were sold for saltwater angling. Most that were being manufactured at this time were targeted for sales in the Southern Gulf Coast states. The rather unspectacular-looking Bagley Salty Dog and Boone Tout were some of the first lures of this material to find their way West. These baits were nothing more than thick chunks of soft plastic with a flat tail section. They were fished on a lead head and supposedly mimicked a shrimp hopping along the bottom.

Local deckhands in Southern California's party boat fleet began using these lures, initially on sand bass. They found that a chunk of plastic bounced off the bottom would also nail calico and white sea bass, halibut, and a smorgasbord of shallow-water rockfish.

At about this same time, another hearty band of fishermen were working the breakwalls in the Long Beach-San Pedro Harbors at night. These "wallbangers" began experimenting with various soft plastic worms and jig trailers normally used for freshwater largemouth bass. They soon discovered that hungry calicos and sand bass would readily jump on these baits fished off the rocks at night.

Finally, a third group of anglers was exploring the possible effectiveness of soft plastics in coastal harbors and bays. The advent of the curl-tail worm extensively promoted by Mr. Twister ushered in still another application of soft plastic lures in saltwater. Spotted bay bass, sandies, halibut, croaker, and even perch, sargo, and corbina, were found to like these strange new worms in places like Newport and San Diego Harbors.

Nowadays, the saltwater buff can visit any tackle store and have an awesome array of soft plastics from which to choose. Let's review some of the options available and how and where these different lures are best used.

Fork-Tails

This bait basically evolved from the body design of the early Bagley Salty Dog. The Scampi was one of the first to expand upon this lure shape, by adding a double-tail section to the bait. The thick thorax portion of the Salty Dog remained intact with the Scampi design. Other manufacturers followed Scampi with a variety of other fork-tail models. These included the Mojo, Haddock's Lunker Thumper, and Shabby Shrimp.

You will find some of these models to be mass-produced through the injection-molding process. Other fork-tail lures are made from a more labor intensive, hand-poured procedure. The latter type of bait is usually characterized by more elaborate, multi-layered color schemes and a distinctively softer body. Hand-poured plastic lures in this genre are frequently more potent than the standard fare represented by the harder, more bland-looking injection-molded baits. Expect to pay more for the soft plastic models and to lose them more frequently because they become torn up more easily by toothy critters.

Soft plastic baits made from either of these processes excel for calico and sand bass fishing along with rockfish and ling cod. They can be casted, yo-yoed, or drifted along the bottom. Deep-water rock codders have also found that the jumbo-size fork-tails fished on a 10 to 16 ounce lead head can be dynamite on big ling cod, salmon grouper, and "cow" cod.

One little tip is worth mentioning again here when using these lures. Cut a strip of frozen squid about 2/3 the length of the plastic and pin it onto the jig head hook. The squid trailer will ride above the plastic tails, but it will not affect the action of the bait. This serves as a "tantalizer" of sorts, when the bass seem finicky and won't eat the straight plastic offerings. Do this with both injection-mold and hand-poured models.

Another ploy to use with these lures is to add a plastic or vinyl skirt behind the jig head. This skirt should be reversed to make the strands of vinyl or plastic flair out when the bait sits on the bottom. The addition of the skirt will also make these lures fall more slowly through the water. This is an excellent option to try when the fish are hitting the offering on the "sink."

Skirts will also add a nice contrast to these baits, especially the less-spectacular, injection-molded models. You can purchase the skirts from most coastal tackle stores. They are the same type used with freshwater bass spinners. Be creative here, mixing and matching colors of the skirts and the plastic fork-tails. Quite frequently you may come up with a super "hot" customized combination that no one else will have on the boat that day!

Freshwater bassers should also consider bringing out the light gear and some of their miniature counterparts in fork-tail jigs when fishing off the rocks, breakwalls, bays, or jetties that dot the coast. Lures such as Garland's Spider Jig, Canyon Lures' Cap'N Gown, and Haddock's Kreepy Krawler are excellent calico and sand bass baits when fished on + to 5/8 ounce lead heads and 8 to 20 pound test. They are also perfect for light tackle rock fishing in northern kelp beds and reefs using freshwater bass gear.

In the Southland, hard-core breakwall fishermen have been tallying some hefty limits on mixed catches of calicos and sandies tossing these three freshwater lures along the rocks at night on the various breakwalls. Here too, as was recommended to do with saltwater fork-tails, it helps to add a 1x3 inch piece of cut squid as a trailer to these smaller baits.

As a bonus, you will most likely find an awesome array of colors available in the freshwater fork-tails since they are in considerable demand among tournament bass fishermen.

Tube Baits

Hollow-bodied tube baits clearly evolved from freshwater bassin' circles. Lures like Bobby Garland's Fat Gitzit have become legendary bass killers on Western impoundments. These and other versions of the "tubes" often produce sensational results in the marine environment as well. More and more saltwater tackle stores are adding both freshwater and larger size "tubes" to their floor stock.

You can start out by using the basic freshwater 2 to 3 inch models with an 1/8 ounce jig head inserted inside the hollow body. This size tube bait is perfect for pitchin' around the docks, pilings, and boat moorings found in harbors up and down the coast. All sorts of perch, croakers, halibut, as well as bay and sand bass will bushwhack these tubes as they sashay down along a piling.

Larger 4 to 6 inch tube baits produce on deeper outside waters. These soft plastic lures replicate a slow-moving squid when they are either drifted or casted. Models like A.A.T.'s Caba Caba Tube and Crappie John's Turbo Jig are perfect for salmon, stripers, calicos, sand bass, bonito, barracuda, halibut, ling cod, a wide variety of rockfish and, believe it or not, deep-water yellowtail!

Southern California engineer and lure designer, Leonard Hashimoto, markets his Caba Caba Tube, in a huge, 8 inch size, representing the largest offering in this style of lure. This tube bait has been generating spectacular catches from the Farallon Islands to below Ensenada, Mexico on ling cod and other rockfish. On an outing to the Farallons, for example, all the jackpot contenders were caught on the giant Cabas. Similar results have occurred when rockfishing in more southern waters. This tube bait is an absolute "hawg hunter"!

You can also run your line through the head of the giant Caba Caba Tube and then through a series of egg sinkers shoved into the hollow body. Tie the line onto a larger single Siwash hook and you have an intriguing new trolling lure. This is an interesting alternative to trolling with feathers for larger offshore species. Tuna, albacore, yellowtail, and wahoo will strike this magnum-size tube bait on a relatively fast troll.

Saltwater tube baits can be even more potent if the hollow cavity is filled with liquid fish attractant. Stuff a small cotton wad up into the tube and soak it with some Berkley Saltwater Strike. As the tube glides through the water, the bait will emit a "chum slick" of the scent. This may again generate strikes when the fish seem especially hook-shy.

One other rather unusual application for saltwater tube baits is to use them to construct the "soft spoon." This is simple to make. Take a slender narrow-bodied spoon like the Crippled Herring, Dungeness Stinger, or Haddock Jig'n Spoon and carefully slide a medium-length tube bait over the lure. Push the line eyelet at the head of the spoon up through the nose of the tube bait. What you now have is a metal spoon encased in a soft plastic tube.

As the spoon is either casted and retrieved below the surface or yo-yoed off the bottom, the tiny tentacles in the tail section of the tube bait seductively flair in and out. The weight of the metal lure will help it sink faster or cast further than a tube bait on a lead head, yet still resemble a squid on the retrieve. Furthermore, when the fish strike the soft plastic outer cover, it will feel more lifelike compared to a hard metallic surface.

Tube Driftin'

Tubes are excellent as a drift bait. Both party boat anglers and private craft fishermen can cover a lot of terrain by slow-drifting tubes. The secret is to make solid bottom contact. As the lead head bounces along, the lure will sort of rise and fall with the tentacles flaring similar to a live squid. A typical drift for halibut, sand or calico bass, salmon, stripers, or even white sea bass requires using a 1 to 3 ounce lead head with the tube bait bottom bouncin' in 60 to 120 feet.

Start with the lighter head. If the current picks up, switch to the heavier jig heads. The motion of the waves and the current is usually enough to impart the necessary action to this kind of lure. However, to enhance the effectiveness of the tube, squirt some liquid fish attractant up into the hollow cavity. As you drift with the lure, the scent is slowly emitted, creating a chum slick of sorts to call in the fish.

Tube baits are terrific on a cast-and-retrieve strategy. Occasionally, a more aggressive fish may nail the lure on a straight wind such as a bonito or tuna. Invariably the

more potent method is to carefully "pump" the tube back to the boat.

To do this, let the lure sink to the desired depth. Then lift the rod tip from the 3 o'clock position. Drop the tip back down parallel to the water, allowing the tube bait to slowly fall. "Pumping" the tube in this manner has the effect of making the lure kind of dart up and down while the tentacles seductively pulsate on this type of stroking retrieve.

Bottom dwellers such as ling cod, halibut, and shallow-water rockfish frequently chase down the tube "pumped" like this off the bottom and viciously attack the lure. More surface-feeding species such as calico bass, bonito, barracuda, and even yellowtail and tuna will strike a tube slow-pumped through 15 to 60 foot depths.

The S-L-O-W Yo-Yo

Tube baits also excel with the vertical yo-yo technique. Here too bottom contact is essential. After the lure reaches the bottom, throw the reel into gear and lift the rod tip up anywhere from 1 to 8 feet. Let the tube slowly sink, hit the bottom, then start the lift-and-drop sequence all over again.

There are times when the more exaggerated yo-yoing works best with the tube bait jumping 6 to 8 feet off the bottom. Invariably, most of the strikes will occur on the fall. Look for any sudden dramatic slack in the line. This usually signals that a fish has inhaled the tube on the sink. Swing and set!

Often in colder deeper water a very subtle short rod lift, perhaps not more than 1 to 2 feet, is most effective. The fish may not want to move too far or too fast in the colder environment. Thus, the S-L-O-W vertical yo-yo makes the tube an easy target to attack. This yo-yo tactic with tube baits has proven effective not only on shallow-water rockfish but on prize gamefish as well. Both yellowtail and white sea bass will sometimes annihilate one of these squid-like soft plastics when they are feeding in deep water on schools of "squirts."

Larger 8 to 10 ounce Caba Caba Tubes can be yo-yoed in much deeper 30 to 50 fathom water for larger rock cod. Better yet, attach a dropper loop about 18 inches above the jumbo Caba Tube and hitch on a smaller 1 ounce Berkley Power Tube as a trailer. This can be a dynamite one-two punch for red rockfish, salmon grouper, and ling cod. Often a smaller fish might hit the little Tube only to have a larger predator strike the big Caba Caba on the way up. Catching two deep-water rockfish on one drop is quite common with this double tube bait setup.

You can also thread small to medium-size brightly colored Berkley Saltwater Power Tubes onto the multiple hooks of a rock cod gangion. Definitely add either live or cut bait to the hook along with the colorful tubes. If the deep-water species steal the bait, the soft plastic tubes will act as a backup offering. You can thus keep the gangion rigs down for longer periods without having to reel up from these greater depths.

Knob-Tail Shads

These fish-shaped lures probably had their origins back with the French-made Vivif or the Weber Hoochy Toad. These were fairly hard plastic replicas of mackerel with big double hooks and a whippy knob-tail. They were super big fish killers for "bull" calicos and yellowtail. Neither of these baits are made today.

Instead, soft plastic manufacturers have a series of knob-tail models that have greater utility for a spectrum of gamefish. These lures are fished on a lead head jig similar to fork-tails. They are basically designed as cast-and-wind baits with the knob-tail pulsating and shaking on the retrieve.

Smaller 3 inch models such as A.A. Worm's Shad have been the rage among bay fishermen in Southern California. These are effective on practically all species of gamefish found in these harbors. They are best worked on a slow retrieve with a 1/8 ounce, darter-head jig teamed with 6 to 8 pound monofilament.

Larger size knob-tails like the A.A. Worm's Super Shad are made to look like small tom cod, herring, or queenfish. These "brown bait" look-alikes can be highly productive on calicos and sand bass when the fish seem to be keying in on a larger offering. I want to emphasize, however, that the knob-tails clearly are most effective with a relatively S-L-O-W retrieve, with barely enough speed to keep the tail throbbing.

Whip-Tail Grubs

These soft plastic lures have also garnered a reputation among freshwater bassers. Most of the models used on our Western bass lakes will work in saltwater, primarily in the harbors and back bays, and off the rocks or piers.

Grubs also fish best with light line and tiny 1/8 to 1/4 ounce jig heads. Models such as Kalin's Lunker Grub, the Mr. Twister Grub, and the new Berkley Power Grub are excellent baits to fish in moving water such as the eddies found in Newport Harbor all the way to Coos Bay.

Grubs featuring these prominent tails can also be rigged with freshwater plastic worm hooks combined with sliding bullet sinkers. The hook is re-embedded back into the thick body of the grub, making this plastic bait particularly weedless.

Both shallow-water rockfish enthusiasts and dedicated deep-water rock codders would be wise to carry some of these little grubs in their offshore tackle boxes. A whip-tail grub added onto either a gangion or dropper loop hook will add considerably more action to a piece of strip bait as it dangles from the same hook.

Sickle-Tails

A lesser known class of soft plastic lures are distinguished by long, narrow sickle-shaped tails. These are usually single-tail variations of the fork-tail baits utilizing the same basic head and thorax design. Only the shape of the tail differs.

A.A.T.'s Salty Magic exemplifies this genre of soft saltwater plastics. After many years of experimenting with these lures, I can state with accuracy that there are definitely times when the diverse species key in on the sickle-tail and won't make the slightest pass at the more popular fork-tail models.

Sickle-tail lures have caught sand bass, calicos, halibut, lings, and rockfish drifted or retrieved along the bottom. Interestingly, these soft plastics also perform quite well at time with other pelagic species.

Barracuda will eat them on a slow "pump." Bonito will nail them on a fast grind. Yellowtail, albacore, skipjack, dorado, and yellowfin tuna have all been taken on sickle-tail lures like these primarily on the "slide" as the boat came to a stop following a jig stop on a trolling feather. However, there were also occasions, when shrewd anglers casting from the bow with light tackle, caught these exotics dragging a sickle-tail lure near a floating kelp paddy.

Split-Tail Grubs

Even less common than the sickle-tail design are those saltwater plastic lures which feature tails that are split in half or sometimes even into quarters. Haddock's Split-Tail Grub and Calico Bagger illustrate this type of subtle tail configuration.

These lures are used off the breakwalls for nighttime calico and sand bass safaris. However, I have personally found the split-tail grubs to be highly effective as bottom-bouncing baits, working drift patterns in 45 to 100 feet of water. Practically anything that is near or on the bottom will eat these lures, especially if they are tipped with a piece of cut squid. This is an excellent shallow-water rockfish offering!

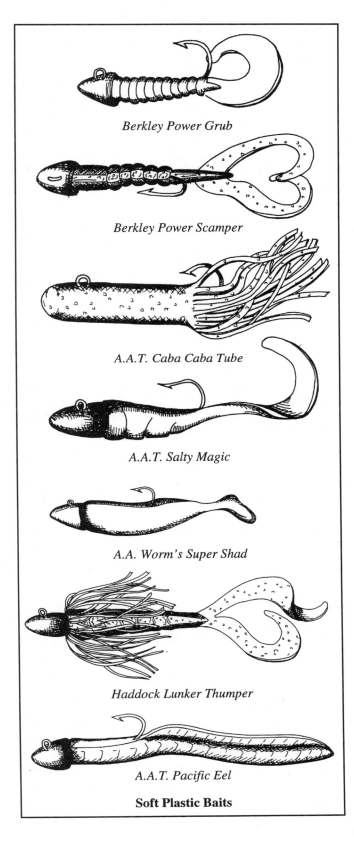

Berkley Power Grub

Berkley Power Scamper

A.A.T. Caba Caba Tube

A.A.T. Salty Magic

A.A. Worm's Super Shad

Haddock Lunker Thumper

A.A.T. Pacific Eel

Soft Plastic Baits

Split-tail grubs have minimal action compared to other soft plastics. During the winter, the pelagic bass species will typically be in a slow-down mode and so won't always attack a lure with more vigorous erratic tail action. Try the split-tail grubs under these conditions, with or without a single skirt. Some of the largest "bull" calicos and "grumper" sand bass I have ever caught came on these split-tails while slow drifting in the dead of winter!

Versatile Lures!

So there you have it—a full parade of soft plastics widely used by the Pacific fishermen. As you can see, these soft plastic baits are extremely versatile lures for marine conditions. Try to work these lures with as light as line as you can possibly use. The tail action of these baits is greatly enhanced with the fine diameter monofilament.

More on Lead Heads

I love lead heads. As a longtime freshwater bass fisherman, I learned to fish everything from the pig'n jig to the Spyder and the Kreepy Krawler. Anyone who chases largemouth bass the West quickly comes to realize that there is nothing better than plowing a lead head jig across the bottom for locating fish holding on deep structure.

Well guess what? These simple lures have even greater utility in saltwater. Armed with a coffee can full of lead heads in 1 to 3 ounce weights, the Pacific angler is ready to tackle anything from sand bass, rockfish and even yellowtail and ling cod.

Lead heads are cheap to buy and even less expensive if you cast your own. The trailers that you lace behind them vary from soft plastic grubs and fork-tails to frozen squid and live herring. The various lures you can assemble from the basic lead head jig are practically endless and extremely simple to put together. Here are some of my favorite combos:

Squid'n Jig. This is one of my longtime favorites. In the "old days" we used to use Bomber Gumpy Jigs with the nylon tail bristles and a whole frozen squid pinned on tail first. The Bomber or any other colorful lead head with feathers or plastic skirt will still work with this squid'n jig combo. As simple as this sounds, you can produce good catches of bass and rockfish by using a cheap, unpainted lead head with the whole squid.

Brown Bait Plunker. Take a lead head and lace the hook through the upper and lower lip of a live small to medium-size tom cod, herring, or shiner perch. This rig doesn't look too attractive but it gets the "brown bait" down deep where the big "bull" calicos, halibut, and ling cod live.

These are just two of my favorite tricks using lead heads above and beyond combining them with soft plastic trailers. Keep plenty of these jigs on hand. When you bounce the bottom, you are going to lose some. They are fairly inexpensive and it won't take a huge investment to assemble an awesome lead head arsenal. Keep it simple—fish lead heads!

Also, be certain to pre-sharpen all the hooks used with lead heads. Many lead jig heads are poured with cadmium hooks. These are not as sharp as bronze hooks but they won't rust as quickly either. Many times our local species will gently "mouth" the soft plastic, so solid hook penetration is necessary.

On this note, consider using a graphite rod to increase your hook-to-strike ratio with lead head combos. Because the "strike" is not often so pronounced, the graphite blank is more sensitive and responsive to nail those delicate feeders. Many anglers are now stepping onto sportfishing boats additionally armed with 7 or 7 1/2 freshwater graphite bass trigger-grip rods, and light level wind baitcasting reels spooled with 10 to 15 pound string strictly for fishing soft plastics and lead heads.

Pumpin' the Eel

I am fortunate to be both an outdoor writer and the director of the Eagle Claw Fishing Schools program. Frequently, I have the chance to preview, test, and help refine a variety of new products over the seasons. In past years, students in our on-the-water seminars have had the opportunity to be among the first to try the now popular Caba Caba Tubes. Next came the soon-to-be marketed Salty Magic curl-tail baits, the Rapala jumbo Shad Raps, Berkley Power Grubs, Tubes and Scampers and, most recently, the hot new U.F.O. Pacific Lights collection of surface irons. We have tried them all, and they have all performed quite well in our schools.

At one of our land-based Penn Fishing University symposiums, one of my guest speakers, Mike Gardner, a renown light-tackle saltwater guide, handed me some of the most bizarre-looking lures I had ever seen. These were 10 inch long, hand-poured, soft plastic eels. Now I've used eels before in freshwater bass lakes, but they were smaller 6 inch specimens. I might add that I was first introduced to these baits back in the mid 1960s and I rarely ever see eels sold in the West anymore—until now.

Gardner's monster versions were made by Tony Pena of AA Worms. They were obviously created to resemble rainbow trout, a natural prey for big largemouth bass at Lake Castaic outside Los Angeles. So, to be polite, I took the sample baits and stashed them in my saltwater box.

A few weeks later, I was leading one of my schools down to San Martin Island about 155 miles south of San Diego. We had been picking at log size 'cuda, a smattering of yellowtail, and some calico bass all day. In the late afternoon, we anchored on a high spot in about 180 feet of water. This was a recognized pinnacle for big red rockfish and sometimes ling cod. The bite was especially slow. Scrounging through my tackle box, I found one of the AA eels—in rainbow trout color no less—and laced it on a 3 ounce lead head. I fished the eel on 12 pound string, matched with a graphite 7 foot freshwater poppin' rod. On the first drop, I was hammered. I slowly wound up a nice 7 pound red rockfish. The next drop I was nailed again by a red of equal size. Initially, both my instructors and deckhands alike snickered at my weird eel. After the second big red hit the deck, and coughed up a 6 to 8 inch "real" baby eel, my skeptics soon asked if I had any more of these new baits.

This story has been repeated many times as I take my eels to sea. Big chuckleheads, lings, "grumper" sand bass, and toad "bull" calicos will also eat them. As I discovered, bass like most bottom grabbers, such as reds, lings, whitefish, and halibut, feed on small eels in their natural habitat. It's not so strange then that the soft plastic imitation works so well.

The soft plastic eels are big fish baits. Don't worry about short strikes—the keeper fish bite the eel at the head. Don't fool around with tricky stinger hooks in the tail. As for colors—I've used about every pattern sold and all work fine. It's the size, silhouette, action, and uniqueness of these new eels that makes them so effective!

Saltwater Scents

Saltwater angling, like other sports, has evolved into a hi-tech industry. We now have everything from big game reels with lightning-fast gear ratios and sophisticated lever drag mechanisms to lines made out of Kevlar. There are electronic fish finders that scan from side to side as well as supplying a vertical picture of the bottom. Hooks are now manufactured with laser technology and lures are marketed with incredible natural fish-like finishes. Everything is going hi-tech.

A somewhat less glamorous member of this cavalcade of hi-tech tackle is the multitude of fish scents and attractants that are now on the market. You can purchase waxes, liquids, and solid compounds that are designed to encourage the fish to bite your offering. Much of this emergent scent technology, however, was spawned in the freshwater bass and trout fraternities. It has only been recently that anglers have been taking a serious look at these mixtures and how they might have application in a marine capacity.

As director of the Eagle Claw Fishing Schools, I have had the opportunity to investigate many of these compounds while conducting our various on-the-water seminars in California, Baja, Hawaii, and the Florida Keys. I also have a strong background using scents and attractants on freshwater lakes while running my bass and trout guide service in the Southland. My freshwater experience has been especially helpful, I might add, for generating a myriad of applications for these concoctions for my instructors to use while at sea. Here are some of the more intriguing applications we have discovered.

Home Remedies

Some of the best fish attractants for saltwater are actually products of home experimentation, passed on from one angler to another and are fairly simple to put together.

An example of this is what veteran lure manufacturer, Bob Suekawa, of Haddock Tackle, does when preparing to use soft plastic grubs and jigs fishing the Long Beach Federal Breakwater at night. Parlaying the propensity of both calico and sand bass to key in on smell during a nocturnal bite, Suekawa frequently pre-soaks his lures in squid juice during and prior to the trip.

"The stuff is simple to extract," notes Suekawa. "I just let a block of frozen squid thaw out and collect the natural juices in a bucket. I then let my Kreepy Krawlers and split-tail grubs soak for a while in the natural juice. This produces a lot of strikes when I fish the "Wall"—more so, than if I fish plastic lures without the juice."

Other natural sources also produce "juices" that are excellent when applied to soft plastic baits. One in particular is the result of crushing fresh rock mussels and collecting the juice. Small curl-tail grubs dipped in this scent will perform along the surf line, off the piers, and along the docks and pilings in secluded harbors and bays.

For years, freshwater bassers have relied upon oil of anise as a "secret sauce" of sorts. This oil not only gives the lure the distinctive licorice odor, it also "greases" the bait, giving it a slick lifelike appearance. Small tube baits like the Fat Gitzit or Fatzee are excellent when pitched under docks, piers, and moored boats in the backwaters of Southland harbors. Dip these soft plastic lures as well as curl-tail grubs and knob-tail minnow-like baits in the anise oil for greater effect.

You can also create some unique, one-of-a-kind, custom smelly soft plastic lures by putting a variety of different baits into a poly bag with a spoonful of anise oil. Seal the bag and let it sit in the sunlight for a few days. A virtual rainbow of interesting patterns will develop as the different colors of soft plastic bleed into one another. The oil seems to facilitate this "bleeding" process with the by-product of having the anise scent permeate more deeply into the soft lure.

This little trick is a good way to recycle some of those old, torn-up plastic worms that may be stashed away in your freshwater bassin' box.

Liquid Blends

Far and away, the most prominent representation of fish attractants and scent is in liquid form. Some of the popular varieties include Berkley Strike, Dr. Juice, Fish Formula, Sparkle Scales, and Baitmate.

Some of these mixtures like Fish Formula are oil-based, creating that slick-looking effect similar to the anise-soaked baits I mentioned. Others, like Berkley Strike, are water soluble, creating a less spectacular effect as far as lure finish is concerned, but presumably emitting a particular chemical to encourage the fish to attack the bait.

The manufacturers of true liquid scents and attractants have also been careful to market all these products in different odors to be employed for a particular species. Dr. Juice, for example, comes in a saltwater, trout, salmon, panfish, or catfish blend.

Like the home remedies discussed, the liquid formulas would seem to have greatest utility in conjunction with soft plastic baits. The simplest technique is to either spray on or add a drop or two of the liquid to the saltwater lure. Most of these mixtures are relatively expensive and highly concentrated. In my experience, it doesn't take a lot of the liquid scent or attractant to dress up the lure.

One thing worth noting, however, is to be sure to apply the liquid especially to the head and mid-thorax portion of the bait. Popular soft plastic lures like the Mojo, Lunker Thumper, Scampi, or A.A. Shad will commonly be attacked near the head section of the bait. If you add too much oil to the tail portion of these lures, expect to see a lot of little fish short-striking the bait, ripping at the tail.

These liquid formulas should also be used in conjunction with a natural bait trailer or with natural bait by itself. For instance, a common ploy is to add a small 1x3 inch strip of cut squid to the hook on a soft plastic bait as an added attraction if the lure is not drawing strikes. Better yet, add a few drops of your favorite scent for even greater potency. Again, this stuff is expensive and a few drops will go a long way.

Another intriguing tactic we pioneered on our Eagle Claw Schools was taken directly from our freshwater bass guide logs. For years, so-called "finesse" bassers have been injecting both plastic worms and grubs with liquid scent or attractants using a hypodermic syringe. A less unusual version of this little ploy is to fill the hollow cavity of popular tubular lures with these liquids.

Take a medium-size Caba Caba Tube or a Crappie John Turbo Tube and fill it with an ample amount of one of these liquid compounds. As the soft plastic tube glides down on the sink, it emits a sort of "vapor trail" of the liquid scent, calling the fish in to investigate. This strategy has produced stellar catches of sand bass, calicos, barracuda, shallow-water rockfish, ling cod, and even deep-water yellowtail. Through informal controlled tests, my instructors and I firmly conclude that the "tubes" injected with the liquid attractants or scents overwhelmingly get bit better than those that are fished "dry."

A variation along this theme is also worth noting. To conserve on the liquid along with creating perhaps a longer time-release effect, many anglers now stuff a small amount of cotton into these hollow tube baits. Then they saturate the cotton plug with the various liquid formulas. While once participating in a major billfish tournament, an enterprising angler drilled out small portion of the core of a marlin jig head. Then he inserted a cotton plug soaked in liquid attractant. On a slow-trolling program, the liquid would again be released gradually presumably creating a chum slick around the lure.

Liquid scents can also be used in conjunction with natural bait to create an even more potent chum concoction. One proven trick is to take strips of bonito, mackerel, barracuda, or pieces of squid. Put them into a milk carton and mix in a few cups of sand. Then add an ample amount of liquid fish attractant. The scent adheres to the sand while the sand adheres to the slimy natural bait. You can then throw out pieces of this combo as chum, similar to the way East Coasters "chunk," utilizing portions of cut bait to bring the fish to the boat. The attractant is slow to leave the natural bait, since it is mixed in with the sand that coats the bait. This specialized "chum pot" works great for sand bass!

Pastes and Slime

One of the problems in using liquid fish attractants is that they will not adhere properly to hard baits such as cast-metal jigs, spoons, or plastic plugs. Some time ago, the people at Berkley marketed a powdery substance called "Alive." It comes in a canister, and if you run across some on a dusty shelf, buy it! When mixed with water, Alive produces a thick syrupy slimy solution into which you can dip hard baits. It is still basically a water soluble product like Berkley's liquid Strike, but it is much more sticky.

The late Bob Bringhurst, a former world record holder and renown big fish expect, started coating his trout-colored plastic plugs with this stuff while stalking trophy rainbows and browns. He shared this little trick with me, and I soon found that Alive would also work in saltwater. For example, I took a group of students to fish giant amberjack in Key Largo on the "iron." Our 83 pound jackpot fish was nailed when I recommended the angler dip his heavy jig in a bucketful of Alive.

Two new compounds are now available that are similar to the slimy Alive. Both Smelly Jelly and Scent Wax approach a more solid state. Each of these mixtures will, to a great degree, adhere to smooth metal surfaces like those found on a saltwater spoon. Similarly, both the wax-like and gel attractants can be used to coat a jig or a plastic minnow-shaped plug.

Built-In Scents

Perhaps the most intriguing application for scent technology in the saltwater field has been the recent proliferation of soft plastic lures that feature "baked in" attractant. For years, freshwater bass fishermen have experimented with this technology by hand-pouring their own plastic worms with everything from vanilla extract to salt crystals added into the molten plastic. The theory behind this concern for built-in scents is twofold: 1) the scent will mask human odors and 2) it will also actually attract fish into striking the artificial lure.

A soft plastic bait impregnated with one of these substances also presumably has the added benefit that the fish will actually hold onto the lure longer than if it was simply plain, unadulterated plastic. Berkley led the way with the advent of their "Power" series of grubs, worms, and tube baits. Experimenting with these basic freshwater bass lures on our saltwater schools has produced remarkable results!

My instructors and I have found that everything from sand bass and calicos to ling cod and halibut will viciously strike the Power Grubs, Power Scampers, and Power Tubes. Many jackpot fish were taken this past season when anglers fished one of these soft plastic lures which are essentially impregnated with the same materials as those found in the liquid Strike compound.

Not to be outdone, three other manufacturers have also entered this built-in scent market. The Zaxis company in Ohio has also designed their Trickle Baits with built-in flavor and scent enhancers.

Upon immersion, the plastic-like Trickle Bait lures release an invisible cloud of enhancer and then continue to deliver the "flavor cloud" into the water for up to 5 to 6 hours. The scent compounds in the Trickle Bait lures last even longer, giving this type of artificial lure a deadly one-two punch. The Trickle Bait products are also biodegradable.

Jim Bloomfield and Reuji Suenaga are in the business of hand-pouring soft plastic bass baits. Also concerned with eliminating messy external applications of scent, Bloomfield and Suenega started adding Smelly Jelly to their Bonzai Worm products.

Another entry into this saltwater attractant market is the series of Culprit Shrimp Tidbits, Sea Ray I, and Shad Tail Grubs. These soft plastic lures also have scent and flavor enhancements built in to product harder, more pronounced strikes. These are basically shrimp-like or knobby-tail designs.

Trickle Bait, Culprit and Bonzai baits have also produced spectacular results on recent Eagle Claw Fishing Schools targeting shallow-water rockfish. As with the Berkley Power series of baits, we have found the lings and other rockfish to readily attack these most recently introduced scent-laden lures.

The most effective way we have devised to utilize these soft plastics with the built-in scent is on a dropper loop rig. Tie on either a heavy cast-metal jig or spoon with a dropper loop about 12 to 18 inches above the lure. Attach a #4/0 live bait hook to the loop then thread on one of these smelly grubs, worms, tubes, or leeches. Proceed to "bounce" the jig or spoon off the bottom. Invariably if you stick only one fish, it will be on the dropper loop and the soft plastic bait. Double hook-ups are frequent with the soft plastic lure usually accounting for the larger of the two fish. These scent-laden baits are also sensational thrown on light bass-casting gear while fishing harbors and bays or coastal reefs and rock piles. Any bottom-dwelling fish might eat one of these lures laced on a lead head and retrieved or drifted slowly.

You can also take the tiniest Power Tubes and insert one over each of the points of a big treble hook on a jig or spoon. Now the lure has acquired a modicum of "smell" without jeopardizing its performance. A jig or spoon with three miniature tubes sticking off the treble hook looks rather weird—but it definitely gets bit!

Be Creative!

As you can see, there are endless applications for using fish scent in saltwater. I have touched on only a few tricks I have come across this past season. Undoubtedly, there are many more to be discovered.

I must confess that I, like most anglers, also use only the compound prescribed by the manufacturer for a single gamefish species. This obviously facilitates more multiple sales for the scent and attractant companies. I certainly encourage you to be innovative and perhaps try some freshwater compounds in the marine environment. It just might lead to some interesting results as a halibut homes in on a grub soaked in rainbow trout scent!

South Coast Trolling

Trolling is one of the most productive ways to catch the major pelagic species in Southern California and Baja California waters. This is especially true for small private boats that have limited chumming capabilities. Even sportfishing skippers will attest that there are situations when trolling allows them to cover expanses of open water efficiently in an effort to locate schools of marauding gamefish.

The five major surface species caught in the Southland—bass, bonito, barracuda, yellowtail, and tuna—will all strike an artificial lure dragged behind the boat. Here is a brief rundown of how to set up a trolling program for each of these distinct gamefish. Keep in mind that some of this material is repeated in greater detail in the individual sections on the different gamefish species. This is merely a basic "primer" on trolling.

Bass on the Troll

Many anglers are remiss in not trolling for bass when the opportunity arises. Both calicos and sand bass can be tallied with this technique. Calico bass will frequently nail the "iron" as a cast-metal jig is slowly pulled behind the boat. The emphasis here is S-L-O-W-L-Y. Jigs in this genre will have a tendency to spin if they are trolled too fast. You can throttle down to a plodding 1 to 3 knots if you want to drag the iron.

Two kinds of jigs will work on calicos with the trolling strategy. If you are cruising along the outside kelp lines, I recommend a small compact "heavy" model such as a U.F.O. #2 or Salas Christy 2. These jigs pull nicely on 20 to 30 pound mono and, at least initially, they should be tied directly to the line. If the jig begins to spin even with a slow trolling speed, use a ball-bearing swivel with a leader. Tie your main line to the ball bearing swivel and add a 4 to 6 foot length of leader. Then tie your jig directly to the other end of the leader line. Don't snap a swivel to the split ring on the jig. This usually kills the distinctive side-to-side swimming action of the "iron."

As for colors, these smaller jigs are made to replicate mackerel, sardines, or anchovies. Time-proven patterns are blue/white, blue/chrome, and definitely green/yellow for calicos.

There are other times when the calicos—particularly the bigger "bull" bass—are up feeding near the surface of the kelp stringers. This is an excellent opportunity to slow-troll a lighter surface jig. Larger models like the Salas 6X or 7X or Tady 45 in a "light" weight are perfect for this type of trolling. Consider switching to the less popular single hook versions in these jigs. They will swim through the kelp stringers better than conventional treble hooks models with less snagging. With these longer jigs, a blue and white pattern with a painted black underbelly is a terrific pattern used by many of the big calico experts. Another "sleeper" color is a dull, almost General Motors green jig.

A prime situation to drag one of these larger jigs is on a party boat while the deckhand is setting up a chum line. The skipper will typically circle a prime spot while chum is tossed out to bring up the fish. Troll one of these larger surface jigs through the initial chum—you just might get nailed by a big bull bass!

Both calicos and sand bass will also strike a big soft plastic tail-swimming lure on the slow-troll. Small boats can cruise near the bank keeping an eye open for so-called "boilers." These are small, rocky outcroppings that the surge will crash over at low tide. Calicos and sometimes sandies will be found in the foamy water created by the "boiler." Pull a larger fork-tail Scampi, Mojo, or Lunker Thumper near the white water. The single hook lead head used with these soft plastics makes the lure practically weedless. Soft plastics like these also slow-troll well along the kelp stringers or through a chum circle. Stay with the ever popular root beer/flake, chartreuse, or smoke/sparkle colors with the fork-tail lures.

Sand bass, more so than calicos, will often stratify or suspend. It is not uncommon to meter sandies stacked up from 20 to 40 feet above a 100 foot bottom. One seldom used method is to slow-troll a weighted plug through these deeper strike zones. Using 20 to 30 pound line, tie your main line to a ball-bearing snap-swivel. Clip the swivel to the ring on a 10 to 16 ounce torpedo sinker. Clip another snap-swivel to the other ring on the sinker. Next add a 4 to 6 foot length of lighter 12 to 15 pound line tied onto the swivel at the bottom of the sinker. Lastly, tie on a medium-size, minnow-shaped plug such as a Rapala CD-11, CD-13, or CD-14 Magnum model.

On a moderate slow-troll, the torpedo sinker will take the lightweight plug down fairly deep. The sand bass readily attack the anchovy look-alike providing the boat skipper with an excellent means to target suspended bass!

Troll for Bonito

"Bongos" are by far the easiest of the pelagics to fool with a trolling program. Like calicos, they will eagerly attack a smaller metal jig when it is slow-trolled. The heavier U.F.O. #1 and #2, Yo Ho Ho #1 to #3, along with the Salas Christy #1 and Pee Wee models, are great for this slow-troll strategy. Blue and white as well as solid chrome patterns would be hard to beat.

Bonito will also annihilate smaller minnow-shaped plugs. The Jensen Minnow, Rapala CD-9, CD-11, and CD-13 Magnum lures are excellent choices when trolling for bongos. Usually these artificial minnows produce best for this species tied directly to the line and pulled a few feet below the surface. These plugs are also small enough to be trolled with freshwater bass gear, producing terrific light-line sport on 10 to 12 pound spinning or baitcasting outfits.

Surprisingly, soft plastic baits can also be trolled for bonito and at a fairly fast speed—well over 6 to 7 knots. The classic fork-tails work well along with the recently introduced Caba Caba Tubes. Pull brighter shades such as fluorescent lime, chartreuse, blue, or red while trolling soft plastics for bongos.

Metal spoons are also a viable option. More than ever, with these lures, S-L-O-W is the word if you want to troll them. The slab-shaped models like the Crippled Herring, Dungeness Stinger, Nordic, and Haddock Jig'n Spoon will erratically dart back and forth near the surface on the slow-troll. The wobblers with their curvier wider bodies such as the Krocadile and Hot Shot series most definitely must be pulled S-L-O-W-L-Y. Avoid adding a snap-swivel to these spoons—it will kill their slow-seductive action.

All of these spoons are available in chrome or prism-scale finishes. Both patterns seem to work equally well. A lot of times the bonito will eat a slow-trolled spoon when faster-moving less subtle lures are producing.

Day in and day out, however, it is hard to beat feathers as your best overall option for trolled bonito. The old standby—a chrome, single-hook, lead head with turkey feathers—still works. It can be pulled fast or slow, rides fairly weedless, and persists in getting bit. The basic array of colors still produces with these feathers: blue/white, red/white, and green/yellow.

If you feel that you may be getting into some larger bonito, perhaps in double-digit weights, you might consider trolling a large, more conventional 15 mm tuna feather. These lures are sold rigged or unrigged, usually with a strong double hook. Particularly while running offshore near the outer banks and around the islands, a larger tuna feather like this might result in a big monster bonito or tuna! More on this strategy shortly.

Barracuda on the Troll

Rounding out the three B's, barracuda are also prone to attack a lure slowly trolled. Barries will eagerly hit soft plastics, small to medium size iron, feathers, spoons, and minnow-shaped plugs on the troll. With soft plastics, switch to Mojos and Lunker Thumpers in fluorescent lime or smoke/sparkle. A small Tora Tube in blue/flake is dynamite on the 'cuda pulled slowly behind the boat. Barracuda like a solid white jig slow-trolled. My favorite choices in this situation would be a U.F.O. #2, #3, or #4, or a Salas Christy 1, 2, or 6x Junior in heavier versions. Blue and white, along with blue and chrome models, can also be effective, but solid white in the "iron" remains the inside secret of the 'cuda experts.

Barries will also tear up your smaller plugs on the troll. You will get a lot of action and great sport using 10 to 12 pound string but be prepared to lose some of your lures with these toothy critters. You might be better off dragging plugs on 15 to 20 pound mono when it comes to 'cuda.

The CD-13 Magnum Rapala is a staple for barracuda on the slow-troll. However, some of the large 7 to 9 pound "stove pipes" will be scored trolling a longer and distinctively larger Rapala #SL-20 "Sliver" model. These are elongated, jointed-minnow plugs that can sometimes drive a barracuda crazy. Troll the Slivers in the more opulent fluorescent orange and chartreuse finishes while staying with the traditional blue or black models in the CD-13 Rapalas.

'Cuda will also sometimes nail a single-hook bonito feather slow-trolled especially in colder water conditions. Longtime barracuda aficionados will attest that the solid white feather with the chrome head and red glass bead eye would be the one to pull.

As for spoons, the same arsenal cited for bonito will work equally well for barracuda on the slow-troll. However, don't hesitate to experiment, scaling up considerably in size, trolling a large 2 to 4 ounce Krocadile or 2 1/8 ounce Haddock Jig'n Spoon. Again, the trick is to keep your trolling speed down but don't go so slow as to eliminate the action from the spoon. Dragging a big spoon like this may result in a "log" barrie that may home in on a bigger morsel while smaller school 'cuda are chasing 'chovies.

Drag Lures for Yellowtail

Many anglers fail to take advantage of a trolling opportunity when it comes to stalking 'tails. Trolling will often generate catches—both on shore and off—when fishing is especially slow or the yellows are scattered over a large area. The best overall strategy is to either drag tuna feathers or plugs for yellowtail. A basic 15 mm head is the appropriate size feather to troll alongside offshore kelp paddies. The 'tails will frequently race out from under the floating kelp to strike the tuna feather.

This same basic feather combo can also be pulled while cruising for breezing fish. This method works especially well inshore when you are working in the general vicinity where yellows have been sighted.

Sometimes, however, these "breezers" will be in a sub-surface mode. Tie on a 10 to 16 ounce ringed torpedo sinker about 4 to 6 feet above the feather. Rig the sinker with ball-bearing swivels at each end as previously discussed. The torpedo weight will drag the feather into slightly deeper strike zones. This subtle trick often produces bonanza catches on "breezers." Traditional tuna colors—blue/white, red/white, and green/yellow—are suitable for yellowtail trolling.

'Tails will also chase a minnow-shaped plug pulled at 3 to 6 knots. Smaller CD-13 Rapalas match well for 6 to 10 pound "peanut" class yellows. Drag the larger CD-14 and CD-18 Magnum Rapala or the giant #SL-20 Rapala Slivers if you are looking for bigger fish. The saltwater version of the Rapala Shad Rap also works for yellowtail on the troll. It has to be dragged fairly slow but it really mimics greenback and Spanish mackerel in size, color, and shape. Usually you won't be able to troll both feathers and plugs together. Drag either one class of lure or the other. Trolled together, the plugs may track too close to the feathers on their natural swimming motions and inadvertently cross lines.

Although it is rarely practiced, yellowtail will also respond to a large size candy bar style jig trolled at a fairly slow pace. A hefty size Salas 6x or 7x, a Tady 45 or a U.F.O. #3 or #5 may prove effective on the slow-troll. Stay with the lighter versions and definitely drag them in the stern as you set up the chum. Pull blue/white, mackerel, sardine, or scrambled egg colored jigs for yellowtail.

Tuna and Dorado on the Troll

Like yellowtail, almost all the major tuna species will home in on a trolled feather or plug. Historically, in the last decade or so the albacore as well as the yellow, bluefin, and skipjack tuna seem to overwhelmingly prefer a 15 mm head. These can be rigged with the traditional double hook or with a single Siwash model.

Popular tuna feather colors include "the basics"—blue/white, yellow/green, and red/white—along with more exotic combos such as purple/black, black/green, sold white, "Mexican flag" (yellow/red/green) or "zucchini" (yellow/orange/red). All the major manufacturers such as Braid, California Lures, and Zucker market tuna feathers in these combinations. Not all of these feathers are actually "feathers," per se. The tail portion of these trolling lures might also be plastic or vinyl.

Over the years, I have experimented by stacking two 15 mm heads on top of each other. This produces numerous, sometimes unusual, custom color combinations. For example, one of my favorites is to stack a red/white feather on top of a blue/white model. I call this hybrid the "Fourth of July." Stacking smaller feathers like this also creates a "joisted" or hinged effect with the lure. This increases the motion of the jig and gives the fish something new and different to look at.

Also keep in mind that there are different head shapes in these trolling feather lures that you can try. Braid, for example, markets a blunt-nose Wombat and a pointed cone-head shape Albie Teaser. There are also metal heads with holes drilled in to generate a stream of bubbles behind the lure. Popular models are made by J.P.R. and Mako.

Larger 25 mm class feathers are used for the big eye tuna. These 40 pound(+) fish prefer a bigger offering. However, there are times when they may want a sleeker, longer lure without the bulky 25 mm head. Here is where two stacked 15 mm feathers may be the hot ticket. I might add that I have even had striped marlin hit the slim profile double-stacked jig!

Other somewhat larger feathers or models with plastic skirts will also produce catches of big eye. The Zuckers "3.5" was designed primarily as a striped marlin jig. Big tuna and dorado will eat these large lures readily if they are in the area.

The members of the tuna family also attack trolled plugs. The large Rapala CD-14, CD-18 Magnum, and #SL-20 Slivers are excellent options to feathers if the fish seem to be highly finicky and reluctant to bite. The Braid Speedster and Reflecta models, both lipless plugs, are

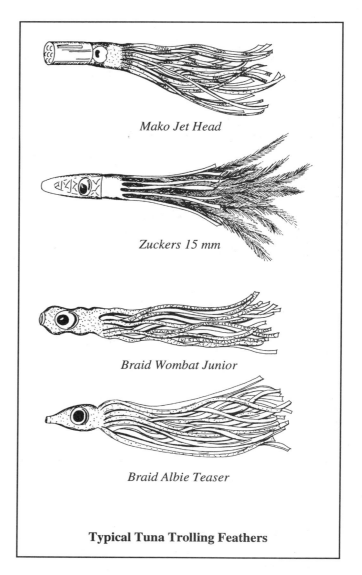

Mako Jet Head

Zuckers 15 mm

Braid Wombat Junior

Braid Albie Teaser

Typical Tuna Trolling Feathers

recent additions to the parade of trolling plugs and have enjoyed success with tuna on both local and long-range trips.

Even more important than the double or single Siwash hooks commonly used with trolling gear, the treble hooks on many of these big minnow-shaped plugs must be pre-sharpened before you drag the lure. Tuna and dorado caught on the troll can apply tremendous leverage and force against the hooks combined with the boat traveling in the opposite direction. Insure solid penetration by taking the time to sharpen these big trebles.

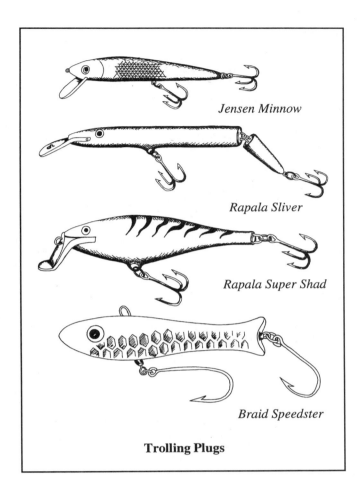

Jensen Minnow

Rapala Sliver

Rapala Super Shad

Braid Speedster

Trolling Plugs

More Trolling Tips

Irrespective of which pelagic species you are trolling for, always make sure that your rod and reel are secured to withstand the sudden impact from that initial strike. You may want to use auxiliary ropes tied to solid brass or stainless steel clips that attach to the posts of your conventional reel for extra insurance. The ropes are hitched to the railing in the stern of the boat.

On that note, you don't always have to troll with casting gear. I have had some outstanding sport dragging light jigs, plugs, spoons, plastics, and feathers on spinning tackle. If you want to troll with a spinner, be certain to use a reel with a quality drag system; otherwise many fish will be lost following that initial surge with a sticky drag that can happen with an inexpensive spinning reel. Similarly, check your baitcasting reels. These drags must also be in top-notch condition for a trolling program.

Another tip is to always monitor your boat speed and the distance from the boat where the lure is riding. After you get bit and wind the fish in be careful to duplicate the same trolling program. Let out the same amount of line and maintain the identical boat speed. Many novice trollers forget to account for these factors, which often produce only random success at best.

Finally, trolling is far from an exact science. Be experimental! Work with the entire menu of lures for a particular species. However, be careful in mixing different classes of baits at the same time. Usually spoons won't troll well next to plugs, or plugs with feathers. Always check your trolling lures to ascertain that they are "swimming" properly to generate the maximum results. Good luck!

Spoonin' the Pacific Coast

Metal spoons are one of the most versatile but underrated lures in a Pacific angler's tackle box. Spoons are an all-season lure. They will catch everything from pelagic species like bonito, barracuda, salmon, striped bass, yellowtail, and even tuna, to bottom dwellers including almost every kind of rockfish, halibut, and ling cod. Spoons are relatively simple to use once you understand their basic design and application.

Types of Saltwater Spoons

Spoons can be divided into two basic shapes: 1) wide-bodied wobblers and 2) narrow slab-shaped spoons. These are the simple yet fundamental styles we use here along the Pacific Coast from the north to the south.

Wide-Bodied Models. These spoons are larger versions of popular models often seen in Western trout circles. The spoon most widely used for marine conditions is the ever-popular Luhr Jensen Krocadile. Spoons in this design feature a fairly wide metal body that wobbles from side to side on the retrieve. This kind of spoon also has terrific fluttering action, mimicking a wounded baitfish as it slowly sinks. Other wide-bodied spoons that are highly suitable for Pacific coastal and offshore saltwater fishing include the Flutter Spoon, Diamond King and Mister "J."

Slab-Shaped Models. These spoons are characterized by their narrow bodies and sleek appearance. Models like the Hopkins, Dungeness Stinger, Nordic, Haddock Jig'n Spoon, and Crippled Herring spoons have tremendous wind resistance and can be cast great distances. Slab-shaped spoons are designed to sink quickly and bounce off the bottom. However, these spoons may also prove to be deadly as surface lures. Let's look at some of the major gamefish species found off the Pacific Coast and how to catch these fish using simple spoons.

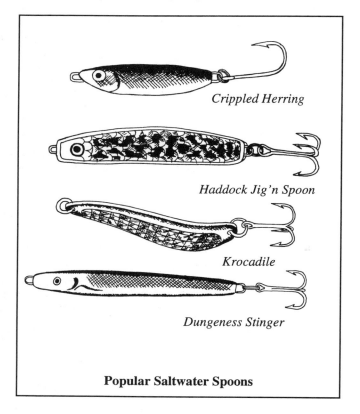

Crippled Herring

Haddock Jig'n Spoon

Krocadile

Dungeness Stinger

Popular Saltwater Spoons

Bass on Spoons

Calico and sand bass comprise an integral component of the yearly catch for sportfishing fleets in southern California. Both of these saltwater bass species will readily attack a shiny spoon.

In the colder months, both calicos and "sandies" will be situated near the bottom structure at 60 to 90 foot depths. One of the best ways to reach these fish is with a slab-shaped spoon vertically yo-yoed off the bottom. The trick is to make good bottom contact. Depending upon wind and current, fish either a Dungeness Stinger or Crippled Herring spoon in 1 to 3 ounce models. Watch for sudden slack in the line as bass suspended off the bottom may strike the spoon as it is sinking. Once on the bottom, use an exaggerated lift-and-drop sequence, raising and lowering your rod tip from the 3 to the 12 o'clock position. The object is to make the spoon literally "jump" off the bottom, then flutter down replicating a dying squid, anchovy, mackerel, or sardine.

For bass, use the Dungeness Stinger in pearl/blue back, pearl/green back, or nickel/neon green patterns. In the Crippled Herring series, the blue/over chrome and bluish green back/over chrome finishes are great for calico and sand bass.

As water temperatures warm, switch to a sub-surface cast-and-wind retrieve with a Krocadile spoon. Depending upon the size of the bass in the school, select from 5/8 to 2 + ounce models. Remember, however, "big spoons catch big fish." Occasionally pause in the retrieve to let the "Kroc" lazily flutter down a few feet. Always be prepared for a sudden jolt as a bigger "bull" calico or sand bass practically "inhales" the Krocadile on the sink.

Time-proven colors for this style of saltwater bassin' are chrome, chrome/blue mackerel, chrome/green mackerel, and chrome/silver prism lite. The Luhr Jensen Krocadile spoon is available in all these finishes.

Spoon 'Cuda!

Veteran saltwater buffs in Southern California have known for years that big 'cuda love a shiny spoon! Although a lot of smaller barracuda may be caught on live bait, the trophy 7 to 10 pound "logs" are frequently taken by accomplished spoon fishermen.

In the early spring, the barries can stack up on the bottom all the way down to 120 feet. These fish will be semi-lethargic, but they will eat if a lure is placed right in front of them. Here a heavier 1 1/2 to 3 ounce spoon yo-yoed off the bottom can be deadly. The Luhr Jensen Dungeness Stinger and Crippled Herring along with the large Haddock Jig'n Spoon are perfect for deep-water 'cuda. In addition to the patterns recommended for bass, try a Dungeness Stinger in solid white or pearl/pink back patterns. Barracuda are notoriously fond of white and pearl finish lures. The Haddock models in prism scale finishes all seem to work equally well. Similarly, fish a Crippled Herring in the fluorescent blue back over a pearl white body. This particular pattern should always be a staple in the serious 'cuda fisherman's arsenal.

When the barries are "up" near the surface, it is hard to find a lure better than the Krocadile. The basic patterns used for saltwater bass are also perfect for barracuda. 'Cuda will also go crazy over some other, more esoteric finishes in the Krocadile series that are worth adding to your spoon inventory. The hammered brass/fire stripe has been a longtime local favorite along with the chrome/fire stripe. You may also want to switch to a Krocadile with the optional single hook arrangement. This spoon is a lot easier to remove from a toothy customer like the barracuda, using a single hook instead of the traditional treble hook configuration.

Another well-kept secret is to throw either the Luhr Jensen Super Duper or Hot Shot Wobbler spoon on light line for these fish. The Super Duper and Hot Shot are hallmark lures for Western trouters. Skilled saltwater anglers casting these spoons in brass/fire stripe patterns know that finicky barracuda will also find a Super Duper or Hot Shot Wobbler to their liking!

Bonito Spoonin'

These powerful little members of the tuna family are readily taken on a shiny spoon. "Bonies" in deep water will jump on a Crippled Herring, Haddock Jig'n Spoon, Hopkins, or Dungeness Stinger spoon yo-yoed off the bottom. Any of these models in some variation of chrome finish will perform admirably. Scale down in size, however, from 3/4 to 2 ounces.

When bonito are on the surface feeding on schools on anchovies, start throwing those Krocadiles! A 5/8 to 1 1/2 ounce "Kroc" thrown on a light baitcasting or spinning outfit makes a potent combination on bonito. Here again, almost any finish in the Krocadile series will be effective on the bonies as long as it has some trace of chrome in it.

Yellowtail Spoons

These fish are one of the most prized gamefish sought along the Southern California and Baja coastlines. There are times, particularly when the "yellows" are feeding near the surface, that they will attack a spoon.

With most specimens in the 12 to 25 pound range, don't hesitate to throw a larger 3 1/4 to 5 ounce Krocadile on schools of boiling yellowtail. Be careful not to reel the "Kroc" in too fast. A steady retrieve to keep the spoon from spinning is best for yellows.

The chrome/blue mackerel, chrome/green mackerel, chrome/silver prism-lite, and blue mackerel finishes are favorites when throwing big Krocadiles on feeding yellowtail.

However, don't overlook slow-trolling these big spoons to locate schools of "breezing" yellows. Throttle down the boat speed to a few knots and slow-troll "Krocs" in yellowtail territory. The big spoons will look like errant mackerels or sardines—prime morsels for hungry yellows!

Tuna Spoons

Yes, tuna will definitely nail a spoon on the outer banks! As the boat slides to a stop following an initial strike on the trolling lines, quickly fire off a cast with either a Krocadile, Dungeness Stinger, Haddock Jig'n Spoon, or Crippled Herring spoon. Lure color isn't too critical in this situation when fishing "the slide." Any of these spoons in a variation of chrome finish will work fine. As the spoon sinks away from the boat, charging yellowfin, bluefin, or albacore tuna may intercept it as it is sinking. After the spoon has sunk to roughly 90 to 150 feet if you don't get bit, start a steady retrieve back to the surface.

The offshore strike can be voracious on these lures with tuna in the 15 to 35 pound range. After you catch one on the slide, continue to free-cast the spoons, fishing them fairly deep for the schooling tuna. Some of the largest specimens caught on a tuna trip are invariably taken by an accomplished angler fishing lures like these spoons on "the slide."

Spoon Bottom Grabbers

Halibut, ling cod, and the myriad of shallow-water rockfish found all the way north to Vancouver are eager biters when it comes to the shiny spoon. As was mentioned with saltwater bass fishing, bottom contact will be essential when vertical spoonin' for these bottom dwellers.

The heavier 1 1/2 to 4 ounce models in both the Dungeness Stinger and Crippled Herring spoons are excellent for this type of bottom-bouncin'. The vertical lift-and-drop yo-yoing technique works best. As you fish these spoons below 120 foot depths, color becomes less important to the fish. The key again is to make solid bottom contact, keeping the spoon in the deep strike zone.

I want to reiterate how important it is to occasionally pin on a strip of cut mackerel or dead squid to one of the points on the spoon's treble hook when you start to do some serious deep-water spoonin'. This adds a lot of "flavor," giving the spoon a more lifelike scent at these greater depths where the fish rely more upon smell than sight and color!

Salmon Spoons

Both chinook and coho salmon are eager to strike a trolled spoon as the boat pulls these lures with the current. This kind of lure clearly mimics crippled baitfish which comprise the bulk of the salmon's diet. Wobbling spoons such as the Krocadile are usually the best choice for salmon. You need to have that distinctive side-to-side action to trigger strikes.

Both coho and chinook salmon can be highly temperamental when it comes to spoon color choices. Be prepared to switch back and forth between certain models throughout a day of trolling. Depending upon where the salmon are stratified—and this is where good electronics come into play—different colored spoons will reflect or refract light better than others.

For example, a red spoon trolls best at the surface down to about 30 foot depths. Any deeper, and this color is filtered out. Yellow and chartreuse models in contrast, will be effective down to about 60 feet with green and blue spoons working somewhat deeper. By understanding this simple color gradation, you will be able to select the most effective colored spoon when trolling for salmon off the Pacific Coast.

Compared to other spoonin' strategies, salmon trolling can be done with a wide range of set ups: surface (flat line), keel sinker, Dipsy Diver plane, downriggers, and Dodger rigs. (These tactics are explained in greater detail in the general section on salmon fishing.) Salmon can also be caught slowly drifting spoons in open water. This method is simple to master. Free-spool the spoon to the bottom or desired level. Raise the rod tip from about 6 inches to 6 feet to start the sequence. Then drop the rod tip sharply causing slack line. This allows the lure to flutter back to the starting level. Pause a few seconds after the line tightens up and begins another lift-and-drop sequence.

Spoon Stripers!

Most of the same spoonin' tactics that work for pelagic species such as bonito, barracuda, and calico or sand bass will work equally well for striped bass. In fact, stripers often put on the most voracious surface-feeding frenzies where a well-thrown spoon gets bit instantly. Both wobblers and slab-style models are effective with this northern gamefish.

Like salmon, striped bass can also be spooned on the drift or slow-trolled from the surface to mid-depths utilizing everything from diving plans to downriggers to keep the spoon at specific strata. Proven striped bass colors in metal spoons for medium to deep spoonin' are blue or green in combination with nickel (either hammered or smooth surface). For spoonin' striped bass near the surface use chartreuse green or red in prism scale or pointed finishes as well as standard metallic gold or chrome finishes. Refer to the more detailed section on stripers for additional information.

All-Season Lures!

As you can see, saltwater spoons are truly multi-species all-season lures. Carry an array of these various models in a variety of sizes, shapes and colors with you when fishing the vast Pacific coastal waters.

When other anglers are struggling with live bait, try these spoons! More fish and larger "jackpot" contenders are always a possibility when you start using simple yet effective spoons along the West Coast!

Packing Iron

As the director of the Eagle Claw Saltwater Fishing Schools, I travel around the country to look for new locales to serve as sights for future programs. In my travels to the Florida Keys, Kauai, Kona, and Cabo San Lucas, I have realized that the cast-metal jig or the "iron" as it is termed, is basically a Southern California phenomenon. For example, on a trip to the Keys to sample the giant amberjack suspended in 300 to 400 feet of water, I was amazed to see 45 to 75 pound "ambers" practically inhale a big U.F.O. #6 or Salas 6 or 7x size jig every drop.

Deep-water yo-yoing in this manner is still foreign to most charter boat operations in Florida. When you talk about "jigs," many skippers quickly point to a painted lead head with bucktail feathers. A search through the various tackle stores in the Keys also proved futile—they just don't stock this style of lure.

On a trip to Cabo San Lucas, our students experienced one of those rare days when the marlin simply refused to strike either live bait or a trolled lure. As we were jigging for mackerel (a prime marlin bait), in mid-afternoon, one of the anglers in our party decided to drop a heavy blue and white metal jig down about 200 to 250 feet to see if there were fish below the bait.

Sure enough, almost instantly, he got bit on the yo-yo by huge 10 to 13 pound class skipjack tuna. Soon, we were all yo-yoing the iron for these second-class tuna as a means of salvaging an otherwise long, unproductive day of marlin fishing. Needless to say, we had some great sport fighting these monster "skippies" on light tackle teamed with the heavy jigs. A similar scenario was repeated for yellowfin tuna and dorado while tossing the iron following a Cabo jig strike on the troll.

These are clear examples of why it pays to "pack iron" with you wherever you venture Pacific. You can't go wrong by always having a few of the heavier sinking versions handy. These jigs will allow you to fish the optimal strike zones quickly. They are relatively easy to use, either yo-yoing up-and-down, or simply winding in on a steady retrieve. Salmon, striped bass, ling cod, and rockfish are also prime candidates for the serious jig fisherman working the colder northern waters.

As for color schemes, there seems to be a basic selection of patterns in this sort of lure that are effective on the Pacific coast. Keep a few jigs in chrome, blue and white, green and yellow, and solid white in your tackle box at all times. These are popular colors for most pelagic species. As an added trick, throw a few marking pens into your tackle box. Using permanent black, blue, red, or green ink, you can custom-color almost any one of the basic jig patterns while in the field to adjust for particular species preferences.

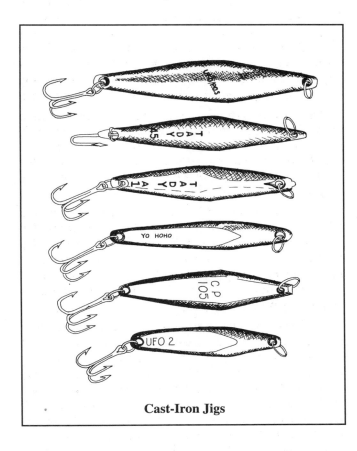

Cast-Iron Jigs

Bottom dwellers also chomp on solid chrome, blue/ white, scrambled egg, green or blue/chrome, mottled purple, orange or red, and solid white. As for the "light" versions, or surface jigs, the color menu includes solid white or chrome, scrambled egg, blue/white, and green/ yellow. Here is a succinct listing of the most popular models, weights, and colors of cast-metal jigs we routinely use on the Eagle Claw Fishing Schools with great success.

Species	Recommended Jig Models	Preferred Colors
Calico bass	U.F.O. #2 Salas Christy 2 (H) Tady 45 (L)	blue/white, green/yellow, General Motors green
Sand bass	U.F.O. #2 Salas Christy 2 (H)	blue/white, blue/chrome, solid white, solid chrome
Striped bass	U.F.O. #2, #3, #5	solid white, solid chrome
Bonito	U.F.O. #1, #2 Yo Ho Ho 1-4	blue/white, blue/chrome, green/chrome
Barracuda	U.F.O. #2, #4 Yo Ho Ho 1-4 Tady A1 (H) Salas 6xJR (H)	solid white, blue/white, blue/chrome, scrambled egg
Yellowtail	U.F.O. #3, #5 and P.O.S.(L) Tady A1(H) and 45(L) Salas CP105	scrambled egg, blue/white, solid chrome, dorado
Yellowfin tuna	U.F.O. #3, #5 Yo Ho Ho #2, #3 Tady A-1(H) Salas CP105	scrambled egg, blue/white, blue/chrome, dorado
Bluefin tuna	U.F.O. #5, #6 Yo Ho Ho #3 Tady A1 (H) Salas CP105 Yo Yo #4	blue/white, blue/chrome
Albacore	U.F.O. #3, #5 Yo Ho Ho #3 Tady A1 (H) Salas CP105 Yo Yo #4	blue/white, blue/chrome, scrambled egg, red/white
Dorado	U.F.O. #3 Yo Ho Ho #3 Tady A1 (H)	dorado, blue/white, scrambled egg, blue/ chrome
White sea bass	U.F.O. #5 and P.O.S. (L) Salas 6x and 7x (H and L)	solid white, blue/white, solid chrome
Ling cod	U.F.O. #5, #6 Salas 6x, 7x (H)	solid white, blue/white, blue/chrome, solid chrome
Rockfish	U.F.O. #2, #5, #6 Salas 6xJR Yo Ho Ho 1-4	solid white, solid chrome, blue/white, scrambled egg, blue/chrome, green/chrome

Favorite Times and Places

Over the years we have traveled to may different locales to teach anglers the insiders' perspective on how to catch more and larger saltwater species. In this section I want to select some of the most popular times and areas we routinely fish on our Eagle Claw Schools, plus a few "hot spots" that especially cater to the small boater. I'll elaborate on how to increase your catch from these "honey holes" employing many of the strategies highlighted in previous chapters. These are the times and places where you can put your lessons to good use!

Small Boats and Moonlight Madness

With the reflection of the moon glistening on the water, I felt the hard "thump" of a bass inhaling my jig as it bounced off the rocks. I reeled up the slack quickly and reared back on the 7 1/2 foot graphite casting rod. I could feel that I had some good "metal" on this fish as the stiff rod bent in two and the 17 pound mono started to peel off the reel. After a few minutes a fat chunky 4 pounder was placed in the "live well motel."

This was not a scene from an exotic night bite on some bass lake. Rather, we were fishing the Long Beach Federal Breakwater for those super strong saltwater counterparts to the freshwater largemouth calico and sand bass. My guide was Bob Suekawa, longtime local and manufacturer of the popular line of Haddock lures. Suekawa has been fishing this expansive rocky structure for over 20 years. He is considered to be an authority on challenging the breakwall in the middle of the night.

The Federal Breakwater is actually divided into three distinct rocky jetties, each separated by a channel leading to the open sea. The three rocky strands are known as the San Pedro, Federal, and Long Beach Walls. Local anglers collectively refer to the three structures as the "Wall." They are located about 1 1/2 miles from the shore and are accessible by private boat from a variety of small craft harbors including Cabrillo Beach, Golden Shores, and San Pedro.

Most anglers visiting the Wall are recreational fishermen who work it primarily in daylight hours. There can be a modest bite on perch, halibut, rockfish, and a few scattered sand bass, as well as the occasional bonito or barracuda. However, the real secret is to fish the Wall after dark. By sunset, pleasure boat traffic has dwindled down completely. Winds have usually subsided and the water surrounding the jetties can assume an eerie calm. This time of day calico bass are the prime targets of veteran Wall fishermen working from small skiffs and larger private craft. These are very tough fighters, sometimes reaching weights over 10 pounds. A 5 pounder caught off the breakwater is a true trophy.

Many Wall regulars feel that both calicos and sand bass put on a stronger fight in the darkness and along the breakwater than when caught in the offshore ocean waters. Locals theorize that some of the calicos in particular become "home guard" fish, living only in the sanctuary of the rocky crevices. The growth of calico bass is very slow compared to other pelagic species of saltwater gamefish, so calicos over 7 to 8 pounds have

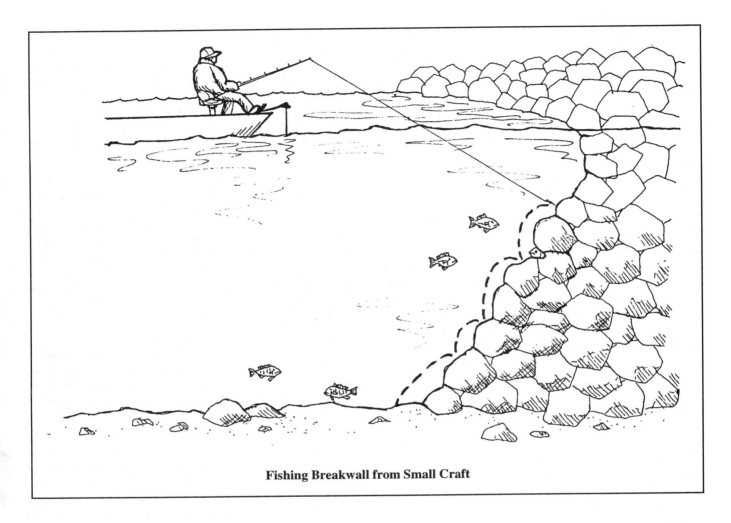

Fishing Breakwall from Small Craft

probably lived along the Wall for over 10 years. They are wary and very smart, but they are also nocturnal feeders, giving the "hawg hunters" a better shot at the bigger specimens.

Wall fishermen have the choice of sampling either the "inside" or the "outside" of the Wall. The inside waters are calmer, with the wave and surge action broken by the shelter of the rocky Wall. Many anglers fishing out of small aluminum or fiberglass boats feel safest working the "inside." On the other hand, the "outside" may hold the bigger fish. There is less fishing pressure on the outside, plus there is more food washed off the rocks into the foam by the pounding of the waves. However, it is clearly more dangerous.

Most Wall fishermen rely upon electric trolling motors to keep moving along the jetty, casting to the rocks, and retrieving the bait back to the boat. Suekawa points out one very interesting feature about fishing the Wall. He

notes that often you can motor and cast down one side without any strikes. Then, you might reverse and work your way back along the same stretch and the action becomes "wide open." He speculates that even the slightest change in tidal flow can activate the bite like an "On-Off" switch. The best activity seems to occur with a full moon, prominent current, and at the height of the solunar tables.

The large rock slabs and boulders that comprise the breakwalls actually extend out some distance under the water in a staircase-like fashion. The calicos are typically found up tight in the broken rocks and will often attack the lure the instant it hits the water. In contrast, the sand bass seem to congregate just at the edge where the rocks meet the hard-packed, sandy bottom. It is important to work your lures all the way down the incline of the Wall, checking for calicos against the rocks, and sandies out in deeper water all the way out to the boat.

Interestingly, on some super calm evenings, you can actually employ a saltwater version of the flippin' method used by freshwater bass fishermen to fish shallow areas. Using longer 7 1/2 to 8 foot rods, motor carefully on the inside of the Wall just to the edge of the submerged boulders. Believe it or not, you can gently pitch or flip lures in an almost vertical presentation directly into the rocks. Without substantial tidal surge, the calicos in particular will root right into the boulders. The vertical flippin' technique puts the jig straight down into the cracks and holes where the bigger fish live. Be prepared for a jolting strike and swing hard!

As for the proper tackle for this type of moonlight safari, stout rods and baitcasting reels are a necessity. Heavy-duty freshwater bassin' gear is usually adequate. Strong graphite or fiberglass rods in 6 to 7 1/2 foot lengths are ample for making the 50 to 60 foot long casts to the rocks. Baitcasting reels spooled with 15 to 20 pound monofilament are matched with these stronger rods. Casting reels with some type of magnetic breaking system can be a real boon for this type of night fishing. Turn the anti-inertia setting up a little higher than normal to minimize the chance of bothersome backlash in the dark.

Drags are usually locked down fairly tight. With calicos, in particular, you don't want to have these fish run back into the sharp rocks. Be prepared to lose a lot of lures over the course of an evening's fishing. Invariably even the heavier monofilament will become frayed and nicked from contact with the rocks. You should recurrently check the last 18 inches of line and re-tie as necessary.

Also many anglers have some initial problem with night vision and depth perception when fishing the Wall. It may take some practice to consistently make a cast that will land tight up against the Wall, without overshooting and embedding the lure into the boulders.

In addition, you can't let the bait sink too far. As with freshwater bassin', the Wall fisherman will have to develop a sensitive feel that allows him to either "hop" the lure over or to "swim" it just above the rocks. Try to maintain a moderately tight line to get a good strong hookset on these tough saltwater bass.

Both species—calicos and sand bass alike—are very tenacious fish. The strike can be vicious. However, once hooked near the Wall, count on these bass to make a beeline right back to the boulders. Hence, it is important to keep steady pressure on the fish, heading them away from the rocks.

Most seasoned breakwater fishermen use artificial lures in stalking nighttime sandies and calicos. Plastic baits are overwhelmingly the choice of locals who fish these rocks. Popular swimming lures such as the Scampi, Mojo, Shakin' Shrimp, and Shakin' Shad produce quite well. Preferred colors include root beer flake, lime, hot pink, and smoke. Twin T's made a lure years ago called the Lunker Legs that also excels as a swimming bait if you can find any on some dusty shelf.

More conventional freshwater bass lures also take their share of these nocturnal feeders. Haddock Kreepy Krawler and Garland Spider jigs work if the fish are keying on a swimming bait. Large curl-tail plastic worms also produce when fished on an open-hook jig head. Similarly, Berkley's Power Grub that is widely used in freshwater bassin' circles has produced some sensational nighttime catches on the Wall. Pink, green, orange, salt'n pepper, silver, black, motor oil, root beer, and red seem to all work at one time or another.

Suekawa prefers his own unique Haddock Split-Tail Grub as perhaps the "sleeper" bait of the lot. The Split-Tail Grub is a thick, fat-bodied bait with a tail divided into four separate sections. This effect creates a very slow, subtle swimming action in contrast to more active curl-tail or fork-tail lures.

But here's the key secret that Suekawa passes along: no matter what plastic lure you select for using on the Wall, tip it with a strip of frozen squid. What he does is to take about a pound of whole frozen squid, thaw it, and strip it into small 3x1/2 inch tippets. These are all pre-cut and placed in a small bait bucket before he reaches the Wall. It is tough enough fishing in the dark, let alone having to filet out frozen squid. The "jig'n squid" combo is reminiscent of the way in which freshwater bassers use pork rind trailers with their assorted jigs. (Some "old timers" still use pork rind-tipped jigs out on the wall with consistently good results.) For an added attraction squirt some saltwater Berkley Strike onto the jig'n squid. There are times when this extra scent seems to stimulate the bass into a more active feeding mode.

For anglers who prefer to use natural baits, Suekawa recommends two options. Large, whole frozen or fresh squid can be sensational at times pinned onto a 3/8 or 5/8 ounce plain jig head. Live mudsuckers fly-lined into the rocks would be the other choice. With either, don't be surprised if you tie into a real "hawg" some night, as a wayward white sea bass bushwhacks the bait.

With regard to the jig heads themselves, Suekawa recommends anywhere from 3/8 to 3/4 ounces of lead depending on tidal conditions. The lighter heads will fall slower which sometimes triggers more strikes than a heavier, faster-falling jig. The larger lead heads however are somewhat easier to cast and control when there is a lot of surge. A compromise is to take a vinyl spinnerbait skirt and slide it onto the heavier jig head. This adds bulk to the lure making it displace more water. It also gives the bait a more prominent silhouette in the darkness that can be very beneficial for this kind of night fishing. The vinyl skirt also permits the jig'n squid to fall somewhat more slowly, tantalizingly drifting just above the rocks.

Most pros who fish the Wall also prefer to use jigs with the heavier gauge cadmium hooks instead of the more traditional wire hooks found on freshwater baits. The thinner wire hooks will certainly provide better penetration on the hook-set. However, they will become either blunt or bend too easily after repeatedly bumping into the rocks.

The cadmium-plated hooks, although much duller than the wire versions, are very strong. Suekawa notes that the bass along the Wall are remarkably aggressive fish. As is often the case, they actually impale themselves on the lure as they ambush the jig and head back to the rocks. Thus, the cadmium hooks seem to work just fine even without any pre-sharpening. Also jig heads with the wire hooks become severely rusted after just one night's fishing in the salty air. This won't happen with the cadmium-plated models.

The Federal Breakwater can be an exciting alternative to more traditional offshore party boat fishing. The Wall produces all year long. Suekawa feels that it is best in late spring and early summer during the spawning season when droves of sand bass move into the shallow waters. Even the dead of winter can be productive with the right combination of moon and tidal action.

You must remain constantly alert when fishing this area in the dark. Running lights are essential. Private boaters can be expected to be visited by Coast Guard patrols if navigational lights are not turned on. There is also a lot of flotsam and floating debris at times in the harbor. Keep your speed down and motor out to the Wall with caution.

Once there, keep an eye out for shifts in tidal conditions. If you prefer to work the outside, be especially on guard for unexpected swells created by the taxi boats that run all night long shuttling back and forth to the offshore oil rigs. If the winds kick up and the sea becomes too rough on the outside Wall—don't fight it! You can still salvage much of the outing by seeking protection on the calmer inside rocks.

One further note: it might be wise to keep a compass in your boat. The coastal fog can become really thick all of a sudden, turning a clear night into a navigational nightmare. Many veteran Wall jockeys dress in foul weather gear, since the nighttime air can become very misty and wet.

The Wall usually holds plenty of calicos and sandies but they are not always lunkers. Some evenings the pesky little ones will mount an all-out attack on your jigs, while the "toads" seem to be hiding in the rocks. Consider keeping a lighter spinning outfit spooled with 6 to 8 pound mono. Even the "shorts" offer one of the best fights pound for pound of any fish I've caught on light tackle. You will experience that the ratio of fish caught per angling hour spent on the Wall is one of the highest found anywhere in the West!

A Bay Bonanza!

Located one hour south of downtown Los Angeles, Newport Bay is a recreational mecca for many Southern Californians. This is one of the most productive places to find a myriad of saltwater species. Locals are able to catch everything from spotted bay bass and halibut to spotfin croaker and bonito on a year-round basis in this busy harbor. Tourists visiting the Southland will also enjoy the nearby charm of Balboa Island with its quaint shops and variety of restaurants. You can take a swim at Newport Dunes and Balboa Peninsula or hike around the back bay wilderness preserve and encounter numerous species of coastal waterfowl.

Look for Moving Water

You usually can't go wrong fishing moving water in Newport Harbor. By "moving" I am referring to tidal flow, backwashes, whirlpools, and eddies. I have fished numerous times, for instance, in the bay with local experts like guide Mike Gardner and freshwater bass pros, Jim Emmett and Larry Hopper. Even when using strictly artificial lures, these anglers are always on the lookout for flowing water. All types of gamefish found in this particular harbor are attracted to areas like this. The trick is to watch for junctures where the currents cut into otherwise still water.

The mouth of this bay leads to open ocean. This is also a place where the outside currents collide with calmer waters. Pelagic species such as bonito can frequently be taken in this outermost portion of Newport Bay. Colder ocean currents often push the schools of anchovy baitfish into the warmer waters of the middle harbor area. Gamefish will typically follow, sometimes traveling some distance all the way into the backwaters.

The main channel in Newport Bay can have considerable current ripping through it. Numerous species traverse the channel looking for morsels of food swept up in the current. The sand bass and halibut in particular can be found here all through the year.

Electronics can be a tremendous help. The deeper channel is marked with navigational buoys in most areas. By monitoring graphs and LCRs for dramatic changes in depth, private boaters can find the edge of the channel. This topographical "break" or drop-off is where different gamefish lurk waiting to ambush schools of bait.

Always pay attention to tide tables. For Newport Bay, your chances are maximized fishing on a fast-moving incoming tide. Fishing here is always best with a lot of water being exchanged with the tides.

Fish Structure

There can be extensive structure in this harbor that will attract fish in the quiet waters. Both functional and deteriorated wooden or concrete pilings used for supporting wharves, docks, or bridges are excellent spots to try. Rocky outcroppings and scattered chunks of broken concrete block are equally good fish-holding areas.

The boat moorings themselves provide shade and cover for gamefish. They can hide in the darker water created underneath moored boats lying in wait to ambush an errant baitfish or crustacean. Boat docks and moorings are often situated in deeper water so that sailboat skegs and power boat motors won't scrape the bottom. Sometimes this difference in depth, especially when it is near the bank or dock, can form feeding pockets for larger harbor residents.

The fuel dock on the east side of the main channel can similarly be a phenomenally good place to try. Too often anglers falsely assume that because of all the boat traffic, fish won't move into the waters under this structure. Gamefish that have resided in Newport Bay for long periods of time become acclimated to the commotion created by passing boats. The wood, concrete, and similar material used to build this floating gas station can play host, once again, to barnacles, mussels, crabs, and schools of bait. Spotted bay bass—one of the toughest of all marine gamefish—will gravitate to all of these diverse structures.

A bait receiver can also be an "oasis in the desert" for an expansive harbor such as Newport. Invariably, baitfish minnows escape from the holding tanks or transfer nets. These baits will typically remain in close proximity to the floating receiver located in front of the Balboa Pavilion. It is always a good gamble to investigate the water in this area, especially if the halibut are on the move.

Basic Tackle

Heavier freshwater outfits such as baitcasting reels and stouter popping rods have excellent utility in Newport Bay. They are strong enough to tame a halibut, bonito, or even a big bat ray. They are also lightweight and can provide a lot of sporting fight with the spotted bay and sand bass. Heavy freshwater or lighter saltwater outfits like these are also perfect for trolling in the harbor. Bonito or bay bass can put up quite a tussle when caught while trolling this bay. Saltwater species of this genre strike a trolled lure hard—even the 1 to 2 pounders—so a few broken lines will result with ultralight tackle.

Lures for Fishing Newport Bay

It is important to fish the moving water with lures. In the flowing water, gamefish—and the bigger specimens at that—are often more likely to strike the artificial over a live offering. This is probably due to both the unique appearance and swimming action of the lure. Bass, halibut, or croaker feeding in current don't have time to study the bait. If they wait too long, the morsel will be swept away. (This is analogous to stream fishing for trout.) If the fish sees the lure erratically moving in the current, it will often strike with a vengeance, fearful that its food will quickly move out of range. Lures should definitely be trolled or bounced along the edge of the channel. Positioning the boat on the outside lip of the break and casting to deep water, bringing the lure up the side, works for many gamefish found inside Newport Harbor.

Gently "parachute" your lures down the side of pilings and docks, looking for the scrappy spotted bay bass. Locating and using structure is the foundation of a lot of free-casting with lures while sampling Newport Bay. Pinpoint accuracy is essential in presenting your artificial baits along the pilings, docks, moorings, and similar structure.

As with freshwater stream fishing, bay species will face the current as it washes food down in their direction. So with artificials make your presentation up above the fish and retrieve it directly in front of them. Time is wasted if the angler can clearly discern the direction of the current but ends up casting his lure to the fish's back.

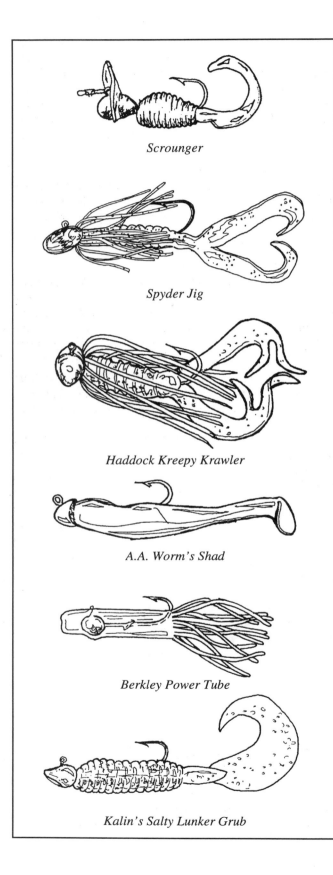

Scrounger

Spyder Jig

Haddock Kreepy Krawler

A.A. Worm's Shad

Berkley Power Tube

Kalin's Salty Lunker Grub

Plastics, Cranks, and Spoons for the Bay

Many soft plastic baits work quite well in the quiet waters of Newport Harbor. Ultralight tube lures like tiny Fatzees or Gitzits are excellent. Scroungers, Berkley Power Grubs, and plastic worms can also be sensational on all kinds of bay residents. Perch, croaker, turbot, corbina, halibut, stripers, as well as sand and spotted bay bass, will eat these soft plastics. Plastic lures in this genre are also highly effective slow-drifted in these areas. The easiest technique is to use two or three different rods per angler with assorted baits. Lean the rods on the side of the boat and let the drift and current work the lures in a slow, bottom-bouncing action.

Slow-swimming knob-tail baits like A.A. Worm's Shads have also put a major dent into the population of bay gamefish, especially the smaller species such as turbot, perch, croaker, sargo, and spotted bay and sand bass. Most of these fish-like replicas are made from hand-poured soft plastic. They are meant to be casted or drifted on a 1/8 ounce lead head. The tantalizing tail action imitates a small perch or anchovy. The results can be fantastic using a knob-tail bait and lighter 6 to 8 pound monofilament. Don't hesitate to fish these miniature lures through shallow areas with a lot of current.

Assorted crankbaits normally associated with freshwater bassin' also produce in this water. Some anglers cast and retrieve these lures towards shoreline targets. Others prefer to set up trolling patterns, dragging the crankplugs along the edges of the channel. Deep-diving plugs such as Bomber Model As, Hellbenders, Rapala Fat Raps, and Waterdogs, can really stir up some commotion as they plow the 10 to 20 foot depths of the bay. Likewise, don't overlook the wide range of possibilities for casting or trolling medium-to-deep CD-9 to CD-13 Rapala minnows in the harbor. Larger gamefish will definitely zero in on these 'chovy replicas.

More traditional spoonin' tactics also work inside these sheltered zones. Basic cast-and-retrieve or slow-trolling with spoons account for numerous tallies of bonito and small barracuda. These pelagic gamefish are accustomed to attacking a more active lure as they do in open ocean. Krocadiles, Hot Shots, Haddock Jig'n Spoons, or larger Hopkins models can be used to lure these more aggressive species when they migrate into Newport Bay.

Bay Baits

Live anchovies are overwhelmingly the best natural bait to use in Newport Bay for the bass, bonito, barracuda, and halibut. The anchovies can be purchased at the Pavilion on the west side of the main channel. The rental boats also come with a supply of live 'chovies. Other viable natural baits include blood worms, fresh bay mussels, ghost shrimp, and Pismo clams. Perch, sargo, croaker, and corbina will readily attack these natural offerings. Fish these with either a medium-size split-shot crimped 18 to 24 inches above the baits or fish a sliding egg sinker rig similar to the one used for trout or catfish. Local bait shops on the Newport Pier and Balboa Pavilion areas sell these and other natural baits.

A Year-Round Bonanza

Newport Bay provides some of the best light tackle sport to be found in either coast. Veteran bay busters like guide Mike Gardner emphasize to stay with light line, preferably 6 pound test monofilament for the best results. The natural baits and lures will swim better with the fine diameter mono. Keep trying different spots and always look for moving water. This is truly a year-round bonanza!

The Farallons

Located about 2 1/2 hours west of San Francisco's Golden Gate Bridge, the eerie rocky outcroppings collectively known as the Farallon Islands serve as the prime fishing grounds for the Bay Area party boat fleet. In actuality, the expansive Gulf of the Farallons, located midway between the islands and the mainland, is perhaps one of the finest salmon trolling areas in the entire West Coast from mid-February to mid-November. Both chinook and coho (silver) salmon are possibilities. Albacore tuna are even caught due south of the rocks from August to October during many years.

It is, however, the awesome ling cod and shallow-water rockfish population at the Farallons I want to talk about here. The first seminar I conducted while fishing the Pacific Ocean's version of Stonehenge was indeed a memorable experience.

A Shallow-Water Haven!

The most surprising thing about the Farallons is perhaps how shallow you can fish compared to locales further south. Sportfishing skippers routinely anchor at depths ranging from 6 to 20 fathoms. The bottom can be very rocky, the water typically cold, and the bottom grabbers very willing to bite.

Ling cod, vermilion, yellowtail, copper, and blue rockfish, as well as johnny bass (olive rockfish) and bocaccio (salmon grouper), round out the Farallons menu.

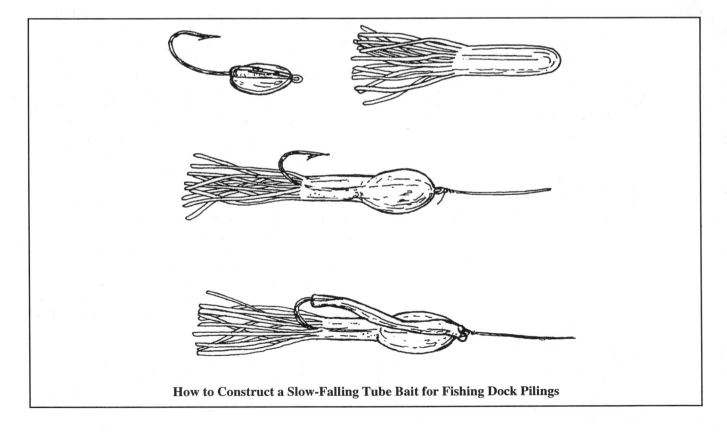

How to Construct a Slow-Falling Tube Bait for Fishing Dock Pilings

Dividing the species into lings and shallow-water rock-fish, let me share with you some of the best methods to use when exploring these strange rock formations.

Farallons Ling Cod

If the boat has live anchovies available for chum don't be surprised to see ling cod come up and actually boil in the chum line like tuna! It is an awesome sight to see these turquoise-bellied monsters crashing on the surface for bait in less than 50 feet of water!

At times you can indeed catch ling cod fly-lining live bait. Pick out the largest specimens you can find from anchovies, smelt, herring, or small perch. The bigger the bait, the bigger the ling. Use an anal hooking technique with a large Eagle Claw #318-N 4/0 to 6/0 hook for these voracious bottom fish.

The Farallon lings also annihilate the big Caba Caba Tubes. This is a highly potent lure, especially when the ling cod are near the bottom, The best color schemes for throwing the Cabas seem to be darker patterns including black/orange, black/red, dark blue, and root beer/flake. Add a strip of small rockfish filet, a piece of cut squid, or a wedge of mackerel, to the Caba Caba Tubes and you have one of the best ling cod killers in the Bay Area!

The ling cod off these rocks will also readily eat the iron. You don't have to necessarily fish the big jigs, just make sure you are using the heavy models in the medium-size lures. Models such as the Yo Ho Ho #3 or #4, U.F.O. #3 and #5, and Salas Christy 2 and CP105 are perfect for Farallons lings. I like to bounce these jigs in solid chrome, blue/chrome, or green/chrome finishes. As with any bottom-bouncin' jigs, a strip of meat or a whole frozen squid pinned onto one of the treble hooks increases the effectiveness of the lure.

If the Caba Caba Tubes or the iron fail to produce then fish the lings using standard dropper loops and live, strip, or cut bait. As I mentioned in regard to fly-lining for the ling cod, don't think twice about using a big bait on the dropper loop setup. I prefer a fairly large strip of small rockfish with lots of skin showing or a whole smelt, mackerel, or herring. I might even try a whole small rockfish or a large #6/0 to #8/0 hook. Keep in mind that especially in the fall, it is not uncommon to see sportfishing boats score one to two lings per day between 40 and 60 pounds!

Rockfish on the Rocks

The shallow-water rockfishing at the Farallons can be equally awesome using artificials. Because much of the action occurs at a mere 6 to 20 fathoms, this can be a light-liner's heaven, especially tossing soft plastics.

The full array of plastic/lead head combos work on the rockfish population: Scampi, Mojo, Power Scamper fork-tails, Salty-Magic sickle-tails, Super Shad knob-tails and, of course, Caba Caba Tubes in the smaller 1 to 3 ounce models. The soft plastic eels will rack up some nice catches, especially on the vermilion rockfish and salmon grouper.

A colorful shrimp-fly gangion is also effective for Farallon rockfish. With a torpedo sinker on the bottom, the brightly colored flies above the weight should be trimmed with either a single anchovy or a sliver of strip bait per hook. The blue, yellowtail, and copper rockfish, in particular, readily climb on this shallow-water gangion with anglers often pulling up 4 to 5 bottom grabbers per "drop." Of course, basic dropper loop rigs combined with Berkley Power Grubs or Power Tubes will also tally nice limits of the Farallon rockfish species. Here too, always try to add a small piece of squid or an anchovy to the Power Bait.

Don't overlook doing some serious shallow-water spoonin' at the Farallon Islands. Smaller 1 to 2 ounce Krocadile, Nordic, Dungeness Stinger, or Crippled Herring models can be dynamite fished either alone or in conjunction with a dropper loop and a small Power Grub. Here again, the angler proficient with heavy freshwater bassin' gear and 10 to 12 pound test line can have a field day bouncin' a smaller spoon in less than 120 feet of water for these rockfish!

Viva Los Coronados!

Lying 14 miles south of San Diego, the Los Coronados Islands offer some of the finest autumn action to be found in Southern California. Long regarded as the yellowtail mecca of the West Coast, these islands also produce stellar catches of bonito, barracuda, and sometimes blue-fin tuna in the fall.

The Coronados are divided into three major outcroppings: north and south islands and the middle ground rocks. The pelagic species seem to concentrate in one primary area on any given day. For example, in the months of September and October, you may encounter the yellows "breezing" through the middle grounds on one day. The next day, the bite may concentrate on north island's infamous "pukey point."

Thus, it is imperative to remain flexible and mobile in exploring the Coronados during this season. Always be on the lookout for signs of activity—particularly when going after yellowtail—as birds crash on meatballs of bait among surface boils of hungry 'tails, tuna, barracuda, or bonito.

Here is a basic menu of tactics to try for fall action at the Coronados once you have spotted the fish.

Trolling

To begin with, small boaters with limited chum capacity can troll between the islands in order to locate both yellows and bonito. I should add that party boat skippers also employ this strategy from time to time if the fish seem to be relatively scattered through the area.

Balsa wood Rapala minnows are one of the key lures to use for the trolling program. The larger CD-13, CD-14 and CD-18 Magnum sinking models are recommended. These have pronounced diving lips that keep the plugs at least 5 to 6 feet below the surface even on rough seas. Lures in this genre troll best at roughly 3 to 5 knots tied to 15 to 20 pound test monofilament. The large saltwater Rapala Shad Raps will also nail yellowtail here, particularly on a slow-troll through a chum line. Sometimes tuna feathers can also be effective in the smaller 15 mm head size.

The trick here is to intentionally weight the feather down so it rides 5 to 8 feet below the surface. Here is a simple rigging technique that will keep the feather deep for the yellowtail troll. Tie your 20 to 40 pound test line coming off your reel to a large snap-lock swivel eyelet. Open the snap and attach it to the ringed eye of a 10 to 16 ounce torpedo weight. Add another snap-lock swivel to the other ringed eye of the sinker. To complete the setup, tie a 5 to 6 foot length of 30 to 40 pound monofilament to this swivel eyelet. Run the remaining loose end through the 15 mm feather tied off to a double hook.

This deep-feather trolling ploy allows you to cover a lot of territory, especially when the 'tails are breezing or chasing bait. Interestingly, the schools frequently follow the jig fish up to the stern just like albacore. Be prepared to chum and get a baited hook in the water once the trolling fish is boated.

Another trolling tip is worth noting. You can sometimes catch 'tails at the Coronados in the fall slow-trolling surface "iron." I emphasize S-L-O-W trolling. Use 30 to 40 pound test line for this method and don't add swivels to the jigs. Try the U.F.O. "P.O.S." series, a Salas 6 or 7x light or a Tady 45. Stay with the basic yellowtail menu: blue/white, scrambled egg, solid white, or chrome, and sardine finishes in the iron.

Bonito can similarly be taken on the troll, dragging the Rapalas and smaller feathers. You can also slow-troll shiny spoons or more compact cast-iron jigs for "bongos."

Live Bait

An overwhelming majority of the sportfish landed at the Coronados in the fall are caught on live bait. Anchovies are the staple for autumn 'tails. Sometimes the bait this time of the year is on the small "pin-head" size. Be prepared to switch to a tiny #6 live bait hook if the 'chovies are tiny specimens. Fish the anchovies on 12 to 20 pound line. They can be either fly-lined on the surface or plunked deeper with a large split-shot sinker attached 18 to 24 inches above the hook. Scale down to 10 to 15 pound test when using 'chovies for bonito or barracuda.

Sardines are often available in the fall. Scale up to #2 to #4/0 live bait hooks depending upon the size of the 'dine. Let the fish run further with the sardine than you would when fishing with an anchovy. A slow count of 1-2-3-4-5 is commonly recommended by party boat skippers before setting up on a 'tail munching a 'dine.

Both Spanish and greenback mackerel along with smelt, tom cod, and pompano will also produce for autumn yellows. When these fish decide to eat the larger baits, don't hesitate to cast with 25 to 30 pound line. The smaller mackerel, smelt, tom cod, and pompano can be fly-lined on the surface pinned to a #1/0 to #2/0 short-shank live bait hook. As with sardines, be patient following the initial sensation of the yellowtail picking up the bait. Use the "five count" again, then swing and set hard!

For the larger mackerel, many party boat skippers now have their passengers fishing with #4 to #4/0 treble hooks. The way to do this is to carefully run only one of the three points through the nostrils of the mackerel. You will have two remaining points of the hook totally exposed. Granted, this does not appear to be a cosmetically "clean" rigging. However, greater catch-to-hook ratios typically occur when you switch to the treble hooks. This type of hook does not seem to impede the movement of the baitfish in any way.

There is always a remote possibility that bluefin tuna may show at the islands this time of year. Party boat captains view these gamesters as absolute "talent" fish. That is, it will take an accurate presentation of the bait combined with precision tackle and fish-fighting savvy to land a 15 to 30 pound bluefin. (For additional details check the previous section, "Bluefin Blues.")

Anchovies are the primary bluefin bait. Usually, these fish shy away from anything heavier that 15 pound test line. Equally important is the size of the hook. Most veteran anglers fish a small #6 to #8 live bait hook for bluefin, irrespective of how large the 'chovies are.

These fish are typically extremely sensitive feeders, but when they eat the bait, expect a scorching run and a tough battle. Reels should be spooled with no less than 300 yards of monofilament for island bluefin.

Iron, Spoons, and Plastics

Jig fishermen enjoy the autumn action at the Coronados. The bonito and barracuda usually attack the "iron." If either of these species are eating fly-lined 'chovies, then definitely make a few casts with a light surface jig. If you sight surface boils of hungry 'tails, throw larger surface "iron" in the lighter aluminum alloy versions. Best colors here are blue/white and scrambled egg.

Barracuda, bonito, and yellowtail can also be taken on a deeper "yo-yo" grind during the fall. The strategy is simple to master. Drop a "heavy" cast-iron jig down to the bottom. Then reel fast all the way back to the surface. For yellowtail, medium-size jigs are perfect for this drop-and-wind technique. Smaller models are better for bonito and "scooters" holding in deeper water. Stay with blue/white and scrambled egg in the yo-yo program.

Another popular type of lure is the narrow-bodied spoon for the Coronados bite. This highly versatile spoon weighs about 1 to 1 1/2 ounces and is available in numerous prism or scale-like finishes in models like the Haddock Jig'n Spoon, Crippled Herring, Nordic, and Dungeness Stinger. They fish exceptionally well on light 10 to 15 pound line, functioning as both a surface and deep yo-yo lure. Bonito and 'cuda often annihilate this style of spoon when live bait action sputters.

These islands have historically had only sporadic activity for calico and sand bass. However, the soft plastic lures commonly used for these fish sometimes become real "sleeper" baits for fall bonito, barracuda, and possibly yellowtail.

Soft plastic fork-tail lures occasionally give the bonies and barracuda something different to look at. Scampis, Mojos, Lunker Thumpers, and Power Scampers are staples. Hollow-bodied Caba Caba Tubes also sometimes produce excellent results on the surface feeders, slowly "pumped" back in following a long cast.

Whatever your fancy, the Coronados provide both the small craft owner and party boater alike the opportunity to experience solid fall action. You name it—trolling, live bait, jigs, spoons, or plastics—the pelagic species at these islands can be caught using a variety of methods. Crowds dwindle and the weather is mild for autumn fishing at the Coronados!

A Day on the Cortez

As I boarded the charter boat "Dreamer" out of Los Angeles Harbor Sportfishing, I asked Captain Allan Watson not to wake me until we neared our destination some 10 hours later. This mid-autumn exploratory run was my first trip to the Cortez Bank.

On this particular outing, the owner of the "Dreamer," veteran skipper Tom Schlauch, invited a collection of "hired guns" to sample the infamous Cortez. Along with Schlauch, Watson and myself were tackle dealer Ron De La Mare, sales rep Mike Callan, and deckhand Cindy White—one of the finest female anglers in the Southland.

The Cortez Bank lies roughly 95 miles due south of L.A. Harbor. The ocean bottom on this ridge varies from about 600 feet on the edge to nine fathoms (54 feet) on the high spot. Actually the Cortez is comprised of at least two shallow plateaus, each rising to the nine fathom mark. One is marked by a prominent buoy; the other lies 41 miles due west along this expansive edge. "There are times," notes Captain Schlauch, "that the buoyed high spot will actually have water breaking over the rock at low tide with a big swell creating a wash effect."

Great Surface Action!

On this particular trip Captain Watson, long regarded as one of the foremost tuna and yellowtail experts on the Coast, wanted to target big fish. That day I experienced one of the most spectacular bites I have ever encountered north of San Diego.

To start off, we anchored near the buoy in the morning and fly-lined a combination of live mackerel and squid. Callan was the first to hook up with a solid 20 pound yellowtail. After sighting marauding schools of 'tails chasing big meatballs of mackerel, we pulled anchor and slow-trolled the ridge. I was the next one to nail another solid twenty pounder on mackerel. Watson then proceeded to re-anchor. This is when the bite slowly began to build up.

I got bit again and this time I knew I was on a much larger fish. I was soaking squid on straight 40 pound test mono. After about 20 minutes, Watson gaffed a 33 pound yellowtail. This was by far my personal best for Southern California. Next, Callan set up and he too acknowledged a big fish had inhaled his mackerel. After another 20 minute battle, Callan brought a 35 pound 'tail to gaff.

Not to be outdone, De La Mare was soon on a "toad" that ate a squid on 50 pound string. This fish was clearly bigger than the two yellows Callan and I had landed. After another lengthy fight, Watson stuck De La Mare's 40 pounder—another personal best for this angler in Southern California waters. The action pretty much continued like this for over two hours, until deckhand Cindy White leaned into a fish that would soon pin her to the bow for the next half hour.

In the mean time, the bite shifted at the stern and I began to experience a scorching run unlike the "hawg" yellowtail we had been catching. After 15 minutes, Watson brought over the rail a chunky 28 pound bluefin tuna that had eaten a live squid on my 40 pound gear. Shortly after that, White lost a bluefin estimated at over 60 pounds as the hook pulled out right at "color."

This type of moderate yet steady action continued all the way into late afternoon. One or another member of the group would pick up either a yellowtail or a blue fin every 20 to 30 minutes or so. The big fish of the trip turned out to be De La Mare's 48 pound bluefin although other larger specimens were lost. By sunset, our small scouting party had tallied over thirty yellows and bluefin combined, with almost all of the fish over 30 pounds.

According to Watson, this was only a sample of how good the fishing can get on this remote bank. There are days, claims Watson, when all the yellows are pushing 40 pounds and the bluefin consistently top the 50 pound mark!

Cortez Strategies

The yellowtail on the Cortez can be caught on a variety of methods including fly-lining live bait, drifting and trolling, and sometimes either deep yo-yoing or winding a jig across the surface. "Always pick your spots when it comes to fishing these big yellows on the Cortez," observes De La Mare. "Look for fish coming up to the surface, pushing big schools of bait. Don't hesitate to throw the 'iron' in this situation."

Those who know the Cortez usually prefer to anchor on top of the bank, primarily in the autumn period. Typical yellowtail tackle consists of 25 to 60 pound outfits and is similar to long range gear. Most of the tuna action on the Cortez focuses on bluefin. However, Callan warns, don't be surprised to encounter some large yellowfin or even big eye tuna while either trolling feathers or fly-lining bait

at anchor when on this ridge. "Also, don't overlook the possibility of albacore on the Cortez," says Callan. "This happens quite frequently right outside the bank, between the Cortez and the 43 fathom spot trolling along the edge and towards the east end of Clemente."

Interestingly, Callan, one of the premier bill fishermen in the West, also emphasizes that the Cortez Bank can host a good population of striped marlin and broadbill swordfish. "The problem," claims Callan, "is that you rarely hear about the concentrations of billfish found on the Cortez because it is so far away."

Although the Cortez bank is recognized as a big fish mecca primarily in the fall, you can actually experience a year-around rockfish bonanza along this ridge. Some landings run multi-day, so-called "freezer special" trips to sample the outstanding bottom fishing at the Cortez. In the shallower zones, you will find reds, starry rockfish, and some magnum-class johnny bass and whitefish. Although not many anglers intentionally fish for this species, it is not uncommon, according to Watson, to hook into a black sea bass while soaking a large whole mackerel on the high spot.

Cut squid on dropper loop-sinker setups along with heavy chrome Diamond, Salas 6X, or U.F.O. #6 metal jigs will produce stellar rockfish limits on the Cortez. Look for larger reds and cow cod as you drift off the edge into 240 to 360 feet of water. Different portions of this bank will hold different species of bottom fish. Move around to explore your options.

A Dangerous Bank!

As mysterious and bountiful as the Cortez may appear, the fact remains that this can be a dangerous journey for inexperienced skippers in small craft. Captain Schlauch emphasizes the ominous nature of this outer bank with the following warning: "The best time to fish the Cortez is during a Santa Ana Wind condition. Understand that there is nowhere to run out here if you are caught in rough water typical of many days on this bank. You are 45 miles from the West End of San Clemente Island which is probably your nearest sanctuary. The Cortez is no place for a small boat. You are almost 100 miles out to sea. Even using your radio to put out a "May Day" signal may not be good enough if no one can hear your transmission."

Thus, treat a trip to the Cortez Bank as a miniature offshore long-range expedition. Make the journey in a boat large enough and with the appropriate safety equipment typically found on a long-range vessel. It's a long way back from the Cortez!

Tackle for the Cortez

The recommended tackle for fishing the Cortez Bank includes basic yellowtail and tuna stand-up gear. The 'tails will be caught on baits ranging from anchovies and sardines to squid and mackerel. Match hook sizes from #1/0 to #6/0 to the size of the live bait selected. Casting reels spooled with 20 to 60 pound monofilament will handle the larger yellows as they head into the rocks. Rods should be standard 6 to 7 foot, heavy-duty casting models, capable of throwing large baits or cast-metal jigs.

Similar gear will be suitable for smaller yellowfin and bluefin found on the Cortez. However, scale up with larger Penn 4/0 class reels (e.g., 113HL, 45GLS, 12 or 30T Internationals) and 50 to 80 pound line for both trolling and even fly-lining baits for big yellowfin and bluefin tuna along with big eye and possibly striped marlin.

Bottom fishing tackle may vary from shallow-water outfits for fishing smaller whitefish and reds on 15 to 30 pound line to heavy-duty roller tip rods and 4/0 to 6/0 reels for working 250 to 600 foot depths for bigger cow cod.

The Lucky Horseshoe Kelp

Less than 45 minutes out of Los Angeles Harbor, anglers can fish one of the most bountiful inshore spots to be found along the Pacific rim. The Horseshoe Kelp is a massive complex of diverse fish-holding structure with a myriad of rock piles, sunken wrecks, and various so-called "high spots." The kelp itself is seen, if at all, only on rare occasions. Much of the once-prominent kelp bed is either depleted or remains mostly submerged.

Still the "Shoe" is perhaps the most productive region for scoring on the major coastal pelagic species on a year-round basis. Lucky anglers on a given day may encounter both sand bass and calicos, barracuda, bonito, possibly yellowtail, and maybe even a wayward white sea bass or halibut. The Horseshoe Kelp consistently kicks out some of the best limit-fishing of the "three B's"—bass, barracuda, and bonito—to be found in Southern California within a one-day range of the local landings.

Here then is a synopsis of how to catch the "three B's" while fishing the "Shoe."

Big Calicos

The big "bull" bass are perhaps the main attraction for the veteran anglers who work the Horseshoe Kelp. These bass

are highly structure oriented. Pinpoint accuracy is needed with regard to boat position when setting up on a rock pile or submerged wreck. The current has to be right and the anchor set properly so that the chum will drift over the edge of the high spot bringing the bull bass up, sometimes from greater than 120 foot depths.

It is common, I might add, to watch the more knowledgeable party boat skippers anchor and re-anchor on the "Shoe" in order to adjust for changes in current so that proper position is maintained at all times.

When fishing the more compact rock piles, I have been on smaller charter boats where position became so critical for fishing the bull bass on these pinnacles that one side of the boat might get bit while the other side, slightly off center from the high spot, was stymied.

There are a number of strategies that will work for catching calicos on the Horseshoe. However, if you are targeting the larger 6 to 10 pound "bulls," learn to think "BIG." The smaller 12 inch class bass will readily eat a fly-lined 'chovy. The bull bass, in contrast, seem to hang at deeper strike zones, preferring a well-presented and substantially larger morsel. On many occasions, I have fished the Shoe with veteran skipper Alan Watson. Here is a man who is a firm believer in the adage "Big Baits = Big Fish."

Watson usually likes to fish the "junk" for these big bull bass. This is your typical mixture of brown baits including herring, tom cod, queen fish, and small shiner perch. This collection of larger baits can be fished in a number of different ways.

To begin with, you can try nose-hooking the brown bait or run a large #4/0 live bait hook behind the dorsal fin. Either of these methods work for fly-lining the tom cod or herring on heavier 20 to 30 pound line. This tactic is productive if the bass are up near the surface, boiling in the chum.

More often than not, a better approach is to get the brown baits down where the trophy size fish live. The simplest way to do this is to run your live bait hook across the anal pore of the tom cod or herring. This ploy forces the baitfish to swim downward rather than staying near the surface. No cumbersome sinker is necessary with this technique so the brown bait swims essentially on a deep fly-line program.

The other strategy I have seen skippers like Watson, Tom Schlauch, Russ Izor, and Mike Callan employ is so simple it borders on the ridiculous! They take a 1 to 3 ounce lead head and pin the brown bait on by running the hook through the upper and lower lip. When you see this

Hooking "Brown (Junk) Baits"

calico killer setup for the first time, it appears extremely crude and doesn't look like anything that would fool a fish that may be over a decade old.

Nevertheless, this little trick really works, as I learned when I watched Captain Watson nail a limit of big fish including a 10 pound bull on consecutive casts one morning. It is obvious that the big calicos are less interested in how cosmetically "clean" the lead head and brown bait combo looks. It is more important that this rug gets the bait down into those deeper ranges where the larger bass are holding.

The big calicos on the Shoe also eat squid. During the winter months, the bass will be holding at greater depths. Pin a live squid onto either an Eagle Claw #118MG or #318-N bait hook in size #4/0 with a 1 to 2 ounce sliding egg sinker resting above the hook eye. After you make the cast, the live "candy" darts and dances as it swims towards the bottom dragging the sliding egg sinker. The bass may strike the squid anywhere from sub-surface depths all the way to the bottom.

Other experts on the Shoe will fish the live squid pinned onto a simple unpainted lead head. Again, nothing fancy. The 3/4 to 3 ounce jig head will get the squid down fairly quickly.

Either the sliding sinker or simple lead head strategy will also work with dead squid. The trick here is to sort of "pump" the bait in, lifting the rod tip a few feet then letting it drop. This will provide the dead squid with some movement, giving the illusion that it is alive under water.

The calico bass on the Shoe will also eat two other offerings, especially in warm weather. Try soft plastic tail-swimming jigs like the Mojo, Lunker Thumper, or Salty Magic on lighter 10 to 15 pound line. Look for a lot of strikes to occur following the cast as the lure flutters downward.

Finally, also consider fly-lining Spanish or greenback mackerel for bull bass. These two baitfish can produce some real trophy calicos when the big fish are boiling in the chum line.

Sand Bass

The Horseshoe Kelp area produces a good portion of the Southern California sand bass totals each season. With the sandies, almost anything goes here when the fish are stacked up thick in the spring and summer. There are, however, a few insiders tips worth noting in your hunt for a larger "grumper" sand bass in the 6 to 10 pound range.

For instance, Captain "Cookie" Cook running for Sport King out of L.A. Harbor Sportfishing routinely puts on a convincing demonstration of the potency of a dropper loop setup on the Shoe. Cook's strategy is simple enough: a 2 ounce torpedo sinker with a dropper loop about 10 to 12 inches above the weight. Use an Eagle Claw #318-N in size #1 or #2 live bait hook and 'chovies with the dropper loop setup.

Soft plastic lures are another staple for the sandies on the Horseshoe. If you want a shot at the larger "grumpers," fish a small Caba Caba Tube in either milky glow or chartreuse with black flakes. Both of these colors in the Caba seem to produce the better quality sand bass. Maintain good bottom contact with a 3 ounce lead head when fishing the Caba Caba Tube here. Usually the "grumper" class bass will be deep.

Spoons are yet another well-kept secret for big sandies on the Shoe. The heavier 2 to 4 ounce chrome Krocadile models laced with a chunk of squid are real sand bass killers at times. The wide metallic surface gives off a lot of flash. Add a squid tippet, and the fluttering action of this combo on the fall presumably appears to be an erratic squid tumbling towards oblivion.

Although the sand bass are usually found on hard muddy bottoms, they will definitely hunker down on the reefs and rock piles found in the Horseshoe Kelp. You will find that these are frequently the larger specimens in the dock counts.

Bonito

There are times when the bonito action on the Shoe is nothing short of fantastic. There are some occasions where magnum-class, 8 to 10 pound bonies readily cooperate, assuming there is plenty of live bait for chum.

Quite frequently, anglers departing for the Shoe at 1:00 or 2:00 in the morning will be able to acquire only puny-size anchovies from the bait vendors. However, if you are willing to delay your departure until 5:00 or 6:00 a.m., there is a better chance that the bait boats have netted larger anchovies. One explanation for this is that the larger baitfish seem to congregate in the shallower water near the coastline in the hours before dawn.

Obviously, live 'chovies fly-lined will always be a particularly prime offering for big bonito at the Horseshoe. However, a number of other strategies will work as well.

First of all, if you end up with a tank full of pinheads, try using a large, clear Cast-a-Bubble filled halfway with water in place of a sliding egg sinker. Let the plastic float butt up against a simple swivel. Tie a 4 to 6 foot length of leader to the other end with a small Eagle Claw #318-N live bait hook in sizes #4 to #6.

The clear plastic bubble filled with water will give you ample weight to make a long cast to the outside chum where the bonito may be feeding. When the bonie picks up the pinhead 'chovy, the leader slides through the float with minimal resistance. This simple little trick will often save the trip when you are stuck with tiny bait.

The bonito on the Shoe will also attack a small white feather with the old-fashioned chrome lead head. The secret is to "pump" the feather back to the boat, using long rhythmic sweeps of the rod tip, and without any other weight added. Look for strikes to occur in between "pumps" as the feather falls.

Horseshoe-bred bongos will also chase basic blue/white, blue/chrome, or green/yellow jigs. Scale down with your selection of iron with this species. Try the U.F.O. #1 or #2, Yo Ho Ho #1 to #3, Tady AA, or Salas Christy #1 or #2 for bonito on the Shoe.

Similarly, the ever popular Krocadile spoon in 1 to 2 ounce models as well as the Dungeness Stinger or Crippled Herring in the same weight range will nail plenty of bonies here. Popular colors are chrome, blue/chrome, or mackerel finishes.

Finally, don't overlook trolling this area for bonito. You can slow-troll spoons or feathers, but better yet, switch to a small minnow-shaped plug. The Rapala sinking CD-11 or CD-13 series along with the chrome finish floating-diving Jensen Minnow are winners on a medium troll at 2 to 5 knots. Almost any pattern will work, especially in the blue/silver foil color.

Barracuda

Historically, the Horseshoe kelp produces sensational barracuda action. The 'cuda will always home in on a fly-lined 'chovy or the same bait fished behind a 1 to 2 ounce chrome torpedo sinker with a 24 inch leader if the fish are holding deep. However, the best barracuda fishing on the Shoe is usually with a narrow repertoire of artificial lures.

Start by "pumping" a solid white or red/white chromed feather. Use the same rod-lift technique I mentioned for bonito. Next, try grinding the iron for the 'cuda. A small to medium, heavier jig in blue/white or blue/chrome is hard to beat. Bring out your jig stick and throw the big surface iron in the same color schemes if the big "log" barries start boiling on the surface.

The larger 2 to 4 ounce chrome, blue/chrome or prism scale colored Krocadile spoons are real killers on the bigger "stove pipe" class barracuda on the Shoe. Let this spoon sink all the way to the bottom then wind it in intermittently pausing to let the lure sink. As you would expect, many bites occur while the "Kroc " is sinking.

Recently, a red hot bait we discovered on our Eagle Claw Schools has been to fish the Horseshoe barracuda population with a small blue Caba Caba Tube. The "blue tube" as we call it has produced stunning limit catches, especially on bigger specimens when both live bait and traditional hardware fails to get bit.

All Year Long!

The Horseshoe Kelp region remains a remarkable all-year fishery, especially for the "three B's." Limit-type fishing is possible for both bass species during the winter and early spring. The sandies will usually go "wide open" by mid-June through late summer, while the calicos move up to the surface, hungry for big baits.

The barracuda and bonito are primarily a summer through fall surface proposition here. There is always an outside chance of finding a smattering of each of these two gamefish almost any time if you look to deeper water on the Shoe.

Learn this area. Fish with both the top charter and sportfishing fleets. There are lots of prime spots to fish on the Horseshoe, but only the veteran skippers know how to position their vessels to take advantage of these rock piles, pinnacles, and sunken wrecks.

Fishing the El Niño

Most Southland anglers have heard of it; some have experienced it. But, for the most part, the El Niño phenomena remains an enigma. An El Niño condition may exist when an extraordinary mass of warm water is pushed up from southern Baja into the Southern California region. This is when barracuda are caught off Monterey and yellowtail show up in San Francisco Bay.

Some More Strange Phenomena

While interviewing a number of local experts, I was told of some intriguing phenomena they encountered in past El Niños.

Captain Russ Izor, one of the foremost authorities on the Southern California fishery, talked about the El Niño of 1958-59 as perhaps the most fantastic of all in recent local angling history. "I remember how in the early spring of 1958, the entire Southern California area from Newport Beach to Paradise Cove was loaded with 10 to 12 pound yellowtail. The run lasted for about three weeks, but at least 2500 yellows in this weight class were caught every day!"

Izor notes that these fish were caught primarily in "ugly, green, 54 degree water." These are not conditions normally associated with a wide-open yellowtail bite. Izor believes that the El Niño condition, as well as the availability of sardines for bait, brought this mass of fish up into the Rocky Point area. "These fish," notes Izor, "simply bit in conditions that no one would believe. When I see spectacles like this, it just blows my mind!"

It wasn't only the hoards of yellowtail that impressed Izor during the El Niño of 1958-59. This veteran skipper related how log-size barracuda moved into this region, the likes of which are rarely seen anymore. "I saw barracuda in the 8 to 10 pound range literally jumping out of the water from Rocky Point to Santa Monica," Izor recalled. "Even surf fishermen caught them—you couldn't get away from them. They were everywhere!"

Izor theorizes that these big 'cuda were actually not the same as the smaller barries typically caught along the coast today. "I think these 8 to 10 pound barracuda caught during El Niño were a different species, otherwise, where did they all go?" says Izor. He notes that currently he can chum up a quantity of smaller 'cuda almost anytime today—but rarely does he ever see the big "logs" any more. It is possible that these fish were another species that hitchhiked up here during previous El Niños.

Lure manufacturer Butch Chapman is a bona fide calico bass expert where it comes to throwing his plastic Mojos. Chapman has witnessed some strange doings during the last El Niño condition. Chapman points out that calicos will rarely eat soft plastic lures in the winter, preferring instead live squid. "During the last El Niño, the fish ate the plastics in the winter," relates Chapman. "Look, I'm not one of those manufacturers who always throws his plastics first over live bait. The fact was the calicos really wanted the plastic lures in this water that was unusually warm for this time of the year."

Working both Cedros and Benitos Islands, about 300 miles south of San Diego, Chapman also encountered huge sand bass and big calicos in the 1987 El Niño. These fish were, again, amazingly willing to attack soft plastics in the dead of winter. "We had a slammer of squid and mackerel on this long-range trip," Chapman recalls. "But the plastics were far and away the best thing going—the plastic lures definitely outfished the live bait in this El Niño condition."

As pilot of the long-range sportfisher, Big Game, out of H&M Landing in San Diego, Captain Irv Grisbeck remembers many El Niños. It is probably 1983 that Grisbeck remembers most: "It started out slow in '83, with some 'cuda and 'tails at the Coronados. In June, we ran into the albacore in a little tiny area off Guadalupe Island. Then we saw the push of the El Niño in July with phenomenal yellowtail fishing on the floating kelp paddies."

Grisbeck looks back on the El Niño of 1983 with fond memories. What offshore skipper wouldn't? It was common, he notes, to have full limits of skipjack, yellowtail, and yellowfin tuna—all off a single kelp paddy! In that year, the yellowfin bit all the way into late November. Believe it or not, angler interest dwindled after so much spectacular fishing through the late summer and fall. By mid-November, the San Diego fleet stopped running one-day trips despite the El Niño tuna, due to lack of passengers.

Interestingly, the following year, boats running 2 to 3 day mini long-range trips continued to catch yellowfin all the way through April 1984. This was compounded with the resurgence of a strong yellowtail explosion at the Coronados Islands also holding through April of that year. All of this was a result of the residual warm water left from the El Niño of 1983.

Grisbeck also speculates that one of the reasons why the fish counts were so astonishing for tuna that year—and particularly big eye—might also have to do with the presence of sardines in the bait wells. "Prior to this El Niño, we wouldn't legally obtain sardines from the bait boats," claims Grisbeck. "It is possible that the big eye were up this way before, but they wouldn't eat the 'chovies. If they ate the anchovies, we couldn't land many big tuna on light mono. Sardines let us start fishing the 60 to 80 pound test line that resulted in more big eye starting with this El Niño."

Local tackle retailer, Ron De La Mare, remembers El Niños for still another unusual phenomena. De La Mare is an expert marlin fisherman. In past El Niños, he relates how the environment seemed to change at Cabo San Lucas. "Blue marlin fishing," observes De La Mare, "was absolutely extraordinary at the Cape in past El Niño conditions in 1984 and 1986. The water temperature was so warm, up to 91 degrees, that we found the blues all the way up to La Paz by Las Arenas. It is definitely unusually to find blue marlin up here on the east Cape."

De La Mare also recalls how tackle sales skyrocket during an El Niño year due to the presence of prized gamefish becoming within easy local party boat range. "During the El Niño we had yellowfin tuna at the 14 mile bank and closer," relates De La Mare. "The same thing for the Huntington Beach oil rigs—during the El Niño, they are loaded with yellowtail."

Perhaps the most spectacular effects of an El Niño condition are those shared by tackle manufacturer's representative Mike Callan. Long regarded as one of the premier big game specialists in the West, Callan tells of a day during the last El Niño in 1986. "Bill Nutt—the former president of Sportfishing Association of Califor-nia—and I headed up to the Santa Rosa Flats off of Santa Cruz Island, about 97 miles from Long Beach. We heard that a net boat was working the 17 fathom spot. When we got to that bank, we saw them with albacore up to 65 pounds and yellowfin topping the 300 pound mark.

"For months, we fished this area for tuna. The yellowfin ate our marlin jigs. They would eat one jig after another. It was absolutely incredible to see marlin, tuna, and albacore together in the Channel Islands. Some days it was hard to leave. Every time we started home, the jigs would get bit. On one day we caught and released 13 marlin up here for just the two of us. That day we had over 40 bites, but with too many multiple hook-ups for just two guys to handle."

Preparing for an El Niño

This writer, too, remembers El Niños. I recall seeing tropical needlefish caught off the Marina Del Rey breakers by jetty jockeys. I remember accounts of barracuda ir Monterey Bay and marlin as far north as San Francisco. As I stated at the beginning of this section, there is a good possibility that similar phenomena may occur anytime when warm tropical seas move north. So how should we prepare for a possible El Niño?

Well, to begin with, don't be surprised to find yellowtail on offshore kelp paddies below San Diego. Quite often, even into late November, there can still be mid-70 degree water 100 miles south of Tijuana. It is probable that this water mass will be pushed northward creating conditions at the kelp paddies advantageous for yellowtail. The presence of these fish under the floating paddies usually signals the start of a potential El Niño. These fish will probably be hungry. They readily eat anchovies or sardines fly-lined initially, then "plunked" at 90 to 120 foot depths with a 1 to 2 ounce sinker.

Don't overlook throwing the iron on the migratory early season 'tails. They will eat a smaller jig like a Salas 6xJR or CP105, U.F.O. #3 or #5, or Tady AA. Yo-yo these jigs in blue/white, blue/chrome, or scrambled egg finishes to start the season. Expect to see early season action more locally at the Coronados on barracuda and some yellowtail. These fish will probably be surface biters, keying in on 'chovies and mackerel.

Yellowtail action will extend further up the coast. Prepare to target Catalina and San Clemente Islands, along with the Huntington Beach oil rigs. The island fish will be keying in on squid. Yellowtail on the rigs will home in on live mackerel or squid if available. Don't hesitate to fish the heavy 25 to 30 pound line around the oil rigs. By midsummer, be on the lookout for yellows underneath paddies possibly all the way north to Malibu.

The barracuda will follow the warmer currents as well. It is likely that Ventura, Santa Barbara, and possibly north to San Simeon on the central coast will have good action on the 'cuda. I cannot emphasize enough to throw the hardware if you are looking for one of those trophy "log" size 'cuda that visited the coast in past El Niños. Smaller blue/white, blue/chrome, and solid white U.F.O. #2 and #4, Tady AA, and Salas Christy 1 or 2 are perfect for the bigger barracuda. Krocadile, Crippled Herring, and Haddock Jiggin' spoons are the other class of lures to gear up for when it comes to "stove pipe" 'cuda.

By midsummer, don't be surprised to find sporadic yellowfin tuna action within 30 to 45 miles off the Coronados. If—and it's a big "if"—an El Niño proves to be a more prominent mass of water, then yellowfin tuna and even albacore might range into the Catalina channel!

Expect an El Niño to usher in a major big eye tuna scare, with a lot of the action within one-day range of the Southern California fleet. Remember one important thing during a possible El Niño condition: when you fish south of San Diego or west of Catalina, never leave home without your *big gear*! I'm talking about the 50 to 80 pound class outfits normally associated with long-range trips. Again, if the water temperatures push over that 70 degree mark, big eye tuna may start cruising the Tanner, Osborne, Cortez, 14, and Farnsworth banks—all well within a one-day trip.

Of all the pelagic species that accompany an El Niño, dorado would seem to be the most mysterious. During great warm water years, the mahi will often be easily within one-day range of the San Diego fleet. These fish will also heavily gravitate to floating kelp paddies. However, look at the end of 1990. This was a fairly good offshore season but technically not an El Niño condition per se. Still, a major concentration of dorado was located in late summer that year. Interestingly, they were caught in great numbers during a 10-day span from Dana Point to the Catalina Channel. Half-day boats were even able to nail limits of these exotics.

Most El Niños usher in at least modest mahi-mahi action south of San Diego. I would always be prepared, however, to toss a live anchovy on any paddy all the way north to Malibu in case both yellowtail and dorado are sharing residence on the floating kelp.

So there you have it—suggestions on how to fish future warm water years. You can count on one thing—fishing the California coast will be incredibly exciting any time those massive warm currents push the El Niño up the coast along Southern or even Central California.

The Mesquite Reefs

Sportfishing in waters offshore from San Diego can be spectacular at times, particularly during the warmer months. As surface temperatures approach 70 degrees, party boat skippers will target yellowtail and tuna found 14 miles south of the landings at the Los Coronados Islands.

During the late fall through late spring, or anytime surface temperatures drop, these same waters can become a virtual "dead sea" with minimal action for pelagic species. It is during these colder periods that a shallow-water bonanza awaits those anglers willing to venture a little further south into Mexico to the Punta Mesquite region.

"Mesquite," as the skippers term this area, is comprised of a series of reefs that extend out about 1 1/2 to 2 miles from the coast roughly 40 miles below San Diego. These rocky pinnacles play host to a smorgasbord of both surface-feeding species and shallow-water rockfish found at 60 to 150 foot depths.

These reefs receive minimal pressure from private boats, sportfishers, or the commercial fleet. It is not uncommon to catch calico and sand bass, ling cod, whitefish, sheepshead, sculpin, a dozen varieties of rockfish, and an occasional white sea bass—all in a single day's outing at Punta Mesquite.

Here then are some of the key strategies for fishing these shallow reefs.

The Dropper Loop

This is the most effective setup used with bait at Punta Mesquite. Simply tie a 4 to 6 ounce ringed torpedo sinker to 20 to 30 pound test line. Add a dropper loop about 18 to 24 inches above the weight with an Eagle Claw 318-N #4/0 live bait hook. Before baiting up, however, thread a small plastic curl-tail grub onto the hook. Then, pin a live anchovy or strip of cut squid onto the hook together with the grub.

The heavy sinker keeps the rig near the bottom, even in the strongest current. The dropper loop keeps the bait from snagging into the rocks as it rotates around the main line, allowing the bait to suspend off the bottom. The plastic grub adds some color to the bait at these depths.

Also, if a fish steals the 'chovy or squid, it may still strike the grub as it lazily "swims" along. Almost any species found at Punta Mesquite can be caught on this dropper loop setup.

As I previously mentioned in the section on ling cod, don't always fish this dropper loop setup at anchor. Sometimes at Mesquite the red snapper, salmon grouper, and ling cod will instantly change from a lethargic mood to aggressive feeders if you slowly drift it over the reefs with your bait. The additional movement frequently triggers the bite!

Spoons and Iron

The bass, ling cod, and larger rockfish will readily attack a fairly big jig vertically yo-yoed off the bottom at Mesquite. A heavy action rod teamed with a conventional reel and 25 to 30 pound mono is recommended for working the "iron" over this rocky structure.

Drop a cast-metal jig such as a U.F.O. #5 or #6 or a Tady #6x JR in heavy versions to maintain good bottom contact. Solid chrome, chrome and blue, or blue and white patterns in these jigs are perfect for fishing the reefs.

Usually expect to get bit as the lure is sinking or as the jig starts to flutter downward while you are lifting and dropping your rod tip during the yo-yo sequence.

Larger shiny spoons such as the 4 ounce Krocadile or Crippled Herring models are equally productive with the yo-yo strategy at Mesquite. Sometimes it also helps to thread a whole squid onto the spoon's treble hook for added attraction. This spoon-and-squid combo can be especially potent on big ling cod here.

Soft Plastics

Switch to lighter baitcasting tackle or spinning outfits and try an array of soft plastic lures on a 1 1/2 to 3 ounce lead head. Fork-tail models like the Scampi, Mojo, or Lunker Thumper are excellent options for the calico and sand bass. Add a small 1x3 inch piece of squid as a trailer for extra effect.

Tube baits have proven to be a big fish lure at Punta Mesquite. The hollow-bodied Caba Caba Tube can be casted on heavier 20 to 30 pound line and the "pumped" back to the boat, by lifting and dropping the rod tip during the retrieve.

While "pumping" these lures, the tiny tail tentacles flare out and pulsate, giving the Caba Caba Tube a squid-like appearance. Squirt some liquid fish attractant into the lure's hollow body. As you pump the "tube" back in, it will give off a "vapor trail" of scent for the bottom fish to home in on. The Caba Caba Tube is a dynamite lure for the ling cod, big bull calicos, and grumper sand bass that live at Punta Mesquite.

Punta Colonet

As I rigged my jig stick on the deck of the Trilene Big Game, skippers Irv Grisbeck and Jack Slater carefully maneuvered the boat to the edge of the drop-off. We had been running all night on our first Eagle Claw School featuring a 2 1/2 day mini long-range format. The object was to introduce recreational anglers to an extended fishing trip without the extensive days of travel and possibly rough seas. Captain Grisbeck had promised my instructors and myself that we would be in for some unbelievable shallow-water rockfishing.

After anchoring on the reef, Captain Slater announced that we were sitting on the edge of a 180 foot deep ledge. I tied on a magnum-size Caba Caba Tube laced on an 8 ounce lead head. Normally, I will always add a strip of dead squid as an enticing trailer when I fish plastics. I was eager to test the waters, so I quickly made a lob cast with the big Caba minus the squid.

The huge tube bait must have sunk to about 60 feet when I felt a resounding "thunk" on the end of the line. I quickly gathered up the slack, swung and set on what felt like a pretty good fish.

The strike itself caught me by surprise. I chose the jumbo Caba Caba Tube so I could reach the bottom in a short amount of time then maintain solid contact looking for a big ling cod. I didn't expect anything to hit the bait on the sink so close to the surface.

In a few minutes I bounced an awesome 8 pound whitefish onto the deck! Grisbeck had told me that this "poor man's yellowtail" often reaches an astonishing double-digit weight at Colonet. This first drop made me a believer.

This scenario was repeated many times over past seasons on our Eagle Claw Fishing Schools to Punta Colonet. Each sell-out charter has produced a myriad of species including ling, whitefish, calico, sand and white sea bass, reds, bocaccio, bank perch, johnny bass, and even silver salmon and a mako shark for good measure.

The interesting thing is that Colonet is 120 miles south of San Diego, but few sportfishers or commercial operators ever fish these reefs. The sport boats pass it by on their way to further long-range destinations. It is out of range for the one-day fleet, and commercials seem to like to fish the deeper 360 to 900 foot depths. Colonet remains virgin territory.

Let me give you a brief run-down of how to fish these untapped reefs focusing first on the tackle, then on the specific species themselves.

The Gear

The optimal combination would be to have three outfits for fishing Colonet. Starting with the lightest, a freshwater poppin' or flippin' rod in a 7 to 7 1/2 foot graphite blank with a small baitcasting reel spooled with 12 to 15 pound test is my favorite. You can throw practically anything in a soft plastic bait with this rig up to about 4 ounces. Smaller 1 to 3 ounce spoons are also perfectly matched with this type of freshwater bassin' gear.

Your next outfit should be a standard 20 pound test combo. Casting reels are recommended but a quality spinner will also perform well down to the 180 foot range. This rig will also let you throw larger lead heads with the soft plastic lures, heavier 4 to 6 ounce spoons, and medium-size cast-metal jigs like the U.F.O. #3 and #5, Salas 6xJR or Tady AA—all in heavy versions. This 20 pound class gear is also perfect for fishing the 4 to 6 ounce dropper loop sinker rig that I'll discuss in a moment.

As a final option, keep a 30 to 40 pound outfit handy. This stouter gear will handle an 8 ounce lead head, a 10 to 12 ounce torpedo sinker if the current is ripping, and heavier jigs like the U.F.O. #6, Salas 6x and 7x heavy, or the Tady PL78 or 45 heavy.

Lures

There are a number of lures that perform at Colonet on various species but I give the overwhelming nod to soft plastics. The classical fork-tail baits such as the Mojo, Lunker Thumper, or Shabby Shrimp are excellent at the shallower 90 to 120 foot depths on light tackle and a 1 to 2 ounce lead head. Larger fork-tails, the single-tail Salty Magic, and the smaller Caba Caba Tube are perfect for probing the bottom down to 180 feet with 3 ounce heads.

The Berkley Power Grubs, Power Scampers, and Power Tubes are impregnated with a fish attractant initially designed for freshwater species. My instructors have found these new hi-tech soft plastics to have great application at Colonet. They are now a staple bait on our Eagle Claw Schools to these remote reefs.

As for spoons, don't overlook these versatile lures at Colonet. The narrow-bodied Dungeness Stinger, Crippled Herring, and Haddock Jig'n Spoon in 1 to 4 ounce models

have all produced solid results off these reefs.

A secret killer for big lings is the 4 ounce Krocadile spoon. This wider-bodied model will take a longer amount of time to reach the bottom with its prominent fluttering action. Once down there, a big "Kroc" can be a killer on quality size rockfish and the lings.

You should also take along a good stock of iron for your trip to Colonet on 20 to 30 pound outfits. A medium-size jig can be dynamite here bounced on the bottom. In addition to conventional iron, you might also want to throw in a couple of solid chrome diamond jigs in 4 to 8 ounce weights while exploring the reefs.

Terminal Gear

Hooks and sinkers for this type of light-line rockfishing are fairly simple to assemble. Day in and day out, an Eagle Claw 318-N #4/0 live bait hook provides a large enough gap to lower it to the bottom with a chunk of squid, a strip of cut mackerel, or 2 to 3 smaller anchovies pinned on.

On these schools, we have found, however, that our students seem to catch many of the jackpot lings on large, live sardines. In this situation, you may want to switch from a #4/0 live bait hook and replace it with an Eagle Claw #1 to #2 treble hook.

Depending upon current, a 4 ounce ringed torpedo sinker will be your best all around weight for maintaining bottom contact at 90 to 120 feet. As you venture deeper off the edge of the reef, you may need a 6 to 12 ounce torpedo sinker to reach the bottom, especially if there is a lot of current.

So this pretty much comprises your tackle arsenal for fishing Punta Colonet. Now let's look at some of the key species found on these reefs and some of the tactics used to catch them.

Lings

The ling cod are the most sought-after gamefish on our Colonet charters. They are aggressive, mean, and are frequently caught over the 15 pound mark. Unlike other deep-water species, the lings will fight you all the way to the top without "blowing up" from decompression.

As I noted, a large 4 ounce Krocadile spoon is one offering the bigger lings will jump on. The trick is to add either a whole squid or a lengthier strip of cut mackerel onto one of the spoon's trebles before making your drop. Yo-yo the "Kroc" with prominent rod lifts to make the spoon rise and fall like an errant baitfish. Ling cod at Colonet will also attack a cast-metal jig yo-yoed off the bottom. The U.F.O. #6 in blue/chrome, a Tady PL78 in scrambled egg, or a Salas 7x heavy in blue/white would be good choices. Here too, it pays to add a strip of mackerel or a whole squid as a trailer.

Soft plastics will also account for many of the lings tallied on one of our Eagle Claw Schools at Colonet. For a while, the large Caba Caba Tubes in milky glow or root beer flake were scoring many of the jackpot ling. Then the smaller Cabas with a 3 ounce lead head in the same colors were the hot ticket.

A large root beer flake Mojo or a Salty Magic in black/silver flake or motor oil green have also produced some outstanding catches on the lings here. Again, use a piece of strip bait to spice up the flavor of these tail-swimming baits.

Also, whenever you use these soft plastics at Colonet, always squirt some Berkley Strike fish attractant on the lure, then on the squid or mackerel strip. Interestingly, we have found that on many occasions, the larger lings were caught on soft plastics that had this fish scent applied before the cast was made.

A final option is to fish a dropper loop rig with the torpedo sinker for the ling. Although this particular bottom setup is a mainstay on any long-range trip and is even used for yellowtail fishing, it will catch practically anything at Colonet. What my instructors like to do is to have the students lace on a Berkley Power Grub or Power Tube onto the #4/0 hook then add the strip bait.

Ling are notorious bait stealers. If they hit the dropper setup and pull off the strip of mackerel or squid, they will return to viciously strike the heavily scented Power Tube or Power Grub that remains on the hook.

The Rockfish

A combination of white fish, reds, salmon grouper, johnny bass, bank perch, chuckleheads, convict bass, and starry rockfish will attack the dropper loop rigs at Colonet. Continue to lace the hooks with the scented grubs and tubes, but pin on one to two live anchovies instead of the squid or mackerel strip. You will find that these smaller rockfish will frequently be less reluctant to strike a smaller anchovy than dead, cut baits.

This smorgasbord of shallow-water rockfish will also readily eat the soft plastics. Mojos, Lunker Thumpers, and Salty Magics will also produce results, especially in a root beer flake color scheme. The smaller Caba Caba Tube in milky glow color remains the best option in this class of lures.

Pin on a smaller 1x3 inch long piece of cut squid or mackerel or 1 to 2 small to medium anchovies as a trailer

for these medium-size rockfish. The narrow-bodied spoons previously discussed are excellent for these different rockfish. So are the more compact yellowtail-style jigs in the heavy versions.

Calico, Sand, and White Sea Bass

Like the rockfish, all of these species will also be caught—though more infrequently—on the dropper loop setups. The key is to use a live bait such as a large 'chovy, sardine, mackerel, or squid. Anchovies in particular will sometimes be more effective than anything else when these three bass species move onto the reef.

Usually all three—calicos, sandies, and whites—are found on the edge of the break in 60 to 90 foot depths. Sand bass have been taken however on our Colonet charters all the way down to 120 feet. Instead of the dropper rigs, you may be better off using a 2 to 3 ounce sliding egg sinker for the bass here. Let the slider rest right up against the hook for best results.

All three kinds of bass will also attack the artificials. The small Caba Caba Tube in the milky white flow pattern is especially effective with a small strip of squid.

The bass will also eat the iron yo-yoed off the shallow portions of the reef. The U.F.O. #3 in "mack attack" or blue/chrome is effective as is the Salas 6xJR in blue/white or scrambled egg.

More Exotics?

The reefs at Punta Colonet may host other species besides the lings, rockfish, and the bass varieties. It is not the uncommon for the bite on these species to suddenly shut off then almost immediately for the rods to go full B-E-N-D-O as a school of marauding yellowtail moved into the 90 to 120 foot spots. The dropper loops with live 'chovies, sardines, squid, or mackerel will readily nail 'tails at these deeper strike zones along with the iron and Krocadile spoons.

We have also had some pretty strong tallies of deep-water barracuda in this region while running our Eagle Claw Schools in the winter months. The barries will strike the dropper rigs, the jigs, the spoons and, interestingly, the slow-moving soft plastics in sub-60 degree water at 120 foot depths. I might add that these are frequently fat, lazy wintertime log-size 'cuda in the 7 to 8 pound range!

Our most exotic catches to date at Punta Colonet have been mako shark and silver salmon. Both species eat the small Caba Caba Tubes. There are a lot of bottom dwellers off these reefs so the presence of the mako is understandable.

Coho salmon, on the other hand, have been caught this far south of the border, hitchhiking along ultracold currents that are found this close to the beach in this part of Mexico, sometimes all year long. Punta Colonet is a virtual bonanza. It is a place where even the most novice angler can catch a lot of great-eating fish, plus hone their skills using a full arsenal of artificial lures!

Quiet San Martin

San Martin Island is without a doubt one of the most unpredictable places I have ever fished. Located approximately 155 miles south of San Diego, Baja travelers recognize it as the small archipelago that local Mexicans fish out of San Quintin.

In recent years, I have targeted San Martin for my Eagle Claw Fishing Schools as an area to introduce anglers to a 2 1/2 day mini long-range trip. At 155 miles due south and 1/4 the size of Catalina, this island is too far for the one-day boats to hit, and of little interest for those multi-day operators who pass by San Martin on the way to Cedros or Benitos Islands.

The island is without a doubt a year-round fishery. I have explored it from the surface to the bottom, from winter all the way back to fall. San Martin does seem to be affected more by inshore up-wellings of cold water, more than any other area I have fished.

For example, in April we found a large school of yellowtail in 61 to 63 degree water. The next week, a massive up-welling occurred, and the surface temperature dropped to 53 degrees. The yellows obviously high-tailed it south, picking up a warmer current, leaving San Martin a surface fishing desert.

Nevertheless, San Martin Island remains an intriguing spot to fish due to its diversity of species, with overall minimal commercial pressure. Mexican skiff operators do motor out of San Quintin to work the island. Overall, their impact on this fishery is minimal at best.

Let's look at the different gamefish species that are on tap at San Martin, and the ways to catch them.

Yellowtail

These are the prized gamesters sought at this tiny offshore island. As a rule, the 'tails are actually found some distance from the island, usually on one of the many high spots, clearly indicated on nautical charts, within five miles of San Martin. Occasionally the yellowtail will be on the surface, eagerly attacking chummed anchovies or sardines. Usually, however, it is not that simple.

At this remote Mexican island, it nearly always seems that the 'tails are unsettled and in a marauding "breezing" mode. One method is to meter the fish then drift over them yo-yoing heavy cast-iron jigs. Popular patterns include the Tady AA, Salas 6XJR, CP105, and Hacker #4 in blue/white, scrambled egg, and blue/chrome finishes. These yellows will be schooled at typically 90 foot depths. When they are on the "iron" bite, the action can be sensational!

More often, a basic long-range torpedo sinker dropper loop rig is going to produce more yellowtail. A 4-8 ounce sinker, an Eagle Claw #118MG or #318-N #4/0 to #6/0 hook, and either a sardine or mackerel on the dropper loop will do the trick. Also, there is no need to let these Mexican yellowtail run with the bait when you feel a strike. Fish 30-50 pound test mono, with your reel *in gear*. Swing and set hard when your rod tip starts to bend towards the water!

Another critical tactic worth trying on the San Martin breezers is to slow-troll large CD-18 Magnum Rapala plugs. On an Eagle Claw School charter in April, we metered scattered schools of yellowtail for three hours, getting absolutely not one to bite bait or the iron.

As I mentioned in earlier chapters, the local panga fishermen from San Quintin frequently troll the jumbo size Rapalas, so I put one out over the stern to see what would happen while we slow-trolled on the Holiday sportfisher.

Instantly, a 17 pound yellowtail nailed the big plug. Next, I set out another two CD-18 magnums and within seconds we had a double hook-up on similar size "teen-age" 'tails. Still, the fish didn't come to the boat other than those caught on the troll.

Finally, with four of the large Rapalas trolling, we had—you guessed it—a quadruple jig strike! This time the bigger school charged the boat, and the most awesome, wide-open yo-yoing fishing would occur. In less than four hours of steady casting, over 200 San Martin yellowtail were tallied almost exclusively on the yo-yo technique!

Calico and Sand Bass

San Martin also has a year-round, thriving bass population. The calicos are caught primarily uptight, near the kelp strands at the eastern tip of the island. Many of these fish are bigger "bull" bass in the 5-8 pound range.

Both plastics and live sardines will be effective on San Martin's calicos. The shad-like AA soft plastic minnows, along with the Mojo, Haddock Lunker Thumper or Berkley Power Scamper will all produce nicely down here. Add a small piece of frozen squid or a strip of fresh mackerel as a trailer with these fork-tail baits.

At times, the island's lunker "bull" bass will also eat a big surface jig retrieved over the kelp stringers. A U.F.O. "P.O.S. Lite" Tady 45, or Salas 7X light are excellent bull bass killers when the fish are boiling on these kelp beds. The best colors are general motors green, blue/white, sardine or scrambled egg. Work the iron with powerful 8-10 foot long jig sticks and reels spooled with 25-30 pound test line.

Interestingly, the hard muddy flats off the west end of the island host some of the most concentrated numbers of sand bass to be found on this coast. These fish are not too particular and will readily attack jigs, spoons, and soft plastic lures. It is almost a waste of good live bait to fish the sandies with anything but artificials.

For the larger, 6-8 pound "grumper" sand bass, try drifting instead of casting at anchor. It seems like these bigger sandies key on a lure or bait while drifted more aggressively then if you were making casts while anchored.

Barracuda

The 'cuda fishing at San Martin is often nothing less than phenomenal! Even in the dead cold of winter, in chilly 53-56 degree water, we have found hordes of big 6-8 pound "stove pipe" class barries.

Although we have encountered some terrific flurries of surface action on the 'cuda, the best, most consistent pattern seems to be a deep-water approach. San Martin "slime" school deep—90 to 120 feet. The best line of attack is to yo-yo these fish with heavy jigs.

In addition to the jig colors mentioned for San Martin yellowtail, add solid white, white/black, and solid chrome for your 'cuda arsenal. Also, metal spoons such as the Haddock Jig 'n Spoon and Luhr Jensen Krocadile and Crippled Herring, work extremely well on these deep-water barries. Chrome, chrome/blue, prism scale and green mackerel finishes perform best around the island in metal spoons.

I should also note that some of the best scores of big San Martin "log" barracuda have been recorded on our Eagle Claw Schools during the middle of the night! The trick here is to use a fairly heavy jig with a lot of *white* in the finish. Apparently, the big 'cuda pick up the white

"flash" quite easily, often striking the iron as you lift and drop the jig right on the bottom.

Rockfish and Lings

The nice thing about San Martin is that if the surface fishing takes a nose-dive, you can usually slam the shallow-water rockfish. An absolute smorgasbord is available including ling cod, reds, chuckle heads, salmon grouper, bank perch, johnny bass, sheepshead, and whitefish.

Most of this rockfishing occurs at a modest 90-180 foot depth. The "whitefish nation" takes up serious residence at San Martin's 15 fathom spots, and these are big specimens. It is not that uncommon to see 6-9 pound whitefish to come over the rail at San Martin. As you work out into the deeper 180-300 foot range, you'll score on more lings, bigger reds, salmon grouper and chuckleheads.

The rockfishing at San Martin is a light-liner's heaven! We routinely fish this myriad of species with basic 20 pound test live bait outfits—all the way down to 300 feet! I even encourage students to bring out their heavier freshwater bassin' gear for this kind of sensational bottom scratchin'.

The yo-yo bite is at certain times spectacular on the lings and rockfish. Here's another little hot tip: add a Berkley Power Grub about 18-24 inches above the iron jig or metal spoon on a dropper loop hook. Frequently "doubles" result utilizing this combination.

Soft plastic aficionados will also find this facet of San Martin to their liking. All these bottom grabbers, including the ling cod and whitefish, will commonly go nuts over soft plastic lures teamed with lighter 10-15 pound test mono.

The fork-tail baits, tube lures, and, believe it or not, long 10-14 inch soft plastic eels all produce rockfish limits at this island. The AA eels, in particular, have accounted for some of the larger 7 to 8 pound reds brought up from 90-180 feet.

I have also encountered another phase of this phenomenal rockfishing at San Martin, in the form of wide-open night bites. It is not too common to find rockfish to aggressively feed at night further north in Southern California. Down here, the reds, salmon grouper, and big chuckleheads in particular will annihilate a sardine fished on the bottom—note, not on a dropper loop, but more on the bottom for this night bite.

More Options

San Martin Island can also host large marauding schools of yellowfin tuna, not far from the island itself. There is also the possibility of white sea bass and some magnum class, double-digit bonito caught more incidentally than anything else.

Small boaters should be prepared to bring lots of frozen squid, mackerel snag-catching rigs, trolling gear, and plenty of plugs, spoons, soft plastics and heavy iron.

You can launch south of the island out of San Quintin or charter one of the small skiff operators.

San Martin remains a relatively untapped fishery, providing year-round possibilities for the adventuresome "Norte Americano"!

The Inner Game of Fishing

By now you have hopefully garnered some core insights into the technical aspects of fishing a variety of species found along the Pacific Coast. The lessons from the Eagle Claw Fishing Schools concentrate on the real "nitty gritty"—the specific how, when, and where—of how to catch everything from bottom grabbers to major league billfish. The preceding chapters have focused on the specific technical elements of challenging these West Coast species.

To conclude this series of lessons, I want to focus on an aspect of fishing that is equally important—the mental aspect or "inner game" of angling. The accomplished saltwater fisherman realizes that his mental outlook has a strong effect on his fishing success. It may be more important than all the technical information.

Creative Fishing

All fishermen—fresh and saltwater alike—seem to become stuck in a rut at times. We are hung up on tossing the same anchovies, the same jigs, or the same plastic lure trip after trip. Often it simply pays to try something "off the wall," giving the fish a lure or bait that is more bizarre to look at. Let me give you some firsthand examples of this out-of-the-ordinary approach.

On one of our Eagle Claw Fishing Schools we were scratchin' out a few legal size calicos south of Tijuana on the Salsipuedes kelp. One of the students, in the dead of winter, started throwing an old "General Motors" green surface jig on the outside kelp stringers. Wouldn't you know it? A 6 pound bull bass skyrocketed up from one of the kelp pockets to inhale the iron despite the cold water. There was no sign of surface activity. The angler simply wanted to take a shot at throwing something different. A jackpot resulted!

Similarly, on our Eagle Claw Fishing School in Key Largo, Florida, we teach our students to fish giant Atlantic amberjack Pacific Coast stand-up style, yo-yoing the iron. On the third day of fishing, one angler with limits of 65 pound "ambers" decided to pin on an 18 inch long length of strip bonito to the treble hook on his yo-yo iron. The next drop, he nailed an 85 pound amberjack—and you guessed it—the big fish jackpot for the trip.

On one school where we were targeting shallow-water rockfish, I received some miniature Power Tubes from Berkley. These are similar to the tiny tube baits used for freshwater panfish, only laden with Berkley's fish scent. I had all the students lace one of the little Power Tubes onto their live bait hooks or onto the trebles on their jigs and spoons. The rockfish and ling cod annihilated them!

I have been on other trips where shrewd anglers brought out their own private stock of fresh shrimp or even octopus. I watched one fisherman nail one sheepshead after another on the fresh shrimp when nothing else would interest these finicky "goats."

On still another outing, I observed my instructors replacing the trebles on saltwater spoons with single hooks. Then they threaded on a soft plastic curl-tail grub. As bizarre as this spoon-and-grub combo looks, I have seen it catch a lot of bass and rockfish when no other hardware was working.

These are all firsthand examples of how it pays to be experimental, trying unusual lures and baits that might rarely be used otherwise. Let your imagination run wild at times while rummaging through your tackle boxes. Don't worry about what skippers, deckhands, or friends might think—go for it—try something new. A jackpot just might be out there waiting for the guy who takes a chance at fishing the bizarre!

Catching vs. Fishing

On the Eagle Claw Fishing Schools I have encountered an interesting question: Can I guarantee fish? As director of these schools, I charter the best vessels with accomplished captains and veteran crews for these trips. We cannot make the fish appear or more so require them to take the bait if conditions are not favorable. As much as we are in the business of *"fishing,"* we of course want to practice as much *"catching"* as possible. Unfortunately, there are no guarantees in this sport.

There is a myriad of unpredictable variables that can affect a potential bite. Let's itemize a few of the more critical ones.

Water Temperature

Our local waters can be unpredictable and water temperatures can suddenly turn colder when it seems they should by warming up instead. For instance, in the middle of March, we found 61 degree water at San Martin Island, 150 miles south of San Diego. When conditions are right, this is prime yellowtail territory. That day, 160 'tails succumbed to cast-iron jigs in an area that receives relatively little angling pressure.

Three weeks later, with considerable "press" and hoopla, we took another group to this same area with the intention of repeating our previous feat. There was not a yellowtail to be had. An up-welling of cold water hit the island and surface temperatures plummeted to a chilly 55 degrees.

Water Color

Similarly water color can change rapidly and have an equally devastating effect on the bite. One day you may be "catching" tuna in classic dark blue water The next day you are "*fishing*" in a band of dirty green water and the tuna have disappeared. Mother Nature can be highly unpredictable.

Current

Shifts in current can be subtle but even so they can be a killer for inshore fishing. At Catalina Island, for example, you might have all the live squid you can stuff in a bait tank, again with high expectations of a bonanza day ahead. Even this primo bait can be worthless if sub-surface water current is not moving—and in the right direction, I might add—to take the squid to the fish. Here again, you end up "*fishing*" instead of "*catching*."

Bait

Finally, the bait situation can be critical. One week the bait receivers are plum full of frisky hook-size anchovies. The barracuda, bass, and yellowtail go crazy for this hearty bait. The next day, the bait boat fails to score on the anchovies and instead fills the receivers with racehorse-size sardines. Back at the same location, the skipper finds the fish won't give the big hefty 'dines even a glance; so once again it's back to "*fishing*."

So always try to be understanding of the skippers and charter masters who put these trips together. The best operators always try to maximize their chances but the fickleness of nature is obviously something that even these experts cannot control. Unfortunately, this sport does not come with a guarantee.

So plan to enjoy yourself with or without the fish. Remember there is a difference between "*fishing*" and "*catching*" You'll enjoy every trip if you aim to have a great day "*fishing*" and remember that "*catching*" is always a special bonus.

Everyone Welcome

Why are women distinctively absent from most passenger lists on party or charter boat trips? Well, probably because "deep sea fishin'" has been glamorized in the lore and tradition of the past, as one of the last major frontiers for man to battle nature one-on-one. The sea is where men can push their personal strength and stamina to its maximum while combating both the elements and the prey at the other end of the line.

Female athletes on the other hand have penetrated the barriers of most major sports such as golf, tennis, bowling, archery, softball, basketball, volleyball, auto and horse racing and even trap and skeet shooting. But female anglers remain distinctively absent on the "Big Pond."

Well guys, let me share with you some major insights I've gleaned from watching a modest number of ladies fishing on my Eagle Slaw Saltwater School charters. To begin with, the women seem to demonstrate a tremendous amount of inner peace and patience. This is probably due to the fact that the females on these trips don't construct a "man vs. nature" scenario out on the water. Relying upon that kinder, gentler, softer side of human personality, the ladies do not seem to internalize any pressure to prove anything while maintaining respect for nature and the marine environment.

The female angler to be sure is every bit as tough as the male. What she may lack in sheer brute strength, she makes up for in perseverance, stamina, and level-headedness. In all my 40(+) years of saltwater fishing, I have never seen a single woman "lose it" at the rail during a wide-open bite, cursing, yelling, screaming and pouting, like some men do when they lose a fish.

Instead, the ladies I've watched at the rail under heavy "combat" conditions, simply shrug off a lost fish, return to re-tie, bait up again, and get right back into the thick of the action with a smile on their face. Most ladies simply don't consider fighting a fish a life or death proposition, or a "rite of passage" into greater womanhood, as do many of their male counterparts.

Female anglers also seem to have a great sense of touch. They tend to be excellent light-liners, good live bait enthusiasts, with a high level of patience during the slack periods. It is not just luck or mere coincidence why many woman end up winning the jackpot, while males who put a lot of pressure on themselves are often stymied.

Men—we can learn from the so-called "weaker sex" when it comes to saltwater fishing. Study their patience, gentleness, and overall attitude in treating the trip as an occasion to have some fun. The female angler can usually hold her own on a party boat. As novices some may appreciate help or guidance. But this holds true for male or female beginners. One thing the lady fisherman doesn't need is patronizing or being treated like she is a "little girl."

The sportfishing industry depends on bringing more and more "new blood" into the sport. Let's give the women a chance guys—we may learn something from them. Share this idea with someone you love, and bring 'em out on a trip!

"Positive Fish Attitude"

When I was growing up, I devoured every piece of written material about fishing that I could get my hands on. From the campfire lore of Ted Trueblood to simplified fly fishing by Lefty Kreh, I tried to read all the great outdoor authors of that time. Of all the features I collected back in those days, one really stuck with me down through the years.

Unfortunately, I can't remember who wrote the article for I would certainly like to both credit and thank him for the piece. Nevertheless, he talked about what is perhaps the most important ingredient necessary to become a successful angler. The writer termed this component, P.F.A.—Positive Fish Attitude.

What is P.F.A.? Well, basically it is belief that the fish will bite. No matter how bad the weather, how rough the water, or how negative the reports are, P.F.A. means you approach your quarry with victory in mind.

Positive Fish Attitude was coined way before notions such as "visualization" or the "inner game" hit the popular press. But P.F.A. is definitely akin to this type of "affirmative mind set."

I have fished and worked with some of the great fishermen of this past decade. Party boat skippers Jim Peterson, Fred Benko, Steve Giffin, Buzz Brizendine, and Russ Izor certainly are at the top of their sport. World-class trophy hunters like the late Bob Bringhurst and Don McAdams were the best at their specialties. Similarly, western guides like Mike Gardner know how to sustain when the pressure is on.

All of these super fishermen have one thing in common—P.F.A. Even before they set out, they conceptualize a successful game plan for the fishing day. Once on the water, even when things turn sour, they "gut it out." They maintain the strong belief that they not only deserve to catch fish, but that they *will* catch fish. Most importantly, they internalize this positive fish attitude from start to finish—no matter what the prevailing conditions are.

This is not some kind of psychological "mumbo-jumbo" I'm espousing here. By assuming this positive posture, the accomplished saltwater angler is able to assess the situation clearly and draw upon a repertoire of tactics that will work. The motivation level remains high all day long with fishermen of this caliber.

I've seen veteran deckhands, skippers, and "dead heads," for example, continue to fire off casts with as much intensity at the end of the day as when they started. I've watched them go into a "two minute drill" with seconds before the boat pulled up the anchor, meticulously and positively continuing to dissect the water. So many times these saltwater pros will tell you that they "pulled it out" in the last cast. You know why? P.F.A.!

Practice Catch and Release

To conclude this book, I leave you with a simple request. Keep only the fish you are planning to eat—release the rest. The Pacific Coast fishery is not an endless warehouse of the myriad of species I have talked about in this book. Take a look sometime at pictures of the quantities and size of halibut, bass, etc. that were caught earlier in this century and you'll see how greatly this fishery has changed.

More and more it is evident that this is a fragile ecosystem impacted by everything from commercial fishing and pollution to increased recreational traffic. It can take many years for this body of water to replenish diminished stocks of a given species. So don't take this fishery for granted—practice catch and release.

Good Luck!

Saltwater Sportfish Identification Guide

Saltwater Sportfish Identification Guide

The main purpose of this guide is to help identify the species of fish caught off California. Recently, the State of California's Department of Fish and Game (DF & G), in conjunction with several other agencies, published *Marine Sportfish Identification—California*. This publication was instrumental in preparing the information on the following pages, including the "Fishing Information" sections. This fishing info, in most cases, should be considered an adjunct to the detailed material that is the heart of *Saltwater Fishing in California*.

Copies of *Marine Sportfish Identification—California* are available from DF & G offices for approximately $4.00. This version is tackle-box size and includes color reproductions of all 78 species. Speaking of species, there are over 500 species of fish found in California's coastal waters. The most common 78 are described on the following pages.

Spiny Dogfish

a spine at the origin of each dorsal fin

Family: Squalidae (Dogfish sharks)
Genus and Species: *Squalus acanthias*
Description: The body of the spiny dogfish is elongate and slender. The head is pointed. The color is slate gray to brownish on top, sometimes with white spots, becoming white below.

This species and the horn shark are the only sharks along the California coast with spines at the beginning of both dorsal fins. These spines may be mildly poisonous and provide a defense for the spiny dogfish.

Range: Spiny dogfish occur in temperate and subtropical waters in the Atlantic and Pacific Oceans. In the eastern Pacific Ocean they are found off Chile, and from central Baja California to Alaska and to Japan. This species is common in nearshore waters along most of the coast. It is generally found in waters up to 1,200 feet deep though spiny dogfish have been taken to depths of 2,400 feet.

Natural History: The spiny dogfish feeds upon practically all smaller fishes such as herring, sardines, anchovies, smelts and even small spiny dogfish as well as crabs.

The females are larger than the males, and produce from 3 to 14 young at a time and in alternate years. Most adults are 2 to 4 feet long. Spiny dogfish are long lived and non-migratory; as a result, heavy fishing pressure in a given area will lower the population level of this slow growing, low reproductive species quite rapidly.

Fishing Information: You are most likely to catch a spiny dogfish with anchovies or invertebrates on a rock cod jig, They are commonly taken in commercial bottom trawl nets.

Other Common Names: dog shark, grayfish, Pacific grayfish, spinarola, California dogfish.

Largest Recorded: 5.25 feet; no weight recorded; however, a large fat female about 4 feet long will weigh 15 pounds.

Habitat: Shallow Sandy Environment

Common Thresher Shark

Family: Alopiidae (Thresher sharks)
Genus and Species: *Alopias vulpinus*
Description: The body of the common thresher shark is moderately elongate. The snout is rather short, and the mouth crescent shaped. The first dorsal fin is

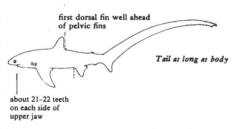

first dorsal fin well ahead of pelvic fins

Tail as long as body

about 21-22 teeth on each side of upper jaw

large, and located midway between the pectoral and ventral fins. The second dorsal and anal fins are very small. The tail is distinctive since it is very long, almost as long as the rest of the body. The coloration may vary from brownish gray, bluish or blackish above to silvery, bluish or golden below. The dorsal, pectoral and ventral fins are blackish and sometimes the pectoral and ventral fins have a white dot in the lip.

The bigeye thresher also occurs off the California coast. It can be distinguished by its large eye; however, if you can count the teeth in the upper jaw, the common thresher has 21-22 on each side while the bigeye thresher has 10-11 on each side.

Range: The common thresher shark occurs worldwide in warmer seas. In the eastern North Pacific, it is found from central Baja California, to the Strait of Juan de Fuca, British Columbia. The common thresher is an inhabitant of the upper layers of deep offshore waters and is most abundant in areas of steep bottom contour along the edges of the continental shelf. During the spring and summer months smaller threshers may occur near shore where they are often seen leaping completely out of the water.

Natural History: The food habits of the thresher are not well known, but on the California coast they feed mostly upon small fish such as sardines, anchovies, mackerel, and squid. They are said to use their long tail as a flail to frighten or stun their prey.

The common thresher shark bears live young and appears to become sexually mature in 6 or 7 years. Four pups are produced annually. A 18 foot female contained four young that weighed 13.5 pounds each and were 4 to 4.5 feet long.

Fishing Information: Most thresher sharks caught off California have been taken on live sardines, anchovies, or mackerel. Best localities

have been the San Francisco Bay area, the inshore coastal water between Point Conception and Port Hueneme, and Santa Monica Bay, especially around Malibu and Paradise Cove.

They are most abundant during the summer months. Considered a fine game species on light or medium tackle, they often put on an aerial demonstration. At other times the battle is entirely beneath the surface and consists of brute strength and shift-towing tactics.

An angler would do well to bait a live mackerel on a 9/0 hook attached to 10 or so feet of heavy wire leader.

Other Common Names: thresher, blue thresher, green thresher, longtail shark, swiveltail, fox shark, sea fox.

Largest Recorded: 20 feet; 1,000 pounds. Largest taken off California by a recreational angler: 527 pounds.

Habitat: Pelagic Environment

Bonito Shark

Family: Lamnidae (Mackerel shark)
Genus and Species: *Isurus oxyrinchus*
Description: The body of the bonito shark is elongate but rather stout. The snout is long

insertion of pectorals well ahead of origin of 1st dorsal fin

and pointed. The first dorsal and the pectoral fins are large, but the second dorsal and anal fins are very small. This species is a deep blue or dark gray above and white below. There is a black spot at the base of the pectorals.

Range: This shark is found worldwide in warm and temperate seas; in the eastern Pacific from Chile to the Columbia River, Washington, including the Gulf of California, but not in the tropics.

Natural History: The diet of the bonito shark includes fishes and squid, often large ones. Whenever possible, the bonito shark takes its food in one gulp. With its tremendous speed, it is unquestionably a dangerous shark. Bonito sharks bear live young.

Fishing Information: The bonito shark is one of the larger sharks to inhabit California waters. By all accounts, it is as dangerous as any shark, and it probably swims faster than most.

The best way to hook a bonito shark is by trolling with a whole tuna, squid or mackerel. You can also use lures, and chumming does help. Watch out, when you catch one, because this is a dangerous fish that will not hesitate to attack you or your boat.

Other Common Names: mako, mackerel shark, spriglio, paloma, shortfin mako.

Largest Recorded: 13 feet; 1,000 pounds. 11.5 feet; 1,030 pounds (California). Largest taken by a recreational angler off California; 299 pounds.

Habitat: Pelagic Environment

Gray Smoothhound

Family: Carcharhinidae (Requiem sharks)
Genus and Species: *Mustelus californicus*
Description: The body of the gray smoothhound is elongate, slender, tapering from behind the dorsal fin to a long slender

midpoint of base of 1st dorsal fin closer to origin of pelvic fins than to insertion of pectoral fins

tail. The snout is comparatively long and flattened. The color is brown to dark gray above and whitish below.

The gray smoothhound can be distinguished from other smoothhounds by scales present on the posterior one-fifth of the dorsal fin and the teeth having sharp points.

Range: This species occurs from Mazatlan, Mexico, to Cape Mendocino, California; and is found in shallow waters to depths of 150 feet.

Natural History: The diet of the gray smoothhound includes crabs, shrimp and small fishes. The female bears the young alive.

Fishing Information: Although the gray smoothhound is of relatively minor importance to sport anglers, it is commonly taken in the surf. It is edible, but not as tasty as the brown smoothhound.

If you're fishing in southern California, you are most likely to catch a gray, and in central California, you are most likely to catch a brown smoothhound.

Other Common Names: shark, dogfish, paloma, sand shark, gray shark.

Largest Recorded: 5 feet 4.25 inches; no weight recorded.

Habitat: Shallow Sandy Environment

Brown Smoothhound

Family: Carcharhinidae (Requiem sharks)
Genus and Species: *Mustelus henlei*
Description: The body of the brown smoothhound is elongate, slender, tapering from behind the dorsal fin to the long slender tail. The snout is comparatively long and flattened. The color is brown or bronze above and silvery below.

The back one-fifth of the dorsal fin is without scales. The teeth are blunt, without sharp points. The brown and other smoothhounds can be distinguished from the soupfin shark since their second dorsal fins originate well in advance of the beginning of the anal fin; while in the soupfin, the second dorsal begins behind the origin of the anal fin.
Range: The brown smoothhound occurs from the Gulf of California to Humboldt Bay, California. It is found at depths from shallow water to 360 feet.
Natural History: The diet of the brown smoothhound includes crabs, shrimp, and small fishes.

Females bear their young live, as do most other sharks.
Fishing Information: The brown smoothhound is a relatively small shark, and is one of the most abundant sharks in the central California sport fishery.

This is a good sport species on light tackle, and can be taken in bays from San Francisco to Point Conception. Good baits to use include crabs, shrimp and small fishes. The brown smoothhound is considered a very good table fish.
Other Common Names: mud shark, dogfish, paloma, sand shark, Henle's shark.
Largest Recorded: 3. feet 1 inch; no weight recorded.
Habitat: Shallow Sandy Environment

Leopard Shark

Family: Carcharinidae (Requiem sharks)
Genus and Species: *Triakis semifasciata*
Description: The body of the leopard shark is elongate, and the snout is short and bluntly rounded. This shark is easily identified by the gray coloration over most of its body, and the black spots and crossbars on the back and side. It is white underneath.
Range: Mazatlan, Mexico, to Oregon. This well decorated species is abundant in bays and along sandy beaches of southern and central California in shallow water. During the fall, large numbers may be found in San Francisco and Monterey Bays.
Natural History: The leopard shark eats a variety of fishes and invertebrates like anchovies, squid or crab, all of which make good bait.

Females, which bear their young live, usually produce 4 to 29 pups in a lifter.
Fishing Information: It is considered a relatively harmless shark and is timid around divers; nevertheless, handle a live leopard shark with care.

The leopard shark is very good eating, and has been compared favorably to salmon.
Other Common Names: cat shark.
Largest Recorded: 7 feet; 70 pounds.
Habitat: Bay Environment

Blue Shark

Family: Carcharhinidae (Requiem sharks)
Genus and Species: *Prionace glauca*
Description: The body of the blue shark is elongate and slender. Its head is slender and the snout is long and pointed. The color is blue or light bluish gray above and white below.

This species has up to three rows of functional teeth in each jaw and there are 14 or 15 serrated teeth in each side of each jaw. The pectoral fins are long and sickle shaped.
Range: The blue shark occurs worldwide. In the eastern Pacific, blue sharks are found from Chile to the Gulf of Alaska, but not in the tropics. It is common off southern California most of the year, but during warm water periods occurs much further north.
Natural History: Blue sharks do not mature until they attain a length of 7 or 8 feet. Of several thousand blue sharks taken on longline gear, the smallest female was 7 feet long.

A female weighing 95 pounds and 7 feet 7 inches long, contained 26 apparently fully developed young ranging in length from 15.5 to 17.75 inches, As many as 54 young have been counted in a single adult female captured in the Mediterranean Sea.
Fishing Information: Most are taken incidentally by albacore or rockfish anglers. Should you wish to specifically fish for blue sharks, they are easily taken once located. Either casting a bait at a previously located fish or chumming in an area known to be inhabited by blue sharks will usually produce results.

Dead fish or squid make excellent bait, and ground up anchovies make good chum. Blue sharks tend to "roll up" on the line, so it is necessary to use a long wire leader to avoid cutting the line on the shark's skin.

The blue shark is not considered a man-eater, but is probably responsible for many attacks upon injured swimmers, after boating, airplane, and other accidents at sea. It should be considered dangerous because of its numerical abundance and attraction for blood, if for no other reasons.

The fish may be eaten, but it is necessary to bleed it while it is still alive. After it is dead it should be cleaned, skinned and soaked as soon as possible to avoid the taste of urea in the meat.
Other Common Names: blue whaler, great blue shark.
Largest Recorded: No length recorded; 231 pounds (California); however, a 5 foot 9 inch male weighed just 49 pounds. A 12 foot 4 inch blue taken off southern California was not weighed.
Habitat: Pelagic Environment

Shovelnose Guitarfish

Family: Rhinobatidae (Guitarfishes)
Genus and Species: *Rhinobatos productus*
Description: The body of the shovelnose guitarfish is depressed and gradually tapers into the tail; the disk is longer than wide. The snout is rather long and rounded at the tip. The color is gray above becoming lighter below.

This species is distinguished from the banded guitarfish by the absence of dark crossbars on the back. It can be separated from most others of this flattened and plated group by the presence of a tail fin and two dorsal fins. Its sharp pointed nose distinguishes it from the other guitarfishes.
Range: Gulf of California to San Francisco, California. The shovelnose can be found, sometimes in large numbers, over sand or mud sand bottoms in colder, shallow coastal waters.
Natural History: The guitarfish diet consists of a variety of crustaceans, worms and clams. They have been observed feeding on sand crabs in water less than 3 inches deep. At times they are left stranded on the beach by receding waves and must wiggle their way back into the water much like grunion.

Shovelnose guitarfish bear live young, with as many as 28 from a single female. Mating takes place during the summer months and the young, apparently born during the following spring and summer, are 6 inch miniatures of the adults.
Fishing Information: Shovelnose guitarfish are caught in the surf, in bays and from piers. They take live or dead bait including clams, mussels, sand crabs and almost any other bait or lure. The flesh, especially the tail and back straps, is considered quite good.
Other Common Names: shovelnose shark, pointed nosed guitarfish, guitarfish.
Largest Recorded: 5 feet 1.5 inches; 40.5 pounds.
Habitat: Shallow Sandy Environment

Bat Ray

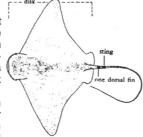

Description: The bat ray has a distinct head that is elevated above the disk. The tail is whip-like and as long or longer than the width of the disk with the sting located just behind the body. The color is dark brown to dark olive or almost black above and white below.

This species can be distinguished from manta rays or mobulas (that rarely occur off California) by the absence of the armlike projections manta rays and mobulas have on their heads.

Range: Bat rays are found from the Gulf of California to Oregon, from surface waters to depths of 150 feet.

Natural History: Bat rays feed chiefly upon mollusks and crustaceans. In bays and sloughs they feed heavily upon clams, oysters, shrimp and crabs. On the open coast they eat abalones and various other snails. When feeding, they swim along the bottom until they encounter currents of water expelled from the siphons of clams. They dig clams by suction created by flapping their wings. The shell of the ingested clam is crushed by their millstone like jaw teeth.

Mating takes place during the summer months and the young are born alive, apparently the following summer, when they are 12 to 14 inches in width and weigh about 2 pounds. The young are always born tail-first with their wings rolled up over the body. They come equipped with a stinger and can cause severe painful wounds.

Females apparently weigh at least 50 pounds and males 10 pounds before they are mature. Females of 50 to 60 pounds usually have two to four young; whereas, females of 130 to 140 pounds may have 10 or 12 young.

Fishing Information: Most sportfishing for bat rays takes place in protected bays and estuaries. Although bat rays may be taken in the open ocean, anglers prefer to catch them in sheltered waters. Heavy tackle is recommended since anglers often encounter large rays. Favorite baits include shrimp, clams, crabs or even cut mackerel.

Other Common Names: sting ray, eagle ray, batfish, stingaree, bat sting ray.

Largest Recorded: Width 4 feet, 9 inches; 181 pounds.

Habitat: Shallow Sandy Environment

Round Stingray

Family: Dasyatididae (Stingrays)

Genus and Species: *Urolophus halleri*

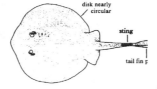

Description: The disk of the round stingray is nearly circular. The back of this species is brown, often mottled or spotted, and the underside is white to orange.

The round stingray is one of six rays found in California waters which have a stinger on the tail. It can be distinguished from the others since it is the only one with a true tail fin. The others have either a whip-like tail or very short tail with no fin membrane.

Range: This species occurs from Panama to Humboldt Bay, California, including the Gulf of California. Round stingrays are most abundant off southern California and northern Baja California at depths up to 70 feet.

Natural History: Round stingrays obtain much of their food by burrowing in the substrate. Their diet includes worms, crabs, snails, clams and small fishes.

It takes 3 months for the round stingray young to develop and they are approximately 3 inches wide at birth. Sexual maturity is reached in 2.6 to 3 years, and mating occurs from May to June and in December. There are one to six pups, depending upon the size of the female.

Fishing Information: Most round stingrays are taken incidentally by anglers fishing for other species. However, should one wish to go after them specifically, marine worms or pieces of clam are good bait. Sandy or muddy bottoms along a beach or in a bay should provide good fishing.

Round stingrays are potentially dangerous because of the wounds they can inflict. If an angler is stung, the wound should be cleaned thoroughly and bathed in water. One should see a doctor if pain persists or infection occurs.

Other Common Names: ray, stingray, stinger, stingaree.

Largest Recorded: 22 inches; no weight recorded; however, a male 20 inches long weighed 1.5 pounds.

Habitat: Shallow Sandy Environment

Green Sturgeon

Family: Acipenseridae (Sturgeons)

Genus and Species: *Acipenser medirostris*

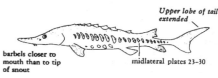

Description: The body of the green sturgeon is long, roughly cylindrical and has five rows of bony plates on its back. The snout is narrow, long, and cone-shaped, and more or less depressed below the level of the forehead. The mouth is toothless, protruding, and sucker-like. Four fleshy projections, or barbers, extend from the underside of the snout. The color is olive green above, whitish below, with olive stripes on the sides.

The green sturgeon can be distinguished by its olive green color, the number of bony plates along the side of the body (mid lateral plates; 23 to 30), a very pointed snout, and the barbels are closer to the mouth than to the tip of the snout.

Range: Ensenada, Baja California, to the Bering Sea and Japan. The green sturgeon is commonly found in brackish water (part saltwater, part freshwater).

Natural History: The green sturgeon sifts muds and silts for food and feeds upon small invertebrates and fishes. Since it has no teeth, it must swallow its food whole. The green sturgeon is anadromous, spending its adult life in the ocean but ascending coastal streams in the winter where it remains to spawn the following summer.

This species appears to reach sexual maturity in 10 or 15 years and may live to be over 100 years old.

Fishing Information: In California, the green sturgeon is regularly caught in San Francisco and San Pablo Bays, but is not considered to be a good food fish.

Other Common Names: none.

Largest Recorded: 7 feet; 350 pounds.

Habitat: Bay Environment

White Sturgeon

Family: Acipenseridae (Sturgeons)

Genus and Species: *Acipenser transmontanus*

Description: The body of the white sturgeon is long, roughly cylindrical, and has five rows of bony plates on its back. The snout is bluntly rounded and more or less depressed below the level of the forehead. The mouth is toothless, protruding, and sucker-like. Four fleshy projections, or barbels, extend from the underside of the snout. The fish is overall gray in color.

The white sturgeon can be distinguished f rom the green sturgeon by its overall grey color, 38 to 48 bony plates along the side, a round snout, and the barbels are closer to the tip of the snout than to the mouth.

Range: This species occurs from Ensenada, Baja California, to the Gulf of Alaska.

The white sturgeon is the largest fish found in North American freshwaters. The white sturgeon is anadromous, and spends more of its time in the brackish (part salt, part freshwater) waters of bays than in the open ocean. Most anadromous fish spend their adult life in the ocean or brackish water, and spawn up freshwater streams.

Natural History: White sturgeon are bottom feeders and their diet consists predominantly of clams, grass shrimp, crabs and herring roe. All can be used as good baits to catch fish that are most commonly under 300 pounds. Rocks, twigs and other odd things have been found in their stomachs and a white sturgeon caught in the Snake River had eaten half a bushel of onions that it had found floating in the river.

This species is long lived and may live to be over 100 years old.

Fishing Information: A good food fish, the white sturgeon in California has been taken commercially in the past for its eggs (caviar).

Other Common Names: Sacramento sturgeon, Oregon sturgeon.

Largest Recorded: 12 feet; 1,285 pounds. Largest recreational caught in California: 468 pounds.

Habitat: Bay Environment

Chinook (King) Salmon

Family: Salmonidae (Salmons)
Genus and Species: *Oncorhynchus tshawytscha*
Description: The body of the chinook salmon is elongate and somewhat compressed. The head is conical. The color is bluish to dark gray above, becoming silvery on the sides and belly. There are black spots on the back and on both lobes of the tail.

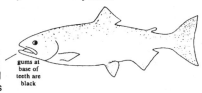

gums at base of teeth are black

While five species of salmon occur along the Pacific Coast, over 99% of all salmon caught in the ocean off California are either chinook or cohos. Chinook and coho salmon can be distinguished by the color of the lining of the gums at the base of the teeth. In chinook salmon, this lining is blackish, while in cohos it is white.
Range: Chinook salmon occur from San Diego, California, to the Bering Sea and Japan. Generally, the fishery begins off San Luis Obispo County, California, and continues north.
Natural History: Chinooks and all salmon are anadromous—that is, they spend part of their life in the ocean and then enter fresh water to spawn. The adults spawn principally in large river systems, primarily from the Sacramento River system north. At spawning time, male chinooks turn very dark and usually have blotchy, dull red splotches on the sides and develops a hooked nose.

Most all chinook spawn when either 3 or 4 years of age but some, predominately males, will spawn at age 2. These precocious males are called jacks, chubs or grilse. Some rivers have large chinooks that do not spawn until 5 or 6 years old.

Sacramento River female chinook salmon produce an average of 6,000 eggs each. This, however, is an unusually high number since female chinook salmon from other river systems normally average only 3,500 to 4,500 eggs each.
Fishing Information: In the ocean, chinook salmon are fished principally by trolling dead bait or artificial lures. Occasionally, live bait will be used while still-fishing or drift-fishing. Chinook salmon normally stay well beneath the surface of the ocean, usually 40 to 250 feet or more and a heavy weight or downrigger is necessary to keep trolled bait at the desired depth.
Other Common Names: king salmon, Sacramento River salmon, spring salmon, black mouth, Columbia River salmon, tyee.
Largest Recorded: 4 feet 10 inches; 126.5 pounds.
Habitat: Pelagic Environment

Coho (Silver) Salmon

Family: Salmonidae (Salmons)
Genus and Species: *Oncorhynchus kisutch*
Description: The body of the coho salmon is elongate and somewhat compressed. The head is conical. This species is dark metallic blue or blue green above, becoming silvery on the sides and belly. There are spots on the back.

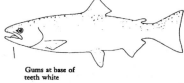

Gums at base of teeth white

The main distinguishing feature between the coho and chinook salmon is the color of the gums at the base of the teeth. Chinook salmon have a blackish lining while coho has a white lining. Cohos also have black spots only on the upper part of the tail fin, whereas chinook tail fins are completely covered with black spots.
Range: Coho salmon occur from Chamalu Bay, Baja California, to the Bering Sea and Japan.
Natural History: Cohos, as all salmon, are anadromous and spawn in fresh water. At spawning time the males turn dusky green above and on their head, bright red on their sides and blackish below. The females turn a pinkish red on their side after they enter fresh water.

Coho salmon enter streams, move upstream, and spawn from September through March. The bulk of spawning takes place from November through January. Adult males enter streams when they are either 2 or 3 years old, but adult females do not return to spawn until 3 years old. Almost all female coho salmon will spawn at age 3. All coho salmon, whether male or female, spend their first year in the stream or river in which they hatch. All adults die after spawning.

Generally speaking, the larger the female the greater the number of eggs produced; however, numerous counts have been made that indicate most females will spawn from 1,500 to 3,500 eggs. The average number produced per female appears to be about 2,500.
Fishing Information: In the ocean, coho salmon are fished primarily by trolling with dead bait (anchovy, herring, etc.) or any of several types of lures. Occasionally, live bait is used while drift fishing. The fish are usually caught within 30 feet of the surface and a heavy weight is normally used to keep a trolled lure at the desired depth. Several devices are used by recreational anglers to detach this weight when a fish strikes or is hooked. Best trolling speed appears to be about 2 knots per hour.

Some coho salmon are taken off southern California; however, the ocean angler is most successful from Monterey Bay north. The bulk of the sport catch contains 6 to 10 pound fish, about 24 inches in length.
Other Common Names: silver salmon, silver sides, hookbill.
Largest Recorded: 38.5 inches; 31 pounds.
Habitat: Pelagic Environment

California Lizardfish

Family: Synodontidae (Lizardfishes)
Genus and Species: *Synodus lucioceps*
Description: The California lizardfish has an elongate cylindrical body with a head

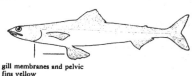

gill membranes and pelvic fins yellow

and mouth which are lizard-like in appearance. The body is a uniform brown on the back and sides shading to tan or white on the belly.

Because of its elongated body and mouth full of sharp teeth, California lizardfish are occasionally mistaken for the California barracuda. The barracuda, however, is silvery rather than brown and has two dorsal fins of approximately equal size with a wide space between them. The lizardfish has only a single dorsal fin with a tiny fleshy fin behind it.
Range: The California lizardfish occurs from Guaymas, Mexico, to San Francisco, California, but is not common north of Point Conception, California. This species generally occurs over sandy bottoms in shallow water ranging from 5 to 150 feet, but has been taken at depths up to 750 feet.
Natural History: The California lizardfish spend most of their time sitting on the bottom with the body at a slight angle, propped up in the front end by the ventral fins. This inactivity ends rapidly when small fishes or squid swim into the area and the fish dart upward to grab one, usually swallowing the prey in one gulp.

This species is believed to spawn during the summer months when adult fish have been observed to congregate on sandy patches. Young lizardfish, less than 3 inches long, are nearly transparent, elongate, scaleless, with a row of large black spots under the skin of the belly.
Fishing Information: The California lizardfish, while not sought by most anglers, is taken incidentally in fairly large numbers by anglers fishing for other shallow water bottomfishes like halibut.

California lizardfish can be caught on a wide variety of cut baits fished on the bottom.
Other Common Names: candlefish, lizardfish.
Largest Recorded: 25.17 inches; no weight recorded; however, it is reported to reach 4 pounds.
Habitat: Shallow Sandy Environment
a Pacific halibut that large. The fish are typically caught on crab, shrimp, squid, and other invertebrates.
Other Common Names: alabato, northern halibut, right halibut, genuine halibut, real halibut.
Largest Recorded: 8.75 feet; 507 pounds.
Habitat: Deep Sandy Environment

Pacific Hake (Pacific Whiting)

Family: Merlucciidae* (Hakes)
Genus and Species: *Merluccius productus*
* Gadidae (American Fisheries Society)
Description: The body of the Pacific hake is elongate, slender, and moderately compressed. The head is elongate and the mouth large.

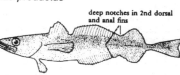

deep notches in 2nd dorsal and anal fins

The color is gray to dusky brown, with brassy overtones and black speckles on the back. The elongated shape, notched second dorsal and anal fin, and the coloration separate Pacific hake from other fish in this group.
Range: The Pacific hake occurs in the Gulf of California (isolated population) and from Magdalena Bay, Baja California, to Alaska and along the Asiatic coast. It is found to depths exceeding 2,900 feet.

Natural History: The diet of this species includes small fishes, shrimp and squid.

Pacific hake spawn in the winter, beginning at 3-4 years of age, off southern California and Baja California, Mexico. After spawning the adults migrate northward to Oregon, Washington and Canada and return to their spawning areas in the fall.

Fishing Information: Pacific hake are most commonly caught incidentally by anglers seeking salmon or bottomfish.

Pacific hake support one of the larger commercial fisheries off the Pacific Coast. Considered a nuisance by many anglers, they are generally discarded if caught. If kept chilled immediately after capture, Pacific hake have good food qualities. However, the fish becomes soft and undesirable if not cared for properly. Pacific hake may be caught with salmon or groundfish baits such as squid, herring or anchovy.

Other Common Names: Pacific whiting, whitefish, haddock, butterfish, California hake, popeye, silver hake, ocean whitefish.

Largest Recorded: 3 feet; no weight recorded.

Habitat: Deep Sandy Environment

Pacific Tomcod

Family: Gadidae (Codfishes)

Genus and Species: *Microgadus proximus*

Description: The body of the Pacific tomcod is elongated, slender and moderately compressed. The head is elongate and there is a small fleshy projection, a barbel, on the lower jaw. The color is olive green above, creamy white below, and the fins have dusky tips.

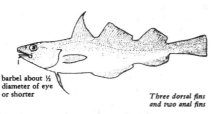

barbel about ½ diameter of eye or shorter

Three dorsal fins and two anal fins

Three spineless dorsal fins and the small chin barbel separate the Pacific tomcod from any similar appearing fish, except its cousin, the Pacific cod. The Pacific cod has a barbel as long as the diameter of the eye while the Pacific tomcod has a barbel that is less than one half the diameter of the eye.

The Pacific tomcod is a member of the true cod family. It is one of the smaller members of the group and is often confused with the white croaker. Again, the three spineless dorsal fins will distinguish this species from the others.

Range: The Pacific tomcod occurs from Point Sal, California, to Unalaska Island, Alaska, in near surface waters to depths of 720 feet.

Natural History: The diet of the Pacific tomcod includes anchovies, shrimp, and worms.

A 10.3 inch female Pacific tomcod contained an estimated 1,200 eggs.

Fishing Information: Pacific tomcod are occasionally taken by recreational anglers in central and northern California. This is usually incidental to fishing for other species of fish. Since these are rather small fish, light line and small baited hooks are the proper gear. Small pieces of cut fish make good bait.

Other Common Names: tomcod, piciata, California tomcod.

Largest Recorded: 12 inches; no weight recorded.

Habitat: Shallow Sandy Environment

California Grunion

Family: Atherinidae (Silversides)

Genus and Species: *Leuresthes tenuis*

Description: The California grunion has an elongate body and head that are more or less compressed. The mouth is small. The scales are small, smooth and firm.

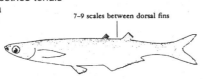

7-9 scales between dorsal fins

This species is bluish green above, silvery below, and a bright silvery band tinged with blue and bordered above with violet extends the length of the body.

Range: The California grunion occurs from Magdalena Bay, Baja California, to San Francisco, California; however, the principal range is between Point Abreojos, Baja California, and Point Conception, California.

Natural History: The food habits are not well known; however, they do eat small crustaceans and fish eggs.

The life span of California grunion is usually 3 years, with some individuals surviving 4 years. The most rapid growth takes place during the first year, at the end of which they are 5 inches long and capable of spawning.

The spawning behavior of grunion is one of the more unusual of all marine fishes. They are the only California fish known to strand themselves on the beach to deposit their reproductive products in the moist sand.

Females, accompanied by one to eight males, swim onto the beach, dig themselves into the sand up to their pectoral fins and lay their eggs. The males wrap themselves around the female and fertilize the eggs. With the next wave the fish return to the sea. During spawning activities, grunion may make a faint squeaking noise.

Spawning takes place from early March through September, and then only for 3 or 4 nights following the full moon during the 1 to 4 hours immediately after high tide.

Most females spawn from four to eight times a year producing up to 3,000 eggs every 2 weeks.

California grunion are non-migratory, and are most often found in schools a short distance from shore in water 15 to 40 feet deep.

Fishing Information: California grunion may only be taken by hand. No appliances of any kind may be used, and no holes may be dug in the beach. The season is closed April and May.

While the California grunion may not be taken during April or May, these are good months to observe spawning activities.

Other Common Names: smelt, little smelt, grunion, lease smelt.

Largest Recorded: 7.5 inches; no weight record; however, a 7 inch female full of eggs weighed less than 2 ounces.

Habitat: Surf Environment

Jacksmelt

Family: Atherinidae (Silversides)

Genus and Species: *Atherinopsis californiensis*

Description: The body of the jacksmelt is elongate and somewhat compressed. The head is oblong and compressed, and the eyes and mouth are small. The color is greenish blue above, silver below, with a metallic stripe bordered with blue extending the length of the body.

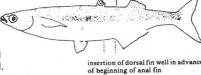

10-12 scales between dorsal fins

insertion of dorsal fin well in advance of beginning of anal fin

Jacksmelt, topsmelt, and California grunion are members of the silversides family and are not considered true smelt.

These three species look very similar except for the location of the first dorsal fin. In the jacksmelt, the first dorsal fin is forward of a line drawn perpendicular to the vent (anus); in the topsmelt, it is just about over the vent and in the grunion, it is behind the vent.

Range: Jacksmelt occur from Santa Maria Bay, Baja California, to Yaquina, Oregon.

Jacksmelt are found in California bays and ocean waters throughout the year. They are schooling fish which prefer shallow water less than 100 feet and are most common in 5 to 50 foot depths.

Natural History: Jacksmelt feed on small crustaceans.

Jacksmelt that are 13 to 15 inches long are 8 or 9 years old. A 16 inch, 1 pound male was 11 years old.

They will spawn first when 2 years old and about 6 inches long. The spawning season extends from October to March. Large masses of eggs, about the size of small BB's, are attached to shallow water seaweeds by means of long filaments.

Fishing Information: Jacksmelt are one of the most common fishes taken by pier anglers, but are also caught in the surf.

Sometimes a number of coiled up worms are found in the flesh. These are intermediate stages of spine headed worms, the adult of which are harmful to sharks, pelicans and other fish predators. The worms are harmless to humans when the fish is thoroughly cooked.

Other Common Names: silverside, horse smelt, blue smelt, California smelt.

Largest Recorded: 17.5 inches; no weight recorded; however, a jacksmelt 16 inches long weighed 1 pound.

Habitat: Bay Environment

Sculpin

Family: Scorpaenidae (Scorpionfishes)
Genus and Species: *Scorpaena guttata*
Description: The body of the sculpin is stocky and slightly compressed. The head and mouth are large, as are the pectoral fins. The

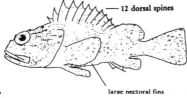

12 dorsal spines

large pectoral fins

color is red to brown, with dark blotches and spotting over the body and fins.
Range: The sculpin occurs between Uncle Sam Bank, Baja California, and Santa Cruz, California, with an isolated population in the Gulf of California. They are caught over hard, rocky bottoms at depths ranging from just below the surface to 600 feet. Some may occasionally be taken over sand or mud bottoms.
Natural History: The diet of the sculpin includes crab, squid, octopus, fishes and shrimp.

Sculpin first spawn when they are 3 or 4 years, and they may live 15 years or longer. Spawning takes place from April through August, and probably occurs at night. The eggs are embedded in the gelatinous walls of hollow, pear shaped egg-balloons. The paired egg-balloons, each 5 to 10 inches long are joined at their small ends. The walls of these "balloons" are about 0.1 inch thick, transparent or greenish in color, and contain a single layer of eggs. Each egg is about 0.05 inch in diameter. The "balloons" are released at the bottom of the sea and rise rapidly to the surface. The eggs hatch within 5 days.
Fishing Information: Sculpins readily take a hook that has been baited with a piece of squid or fish and lowered to the bottom in a rocky area where they are known to inhabit. A lot of rebaiting time can be saved by utilizing a "difficult to steal" bait. At times, a considerable amount of chumming with ground fish will attract sculpins to the surface. Hooked sculpins are not noted for their fighting qualities.

The sculpin is the most venomous member of the scorpionfish family in California. Its dorsal, pelvic and anal fin spines are associated with venom glands and are capable of causing an extremely painful wound. Penetration of the skin by any of these spines is followed almost immediately by intense and excruciating pain in the area of the wound.

Many treatments have been used for sculpin stings, but immersion of the affected part in very hot water seems to be the most effective. Multiple punctures can be quite serious, producing shock, respiratory distress or abnormal heart action and may require hospitalization of the victim.
Other Common Names: spotted scorpionfish, scorpion, rattlesnake, bullhead, scorpene, California scorpionfish.
Largest Recorded: 17 inches; no weight recorded; however, a 15.25 inch female weighed 3.5 pounds.
Habitat: Shallow Rocky Environment

Black Rockfish

Family: Scorpaenidae (Scorpionfishes)
Genus and Species: *Sebastes melanops*
Description: The body of the black rockfish is oval or egg-shaped and compressed. The head has a steep upper pro-

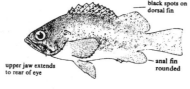

black spots on dorsal fin

upper jaw extends to rear of eye

anal fin rounded

file which is almost straight; the mouth is large and the lower jaw projects slightly. The color is brown to black on the back, paler on the sides, and dirty white below. There are black spots on the dorsal fin.

This species is easily confused with the blue rockfish; however, the anal fin of the black rockfish is rounded while the anal fin of the blue rockfish is slanted or straight. The black rockfish has spots on the dorsal fin, the blue rockfish does not.
Range: Black rockfish occur from Paradise Cove, California, to Amchitka Island, Alaska. They are wide-ranging fish that can live on the surface or on the bottom to 1,200 feet near rocky reefs or in open water over deep banks or drop-offs.
Natural History: The diet of the black rockfish includes squid, crab eggs, and fishes.

Black rockfish are ovoviviparous, like all members of this family—fertilization and development of the embryo take place in the body of the mother. When embryonic development is complete, the female releases the eggs and the exposure to sea water activates the embryo and it escapes from the egg case.

Fishing Information: These fish are commonly caught from commercial passenger fishing vessels and when trolling for salmon. Use similar fishing techniques as for blue rockfish.
Other Common Names: black snapper, black bass, gray rockfish, red snapper.
Largest Recorded: 23.75 inches; 10.5 pounds.
Habitat: Shallow Rocky Environment

Blue Rockfish

Family: Scorpaenidae (Scorpionfishes)
Genus and Species: *Sebastes mystinus*
Description: The body of the blue rockfish is oval or egg-shaped and compressed with similar dorsal and ventral profiles. The head is relatively short and bluntly pointed. The mouth is relatively small with the lower jaw slightly project-

anal fin slanted or straight

ing. The color is dark blue or olive brown to grayish black on the back becoming lighter below; blotched with lighter shades on back and sides.

The presence of five spines on the preopercle (gill cover), easily distinguish this species as a rockfish rather than a perch, a bass or a halfmoon which is of similar color.

The black rockfish can be confused with this species; however, the black rockfish has spots on the dorsal fin while the blue rockfish does not. The anal fin of the black rockfish is rounded while that of the blue rockfish is slanted or straight.
Range: The blue rockfish occurs from Punta Baja, Baja California, to the Bering Sea. It is a schooling species that is often caught in large numbers over rocky bottoms and around kelp beds. It is most commonly caught from the surface to 100 feet, although it has been taken from depths as great as 300 feet.
Natural History: Blue rockfish principally eat small fishes, shrimps, other crustaceans and small pieces of algae or seaweed. Algae may be accidentally ingested while picking up small shrimp and other tidbits.

As with other rockfishes, fertilization is internal and live young are born which are quite small and helpless. A 16 inch female contained just over 500,000 eggs. The main spawning season runs from about November to March. Blue rockfish may attain an age of at least 15 years.
Fishing Information: Blue rockfish can be caught in quantity near rocky shores and around breakwaters, sunken ships, piles of rubble and similar localities along the entire California coastline, especially north of Point Conception. They are caught just beneath the surface in and around kelp beds, but where there is no kelp they live mostly near the bottom. Two or more hooks can be used with good success and almost any kind of cut fish will prove productive bait. Mussel, clam, crab, shrimp and squid strips work almost equally as well, as do some kinds of wet flies and other artificial lures. Blue rockfish are noted for putting up an excellent battle when hooked.
Other Common Names: blue bass, blue fish, reef perch.
Largest Recorded: 21 inches; no weight recorded; however, a 15 inch female weighed 1.75 pounds.
Habitat: Shallow Rocky Environment

Bocaccio

Family: Scorpaenidae (Scorpionfishes)
Genus and Species: *Sebastes paucispinus*
Description: The body of the bocaccio is elongate and compressed. The head is pointed, the mouth large, and the lower jaw greatly protrud-

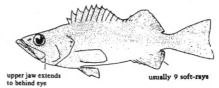

upper jaw extends to behind eye

usually 9 soft-rays

ing. The color varies from shades of brown to reddish and extends down over the belly.

Young fish are generally light bronze with speckling over the sides and back. As they mature, their color generally becomes darker and the speckling gradually disappears.
Range: Bocaccio occur from Punta Blanca, Baja California, to Kruzof Island and Kodiak Island, Alaska. Young bocaccio 1 or 2 years old travel in loose schools and move into shallow water where they may be captured in quantity. With increasing age they seek deeper water and move from near the surface to near the bottom. Adults are commonly found in waters of 250 to 750 feet over a somewhat irregular, hard or rubble bottom. They have been found at depths as great as 1,050 feet.

Natural History: The diet of bocaccio includes mainly fishes such as surfperch, jack mackerel, sablefish, anchovies, sardines, Pacific mackerel, deepsea lanternfish, other rockfishes and sanddabs. Squid, octopus, and crab also are eaten.

Females start maturing when they are 17 inches long. As with all rockfish, fertilization is internal and development of the embryos takes place within the ovaries of the female until they are ready to hatch. A 28 inch female was estimated to contain nearly 1.5 million eggs. The main hatching period runs from December through April. The newly hatched young, about 0.25 inch long, does not completely absorb the yolk from the egg stage for a period of 8 to 12 days.

Fishing Information: Almost any rocky or rubble bottom at depths of 250 to 750 feet will yield good catches of bocaccio. The usual rig is made up of three to six hooks above a sinker that is heavy enough to take the line to the bottom on a fairly straight course. Because of the depths fished, it takes a considerable amount of time to let down and haul up this rig; consequently the bait should be sufficiently tough to remain firmly on the hook while being nibbled and chewed upon by the quarry. Pieces of squid are ideal.

Other Common Names: salmon grouper, grouper, mini-grouper (juveniles), red snapper, Pacific red snapper.

Largest Recorded: 3 feet; 21 pounds.

Habitat: Deep Rocky Environment

Chilipepper

Family: Scorpaenidae (Scorpionfishes)
Genus and Species: *Sebastes goodei*
Description: The body of the chilipepper is slender and rather elongate. The head is elongate, pointed and with no spines; the lower jaw is projecting.

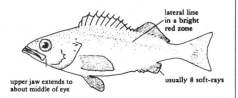

lateral line in a bright red zone

upper jaw extends to about middle of eye

usually 8 soft-rays

The chilipepper is generally pinkish becoming whitish below. The middle of the chilipepper's side, the lateral line, stands out clearly, as a lighter, bright red zone.

In comparison to the bocaccio, it has a smaller mouth with an upper jaw that extends only to about the center of the eye, not past it.

Range: This species occurs from Magdalena Bay, Baja California, to Vancouver Island, British Columbia.

Chilipeppers are not taken as frequently as other rockfishes because they are rarely caught in depths less than 360 feet along the coast of California. They generally occur over rocky bottoms and have been taken as deep as 1,080 feet.

Natural History: Adult chilipepper feed on small crustaceans, small squids, or on such fishes as anchovies, young hake, small sardines, and lanternfishes.

Approximately 50 percent out the males mature when 8.75 inches long and 2 years old; while 50 percent out the females are mature when they are 12 inches long and 4 years old. Chilipeppers may live to be at least 16 years old.

As with other rockfishes, fertilization is internal and live young are born. The number of developing eggs increases from 29,000 in a 12 inch female to about 538,000 in a 22 inch fish.

Fishing Information: The usual rig for chilipepper is made up of three to six hooks above a sinker that is heavy enough to take the line to the bottom on a fairly straight course. Chilipepper are often fished in midwater as well on the bottom. Because of the depths, it may take a considerable amount of time to lower and raise this fishing rig; therefore, the bait should be tough enough to remain on the hook while being chewed upon. Pieces of squid, dried salted anchovies or strip bait, or cut bait as it is commonly known, consists of small strips of flesh with the skin still on from freshly caught rockfish, mackerel or other fishes are ideal.

Other Common Names: chili, red snapper.

Largest Recorded: 22 inches; 5.25 pounds.

Habitat: Deep Rocky Environment

Cowcod

Family: Scorpaenidae (Scorpionfishes)
Genus and Species: *Sebastes levis*
Description: The body and head of the cowcod are

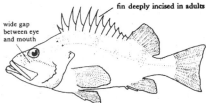

fin deeply incised in adults

wide gap between eye and mouth

somewhat compressed. The head is very large. The mouth is large with a projecting lower jaw.

Adults are uniform pale pink to orange in color. Young fish have four dark vertical bands on their sides which gradually fade into dusky blotches as they increase in size.

Their heads are large and spined, the dorsal fins are deeply notched, and there is an unusually wide space between the eye and the upper jaw. These three characteristics help to distinguish cowcod from other reddish colored rockfish.

Range: Cowcod occur from Ranger Bank and Guadalupe Island, Baja California, to Usal, California. This is a deeper water species occurring at depths from 60 feet (young) to 1,200 feet.

Cowcod are found over rocky bottoms, particularly where there are sharp, steep drop-offs.

Natural History: The diet of the cowcod includes mainly fishes, octopus, and squid. Juvenile cowcod eat small shrimp and crabs.

Like all members of the genus Sebastes, the cowcod gives birth to live young. These are less than 0.5 inches in length and are produced in great numbers.The young are free floating and may be found in shallower water; however, as they grow larger they move to deeper water.

Fishing Information: Because of its large size, the cowcod is one of the most sought after rockfishes in southern California.

Live squid and oversized metal, lead and rubber jigs are often effective baits for this species. Live or salted anchovies or frozen squid are also considered good baits for the cowcod.

Sometimes cowcod are caught while attacking smaller rockfish which have already been hooked and are being brought to the surface.

Other Common Names: cow, cow rockfish, cowfish, red snapper.

Largest Recorded: 37 inches; 28.5 pounds.

Habitat: Deep Rocky Environment

Olive Rockfish

Family: Scorpaenidae (Scorpionfishes)
Genus and Species: *Sebastes serranoides*
Description: The body of the olive rockfish is elongate and compressed. The upper profile of the head is almost straight, and the snout is long and pointed. The lower jaw is projecting.

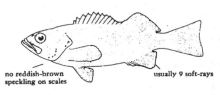

no reddish-brown speckling on scales

usually 9 soft-rays

The olive rockfish is dark olive brown on the back, often with some light areas under the dorsal fin. The sides are a lighter olive green, and the fins are yellow.

This species is very similar in appearance to the yellowtail rockfish. The olive rockfish always has nine soft rays in the anal fin; the yellowtail rockfish usually has eight.

Range: This species occurs from the San Benito Islands, Baja California, to Redding Rock, California.

Olive rockfish are generally caught in nearshore waters. They are found primarily around reefs and kelp beds in water less than 150 feet deep, but have been caught as deep as 480 feet.

Natural History: The diet of olive rockfish consists primarily of fishes; however, crab, shrimp, and squid also are consumed in smaller quantities.

Olive rockfish mature and spawn for the first time when they are 3 or 4 years old. As is true among the other rockfish,fertilization is internal and live young are born. The main spawning season is from December through March and a large female may spawn as many as 500,000 young during the season.

Fishing Information: Olive rockfish may be found in almost every kelp bed along the mainland shore south of Monterey Bay, California.

The best rig employs a single hook on monofilament nylon and calls for a lively anchovy. The bait should be cast directly into the floating fronds of kelp and no sinker should be used. It there are any olive rockfish around they will hit the bait right at the surface, usually so hard that they set the hook themselves. The ensuing battle is excellent in every respect and the larger the fish the better the fight. Olive rockfish will also strike a streamer fly or a properly worked metal lure or small wooden plug.

Other Common Names: johnny bass, johnathans.

Largest Recorded: 24 inches; no weight recorded.

Habitat: Shallow Rocky Environment

Yellowtail Rockfish

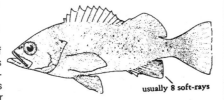

usually 8 soft-rays

Family: Scorpaenidae (Scorpionfishes)
Genus and Species: *Sebastes flavidus*
Description: The body of the yellowtail rockfish is elongate and compressed. The head is rather long and the upper profile is steep and slightly curved. The lower jaw projects, but not beyond the upper profile of the head.

The color is grayish brown above which shades to white below. The sides are finely spotted with yellow. The tail is yellow, while the other fins are dusky yellow. When the fish is fresh, reddish brown speckling is visible on some of the scales.

As with many of the rockfish, identification can be somewhat difficult. Some of the distinguishing characteristics of the yellowtail rockfish include a convex (surface curves outward) space between the eyes, the absence of spines on top of the head, a projecting lower jaw, an anal fin with eight (rarely seven) soft rays and the lining of the belly is white.
Range: The yellowtail rockfish occurs from San Diego, California, to Kodiak Island, Alaska; however, it is most often caught by recreational anglers off of central and northern California. It is regularly found over deep reefs from the surface to depths of 1,800 feet.
Natural History: Adult yellowtail rockfish feed on small hake, anchovies, lanternfishes, and other small fishes, as well as on small squid, and other shrimp-like organisms. These are all good baits to use for the yellowtail rockfish.

A few yellowtail rockfish mature when 11 inches long or 3 years old. Fifty percent are mature when 13 inches long or 5 years old. They may live to be 24 years old.

As with other rockfishes, fertilization is internal and live young are born. The number of developing eggs increases from 50,000 in a fish 12 inches long to about 633,000 in a fish 19 to 21 inches long.
Fishing Information: When fishing for yellowtail rockfish in deeper waters, the typical rockfish rig and bait is appropriate (see bocaccio). Since this species occurs quite often at or near the surface, standard surface fishing techniques and baits such as anchovies or squid fished on a small hook are effective. Small silvery lures or small lead and rubber jigs also work well.
Other Common Names: red snapper, yellowtail.
Largest Recorded: 26 inches; no weight recorded; however, a yellowtail rockfish 24 inches long will weigh about 7.5 pounds.
Habitat: Shallow Rocky Environment

Canary Rockfish

black blotch in fin in fish measuring up to about 14 inches

Family: Scorpaenidae (Scorpionfish)
Genus and Species: *Sebastes pinniger*
Description: The body of the canary rockfish is elongate, moderately deep and compressed. The head is large with an upper profile that is somewhat curved. The

underside of jaw smooth

color is yellow orange with gray mottling on the back and paler, near white, below. The fins are also yellow orange. The middle of the sides are in a clear, gray zone. There is often a black spot near the back of the first dorsal fin in fish shorter than 14 inches.

Although the canary rockfish resembles the vermilion rockfish superficially, the two are easily separated. The underside of the lower jaw of the canary rockfish has no scales and feels smooth to the touch when rubbed from back to front. The vermilion rockfish has scales on the underside of its lower jaw so that it feels rough when rubbed forward.
Range: Canary rockfish occur from Cape Colnett, Baja California, to Cape San Bartolome, Alaska.

Canary rockfish are usually caught at depths of 50 to 300 feet, although juveniles have been taken at the surface and adults have been taken from depths as great as 900 feet. They are found around reefs and over soft bottoms.
Natural History: Adult canary rockfish feed on small crustaceans as well as anchovies, sanddabs, and other small fishes.

The canary rockfish, like all members of the genus *Sebastes*, produces live young. Fertilization and embryo development take place within the body of the mother. The number of eggs increases from 260,000 in a 19 inch female to about 1,900,000 in a female 26 inches long. About 50 percent of canary rockfish are mature at a length of 14 inches, or when they are 5 to 6 years old. They may live to be at least 22 years old.
Fishing Information: The typical rockfish rig and bait may be used for canary rockfish (see bocaccio). This species contributes to the recreational marine anglers mixed rockfish bag.
Other Common Names: red snapper, fantail, canary, orange rockfish.
Largest Recorded: 30 inches; no weight recorded; however, a 24 inch canary rockfish weighs about 7 pounds.
Habitat: Deep Rocky Environment

Vermilion Rockfish

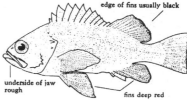

edge of fins usually black

underside of jaw rough

fins deep red

Family: Scorpaenidae (Scorpionfishes)
Genus and Species: *Sebastes miniatus*
Description: The body of the vermilion rockfish is moderately deep and compressed. The upper profile of the head is somewhat curved; the mouth is large, with the lower jaw slightly projecting. The color is bright red on the body and fins; many with black and gray mottling on back and sides. On fish shorter than 12 inches, the mottling is much more apparent and the fins are often edged with black.

The yelloweye and canary rockfishes are similar in appearance to the vermilion, but the bottom of the yelloweye and canary's lower jaws are scaleless and feels smooth to the touch. The vermilion rockfish has scales on the bottom of the lower jaw which make it rough to the touch.
Range: Vermilion rockfish occur from San Benito Islands, Baja California, to Vancouver Island, Canada. They are generally caught over rocky bottoms at depths of 1 00 to 500 feet, although they have been taken from depths as great as 900 feet.
Natural History: The tree swimming young of the vermilion rockfish feed primarily upon shrimp-like organisms, while the larger, bottom-living adults feed almost exclusively upon fishes, squid and octopus. Most fishes that are eaten are other smaller kinds of rockfish.

Vermilion rockfish appear to mature and spawn for the first time when they are 3 or 4 years old. As with all other rockfish, fertilization is internal and they give birth to living young. A vermilion rockfish that was 20 inches long was estimated to contain 282,000 eggs. By this measure a 30 incher might contain as many as 500,000 eggs. The principal reproductive period lasts from December through March.
Fishing Information: Because a good rockfish "hole" often will yield a dozen or more kinds of rockfishes on any given day, it has been said that rockfish fishing is colorful, interesting, productive, and mysterious. Vermilion rockfish usually are found in the bag of "red" rockfish taken from one of these "holes."

The same rig, bait, and technique used for bocaccio works for vermilion rockfish. Again a lot of rebaiting time can be saved by using a tough, difficult to steal bait such as a piece of squid or salted mackerel.
Other Common Names: red snapper, red rock cod.
Largest Recorded: 30 inches; no weight recorded; however, they attain a weight of at least 15 pounds.
Habitat: Deep Rocky Environment

Copper Rockfish

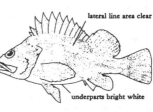

lateral line area clear

underparts bright white

Family: Scorpaenidae (Scorpionfishes)
Genus and Species: *Sebastes caurinus*
Description: The body of the copper rockfish is moderately deep and compressed. The head is large with a slightly curved upper profile; the mouth is large and the lower jaw projects slightly. The color is copper brown to orange tinged with pink. The back two-thirds of the sides are a clear, light pink area; the belly is white.
Range: The copper rockfish occurs from San Benitos Islands, Baja California, to the Kenai Peninsula, Alaska. It is found in shallow rocky and sandy areas, and is generally caught at depths of less than 180 feet; however, some have been taken as deep as 600 feet.

Natural History: The diet of copper rockfish includes snails, worms, squid, octopus, crabs, shrimps, and fishes.

Copper rockfish, like all species in the genus *Sebastes*, give birth to fully developed embryos. Fertilization and development of the embryo take place in the body of the mother. Upon being expelled from the female, the fully developed embryo is released from the egg.

Fishing Information: The copper rockfish is often the last species to die in a bag of rockfish. Some individuals continue to twitch long after members of other species have died.

Other Common Names: never die, whitebelly, chucklehead.

Largest Recorded: 22.5 inches; no weight recorded.

Habitat: Shallow Rocky Environment

Widow Rockfish

Family: Scorpaenidae (Scorpionfishes)

Genus and Species: *Sebastes entomelas*

Description: The body of the widow rockfish is elongate and compressed. The head is relatively short, and the upper profile is slightly curved. The mouth is relatively small, the lower jaw projects slightly.

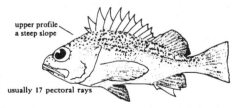

The color is brassy brown over most of the body with the belly generally lighter in color, often with a reddish cast. The fin membranes, particularly in the anal and pectoral fins, are black.

Specimens smaller than 10 inches are lighter in color and are tinged with vague streaks of orange.

Range: Widow rockfish occur from Todos Santos Bay, Baja California, to Kodiak Island, Alaska.

Natural History: Adult widow rockfish feed extensively on small free floating crab-like animals. Occasionally salps, small squids and anchovies are eaten.

A few mature when 12 inches long and 3 years old. Fifty percent are mature when 12.75 inches long or 4 years old. Widow rockfish may live to be 16 years old.

As with other rockfish fertilization is internal and the young are born live. The number of developing eggs increases from 55,000 in fish 12.75 inches long, to about 900,000 in a fish 20 inches long.

Fishing Information: Widow rockfish are generally caught by sport anglers fishing on or just above the bottom in deep water up to 1,200 feet, although young fish may be taken at or near the surface. On occasion, widow rockfish form huge schools in midwater where they feed on small plants. At such times, they are vulnerable to recreational anglers as well as commercial trawling gear and are often taken in great quantities.

Other Common Names: widow, widowfish, red snapper.

Largest Recorded: 21 inches; no weight recorded; however, a 20 inch widow rockfish will weigh about 4 pounds.

Habitat: Deep Rocky Environment

Greenspotted Rockfish

Family: Scorpaenidae (Scorpionfishes)

Genus and Species: *Sebastes chlorostictus*

Description: The body of the green spotted rockfish is elongate and moderately compressed. The upper profile of the head is rather steep with a nearly straight slope. The jaws are even when closed. The color is yellow pink with distinct green spots over the back and top of the head. There are three to five white blotches with green borders along the upper back, and the pectoral fins carry 17 rays. The underside of the lower jaw has no scales and is smooth to the touch.

Two other species, the green blotched rockfish and pink rockfish, are nearly identical to the greenspotted rockfish. Nevertheless, they can be distinguished from the greenspotted rockfish by the small patches of scales on the underside of their lower jaws. These two look-alike species attain a larger size than the greenspotted rockfish, but are not encountered as frequently since they usually inhabitat deeper water.

Range: The greenspotted rockfish occurs from Cedros Island, Baja California, to Copalis Head, Washington.

Greenspotted rockfish are caught around offshore, rocky reefs at depths ranging from 160 to 660 feet.

Natural History: As with other rockfishes, fertilization is internal and live young are born. The young are born during the period of April through July.

Fishing Information: The greenspotted rockfish is a common species in the deep-water rockfish catch. It is not considered very desirable, however, because of its small size.

Other Common Names: chucklehead, red rock cod, bolina.

Largest Recorded: 19.75 inches; no weight recorded.

Habitat: Deep Rocky Environment

Starry Rockfish

Family: Scorpaenidae (Scorpionfishes)

Genus and Species: *Sebastes constellatus*

Description: The body of the starry rockfish is elongate, robust, heavy forward tapering to the tail. The

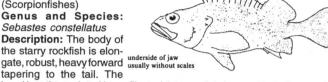

head is rather pointed in profile and the mouth is large with the lower jaw projecting only slightly beyond the upper jaw when the mouth is closed.

The body is red orange and profusely covered with small white spots. There are four or five large whitish blotches along the back. It is a very distinctive fish that is not easily confused with any other rockfish.

Range: The starry rockfish occurs from Thetis Bank, Baja California, to San Francisco, California, and is found around rocky offshore reefs at depths of 80 to 900 feet.

Natural History: As with other kinds of rockfish, fertilization is internal and live young are born. The young are usually born during March through May.

Fishing Information: Starry rockfish contribute to the recreational anglers offshore reef catch. The typical rockfish rig and baits are appropriate gear (see bocaccio).

Other Common Names: spotted corsair, spotted rockfish, chinafish, red rock cod.

Largest Recorded: 18 inches; no weight recorded.

Habitat: Deep Rocky Environment

Sablefish

Family: Anoplopomatidae (Sablefishes)

Genus and Species: *Anoplopoma fimbria*

Description: The body of the sablefish is quite elongate, slightly compressed and tapering to the tail. The head is rather large and elongate. The sable-

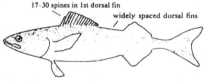

fish is blackish gray on the back and sides, and gray to white below. Two well separated dorsal fins, very small teeth and the uniform coloration distinguishes this species.

Range: The sablefish occurs from Cedros Island, Baja California, to the Bering Sea and Japan; at depths ranging from the surface (juveniles) to 6,000 feet. They are usually taken in 80 to 600 feet of water; however, schools of small individuals occasionally enter shallow areas.

Natural History: The diet of sablefish include marine worms, crustaceans and small fishes.

About 50 percent of the male sablefish are mature by the time they are 24 inches long and 5 years old, whereas 50 percent of the females first mature at 7 years, when they are 28 inches long.

A 28 inch female weighing 6.5 pounds and 7 years old is capable of spawning about 100,000 eggs; while a 40 inch female that is 20 years old will contain approximately 1,000,000 eggs.

Fishing Information: During some years, young sablefish abound in inshore waters and can be caught in large numbers close to the surf zone. Most of the time, however, they live on the bottom in deeper water. There is a tendency for sablefish to move deeper during the winter spawning season; thus, the heaviest catches, which are made during summer months, are made in shallower water.

Considering the depths at which one must fish, a lot of reeling in to rebait can be avoided by using more than one hook and by using bait that is difficult for the fish to steal. Chunks of salted mackerel or fresh squid are both excellent baits. Sablefish are feeble fighters at best, but large fish have a weight advantage that makes hauling them from the depths a back breaking ordeal.

The flesh is pure white and oily with a very mild flavor.

Other Common Names: butterfish, blackcod, coalfish, candlefish, skilfish, coal cod, bluecod, bluefish, deep sea trout, black candlefish, skill.
Largest Recorded: 3 feet, 4 inches; no weight recorded; however, a sablefish 3 feet long weighed 40 pounds.
Habitat: Deep Sandy Environment

Lingcod

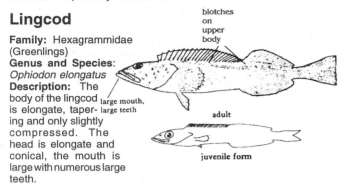

blotches on upper body

large mouth, large teeth

adult

juvenile form

Family: Hexagrammidae (Greenlings)
Genus and Species: *Ophiodon elongatus*
Description: The body of the lingcod is elongate, tapering and only slightly compressed. The head is elongate and conical, the mouth is large with numerous large teeth.

Lingcod are generally dark brown with lots of spots and blotches on the upper part of the body, but come in a variety of colors ranging from blue green to red brown.
Range: Lingcod occur between Point San Carlos, Baja California, and Kodiak Island, Alaska. They are not abundant south of Point Conception except in a few localities. They live at or near the bottom, generally in close association with rocky areas and kelp beds, especially where there is a strong tidal movement. They occur most abundantly at depths ranging to about 350 feet, but will often go into deeper water and have been caught as deep as 2,700 feet off southern California.
Natural History: Young lingcod feed primarily upon shrimp and other crustaceans until they are big enough to eat fish. Once started on fishes, it seems that any kind coming within reach is fair game.

Male and female lingcod first mature when they are 3 years of age and about 23 inches in total length. Nearly all are mature at age 4 when they are nearly 26 inches long. Spawning usually takes place from December through March. The eggs are large (0.17 inch in diameter) and adhesive, sticking in large masses to rocky crevasses, generally on subtidal reefs. The male lingcod guards the eggs after fertilization until they hatch. A female 30 inches long may lay approximately 60,000 eggs; whereas, a 45 inch female may lay more than 500,000 in a single season.
Fishing Information: Lingcod are easily caught on standard rockfish rigs using anchovies or squid pieces. Larger baits such as live squid, mackerel or even small rockfishes often produce catches of very large lingcods. Large chrome-plated metal jigs, large lead-head and rubber jigs, and lead-filled pipe jigs are also favorites of avid lingcod anglers. When sportfishing, live bait is more effective than dead bait, and dead bait usually more than metal jigs. Whatever the bait, it seems more effective if jigged or bounced up and down along the bottom.

Care should be taken when unhooking one of these toothy beasts. The lingcods teeth, as well as the gillrakers, are extremely sharp and can cause serious injury to the fingers of careless anglers. Unless you are wearing heavy gloves, NEVER put your fingers into the mouth or gill chamber of a lingcod. The safest way to pick up a lingcod is to place the thumb and first finger of one hand in the eye sockets and grab the tail with the other hand.
Other Common Names: ling, greenlinger, slinky linky, buffalo cod, cultus cod.
Largest Recorded: 52 inches; 54 pounds (California).
Habitat: Deep Rocky Environment

Kelp Greenling

Family: Hexagrammidae (Greenlings)
Genus and Species: *Hexagrammos decagrammus*
Description: The body of the kelp greenling is elongate and somewhat compressed. The head is conical, blunt in profile, and the mouth is rather small.

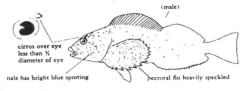

(male)

cirrus over eye less than ¾ diameter of eye

male has bright blue spotting

pectoral fin heavily speckled

Male and female kelp greenling can be readily distinguished by their coloration. The forepart of the body of the male has numerous sky blue spots, each surrounded by a ring of rusty spots. The female is rather uniformly covered with round reddish brown spots. Certainly, the kelp greenling is one of the most boldly colored fishes found along our coast.

The kelp greenling has small, unfringed flaps of skin (cirri) over the eyes and the mouth is yellowish inside; whereas, the rock greenling has a pair of large, fringed flaps of skin over the eyes and the inside of the mouth is bluish.
Range: Kelp greenling occur from La Jolla, California, to the Aleutian Islands, Alaska, but are quite rare south of Point Conception. They live in relatively shallow water along rocky coasts, around jetties and in kelp beds.
Natural History: Included in the kelp greenling's diet are various seaworms, crustaceans, and small fishes.

In British Columbia, spawning occurs in October and November. Pale blue eggs are laid in large masses on rocks. In California, eggs and young have been collected in March suggesting that spawning takes place during the winter months throughout the total range.
Fishing Information: Kelp greenling is one of the major species in the rocky shore angler's bag in central and northern California. The jetties at Eureka comprise the number one greenling "hole" in the state. They can be caught with hooks baited with cut pieces of fish, clams, mussels, shrimp, squid, worms and crab backs. Once hooked, the kelp greenling is difficult to land because of its habit of entangling the angler's line about rocks, crevices or kelp. Kelp greenling are excellent bait for lingcod anglers.
Other Common Names: greenling sea trout, rock trout, spotted rock trout, kelp trout, kelp cod.
Largest Recorded: 21 inches, no weight recorded; however, a male 12 inches long weighed 1 pound.
Habitat: Shallow Rocky Environment

Pacific Staghorn Sculpin

Family: Cottidae (Sculpins)
Genus and Species: *Leptocottus armatus*
Description: The body of the Pacific staghorn sculpin is elongate and scaleless. The head is long and depressed, and the mouth is large. The body coloration often blends

spines in dorsal fin

antlerlike projections or spines just forward of the gill slit on the gillcover

with its environment and shows such varieties as greenish brown or gray above, and white to yellow below. The spinous dorsal fin has an obvious black spot and the pectoral fins are yellowish with dark cross bars. The most striking characteristic of this species is an antler-like spine located just forward of the gill cover.
Range: The Pacific staghorn sculpin occurs from San Quintin Bay, Baja California, to Chignik, Alaska. They frequent California's bays, estuaries, lagoons, and shallow coastal waters, and are wide ranging from the intertidal zone to a depth of 510 feet.
Natural History: The diet of the Pacific staghorn sculpin includes crabs, shrimp, worms, mollusks, and many kinds of juvenile and adult fishes.

These fish become sexually mature when 1 year old. Spawning takes place between October and April. The average sized female produces about 5,000 eggs in a season.
Fishing Information: The Pacific staghorn sculpin is attracted to a variety of baits, preferably small invertebrates. It is not highly prized as a food or sport fish. On the other hand, it is a popular bait fish for the San Francisco Bay Delta striped bass sport fishery. Caution is recommended when handling this species because the spines located on the gill cover can leave nasty cuts if the fish thrashes around in your hands.
Other Common Names: bullhead, staghorn sculpin, smooth cabezon, buffalo sculpin, smooth sculpin.
Largest Recorded: 12 inches (California), 18 inches (Canada); no weight recorded; however, a 10 inch fish weighed 0.5 pounds.
Habitat: Bay Environment

Cabezon

Family: Cottidae (Sculpins)
Genus and Species: *Scorpaenichthys marmoratus*
Description: The body of the cabezon is elongate and stout. The head is large,

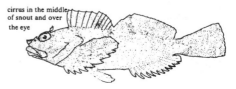

cirrus in the middle of snout and over the eye

broad and the snout is bluntly rounded. The mouth is large. The color is usually dark brown, but a variety of colors ranging from blue green to reddish brown occur and there is much mottling. It looks somewhat like the lingcod, and sometimes has blue colored flesh.

It is a member of the true sculpin family and it can best be distinguished from the similar looking lingcod by: the absence of scales on its body; and by the presence of a small flap of skin, a cirrus, over each eye and in the middle of the snout. The lining of its mouth is a pale to dark blue and it also lacks the large teeth of the lingcod.

Range: Cabezon occur from Point Abreojos, Baja California, to Sitka, Alaska. Cabezon are usually found on the bottom around rocky reefs and kelp beds in water less than 100 feet deep, although they are known to occur as deep as 250 feet.

Natural History: The cabezon's diet is made up of about 50 percent crabs and 50 percent mollusks and fishes. Small abalones are swallowed whole and the shells are regurgitated after some digestion takes place. These shells are sometimes beautifully polished by the action of the acids.

Male cabezon first mature when about 2 years old and 13.5 inches long, females when 3 years old and 17.5 inches long. Females grow faster and attain larger sizes than do males.

Spawning takes place from November through March, peaking in January. The adults tend to congregate at nesting sites. The eggs are laid in large masses on cleared rocks. The individual nest is guarded by the male who will drive away any intruder. A 3 pound female will lay an average of 48,700 eggs and a 10 pounder, 97,600.

The eggs and young are free floating, some having been taken more than 200 miles from shore. The young enter the tide pools and inshore areas during the spring when they are about 1.5 inches long. They then lose their silvery color and take on the pattern characteristic of adults.

Fishing Information: Cabezon are caught by rocky shore anglers in every suitable area from border to border. Larger numbers are caught in the central and northern part of the state. They are one of the most sought-after rocky shore inhabitants.

Suitable baits include abalone trimmings, mussels, clams, squid, shrimp, worms, cut or strip bait, and live bait when available. Here again is a bottom rock dweller that can be most difficult to land if allowed to retreat to the shelter of rocks or seaweeds after being hooked.

Cabezon eggs are poisonous, so do not eat the roe. Consumption of cabezon roe has produced near fatal results in humans.

Other Common Names: bullhead, cab, cabby, bull cod, giant sculpin, scorpion, marble sculpin.

Largest Recorded: 39 inches; 25 pounds.

Habitat: Shallow Rocky Environment

Striped Bass

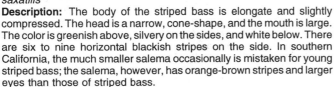

Family: Serranidae (Sea Basses) or Percichthyidae

Genus and Species: *Roccus saxatilis**

* Also known as Morone saxatilis

6–9 blackish stripes along the sides

Description: The body of the striped bass is elongate and slightly compressed. The head is a narrow, cone-shape, and the mouth is large. The color is greenish above, silvery on the sides, and white below. There are six to nine horizontal blackish stripes on the side. In southern California, the much smaller salema occasionally is mistaken for young striped bass; the salema, however, has orange-brown stripes and larger eyes than those of these fish.

Range: Striped bass were brought to California from New Jersey in 1879. They now are found from northern Baja California to Barkley Sound, British Columbia. In California, they most commonly are found in the Sacramento-San Joaquin Delta, San Francisco Bay and adjacent ocean areas.

Natural History: Examination of stomach contents show that shrimp and anchovies are most important during the summer and fall while a variety of small fishes are eaten during the winter.

Females usually mature at 5 years of age when about 24 inches long and many males mature at age 2 when about 11 inches long. A 5 pound fish may spawn as many as 25,000 eggs in one season; while a 12 pounder will spawn 1,250,000 eggs. A 75 pound striper produces as many as 10,000,000 eggs.

Striped bass are believed to spawn only in fresh water in which there is an appreciable current. In California, they spawn from March to July with a peak in April and May.

Fishing Information: By far the largest part of the striped bass catch is made in San Francisco Bay and the Delta. Good fishing occurs during late summer, but is best in the fall. Stripers occur along the coast only during late spring and summer at which time surf fishermen get a chance at them.

A variety of artificial lures and chunks or strips of standard bait fish will attract stripers. The beaches immediately adjacent to the Golden Gate are generally the best coastal spots, but occasional good runs are encountered as far south as Monterey and as far north as Bodega Bay. In San Francisco Bay, trolling with live bait is popular, with common catches under 10 pounds.

Juvenile striped bass have been planted in San Diego, Mission, Newport and Anaheim Bays since 1974 to provide sportfishing.

Other Common Names: striper, streaked bass, squidhound, rock bass.

Largest Recorded: 4 feet; 90 pounds (California); however, in the Atlantic Ocean to 6 feet and 125 pounds.

Habitat: Bay Environment

Giant Sea Bass

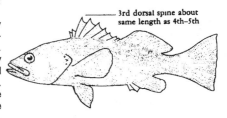

anal fin has 10–12 soft rays

Family: Serranidae (Sea Basses) or Percichthyidae

Genus and Species: *Stereolepis gigas*

Description: The body of the adult giant sea bass is elongate with dorsal spines that fit into a groove on the back. The head is robust, and mouth is large with teeth in the back, Giant sea bass are usually reddish brown to dark brown in color on all but their stomachs and, at times, many have dark spots on their sides.

Perch-like in appearance, juvenile giant sea bass differ radically from adults and are often mistaken for a different fish. Coloring on juveniles is distinct with the body being sandy red with white and dark patches spread along the sides.

Range: Giant sea bass occur throughout the Gulf of California and from Cabo San Lucas, Baja California, to Humboldt Bay, California. In California, the appearance of this species north of Point Conception has been sporadic.

Natural History: Giant sea bass feed upon a wide variety of items. Small fish taken of this species off our coast contained mostly anchovies and white croakers. Pacific mackerel, jack mackerel, sheephead, ocean whitefish, sand bass, cancer crabs, and red crabs have all been found in the stomachs of large giant sea bass. By their very bulk they appear to be slow and cumbersome, yet they are capable of outswimming and catching a bonito in a short chase.

Giant sea bass apparently do not mature until they are 11 to 13 years old. A fish of this age will weigh between 50 and 60 pounds. The ovaries of a 320 pound female weighed 47 pounds and contained an estimated 60 million eggs. This fish was ready to spawn and the larger eggs were about 0.04 inch in diameter. The main spawning season for giant sea bass occurs during July, August, and September.

Fishing Information: There has been a moratorium, which will probably last many years, on landing giant sea bass in California. All fish must be returned alive to the water. Occasionally, fish taken by anglers will "float" to the surface as their gas bladders expand. They may be returned by carefully inserting a hypodermic needle through the side of the fish into the gas bladder and allowing the air to escape.

Please be aware that it is illegal to take or possess giant sea bass.

Other Common Names: black sea bass, jewfish, giant bass.

Largest Recorded: over 7 feet; 563 pounds (Anacapa Island, 1968).

Habitat: Deep Rocky Environment

Kelp Bass

Family: Serranidae (Sea Basses)

Genus and Species: *Paralabrax clathratus*

Description: The body of the kelp bass is elongate and compressed. The head is relatively elongate, compressed and has a pointed snout. The mouth is large. The color is brown to olive green, with light blotches, becoming lighter below.

3rd dorsal spine about same length as 4th–5th

Kelp bass can be easily distinguished from sand bass by the fact that the third, fourth and fifth dorsal spines of kelp bass are about the same length; while in sand bass, the third dorsal spine is much longer than the fourth and fifth spines.

Range: Kelp bass occur from Magdalena Bay, Baja California, to the Columbia River, Washington. They are taken regularly from Point Conception south to central Baja California in depths down to 150 feet.

Natural History: Small shrimp-like crustaceans are very important in the diet of kelp bass of all ages. However, with increase in size there is a corresponding increase in the amount of fish eaten. Anchovies, small surfperch, and other small fishes are part of the diet.

By the time kelp bass are 10.5 inches long and 5 years of age, nearly all are capable of spawning. The spawning season usually extends from May through September with a peak during July. As with most members of the bass family, growth is slow and a 9 year old fish is only about 16.5 inches long.

Fishing Information: Kelp bass are caught primarily with live anchovies fished at or near the surface in and around kelp beds. They may be taken throughout the water column by trolling near kelp beds with live or dead bait. Numerous anglers also catch them on cast plugs, spoons, lures, and jigs. These anglers obtain their best catches with a yellowish, bronze, or white colored jig. In localities where kelp bass are not spoiled by offerings of live bait, they willingly accept hooks baited with strips or chunks of anchovy, mackerel or squid. Kelp bass are noted for their fighting qualities regardless of the type of bait or lure used.

Other Common Names: calico bass, bull bass, kelp salmon, cabrilla.

Largest Recorded: 28.5 inches; 14.5 pounds.

Habitat: Shallow Rocky Environment

Barred Sand Bass

Family: Serranidae (Sea Basses)

Genus and Species: *Paralabrax nebulifer*

Description: The body of the barred sand bass is rather elongate and compressed. The mouth is large and the lower jaw protrudes slightly. The color is gray white on the back, white

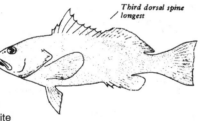

Third dorsal spine longest

on the belly and there are dark vertical bars on the sides. Barred sand bass can be easily distinguished from kelp bass by the height of the third dorsal spine. In barred sand bass, this spine is the longest of the dorsal spines, while in the kelp bass, the third, fourth and fifth dorsal spines are of about equal length. Barred sand bass can be distinguished from spotted sand bass by the lack of spots on the body.

Range: Barred sand bass occur from Magdalena Bay, Baja California, to Santa Cruz, California. This species occurs from shallow water to depths of 600 feet; however, most fish are taken in 60 to 90 feet of water.

Natural History: The barred sand bass diet includes crabs, octopus, squid, and small fishes.

The adults aggregate and spawn during warmer months, The eggs are free floating. The striped young appear in southern California nearshore areas and eelgrass beds during fall and winter.

Fishing Information: Most barred sand bass landed in California are taken between May and October. They are fished in three main areas: Horseshoe Kelp to Newport Beach, Dana Point to Oceanside and the Silver Strand oft San Diego.

The best method for catching barred sand bass is to search a sandy area with an echosounder until a school is located. The boat then can be anchored and fishing commenced with live anchovies. Barred sand bass will usually "build" or gather under the boat when chummed so it pays to wait for awhile before moving.

Other Common Names: sand bass, sandy, ground bass, sugar bass, kelp bass, California sandbass, rock bass.

Largest Recorded: 26 inches; 11.1 pounds.

Habitat: Shallow Sandy Environment

Spotted Sand Bass

Family: Serranidae (Sea Basses)

Genus and Species: *Paralabrax maculatofasciatus*

Description: The body of the spotted sand bass is moderately elongate and compressed. The mouth

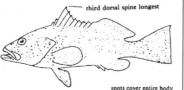

third dorsal spine longest

spots cover entire body

is large and the jaw protruding only slightly. The color is olive brown with round black spots on the body, head and fins.

Spotted sand bass can be easily distinguished from kelp bass by the height of the third dorsal spine. In spotted sand bass and barred sand bass it is the longest of the dorsal spines, while in the kelp bass the third, fourth and fifth spines are of about equal length. Spotted sand bass differ from barred sand bass by the presence of spots that cover the entire body.

Range: Spotted sand bass occur from Mazatlan, Mexico, to Monterey, California.

Spotted sand bass are confined to large bays in southern California. Because of this, they are taken less frequently than kelp or barred sand bass. They may be taken in the open ocean but this generally occurs only when drifting through the kelp.

Natural History: Spotted sand bass eat primarily crustaceans, and a Pacific halibut that large. The fish are typically caught on crab, shrimp, squid, and other invertebrates.

Other Common Names: alabato, northern halibut, right halibut, genuine halibut, real halibut.

Largest Recorded: 8.75 feet; 507 pounds.

Habitat: Deep Sandy Environment

Jack Mackerel

Family: Carangidae (Jacks)

Genus and Species: *Trachurus symmetricus*

Description: The body of the jack mackerel is rather elongate, somewhat compressed. The body tapers to a tail, which is as broad as it is deep. The color is metallic blue to olive green above becoming silvery below.

last dorsal and anal soft-rays rarely separated from fins

enlarged scales

The jack mackerel, which is not a true mackerel, is quite similar to the Mexican scad, but can be distinguished by the enlarged scales along the side and by the last rays of the dorsal and anal fins being attached to the body. These rays are isolated finlets on the Mexican scad.

Range: Jack mackerel occur from Magdalena Bay, Baja California, to southeast Alaska, and from the surface to depths of 150 feet. Adults may be found over 500 miles offshore.

Natural History: Jack mackerel are known to feed heavily upon anchovies, lantern fish, or juvenile squid. Food studies indicated that more than 90 percent of the identifiable items found in the stomachs of jack mackerel are crustaceans and small, free swimming mollusks.

Half of the 2 year old females are sexually mature and will spawn. All are spawning when they are 3 years old. Spawning takes place from March through June, and occurs over an extensive area from 80 to over 240 miles offshore.

Jack mackerel regularly live 20-30 years and weigh 4 to 5 pounds. For fish with such a long lifespan, they become sexually mature at a very young age. They are quite common near the islands and banks off southern California up to 3 or 4 years of age, and then presumably move offshore or northward.

Fishing Information: Younger jack mackerel do not feed extensively on anchovies, do not readily bite on baited hook or lure, and thus are a much less common addition to the catch of a sport angler. They can be jigged, however, on small feathered hooks and frequently are used as a bait for larger game fish by the experienced ocean angler. These younger fish are taken by the southern California commercial purse seine fishery since they occur in large schools.

Jack mackerel are most frequently taken as 15+ year-olds by commercial albacore trollers and bottomfish trawlers, generally in northern California waters and further offshore. These larger, older fish have been found in offshore waters from Baja California to the Aleutian Islands.

Other Common Names: horse mackerel, Spanish mackerel, mackerel-jack, jackfish, Pacific jack mackerel.

Largest Recorded: 32 inches; a fraction of an ounce more than 5 pounds; a 28.5 inch jack mackerel weighed 5.25 pounds.

Habitat: Pelagic Environment

Yellowtail

Family: Carangidae (Jacks)
Genus and Species:
*Seriola lalandi**
* *Also known as S. dorsalis.*

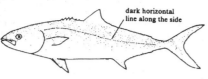

dark horizontal line along the side

Description: The body of the yellowtail is elongate, somewhat compressed, tapering to the sharp snout and the slender tail. The head is more or less conical. The color is olive brown to brown above, with a dark streak along the side of the body. The fins are yellowish. Yellowtail are easily distinguished from other fishes by the darker horizontal stripe along the side of the body, as well as a deeply forked yellow tail.
Range: Yellowtail occur from Chile to southern Washington including the Gulf of California, and from the ocean's surface to depths of 228 feet. Most fish landed in California are taken between Point Conception and the Coronado Islands, Baja California.
Natural History: Yellowtail feed primarily during the day and are opportunistic feeders, eating anything that is abundant in the area. Red crabs, anchovies, squid, and most small fishes are food items.

Spawning occurs from June through October. Many yellowtail are sexually mature in 2 years; all will spawn when 3 years old. A 3 year old female will weigh about 10 pounds and spawn approximately 450,000 eggs; however, a 25 pound female will produce more than 1 million eggs.
Fishing Information: Prime yellowtail areas are found around the Coronado Islands, La Jolla Kelp, the area between Oceanside and Dana Point, Horseshoe Kelp, Palos Verdes Peninsula, Santa Catalina Island and San Clemente Island. Most yellowtail taken by California anglers are landed on boats which anchor at spots where yellowtail are known to aggregate and then chum the fish to the boat with live anchovies. As the fish mill about the boat, anglers then use anchovies, mackerel or squid to catch them. Small boaters may take yellowtail by trolling jigs or feathers in areas where these fish occur.
Other Common Names: California yellowtail, forktail, mossback, amberjack, white salmon.
Largest Recorded: 5 feet; 80 pounds (California).
Habitat: Pelagic Environment

Sargo

Family: Pristipomatidae (Sargos)
Genus and Species:
Anisotremus davidsonii
Description: The body of the adult sargo is a compressed oval shape with the back elevated. The head has a steep, straightish upper profile and a small mouth.

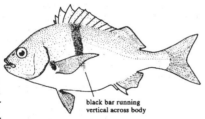

black bar running vertical across body

The color is metallic silvery, with a grayish tinge on the back and silvery below; with a distinguishing dark vertical bar running across the body. Occasionally, sargo are entirely bright yellow, orange or pure white.

Young sargo, up to 4 inches, have several dark horizontal stripes. The vertical bar begins to appear when they are 2 or 3 inches long.
Range: The sargo occurs from Magdalena Bay, Baja California, to Santa Cruz, California, and is found inshore and in bays. Sargo occur from the surface to depths of 130 feet, but are most common in water about 25 feet deep. They are usually found in areas with rock or combination rock-sand bottoms, around pilings or similar submerged structures.
Natural History: Examination of stomach contents indicate sargo are bottom feeders, eating different small shrimps, crabs, clams, and sea snails.

Sargo spawn when they are about 7 inches long and 2 years old.

Spawning occurs in late spring and early summer. The 1 inch young appear in late summer and fall in shallow water, schooling loosely with young salema and black croaker. At a length of 5 inches, when they are about 1 year old, they join adult sargo schools. All through their life they are capable of displaying the striped pattern characteristic of juveniles.
Fishing Information: Sargo are commonly caught incidentally to other fishing, primarily during the summer months. Anglers fishing from the rocks catch a few as part of their mixed fare and good runs are occasionally encountered in southern California bays. Sargo make a piglike grunting sound when pulled from the water.

Almost any type of animal bait, such as clams, mussel, shrimp or pieces of fish, does well. Because of their habit of swimming a few feet off the bottom in loose schools and in shallow water, they are a prime target when spear fishing. Probably more are taken in this manner than by hook and line.
Other Common Names: China croaker, blue bass, black croaker, grunt.
Largest Recorded: 17.4 inches; 3.7 pounds.
Habitat: Shallow Rocky Environment

Queenfish

Family: Sciaenidae (Croakers)
Genus and Species:
Seriphus politus
Description: The body of the queenfish is elongate and moderately compressed. The head is compressed with the upper profile depressed over the eyes. The mouth is large. The color is bluish above becoming silvery below and the fins are yellowish.

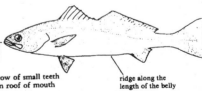

depression of upper profile

base of dorsal and anal fins about same length

Queenfish can be distinguished from other croakers by their large mouth, the base of the second dorsal and anal fins being about equal, and the wide space between the two dorsal fins.
Range: Queenfish occur from Uncle Sam Bank, Baja California, to Yaquina Bay, Oregon. They are common during summer in shallow water around pier pilings on sandy bottoms. They are found at depths up to 180 feet; however, occur more often from 4 to 80 feet.

Queenfish are common in southern California, but are rare north of Monterey, California.
Natural History: Queenfish feed on small, free swimming crustaceans, small crabs, and fishes.

Adult queenfish spawn in the summer. The eggs are free floating. Tiny young queenfish, less than 1 inch long, appear in late summer and fall; first at depths of 20 to 30 feet, gradually moving shoreward until they enter the surf zone when 1 to 3 inches long.
Fishing Information: Queenfish may be caught using live anchovies as bait. They are quite often the most commonly caught fish by anglers from piers.
Other Common Names: herring, kingfish, herring croaker, shiner.
Largest Recorded: 12 inches; no weight recorded.
Habitat: Shallow Sandy Environment

White Sea Bass

Family: Sciaenidae (Croakers)
Genus and Species:
*Cynoscion nobilis**
* *Also known as Atractoscion, nobilis.*
Description: The body of the white sea bass is elongate, and somewhat compressed. The head is pointed and slightly

row of small teeth in roof of mouth

ridge along the length of the belly

compressed. The mouth is large, with a row of small teeth in the roof; the lower jaw slightly projects. The color is bluish to gray above, with dark speckling, becoming silver below. The young have several dark vertical bars.

The white sea bass is closely related to the California corbina, but is the only California member of the croaker family to exceed 20 pounds in weight. They are most easily separated from other croakers by the presence of a ridge running the length of the belly.
Range: White sea bass occur from Magdalena Bay, Baja California, to Juneau, Alaska. They usually travel in schools over rocky bottoms and in and out of kelp beds.
Natural History: The diet of white sea bass includes fishes, especially anchovies and sardines, and squid. At times, large fish are found which have eaten only Pacific mackerel.

At the minimum legal length of 28 inches, the average white sea bass is about 5 years of age, weighs about 7.5 pounds and has been sexually mature for at least one spawning season.
Fishing Information: White sea bass are fished primarily with live bait in relatively shallow water, but they will also take a fast-trolled spoon, artificial squid or bone jig. Live squid appear to be the best bait for a white sea bass, but large anchovies and medium-size sardines are also good.

At times, large white sea bass will bite only on fairly large, live Pacific mackerel.

The young of this species are exceptionally vulnerable to sport anglers for two reasons. The first is that as juveniles they inhabit shallow nearshore areas, bays, and estuaries, and the second is that they are not easily recognized as white sea bass by the average angler. Commonly, these young fish are mistakenly called "sea trout" because of their sleek profile and vertical bars or "parr marks." To add to the confusion, these bars fade as the fish grows.

There is a 28 inch size limit and current fishing regulations should be checked concerning bag limits.

Other Common Names: sea trout (juvenile), weakfish, king croaker.
Largest Recorded: 5 feet; 83 pounds.
Habitat: Deep Rocky Environment

Yellowfin Croaker

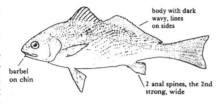

body with dark wavy, lines on sides

2 anal spines, the 2nd strong, wide

barbel on chin

Family: Sciaenidae (Croaker)
Genus and Species: *Umbrina roncador*
Description: The body of the yellowfin croaker is elliptical-elongate with the back somewhat arched. The head is conical and blunt. The color is iridescent blue to gray with brassy reflections on the back diffusing to silvery white below. The sides and back have many diagonal dark wavy lines. The fins are yellowish except for the dark dorsal fins.

The yellowfin croaker differs from other California croakers in having a single fleshy projection, a barbel, on the lower jaw and two heavy spines at the front of the anal fin.
Range: Yellowfin croakers occur from the Gulf to California, Mexico, to Point Conception, California. They frequent bays, channels, harbors and other nearshore waters over sandy bottoms. These croakers are more abundant along beaches during the summer months and may move to deeper water in winter.
Natural History: The diet of the yellowfin croaker consists mainly of small fishes and fish fry; however, invertebrates such as small crustaceans, worms and mollusks are also eaten in large numbers.

Spawning takes place during the summer months when this species is most common along the sandy beaches. Maturity is apparently not reached until the fish are slightly over 9 inches long.
Fishing Information: Yellowfin croaker are most often taken by surf anglers using softshelled sand crabs, worms, mussels, clams or cut fish as bait.
Other Common Names: Catalina croaker, yellowtailed croaker, golden croaker.
Largest Recorded: 20.13 inches; no weight reported. However, an 18 inch yellowfin croaker weighed 4.5 pounds.
Habitat: Shallow Sandy Environment

California Corbina

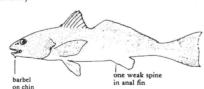

barbel on chin

one weak spine in anal fin

Family: Sciaenidae (Croakers)
Genus and Species: *Menticirrhus undulatus*
Description: The body of the California corbina is elongate and slightly compressed. The head is long and the mouth is small, the upper jaw scarcely reaching a point below the front of the eye. The color is uniform grey with incandescent reflections, and with wavy diagonal lines on the sides.

This croaker and the yellowfin croaker are the only two of the eight coastal croakers present in California waters to have a single fleshy projection, a barbel, on the lower jaw. The California corbina usually has only one weak spine at the front of the anal fin, while the yellowfin croaker has two strong spines.
Range: California corbina occur from the Gulf of California, Mexico to Point Conception, California, and is a bottom fish found along sandy beaches and in shallow bays. This species travels in small groups along the surf zone in a few inches of water to depths of 45 feet.
Natural History: Adults have been seen feeding in the surf, at times in water so shallow that their backs were exposed. They scoop up mouthfuls of sand and separate the food by sending the sand through the gills. They are very particular feeders, apparently spitting out bits of clam shells and other foreign matter. About 90 percent of the food they eat is sand crabs. Other crustaceans and clams are of lesser importance.

Males mature when 2 years old at a length of about 10 inches and females at age 3 when about 13 inches long. Spawning extends f rom June to September, but is heaviest during July and August. Spawning apparently takes place offshore as running ripe fish are not often found in the surf zone. The eggs are free floating. Young corbina, 1 inch long, have been observed outside the surf in 4 to 8 feet of water in August.
Fishing Information: California corbina are caught throughout the year along southern California's sandy beaches, although fishing is at its best from July through September. They are very wary and difficult to hook as many an avid surf fisherman can affirm. Perhaps one reason is that they tend to mouth and chew their food and don't strike solidly very often. Sand crabs (usually softshells) are the preferred bait, though some anglers swear by blood worms, mussels, clams, pileworms, and ghost shrimp.
Other Common Names: California whiting, surf fish, sucker. California corbina should not be confused with corvina which are taken in the Salton Sea.
Largest Recorded: 28 inches; 8.5 pounds.
Habitat: Surf Environment

White Croaker

Family: Sciaenidae (Croakers)
Genus and Species: *Genyonemus lineatus*
Description: The body of the white croaker is elongate and somewhat compressed. The head is oblong and bluntly rounded, with a mouth that is somewhat underneath the head. The color is incandescent brownish to yellowish on the back becoming silvery below. The fins are yellow to white.

(barbel not present)

small black spot sometimes present

The white croaker is one of five California croakers that have mouths located under their heads (subterminal). They can be distinguished from the California corbina and yellowfin croaker by the absence of a single fleshy projection, or barbel, at the tip of the lower jaw. The 12 to 15 spines in the first dorsal fin serve to distinguish white croakers from all the other croakers with subterminal mouths, since none of these has more than 11 spines in this fin.
Range: White croakers have been taken from Magdalena Bay, Baja California, to Vancouver Island, British Columbia, but are not abundant north of San Francisco. White croakers swim in loose schools at or near the bottom of sandy areas. Sometimes they aggregate in the surf zone or in shallow bays and lagoons. Most of the time they are found in offshore areas at depths of 10 to 100 feet. On rare occasions they are fairly abundant at depths as great as 600 feet.
Natural History: White croakers eat a variety of fishes, squid, shrimp, octopus, worms, small crabs, clams and other items, either living or dead.

While the ages of white croakers have not been determined conclusively, it is thought that some live as long as 15 or more years. Some spawn for the first time when they are between 2 and 3 years old. At this age they are only 5 to 6 inches long and weigh less than 0.10 pounds.
Fishing Information: These fish can be caught on almost any kind of animal bait that is fished from piers or jetties in sandy or sandy mud areas. In fact, they are so easily hooked that most anglers consider them a nuisance of the worst sort. If a person desires to fish specifically for white croakers a tough, difficult-to-steal bait, such as squid, is recommended. When hooked, they put up little or no fight. Fishing and catching is good throughout the year.
Other Common Names: kingfish, shiner, Pasadena trout, tommy croaker, little bass.
Largest Recorded: 16.3 inches; no weight recorded; however, a 14.5 inch white croaker weighted 1.41 pounds.
Habitat: Shallow Sandy Environment

Spotfin Croaker

Family: Sciaenidae
(Croakers)
Genus and Species:
Roncador stearnsii
Description: The body of
the spotfin croaker is elongate, but heavy forward.
The upper profile of the
head is steep and slightly
curved, and abruptly
rounded at the very blunt snout. The mouth is underneath the head
(subterminal). The color is silvery gray with bluish luster above and white
below. There are dark wavy lines on the side, and a large black spot at
the base of the pectoral fin.

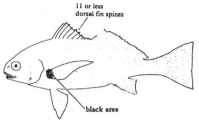

11 or less
dorsal fin spines

black area

The subterminal mouth, absence of a fleshy barbel and the large black
spot at the base of the pectoral fin distinguish spotfin croakers from all
other California croakers. Small "spotties" are sometimes confused with
small white croakers, but a count of the dorsal fin spines will quickly
separate them; the spotfin croaker has 11 or fewer (usually 10), while the
white croaker as 12 to 15. So-called "golden croakers" are nothing more
than large male spotfin croakers in breeding colors.
Range: Spotfin croakers occur from Mazatlan, Mexico, to Point Conception, California, including the Gulf of California. In California, they are
most commonly found south of Los Angeles Harbor. They live along
beaches and in bays over bottoms varying from coarse sand to heavy
mud and at depths varying from 4 to 50 feet or more. They prefer
depressions and holes near shore.
Natural History: Spotfin croakers eat a wide variety of food items.
Apparently they prefer clams and worms. Small crustaceans are also
eaten extensively. They use the large pavement-like pharyngeal (throat)
teeth to crush their food.

Male spotfin croakers first mature and spawn when 2 years old and
about 9 inches long. Most females mature when 3 years old and 12.5
inches long. All are mature by the time they are 4 years old and have
reached a size of 14.5 inches. The spawning season runs from June to
September and apparently takes place offshore, since no ripe fish have
been caught in the surf zone. One inch juveniles do appear in the surf
in the fall.

Spotfin croaker travel considerably but with no definite pattern. They
move extensively from bay to bay. For example, fish tagged in the Los
Angeles Harbor were later taken as far south as Oceanside. Spotfin
tagged in Newport Bay moved to Alamitos Bay and vice versa.
Fishing Information: Although some are caught throughout the year,
late summer is best for spotfin croaker fishing. Good fishing seems to
depend on runs. When a "croaker hole" is found and a run is on, good
fishing can be had by all present whether in a bay, from a pier or in the
surf. Most spotfin croaker caught are small to medium sized fish.
Other Common Names: spotties, spot, golden croaker.
Largest Recorded: 27 inches; 10.5 pounds.
Habitat: Shallow Sandy Environment

Opaleye

Family: Girellidae (Nibblers)
Genus and Species:
Girella nigricans
Description: The body
of the opaleye is oval
and compressed. The
snout is thick with an
evenly rounded pro-
file. The mouth is small.
The color is dark olive
green, and most have one
or two white spots on each
side of the back under the
middle of the dorsal fin.

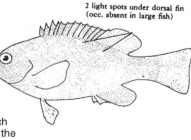

2 light spots under dorsal fin
(occ. absent in large fish)

The opaleye is California's only representative of the nibbler family.
Bright blue eyes and the heavy, olive green, perch-like body quickly
distinguish it from any other species.
Range: Opaleye occur from Cape San Lucas, Baja California, to San
Francisco, California.

Opaleyes are residents of rocky shorelines and kelp beds. Young
ones, 1 or more inches long, live in tide pools, but they seek deeper water
as they grow larger. The largest concentrations of opaleye are in 65 feet
of water.

Natural History: Opaleye primarily eat marine algae with or without
encrustations of organisms. Food items include feather boa kelp, giant
kelp, sea lettuce, coralline algae, small tube dwelling worms, and red
crabs.

Ripe adults have been taken in April, May and June. They form dense
schools in shallower water where spawning takes place. The eggs and
larvae are free floating and at times are found a number of miles from
shore. The juveniles form schools of up to two dozen individuals. When
about 1 inch long they enter tide pools. As they grow they seek deeper
and deeper water. They mature and spawn when about 8 or 9 inches
long at an age of about 2 or 3 years.
Fishing Information: Few fish are harder to hook than the opaleye and
few fish will put up more fight pound-for-pound. Long considered one of
the better sport fish, they take mussels, sand crabs, pieces of fish or
invertebrates on a hook. Since opaleye are primarily vegetarians, some
anglers find it easier to catch them using various "mosses" for bait.
Other Common Names: green perch, black perch, blue-eyed perch,
bluefish, Jack Benny, button-back.
Largest Recorded: 25.5 inches; 13.5 pounds.
Habitat: Shallow Rocky Environment

Halfmoon

Family: Scorpididae* (Halfmoons)
Genus and Species: *Medialuna californiensis*
* *Kyphosidae (American Fisheries Society)*
Description: The body of the halfmoon is oval and compressed. The
head is blunt and rounded and the mouth is small. The color is dark blue
above, shading to blue gray on the sides and becoming white below. The
tail is halfmoon shaped. The soft rays of the dorsal and anal fins are
nearly hidden by a thick sheath of scales. The halfmoon most closely
resembles the blue rockfish, but lacks the 5 spines on the front section
of the gill cover, which are common to all rockfishes.
Range: Halfmoon occur from the Gulf of California, Mexico, to the
Klamath River, California. They are most common in southern California, particularly around the Channel Islands. Halfmoon occur over
shallow rocky areas and in kelp beds. They have been observed as deep
as 130 feet, but are most commonly taken by anglers from waters from
8 to 65 feet deep.
Natural History: Halfmoon feed on a variety of plant and animal matter
such as red, green and brown algae, and sponges. In the turbulent areas
of the rocky coasts they have been seen catching bits of upsurging
seaweed.

Spawning takes place during the summer months. Ripe adults are
taken from July through October. The eggs and young are free floating
and the young, like opaleye, are found some distance from shore. One
inch halfmoon, are found at the outer edges of kelp beds. Only adults are
commonly found in the inshore area. They reach maturity when about
7.5 inches long.
Fishing Information: Halfmoon are abundant throughout the year.
They are scrappy and are good eating. Anglers, fishing from the rocks,
have good success using mussels and shrimp; opaleye anglers occasionally catch them on moss bait. Anglers, fishing offshore, are most
successful using fresh cut bait such as anchovy, sardine or squid.
Other Common Names: Catalina blue perch, blue bass, black perch.
Largest Recorded: 19 inches; 4.75 pounds.
Habitat: Shallow Rocky Environment

Silver Surfperch

Family: Embiotocidae (Surfperches)
Genus and Species: *Hyperprosopon ellipticum*
Description: The body of the
silver surfperch is oval and
strongly compressed. The
head is small and the
mouth is moderately
large. The body is sil-
very with dusky (brown-
ish to gray) coloration on
the back and dusky bars on
the sides. The tail is usually
pink with an occasional orange spot on the anal fin.

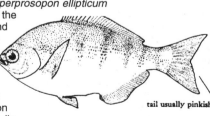

tail usually pinkish

The specific name ellipticum refers to its elliptical body outline. It looks
similar to the walleye surfperch but lacks the black coloration on its
pelvic fins.
Range: Silver surfperch occur from Rio San Vicente, Baja California, to
Schooner Cove, near Tofino, Vancouver Island, British Columbia.

These small surfperch primarily frequent the sandy surf zone although they are also caught among shallow rocks from piers, and in bays.

Natural History: The diet of silver surfperch includes shrimp, crustaceans, amphipods and algae.

As with all surfperch, the young are born alive and are relatively large. Mating occurs during the fall and early winter months. The male approaches the female from below; both swim with vents close for 2 or 3 seconds, then separate and repeat the process. Three to 16 young are born the following spring and summer.

Fishing Information: Silver surfperch rank among the top ten in numbers caught by recreational anglers in central and northern California, even though the average weight is 0.1 pound.

They are plentiful, easy to catch and occur in large numbers in surf, shore and pier catches.

Other Common Names: silver perch, shiner.

Largest Recorded: 10.5 inches; no weight recorded.

Habitat: Shallow Sandy Environment

Walleye Surfperch

Family: Embiotocidae (Surfperches)

Genus and Species: *Hyperprosopon argenteum*

Description: The body of the walleye surfperch is oval and strongly compressed. The head is small and the eyes are large. The mouth is small and slanted downward. The color is silver with faint dusky shading on the back. The tips of the ventral fins are black as are the borders of the anal fin and tail.

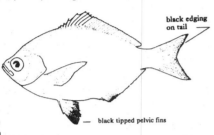

black edging on tail

black tipped pelvic fins

The walleye surfperch can be distinguished from other surfperch by the distinctive black tips on the ventral fins and black borders on the tail and anal fins.

Range: Walleye surfperch occur from Point San Rosarito, Baja California, to Vancouver Island, British Columbia. This species is found in dense schools along sandy beaches, near rocks and around piers. They appear to move into embayments such as Humboldt Bay during summer.

Natural History: Walleye surfperch feed primarily on small crustaceans.

Mating takes place in October, November and December when the usual dense schools break up and the males and females pair off. The encroachment of another male is immediately countered by a quick charge from the courting male toward the intruder's snout. Between 5 and 12 young, depending on the size of the mother, are born the following spring. They average a little over 1.5 inches in length at birth. They reach maturity the following fall and winter; in fact, the largest proportion of the breeding population appears to be young of the year.

Walleyes are probably short-lived as are most other surfperches. A 10.5 inch walleye was only 6 years old.

Fishing Information: Walleyes can be caught in the surf, from rocks, and from piers anywhere along the open coast. They usually are the most abundant surfperch caught from piers. A small hook baited with mussels, pieces of fish, worms, squid or shrimp will catch walleyes any season of the year. Often occurring in dense schools 6 to 8 feet thick, comprised of several hundred fish, the walleye can provide very rewarding fishing.

Other Common Names: walleye surf fish, walleye seaperch, china pompano, white perch.

Largest Recorded: Reported to reach 12 inches; however, largest recorded is a 10.75 inch female; no weight recorded.

Habitat: Bay Environment

Shiner Surfperch

Family: Embiotocidae (Surfperches)

Genus and Species: *Cymatogaster aggregata*

Description: The body of the shiner surfperch is elongate oval and compressed. The head is short and the mouth is small. The

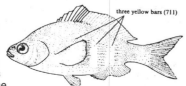

three yellow bars (711)

body is gray to greenish above with vertical lemon yellow cross bars in the shape of a "71 1" and eight horizontal sooty lines along the sides. During courtship and breeding the males are dark gray, almost black, in color and have a black spot on each side of the snout.

The island surfperch is a close relative found around the channel islands off southern California. This species is much more slender than the shiner surfperch.

Range: Shiner surfperch occur from San Quintin Bay, Baja California, to Port Wrangell, Alaska.

They prefer calm water and are most abundant in bays around eelgrass beds and the pilings of wharfs and piers. They have been captured in trawl nets fishing in 350 to 480 feet of water and have been observed by divers at depths as great as 120 feet, but are more numerous in shallow inshore waters.

Natural History: The diet of shiner surfperch consists mostly of small crustaceans and other invertebrates. They are frequently observed around pier pilings nipping off the appendages of barnacles.

Mating takes place during the summer months in most localities, and the young are born the following spring and summer. During courtship, the male closely follows the female, their movements remarkably well synchronized. He will leave her side frequently to chase off other fish, many of which are not the least bit attracted to his mate.

They are apparently short-lived as a 6 inch female (large for shiner surfperch) was only 3 years old.

Fishing Information: Shiner surfperch are caught from shore, docks, piers, rocks, and almost any other fishing area. They are probably the number one fish caught by youngsters along the California coast. They can be taken on almost any type of bait and any type of fishing equipment from handline to spinning gear so long as the hook on the end of the line is small enough for the fish to get in their mouths.

Other Common Names: shiner perch, shiner, shiner seaperch, yellow shiner, bay perch, seven-eleven perch.

Largest Recorded: 7 inches, reported to 8 inches; no weight recorded; however, a pregnant female 6.75 inches long weighed just under 3 ounces.

Habitat: Bay Environment

Redtail Surfperch

Family: Embiotocidae (Surfperches)

Genus and Species: *Amphistichus rhodoterus*

Description: The body of the redtail surfperch is oval and compressed. The upper profile of the head is nearly straight from the snout to the dorsal fin except for a slight depression above the eye. The body color is silver with olive green mottling and bars on the side. The tail is pink to deep purple.

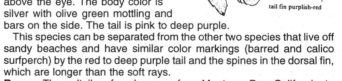

dorsal spines much longer than dorsal soft-rays

tail fin purplish-red

This species can be separated from the other two species that live off sandy beaches and have similar color markings (barred and calico surfperch) by the red to deep purple tail and the spines in the dorsal fin, which are longer than the soft rays.

Range: The redtail surfperch occurs from Monterey Bay, California, to Vancouver Island, British Columbia, and is the most often encountered surfperch from Bodega Bay northward.

Redtail surfperch are predominantly surf dwellers off sandy beaches, but have been taken in rocky areas adjacent to beaches. They are common in estuaries and protected embayments during the spawning season.

Natural History: Small crustaceans are the major food items preferred by this species; however, small crabs, shrimp, mussels or marine worms are also attractive, to redtail surfperch.

Like all surfperch, the redtail gives birth to live young. The young are carried inside the mother until birth when they emerge as miniature replicas of the adults. Males mature at age 2 and females at age 4. They breed in fall and give birth in spring and summer, primarily from June to August. Females contain up to 51 young with the average of 27.

Fishing Information: Redtail surfperch concentrate just before spawning in sheltered inshore waters during the spring and early summer. They are frequently caught in large numbers at this time. The average size of redtail surfperch that an angler usually catches is 1.8 pounds, although 3 pound fish are not uncommon.

Light tackle with No. 406 hooks and crab backs for bait is the preferred method of take in Humboldt Bay. For surf fishing, 20 pound test line and 6 to 80 ounce sinkers are usually used with sand crabs, tube worms or clams for bait.

Other Common Names: rosy surf fish, redtail seaperch, porgie, Oregon porgie.
Largest Recorded: 16 inches; no weight recorded.
Habitat: Surf Environment

Rubberlip Surfperch

Family: Embiotocidae (Surfperches)
Genus and Species: *Rhacochilus toxotes*
Description: The body of the rubberlip surfperch is oval and compressed. The mouth is comparatively large and the lips are extremely thick. The lower jaw is slightly shorter than the upper.

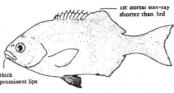

The color is variable but it is generally whitish with brown to brassy overtones on the back fading to tan below. The lips are whitish or pink. Juveniles have one or two vertical dusky bars on the body, although these usually are not found on adults. Its large size and thick prominent lips distinguish it from all other surfperches.
Range: Rubberlip surfperch occur from Thurloe Head, Baja California, to Russian Gulch State Beach, California. They frequent rocky areas, tidepools and kelp beds on the outer coast as well as bays and harbors.
Natural History: Adults feed upon crabs, shrimps and octopus. Juveniles feed on typical surfperch food such as worms, small crabs, mussels, and tiny snails.

Like all surfperch, the rubberlip surfperch bears its young live. A 16.5 inch female, that was 8 years old and weighed slightly less than 3 pounds contained 21 young that averaged a little over 3.5 inches in length.
Fishing Information: While modest numbers of rubberlip surfperch are taken by recreational anglers, it is the leading species of the commercial surfperch catch in the Monterey Bay area.

Recreational anglers catch rubberlip surfperch from skiffs, piers and the shore. The greatest number have been taken from piers in the Monterey Bay area, with the average size caught by sport anglers being 2 pounds. Most hook-and-line catches are made using mussels, clams, sand worms, cut shrimp or similar bait.
Other Common Names: pile perch, rubberlip seaperch, porgee, sprat, liverlip, buttermouth.
Largest Recorded: 18 inches; no weight recorded; however, a 16.5 inch rubberlip surf perch weighed nearly 3 pounds.
Habitat: Shallow Sandy Environment

Barred Surfperch

Family: Embiotocidae (Surfperches)
Genus and Species: *Amphistichus argenteus*
Description: The body of the barred surfperch is oval and compressed. The head is blunt and the mouth is comparatively large. The color is

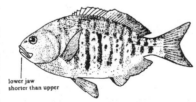

olive green to yellow green on the back becoming silver below; with bronze, brassy or yellow vertical bars and spots on the side.

This surfperch is one of three living off sandy beaches with similar color markings; however, it can be distinguished from the other two (calico and redtail) by its lower jaw being slightly shorter than the upper, and by the absence of red or reddish color on its fins.
Range: The barred surfperch occurs from Plaza Maria Bay, Baja California, to Bodega Bay, California. It is more abundant than the calico and redtail south of Cayucos, California. Barred surfperch are found in the surf zone along sandy beaches where they seem to congregate in depressions on the bottom. They have been taken from water as deep as 240 feet.
Natural History: The major portion of the barred surf perch diet is sand crabs, with other crustaceans, bean clams and small crabs comprising the remainder.

Barred surfperch give birth to living young from March to July. As few as four and as many as 113 have been counted, but the average is 33 per female. They are about 2.5 inches long at birth, and mature when about 6.5 inches long and 1 or 2 years old.

This species is relatively short lived with the oldest males being about 6 years old and 12 inches long. The oldest females are about 9 years old and up to 17 inches long.

Tagging studies indicate barred surfperch move very little, usually less than 2 miles, although movements up to 31 miles have been recorded.
Fishing Information: The most popular bait for barred surfperch is soft shelled sand crabs, but blood worms, mussels, cut fish, and small artificial lures also work. Fishing is usually best on an incoming tide when the perch are feeding inside the breaker zone.
Other Common Names: barred perch, silver perch, surf perch, sand perch, silver surf fish.
Largest Recorded: 17 inches; 4.5 pounds.
Habitat: Surf Environment

California Sheephead

Family: Labridae (Wrasses)
Genus and Species: *Semicossyphus pulcher*
Description: The body of the California sheephead is elongate, robust, and compressed. This species is a "protogynous hermaphrodite"; meaning that it begins life as a

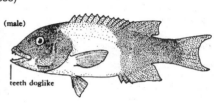

female, but then becomes a male later in life. Females mature at about 8 inches in length when they reach 4 to 5 years of age. Most females transform to males at a length of about 12 inches at 7 to 8 years of age.

This sex change is accompanied by a marked change in appearance. Younger fish (females) are a uniform pinkish red with a white lower jaw. As they age and become males, the head and rear third of the body turns black, the midsection of the body remains red and the lower jaw remains white. In all stages of their development, sheephead have unusually large dog-like teeth.
Range: California sheephead occur from Cabo San Lucas, Baja California, to Monterey Bay, California, with an isolated population in the Gulf of California. They are uncommon north of Point Conception. California sheephead are generally taken in rocky kelp areas near shore, in water from 20 to 100 feet deep, although they do occur as deep as 180 feet.
Natural History: Crabs, mussels, various sized snails, squid, sea urchins, sand dollars, and sea cucumbers are typical food items. The large canine-like teeth are used to pry food from rocks. A special plate in the throat crushes shells into small pieces for easy digestion. Occasionally, large adults have been observed out of the water in the intertidal hanging onto mussels after a wave has receded.

Spawning takes place in early spring and summer. Young about 0.5 inch long occur in late May through late December and do not resemble the adults. They are brilliant red orange with two black spots on the dorsal fin and a black spot at base of tail fin. Pelvic and anal fins are black, trimmed in white. Occasional lemon yellow young are seen.

The young live close to rocks at depths from 10 to well below 100 feet, particularly around beds of gorgonian corals (sea fans). When disturbed, they seek shelter in sea fans or among red seaweed.

The following summer, juveniles are 3 to 4 inches long and have faded to dull pink. At 2 years they are 6 to 8 inches long, have lost all spots, and have a typical female color pattern.
Fishing Information: Sheephead will take a variety of live and cut baits, such as anchovy or squid, fished on the bottom. Those interested in trophy-sized sheephead may try a whole, live mackerel fished on the bottom. The angler who hooks a California sheephead is usually in for a strong, tugging battle. A battle that commonly ends in disaster when the "catch" runs through or around a kelp plant, or under the nearest rocky ledge.
Other Common Names: sheepie, goat, billygoats (large), red fish, humpy, fathead.
Largest Recorded: 36 inches; 36.25 pounds.
Habitat: Shallow Rocky Environment

California Barracuda

Family: Sphyraenidae (Barracudas)
Genus and Species: *Sphyraena argentea*
Description: The body of the California barracuda is very elongate and slender, and almost round. The mouth is large with canine-like teeth. It has a sharply pointed snout with a projecting lower jaw. The color is grayish black with a bluish tinge on the back becoming silvery or

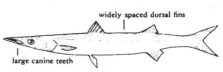

white on the sides and belly. The tail is yellowish and the dorsal fins are widely spaced.

Range: California barracuda occur from Cape San Lucas, Baja California, to Kodiak Island, Alaska. This species is found from the surface to depths of 60 feet, but is rare north of Point Conception, California.

Natural History: The California barracuda's main forage is anchovies and other small fishes. The spawning season in southern California may extend from April through September, but most spawning takes place in May, June and July. An individual probably spawns more than once each season.

About 75 percent of the California barracuda will spawn when they are 2 years old. The ovaries of a 3-inch female weighed 0.75 pounds and were estimated to contain 484,000 mature eggs. Young barracuda up to 6 inches in length are usually found in shallow water close to shore.

Fishing Information: Most California barracuda are taken with live bait fished at or near the surface; however, they will take an assortment of trolled artificial lures. If you see a very large barracuda, in the 10 pound range, chances are it's a female. Positive identification can be made because the female has a charcoal black edge on the pelvic and anal fins, whereas the male fins are edged in yellow or olive.

Three pound barracuda are common, but generally they are large enough to put up a good fight. Caution should be taken when you land a barracuda to avoid their needle sharp teeth.

Other Common Names: barracuda, scoot, scooter, snake, barry, Pacific barracuda.

Largest Recorded: Reported to 5 feet, but recorded to 4 feet; 18.1 pounds.

Habitat: Pelagic Environment

Giant Kelpfish

Family: Clinidae (Clinids)
Genus and Species: *Herterostichus rostratus*
Description: The body of the giant kelpfish is very elongate and compressed. The head is slender, compressed and pointed. The color may vary

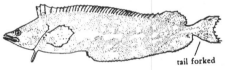

tail forked

from light brown to green and purple with lighter areas of mottling.

Giant kelp fish are easily separated from other family members because they are the only ones with forked tails; other members have rounded tails.

Range: Giant kelpfish range from Cabo San Lucas, Baja California, to British Columbia, and from surface waters down to 130 feet. Rocks covered with seaweed and kelp beds surrounding them provide the forage and habitat giant kelpfish desire.

Natural History: The diet of the giant kelp fish is predominantly small crustaceans, mollusks, and small fishes.

Spawning occurs during March through July. During spawning, which occurs in a territory established by the male, the female releases her eggs on seaweed while she quivers with the male next to her, sometimes head to tail. Pink to greenish eggs are attached to the seaweed by entangling threads that extend from egg coverings. The male remains to guard the eggs. Transparent post larvae appear from April through August, usually in shallow water f rom 5 to 30 feet. Giant kelpfish school until approximately 2.5 inches long when they begin to assume adult colors and become solitary, living close among seaweeds.

Fishing Information: Anglers pursuing giant kelpfish should drift through giant kelp beds since the fish are closely associated with the plants. When fishing for this species, small hooks are recommended since the fish have small mouths. Small shrimp, juvenile clams and other small invertebrates are used as bait. Squid can also be used if cut into small pieces.

Other Common Names: kelpfish, eel, iodine fish, butterfish, kelp blenny.

Largest Recorded: 24 inches; no weight recorded; however, a 16.2 inch giant kelpfish weighed 1.2 pounds.

Habitat: Shallow Rocky Environment

Pacific Mackerel

Family: Scombridae (Mackerels and Tunas)

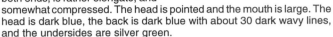

wavy lines extend onto head

4-6 finlets

Genus and Species: *Scomber japonicus*
Description: The body of the Pacific mackerel tapers at both ends, is rather elongate, and somewhat compressed. The head is pointed and the mouth is large. The head is dark blue, the back is dark blue with about 30 dark wavy lines, and the undersides are silver green.

The widely separated first and second dorsal fins serve to distinguish Pacific mackerel from all of the other tuna-like fishes that inhabit our waters, except for the frigate and bullet mackerel. Pacific mackerel and bullet mackerel can be differentiated by counting the dorsal finlets. Pacific mackerel typically have four to six, while bullet and frigate mackerel have seven to eight finlets.

Range: Worldwide in temperate seas; in the eastern Pacific from Chile to the Gulf of Alaska.

Natural History: Larval, juvenile or small fishes appear to be the most important natural food of Pacific mackerel, but there are times when they rely heavily on small crustaceans. They feed upon squid to a lesser extent, and eat whatever other bite-sized organisms they may encounter.

Off southern California, spawning normally reaches a peak during the early spring months, especially March, April and May. Pacific mackerel eggs are about 0.045 inch in diameter and float free in the upper layers of the ocean, usually within 300 feet of the surface. At average water temperatures they will hatch 4 or 5 days after being spawned.

Fishing Information: Pacific mackerel have long been cast in the role of an intruder or nuisance fish by most anglers, especially those seeking larger sportfish like yellowtail or barracuda. Nevertheless, they have been the most frequently caught species on hook and line in California waters in recent years.

Known as a voracious, indiscriminant feeder, Pacific mackerel will devour a live anchovy, engulf dead cut bait, strike readily on lures and often on flies. When in a feeding frenzy it has been known to hit a piece of rag soaked in fish gurg. While it is relatively small in size (3 pounds or 18 inches would be trophy size), it scores high for power (ounce for ounce) and beauty. Pacific mackerel put up an excellent fight against light tackle.

Other Common Names: American mackerel, blue mackerel, greenback jack, chub mackerel.

Largest Recorded: 25 inches; 6.3 pounds.

Habitat: Pelagic Environment

Skipjack

Family: Scombridae (Mackerels and Tunas)
Genus and Species: *Euthynnus pelamis*
Description: The body of the skipjack is cigar-shaped (tapers at both ends). The snout is sharply pointed and the mouth is relatively large. The color is dark blue to purple on the back become silvery

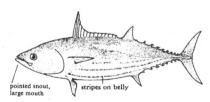

pointed snout, large mouth   stripes on belly

or white below, with four to six dark horizontal stripes on the belly.

Range: Skipjack occur worldwide in warm seas. They are found in the eastern Pacific from Peru to Vancouver Island, British Columbia. Skipjack usually visit California waters in the fall when water is relatively warm (about 68°F) and the currents are from either the south or southwest.

Natural History: The diet of the skipjack tuna includes fishes such as anchovies and sardines as well as squid; however, shrimp eggs and similar organisms are a major component of the diet.

Skipjack tuna do not spawn in waters off California, but further south in the eastern Pacific spawning takes place during the summer months. A skipjack tuna that is 18.5 inches long and weighs 5.5 pounds lays an estimated 113,000 eggs, while one that is 22.1 inches long and weighs 13.1 pounds produces 600,000 eggs. The young fish grow rapidly and when 1 year old are 18 inches long. They rarely live beyond 7 years.

Fishing Information: Most skipjack are taken incidentally to other fishing activities, especially albacore or tuna fishing. They bite a feather eagerly and will readily come to the boat when live anchovies are used as chum.

Most anglers do not actively seek skipjack because of their small size and the undesirability of the meat when fresh. However, skipjack is good if processed and most is consumed after it is canned. Most fish taken off California weigh 2 to 12 pounds, with the vast majority in the 4 to 6 pound range.

Other Common Names: skippies, oceanic bonito, striped tuna, arctic bonito, watermelon, victor fish.

Largest Recorded: No length recorded; 26 pounds (California).

Habitat: Pelagic Environment

Pacific Bonito

Family: Scombridae (Mackerel and Tunas)

Genus and Species: *Sarda chiliensis*

Description: The body of the Pacific bonito is cigar-shaped and somewhat compressed. The head is pointed and conical, and the mouth is large. The color is dark blue above, dusky on the sides becoming silvery below. There is a number of slanted darkish stripes along the back.

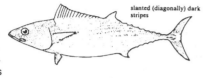
slanted (diagonally) dark stripes

Pacific bonito are the only tuna-like fishes on the California coast that have the slanted dark stripes on their backs.

Range: Pacific bonito occur discontinuously from Chile to the Gulf of Alaska, with the greatest area of abundance in the northern hemisphere occurring in warm waters between Magdalena Bay, Baja California, and Point Conception, California.

Natural History: The preferred food of bonito appears to be small fishes, such as anchovies and sardines. Occasionally, they rely heavily upon squid in their daily diet.

Bonito may not spawn successfully every year in California, but successful spawning does take place further south each year. The bulk of southern California spawning appears to take place from late January through May. The free floating eggs require about 3 days to hatch at average spring water temperatures.

Young fish resulting from local successful spawnings are usually first observed by the various live bait haulers when they are 6 to 10 inches long in the early summer months. These fish will often weigh 3 pounds or more by the fall of the year and by May of the following year many will weigh 6 or 7 pounds.

Fishing Information: Pacific bonito are excellent fighters and have hearty appetites. Once a school is aroused they will take almost any bait or lure that is tossed their way. Most Pacific bonito are taken by a combination of trolling and live baitfishing. The schools are located by trolling feathers and live anchovies or squid pieces are used to bait the fish once located. Fishing for bonito generally takes place offshore in 300 to 600 feet of water, but may occur next to kelp beds when the fish are near shore.

Pacific bonito may arrive off of California as the ocean warms in the spring, but may never show up if oceanic conditions dictate colder than normal water temperatures.

Bonito anglers generally catch 1 to 4 year old fish, weighing between 3 and 12 pounds. Pacific bonito fishing tapers off in the fall as the water cools, but persistent anglers still find good bonito fishing around warm water outfalls associated with power plants.

Other Common Names: bonehead, Laguna tuna, magneto, striped tuna, California bonito, ocean bonito.

Largest Recorded: 40 inches; 25 pounds.

Habitat: Pelagic Environment

Albacore

Family: Scombridae (Mackerels and Tunas)

Genus and Species: *Thunnus alalunga*

Description: The body of the albacore tapers at both ends (cigar-shaped). The head is long and the mouth fairly large. The color is dark gray to metallic blue on the back becoming white to gray below.

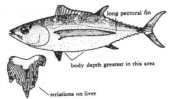
long pectoral fin
body depth greatest in this area
striations on liver

Albacore are easily distinguished from the other tunas occurring off California, with exception of the bigeye, by the extreme length of their pectoral fins (they extend well past the anal fin). Albacore and bigeye can best be distinguished by the characteristics of their livers. The albacore has a heavily striated (covered with blood vessels) liver while the liver of the bigeye is only lightly striated along the edges.

Range: Albacore occur worldwide in temperate seas; in the eastern Pacific they range from south of Guadalupe Island, Baja California, to southeast Alaska.

Natural History: The food of the albacore varies, depending upon where they are feeding in the water column and what items are available at the time and place the albacore are feeding. A majority of the food consists of small fishes, but at times squid, octopus, shrimp-like and crab-like organisms are extremely important.

There are indications that albacore spawning takes place in the mid-Pacific, probably north and west of the Hawaiian Islands. Large specimens caught in that area during late summer on long line gear have had nearly ripe eggs in their ovaries.

The albacore is one of the world's fastest migrant fish. Annual trans-Pacific migrations have been documented by tagging. Fish tagged off California were captured off Japan, nearly 5,000 miles away, 294 days later. Traveling "as the crow flies", this is equivalent to more than 17 miles a day.

Fishing Information: Albacore are the most sought after of the tunas by California anglers. Most fishing for albacore takes place 20-100 miles offshore in central and southern California. They are rarely taken near shore. Albacore have a preference for deep blue oceanic water and mild temperatures. Studies indicate that 57 of every 100 albacore caught are hooked in water ranging in temperature between 60 and 64 F

Albacore travel in loosely knit schools which are located by trolling or observing surface signs (feeding birds, etc.). Once located, they are fished with hook and line using live anchovies for bait. They may also be caught on a trolled feathered jig.

Other Common Names: longfin, albie, pigfish, Pacific albacore, German.

Largest Recorded: 5 feet; 79 pounds (California).

Habitat: Pelagic Environment

Bigeye Tuna

Family: Scombridae (Mackerels and Tunas)

Genus and Species: *Thunnus obesus*

Description: The body of the bigeye tuna is cigar-shaped (tapered at both ends). The head is pointed and the eye is relatively large. The color is dark metallic brownish blue to dark yellow on the back becoming gray or whitish below. There often is a bluish stripe on the side.

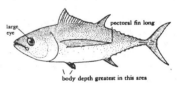
large eye
pectoral fin long
body depth greatest in this area

In most individuals, the length of the pectoral fins should enable one to identify the species properly. Both bigeye and yellowfin tuna look similar, but bigeye tuna have pectoral fins which extend well past their anal fin, while yellowfin tuna have much shorter pectoral fins. Tuna which cannot be distinguished by external characteristics can be positively identified by liver characteristics. Bigeye tuna livers are striated (covered with blood vessels) along the trailing edges, while yellowfin tuna livers are smooth.

Small bigeye tuna also may be distinguished from albacore by the characteristics of the liver. The liver is heavily striated in the albacore while the bigeye tuna liver is only striated along the trailing edges.

Range: Bigeye tuna occur worldwide in warmer seas. In the eastern Pacific these tuna range from Peru to Iron Springs, Washington. They are occasional visitors to California, entering our fishing grounds in June and remaining until November. These fish prefer temperate water in excess of 70°F, but significant catches have occurred in water as cool as 65°F.

Natural History: The diet of bigeye tuna includes fishes, squid, and crustaceans. Like most other tunas, they feed on what is most abundant in the area.

Bigeye tuna do not spawn in waters off California, but spawn further south in the Pacific. Bigeye tuna are approximately 3 years old at first spawning. In the equatorial regions of the Pacific, the peak spawning is between April and September.

A bigeye tuna weighing 159 pounds will produce an estimated 3.3 million eggs per year. The young are fast growing and weigh about 45 pounds when they first mature. They live 7 or 8 years.

Fishing Information: Bigeye tuna generally are not accessible to recreational anglers because they travel tar below the surface during the day. Only rarely are they seen on the surface, and then, only momentarily while feeding. This makes the fish hard to locate since they leave no telltale surface signs nor can they be easily located by trolling. Most bigeye tuna are taken incidental to albacore or marlin fishing.

The best way to fish for them is to troll marlin lures in an area where the fish are known to occur. Most bigeye tuna taken in southern California weigh 50 to 1 00 pounds, with an occasional 150 to 200 pounder landed.

Other Common Names: gorilla, tuna, patudo
Largest Recorded: 80 inches; 435 pounds; 215 pounds (California).
Habitat: Pelagic Environment

Bluefin Tuna

Family: Scombridae (Mackerels and Tunas)
Genus and Species:
Thunnus obesus
Description: The body of the bluefin tuna is cigar-shaped and robust. The head is conical and the mouth rather large. The color is dark blue above and gray below.

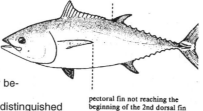

pectoral fin not reaching the beginning of the 2nd dorsal fin

Bluefin tuna can easily be distinguished from other members of the tuna family by the relatively short length of their pectoral fins. Their livers have a unique and definitive characteristic in that they are covered with blood vessels (striated). In other tunas with short pectoral fins, such vessels are either not present or present in small numbers along the edges.

Range: Worldwide in all but the coldest seas. Bluefin tuna range throughout the eastern North Pacific Ocean with fish being taken from Magdalena Bay, Baja California, to Shelikof Strait, Alaska.

Most bluefin tuna landed by California anglers are 1 or 2 year olds and weigh between 15 and 30 pounds.

Natural History: Examination of a number of stomachs indicates that while in California waters anchovies make up the bulk of the diet. Sanddabs, surfperches, and white croakers are also consumed.

Fishing Information: Bluefin tuna are seasonal visitors to California waters. They usually appear in May and depart by October. Since they are temperate tunas, their availability to anglers depends on water temperatures in the 62° to 68°F degree range. They can be located by either trolling feathers or anchoring at a spot known to be frequented by bluefin tuna, and chumming with live anchovies. Once the fish are attracted, anglers must use light line (12# test or less), small hooks (#4's or smaller), and the "hottest" bait available that season (usually live anchovies or pieces of squid).

Other Common Names: leaping tuna, tuna, footballs, tunny, shortfin tuna, ahi, great albacore.
Largest Recorded: No length recorded; 363.5 pounds (California). Weight to 495 pounds in the Pacific Ocean, and 1,500 pounds in the Atlantic Ocean.
Habitat: Pelagic Environment

Yellowfin Tuna

Family: Scombridae (Mackerel and Tunas)
Genus and Species:
Thunnus albacores
Description: The body of the yellowfin tuna tapers at both ends (cigar-shaped), and the head is conical. The color is dark brownish blue to dark yellow on the back becoming gray or whitish below.

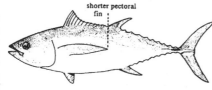

shorter pectoral fin

Identifying tunas can be difficult, especially when yellowfin and bigeye tuna are involved.

In most cases, the length of the pectoral fins can distinguish each species. The yellowfin has pectoral fins which do not extend past the anal fin; while in bigeye, the pectoral fins extend well past the anal fin.

Tuna which cannot be distinguished by external characteristics can be positively identified by liver characteristics. The surface of a yellowfin's liver is smooth while the liver of the bigeye is striated, containing many with small blood vessels along the trailing edge.

Range: Widely distributed in the Pacific Ocean. In the eastern Pacific, yellowfin tuna occur from Chile to Point Buchon, California. They occasionally enter California waters when ocean temperatures are warm. They usually are not taken in waters less than 70°F with best catches occurring in waters above 74°F.

Natural History: The diet of the yellowfin tuna includes juvenile fishes, crustaceans, and squid. They are opportunistic feeders taking whatever is most available in the area.

Yellowfin tuna do not spawn off the coast of California; however, they do spawn further south in the eastern Pacific.

Some spawning takes place during every month of the year, but off Central America it peaks during January and February.

Young fish grow very rapidly and by the time they are 1.5 years old they weigh around 7.5 pounds. At t years old they weigh approximately 150 pounds. The largest yellowfin tuna taken are 10 or more years old. These larger fish sometimes have an elongated second dorsal fin.

Fishing Information: Yellowfin tuna are fished in much the same manner as albacore; jigs are used to locate the schools, and live anchovies are chummed to keep the fish around the boat.

Most yellowfin tuna taken in California weigh 30 to 50 pounds, fish over 200 pounds are occasionally landed. The smaller fish are 1 to 2 years old while the larger ones may be over 10 years of age.

Other Common Names: Allison tuna, ahi, Pacific yellowfin.
Largest Recorded: No length recorded; 239 pounds (California); weight to 450 pounds.
Habitat: Pelagic Environment

Swordfish

Family: Xiphiidae (Swordfishes)
Genus and Species:
Xiphias gladius
Description: The body of the swordfish is elongate and somewhat compressed. The upper jaw is very much extended, forming a long, flat sword. The color is dark gray to black above becoming gray to yellowish below.

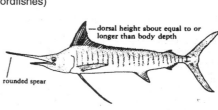

dorsal height about equal to or longer than body depth

rounded spear

Swordfish are readily distinguished from other billfish by their flattened bills, lack of fins on the belly, and the presence of only one keel (small projection) on the base of the tail adjoining the fish.

Range: Swordfish occur worldwide in temperate and tropical seas. Off southern California, they are most commonly encountered between the mainland and the Channel Islands.

Natural History: The diet of swordfish includes fishes such as anchovies, hake, jack mackerel, rockfishes, lanternfishes, pencil smelt, as well as squid.

Swordfish do not spawn off the coast of California, but in 1958 a ripe female was harpooned off Santa Catalina Island. It contained an estimated 50 million eggs.

In areas like the Mediterranean, where spawning has been studied, some females lay eggs during every month of the year, but the spawning peak is in June and July. The eggs take 2.5 days to hatch. While there is little information available on swordfish age and growth, they probably grow quite rapidly and do not live for a great number of years.

Fishing Information: Swordfish are taken from May through November, and occasionally landed in December. The average California recreational fishery take is between 10 and 20 fish per year, but more than 125 fish were landed in 1978, the best year on record.

Most recreational fishing for swordfish involves visually searching for a fish that is finning (presenting itself at the surface) and then maneuvering a baited hook in front of it. Live Pacific mackerel or dead squid are the preferred baits, although some anglers use live California barracuda.

Once hooked, swordfish are strong and stubborn fighters with average encounters lasting more than 4 hours. Some fish are landed in short time (10 to 15 minutes) because the fish may swim within gaffing distance of the boat early in the battle.

Most fish taken off southern California weigh between 100 to 300 pounds. Occasionally, a fish weighing more than 400 pounds is landed.

Other Common Names: broadbill, broadbill swordfish.
Largest Recorded: 15 feet; 503 pounds (California).
Habitat: Pelagic Environment

Striped Marlin

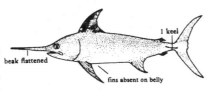

Family: Istiophoridae (Billfishes)
Genus and Species: *Tetrapturus audax*
Description: The body of the striped marlin is elongate and compressed. The upper jaw is much extended, forming a rounded spear. The color is dark blue above becoming silver below, with light blue bars or vertical spots on the sides.

Of the billfishes that occur in California waters, the striped marlin is difficult to confuse with the others. Marlin have scales, fins on the belly, and a rounded spear which set them apart from swordfish which have no scales or ventral fins and have bills that are flat. Sailfish have an extremely high dorsal fin not found among the marlins, and shortnose spearfish do not have the long spear on the upper jaw nor the body weight of the marlin. The striped marlin normally develops conspicuous stripes along the sides of its body after death. This feature is unique to striped marlin.

Range: Striped marlin occur in tropical and warm temperature waters of the Indian and Pacific Oceans. On the west coast of the United States they range as far north as Oregon, but are most common south of Point Conception, California. They usually appear off California in July and remain until late October.

Natural History: The food of striped marlin is predominately fishes, squid, crabs and shrimp. The latter three make up lesser portions of the diet than do fish.

The spear of the marlin is sometimes used both as a weapon for defense and as an aid in capturing food. Wooden boats frequently have been rammed by billfish, and in one instance the spear penetrated 18.5 inches of hardwood-14.5 inches of which was oak. When it uses its bill in capturing food, the striped marlin sometimes stuns its prey by slashing sideways with the spear rather than impaling its victim, as some believe.

Fishing Information: Most striped marlin are taken by trolling artificial lures in are as they are known to inhabit. Blind strikes are generally the rule, but one can occasionally tempt a "finner" or "sleeper" (marlin swimming along the surface) to strike if lures are trolled past the fish. Live bait also works well but requires more effort since the fish must usually be first spotted visually. Once a striped marlin is located, the angler should cast a bait in front of and past the fish so it can be reeled back towards the animal. Strikes usually result from properly presented live bait.

Most striped marlin anglers prefer Pacific mackerel as bait. The best California fishing locality is in a belt of water which extends from the east end of Santa Catalina Island offshore to San Clemente Island and southward in the direction of the Los Coronados Islands.

Other Common Names: striper, marlin, Pacific marlin, spikefish, spearfish.
Largest Recorded: 13.5 feet; 339 pounds (California).
Habitat: Pelagic Environment

California Halibut

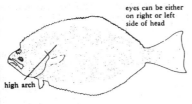

Family: Bothidae (Left-eyed flounders)
Genus and Species: *Paralichthys californicus*
Description: The body of the California halibut is oblong and compressed. The head is small and the mouth large. Although a member of the left-eyed flounder family, about 40 percent of California halibut have their eyes on the right side. The color is dark brown to black on the eyed side and white on the blind side.

Their numerous teeth, very large mouth and a high arch in the middle of the "top" side above the pectoral fin make them easily distinguishable from other flatfish.

Range: California halibut occur from Magdalena Bay, Baja California, to the Quillayute River, British Columbia. A separate population occurs in the upper Gulf of California.

Natural History: California halibut feed almost exclusively upon anchovies and similar small fishes. At times they are observed jumping clear of the water as they make passes at anchovy schools near the surface.

Males first mature when 2 or 3 years of age, but females do not mature until 4 or 5. A 5 year old fish may be anywhere from 11 to 17 inches long. Spawning takes place in relatively shallow water during the months of April through July.

Fishing Information: California halibut are pursued by anglers throughout the year, but the best landings usually occur in the spring. In central and northern California fishing is best in summer and early fall. At that time California halibut move into shallow water to spawn.

Drifting for halibut is the most successful fishing method with anglers using live anchovies, queenfish, white croakers, shiner perch or Pacific mackerel as bait. Artificial lures work well at times although they are not always effective.

California halibut are found over sandy bottoms.

Other Common Names: flatty, fly swatter (small), barn door (large), alabato, Monterey halibut, chicken halibut, southern halibut.
Largest Recorded: 5 feet; 72 pounds.
Habitat: Shallow Sandy Environment

Pacific Sanddab

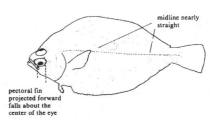

Family: Bothidae (Left-eyed flounders)
Genus and Species: *Citharichthys sordidus*
Description: The body of the Pacific sanddab is oblong and compressed. The head is deep; the eyes are on the left-side and are large. The color is light brown mottled with yellow and orange on the eyed side and white on the blind side.

Although three kinds of sanddabs live in the waters off California, only two are commonly used for food—the Pacific and longfin sanddabs. The third, the speckled sanddab, is so small (only about 5 inches) that it is only important to the diet of other fishes.

The Pacific sanddab can best be distinguished from the longfin sanddab by the length of the pectoral fin on the eyed side. It is always shorter than the head of the Pacific sanddab and longer than the head of the longfin. Sanddabs are always left "handed" (eyes on the left) and can be distinguished from all other left "handed" flatfish by having a midline that is nearly straight for its entire length.

Range: Pacific sanddabs occur from Cape San Lucas, Baja California, to the Bering Sea. They seldom inhabit water that is shallower than 30 feet or deeper than 1,800 feet. They are most abundant at depths of 120 to 300 feet.

Natural History: Pacific sanddabs eat a wide variety of food. In addition to such items as small fishes, squid, octopus, they eat an assortment of eggs, luminescent sea squirts, shrimp, crabs, and marine worms.

During the peak of the spawning season, which is July, August and September, the females spawn numerous eggs. These fish probably spawn more than once during a season.

Fishing Information: If the depth is correct and the bottom suitable, it is extremely difficult to keep sanddabs off the hook. Sportfishing entails the use of small hooks, usually more than one on each line. A variation from the typical rig involves use of an iron ring or hoop around which are dangled several dozen baited hooks of small size. This contraption is lowered on a stout line to a position just off the bottom and allowed to remain a sufficient period to fill all the hooks. Normally this does not require as much time as is needed to rebait the rig after removing the catch. Small pieces of squid or octopus are good baits because they are tough and stay on the hook, but pieces of fish work equally well.

Other Common Names: sanddab, soft flounder, sole, mottled sanddab, megrim.
Largest Recorded: 16 inches; no weight recorded; however, an 11.5 inch female weighed just over 0.5 pound.
Habitat: Deep Sandy Environment

Longfin Sanddab

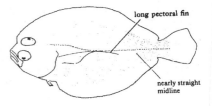

Family: Bothidae (Left-eyed flounders)
Genus and Species: *Citharichthys xanthostigma*
Description: The body of the longfin sanddab is oblong and compressed. The

head is deep; the eyes are large and on the left side. The mouth is large. The color is uniform dark brown with rust orange or white speckles, and the pectoral f in is black on the eyed side; the blind side is white.

The longfin sanddab can best be distinguished from the Pacific sanddab by the length of the pectoral fin on the eyed side. It is always shorter than the head on the Pacific sanddab and longer than the head on the longfin. Sanddabs are always left "handed" and can be distinguished from all other left "handed" flatfish by having a mid-line that is nearly straight for its entire length.

Range: Longfin sanddabs occur from Costa Rica to Monterey, California. These flatfish are usually on sandy, muddy type sea bottoms from 8 to 660 feet.

Natural History: Longfin sanddabs eat a wide variety of food. In addition to such items as small fishes, squid, and octopus, they eat an assortment of eggs, luminescent sea squirts, shrimp, crabs, and marine worms.

Females are larger than males and normally mature when 3 years old and about 7.5 inches long. They produce numerous eggs and each fish probably spawns more than once a season. The peak of the spawning season is July, August and September.

Fishing Information: If the depth is correct and the bottom type is right, it is extremely difficult to keep sanddabs off the hook. Sportfishing entails the use of small hooks, usually more than one on each line. A variation from the typical rig involves use of an iron ring or hoop around which are dangled several dozen baited hooks of small size. This contraption is lowered on a stout line to a position just off the bottom and allowed to remain a sufficient period to fill all the hooks. Normally this does not require as much time as is needed to rebait the rig after removing the catch. Small pieces of squid or octopus are best because they are tough and stay on the hook best, but fish works equally well as a bait.

Other Common Names: sanddab, soft flounder, Catalina sanddab.
Largest Recorded: 15.75 inches; no weight recorded.
Habitat: Deep Sandy Environment

Pacific Halibut

Family: Pleuronectidae (Right-eyed flounders)
Genus and Species: *Hippoglossus stenolepis*
Description: The body of the Pacific halibut is elongate, rather slender, diamond shaped and compressed. The head is elongate and the mouth is large. Both eyes are on the right side of the body. The color of the body is dark brown to black with fine mottling on the eyed side and white on blind side.

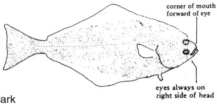

corner of mouth forward of eye

eyes always on right side of head

The Pacific halibut can be distinguished from the California halibut by looking at the end of the jaw. In the Pacific halibut, it extends to the front edge of the eye, while in the California halibut it extends beyond the eye.
Range: Pacific halibut occur from Santa Rosa Island, California, to the bering Sea and the Sea of Japan, at depths from 20 to 3,600 feet. In California, however, most are in nearshore areas from Fort Bragg northward, with the largest numbers being taken by anglers offshore north of California.
Natural History: The diet of the Pacific halibut includes fishes, crabs, clams, squid and other invertebrates. Females become mature at 8 to 16 years of age (average 12); however, males mature earlier.

Spawning takes place from November to January. A large female of 140 pounds may produce as many as 2,700,000 eggs. The eggs and young drift casually with the currents gradually rising toward the surface as development proceeds. When first hatched, the young swim upright; however, they soon start to turn to their left side and the left eye migrates to the right side.

By early spring, the transformation is complete and the young settle to the bottom in shallow waters.
Fishing Information: Recreational anglers have caught Pacific halibut up to 346 pounds, but California anglers would be hard pressed to find a Pacific halibut that large. The fish are typically caught on crab, shrimp, squid, and other invertebrates.
Other Common Names: alabato, northern halibut, right halibut, genuine halibut, real halibut.
Largest Recorded: 8.75 feet; 507 pounds.
Habitat: Deep Sandy Environment

Starry Flounder

Family: Pleuronectidae (Right-eyed flounders)
Genus and Species: *Platichthys stellatus*
Description: The body of the starry flounder is broad, relatively short, somewhat diamond shaped and compressed. The head is relatively short and the eyes and mouth are small, the lower jaw slightly projecting. While a member of the right-eyed flounder family; the majority of starry flounders are left-eyed. The color is dark brown on the eyed side with alternating white to orange and black bars on the dorsal and anal fins; white on the blind side.

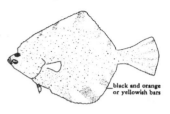

black and orange or yellowish bars

Its name comes from the rough, star-like scales on the eyed-side.
Range: Starry flounders occur from Santa Barbara, California, to Arctic Alaska and the Sea of Japan.

They occur over sand, mud and gravel bottoms in coastal ocean waters, bays, sloughs and even fresh water. Starry flounders are found from depths of a few inches to more than 900 feet.
Natural History: Small starry flounders eat mostly worms and small crustaceans. As they grow they eat progressively more crabs, clams, sand dollars and brittle stars. Large individuals also eat some fishes, among them sardines, sanddabs and surfperch.

Females grow faster and attain larger sizes than do males. Males spawn at the end of their second year when they are about 14.5 inches long, and females in their third year at approximately 16.25 inches. The spawning season extends from November through February with greatest activity in December and January.

Studies in California indicate that spawning occurs in water shallower than 25 fathoms.

Like other flatfishes, the young are born with an eye on each side of the head. By the time they reach about 0.5 inches in length, both eyes are on the same side and they resemble their parents in all respects.
Fishing Information: Starry flounders are one of the most numerous fishes of central and northern California backwaters, particularly San Francisco Bay. Starry flounders can be taken throughout the year but are caught more frequently between December and March. They accept a variety of baits, including chunks of sardine, clams, shrimp, squid, and worms.
Other Common Names: rough jacket, great flounders, grindstone, California flounder, emery flounder, sand paper flounder.
Largest Recorded: 3 feet; 20 pounds.
Habitat: Shallow Sandy Environment

Petrale Sole

Family: Pleuronectidae (Right-eyed flounders)
Genus and Species: *Eopsetta jordani*
Description: The body of the petrale sole is elongate, moderately slender and compressed. The head is deep, and the mouth is large. The eyes are large and on the right side, The color is uniform dark to light brown with dusky blotches on the dorsal and anal fins on the eyed side and white on the blind side.

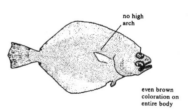

no high arch

even brown coloration on entire body

Petrale sole are often confused with California halibut because of their similar color and large mouths. However, petrale sole have an even, brown coloration and do not have a high arch in the lateral line.
Range: Petrale sole occur from Cedros Island, Baja California, to the northern part of the Gulf of Alaska. They are found at depths of 60 to 1,500 feet.
Natural History: The diet of the petrale sole includes crabs, shrimp, and fishes such as anchovies, hake, small rockfish and other flatfish.
Fishing Information: Although this flatfish is not often sought by recreational anglers, its large size and excellent eating qualities make it a good sportfish. Probably the entire sport catch for this species is taken incidentally by anglers on rockfish trips aboard commercial passenger fishing vessels. These anglers fishing in waters from 100 to 300 feet deep catch petrale sole on the sand surrounding rocky reefs.
Other Common Names: sole, round-nosed sole, Jordan's founder, California sole, brill.
Largest Recorded: 27.5 inches; no weight.
Habitat: Deep Sandy Environment

Ron Kovach

If you enjoyed reading *The Serious Pacific Angler* how about joining Ronnie Kovach on the Eagle Claw Fishing Schools?

Now you can learn more about how to catch fish on our California coast. Become one of the 10 percent of the anglers who catch 90 percent of the fish! These on-the-water seminars are conducted by Ronnie and the expert Eagle Claw instructional staff—many of whom are featured in this book. These schools are first-class, deluxe charters, carrying limited loads. We use only the top vessels and skippers. Crew fishing is not permitted.

Students receive personal one-on-one instruction on all facets of saltwater angling. *Top quality* tackle is provided free for students to use during the trip, including Penn rods and reels.

The Eagle Claw Fishing Schools target Catalina, San Clemente, Santa Barbara, and the Los Coronados Islands on one-day trips. Extended multi-day schools visit San Martin, Benitos, and Cedros Islands deep into Mexican waters. For the adventurer, we offer Eagle Claw Schools in Kauai, Hawaii fighting giant tuna, in Cabo San Lucas for marlin and dorado, and jig fishing for world-class Atlantic amberjack in Key Largo, Florida.

For more information, write:

Ronnie Kovach's Fishing Expeditions
17911 Portside Circle
Huntington Beach, CA 92649